UNCTAD/DITE/4(Vol. XII)

United Nations Conference on Trade and Development
Division on Investment, Technology and Enterprise Development

International Investment Instruments: A Compendium

Volume XII

United Nations
New York and Geneva, 2003

Note

UNCTAD serves as the focal point within the United Nations Secretariat for all matters related to foreign direct investment and transnational corporations. In the past, the Programme on Transnational Corporations was carried out by the United Nations Centre on Transnational Corporations (1975-1992) and the Transnational Corporations and Management Division of the United Nations Department of Economic and Social Development (1992-1993). In 1993, the Programme was transferred to the United Nations Conference on Trade and Development. UNCTAD seeks to further the understanding of the nature of transnational corporations and their contribution to development and to create an enabling environment for international investment and enterprise development. UNCTAD's work is carried out through intergovernmental deliberations, technical assistance activities, seminars, workshops and conferences.

The term "country", as used in the boxes added by the UNCTAD secretariat at the beginning of the instruments reproduced in this volume, also refers, as appropriate, to territories or areas; the designations employed and the presentation of the material do not imply the expression of any opinion whatsoever on the part of the Secretariat of the United Nations concerning the legal status of any country, territory, city or area or of its authorities, or concerning the delimitation of its frontiers or boundaries. Moreover, the country or geographical terminology used in the boxes may occasionally depart from standard United Nations practice when this is made necessary by the nomenclature used at the time of negotiation, signature, ratification or accession of a given international instrument.

To preserve the integrity of the texts of the instruments reproduced in this volume, references to the sources of the instruments that are not contained in their original text are identified as "note added by the editor".

The texts of the instruments included in this volume are reproduced as they were written in one of their original languages or as an official translation thereof. When an obvious linguistic mistake has been found, the word "sic" has been added in brackets.

The materials contained in this volume have been reprinted with special permission of the relevant institutions. For those materials under copyright protection, all rights are reserved by the copyright holders.

It should be further noted that this collection of instruments has been prepared for documentation purposes only, and its contents do not engage the responsibility of UNCTAD.

UNCTAD/DITE/4 Vol. XII

UNITED NATIONS
PUBLICATION

Sales No. E.04.II.D.10

ISBN 92-1-112617-7

PREFACE

International Investment Instruments: A Compendium contains a collection of international instruments relating to foreign direct investment (FDI) and transnational corporations (TNCs). The collection is presented in twelve volumes. The first three volumes were published in 1996. *Volumes IV* and *V* were published in 2000 followed by *Volume VI* in 2001. Four volumes -- VII, VIII IX and X were published in 2002 bringing the collection up to date. The present publication comprises *volumes XI* and *XII*.

The collection has been prepared to make the texts of international investment instruments conveniently available to interested policy-makers, scholars and business executives. The need for such a collection has increased in recent years as bilateral, regional, interregional and multilateral instruments dealing with various aspects of FDI have proliferated, and as new investment instruments are being negotiated or discussed at all levels.

While by necessity selective, the *Compendium* seeks to provide a faithful record of the evolution and present status of intergovernmental cooperation concerning FDI and TNCs. Although the emphasis of the collection is on relatively recent documents (the majority of the instruments reproduced date from after 1990), it was deemed useful to include important older instruments as well, with a view towards providing some indications of the historical development of international concerns over FDI in the decades since the end of the Second World War.

The core of this collection consists of legally binding international instruments, mainly multilateral conventions, regional agreements, and bilateral treaties that have entered into force. In addition, a number of "soft law" documents, such as guidelines, declarations and resolutions adopted by intergovernmental bodies, have been included since these instruments also play a role in the elaboration of an international framework for FDI. In an effort to enhance the understanding of the efforts behind the elaboration of this framework, certain draft instruments that never entered into force, or texts of instruments on which the negotiations were not concluded, are also included; prototypes of bilateral investment treaties are reproduced as well. Included also are a number of influential documents prepared by business, consumer and labour organizations, as well as by other non-governmental organizations. It is clear from the foregoing that no implications concerning the legal status or the legal effect of an instrument can be drawn from its inclusion in this collection.

In view of the great diversity of the instruments in this *Compendium* -- in terms of subject matter, approach, legal form and extent of participation of States -- the simplest possible method of presentation was deemed the most appropriate. With regard to previous volumes, the structure and content are indicated in the table of content which is included below (see pp. ix-xxxviii). As far as volumes XI and XII are concerned relevant instruments are distributed as follows:

Volume XI is divided into the following three parts:

- Part One contains additional multilateral instruments.

- Part Two covers additional interregional and regional instruments, including agreements and other texts from regional organizations with an inclusive geographical context.

- Part Three reproduces investment-related provisions in a number of additional free trade, economic integration and cooperation agreements not covered in previous volumes.

Volume XII is divided into the following two parts:

- Part One reproduces investment-related provisions in a number of additional free trade, economic integration and cooperation agreements not covered in previous volumes.

- Part Two contains the texts of a number of additional prototype BITs not covered in previous volumes.

Within each of these subdivisions and in previous volumes, instruments are reproduced in chronological order, except for the sections dedicated to prototype instruments.

The multilateral and regional instruments covered are widely differing in scope and coverage. Some are designed to provide an overall, general framework for FDI and cover many, although rarely all, aspects of investment operations. Most instruments deal with particular aspects and issues concerning FDI. A significant number address core FDI issues, such as the promotion and protection of investment, investment liberalization, dispute settlement and insurance and guarantees. Others cover specific issues, of direct but not exclusive relevance to FDI and TNCs, such as transfer of technology, intellectual property, avoidance of double taxation, competition and the protection of consumers and the environment. A relatively small number of instruments of this last category has been reproduced, since each of these specific issues often constitutes an entire system of legal regulation of its own, whose proper coverage would require an extended exposition of many kinds of instruments and arrangements.[a]

The *Compendium* is meant to be a collection of instruments, not an anthology of relevant provisions. Indeed, to understand a particular instrument, it is normally necessary to take its entire text into consideration. An effort has been made, therefore, to reproduce complete instruments, even though, in a number of cases, reasons of space and relevance have dictated the inclusion of excerpts.

The UNCTAD secretariat has deliberately refrained from adding its own commentary to the texts reproduced in the *Compendium*. The only exception to this rule is the boxes added to each instrument. They provide some basic facts, such as its date of adoption and date of entry into force and, where appropriate, signatory countries. Also, a list of agreements containing investment-related provisions signed by the EFTA countries and by the EC countries with third countries or regional groups are reproduced in the *Compendium*. Moreover, to facilitate the identification of each instrument in the table of contents, additional information has been added, in brackets, next to each title, on the year of its signature and the name of the relevant institution involved.

Rubens Ricupero
Secretary-General of UNCTAD

Geneva, December 2003

---

[a] For a collection of instruments (or excerpts therefrom) dealing with transfer of technology, see UNCTAD, *Compendium of International Arrangements on Transfer of Technology: Selected Instruments* (Geneva: United Nations), United Nations publication, Sales No. E.01.II.D.28.

ACKNOWLEDGEMENTS

Volumes XI and XII of the *Compendium* were prepared by Abraham Negash under the overall direction of Karl P. Sauvant. Comments and inputs were received from Torbjorn Fredriksson, Sumru Inal, Maryse Robert, Michael D. Urminsky and Dimitri Vlassis. The cooperation of the relevant countries and organizations from which the relevant instruments originate is acknowledged with gratitude.

VOLUME XII

PART ONE

BILATERAL INSTRUMENTS

PART TWO

PROTOTYPE INSTRUMENTS

CONTENTS OF OTHER VOLUMES

VOLUME I

MULTILATERAL INSTRUMENTS

VOLUME II

REGIONAL INSTRUMENTS

VOLUME III

REGIONAL INTEGRATION, BILATERAL AND NON-GOVERNMENTAL INSTRUMENTS

ANNEX A.   INVESTMENT-RELATED PROVISIONS IN FREE TRADE AND REGIONAL ECONOMIC INTEGRATION INSTRUMENTS

ANNEX B.   PROTOTYPE BILATERAL INVESTMENT TREATIES AND LIST OF BILATERAL INVESTMENT TREATIES (1959-1995)

ANNEX C. NON-GOVERNMENTAL INSTRUMENTS

VOLUME IV

MULTILATERAL AND REGIONAL INSTRUMENTS

PART ONE

MULTILATERAL INSTRUMENTS

PART TWO

REGIONAL INSTRUMENTS

VOLUME V

REGIONAL INTEGRATION, BILATERAL AND NON-GOVERNMENTAL INSTRUMENTS

PART ONE

INVESTMENT-RELATED PROVISIONS IN FREE TRADE AND ECONOMIC INTEGRATION AGREEMENTS

PART TWO

INVESTMENT-RELATED PROVISIONS IN ASSOCIATION AGREEMENTS, BILATERAL AND INTERREGIONAL COOPERATION AGREEMENTS

ANNEX A.   INVESTMENT-RELATED PROVISIONS IN FREE TRADE AGREEMENTS SIGNED BETWEEN THE COUNTRIES MEMBERS OF THE EUROPEAN FREE TRADE ASSOCIATION AND THIRD COUNTRIES AND LIST OF AGREEMENTS SIGNED (END-1999)

ANNEX B.   INVESTMENT-RELATED PROVISIONS IN ASSOCIATION, PARTNERSHIP AND COOPERATION AGREEMENTS SIGNED BETWEEN THE COUNTRIES MEMBERS OF THE EUROPEAN COMMUNITY AND THIRD COUNTRIESAND LIST OF AGREEMENTS SIGNED (END-1999)

ANNEX C.   OTHER BILATERAL INVESTMENT-RELATED AGREEMENTS

PART THREE

PROTOTYPE BILATERAL INVESTMENT TREATIES AND LIST OF BILATERAL INVESTMENT TREATIES (MID-1995 — END-1998)

PART FOUR

NON-GOVERNMENTAL INSTRUMENTS

VOLUME VI

PART ONE

MULTILATERAL INSTRUMENTS

PART TWO

INTERREGIONAL AND REGIONAL INSTRUMENTS

PART THREE

INVESTMENT-RELATED PROVISIONS IN FREE TRADE AND ECONOMIC INTEGRATION AGREEMENTS

PART FOUR

INVESTMENT-RELATED PROVISIONS IN ASSOCIATION AGREEMENTS, BILATERAL AND INTERREGIONAL COOPERATION AGREEMENTS

PART FIVE

PROTOTYPE BILATERAL INVESTMENT TREATIES

PART SIX

PROTOTYPE BILATERAL DOUBLE TAXATION TREATIES

VOLUME VII

PART ONE

MULTILATERAL INSTRUMENTS

PART TWO

BILATERAL INSTRUMENTS

PART THREE

PROTOTYPE INSTRUMENTS

VOLUME VIII

PART ONE

INTERREGIONAL AND REGIONAL INSTRUMENTS

PART TWO

BILATERAL INSTRUMENTS

PART THREE

PROTOTYPE INSTRUMENTS

VOLUME IX

PART ONE

INTERREGIONAL AND REGIONAL INSTRUMENTS

PART TWO

BILATERAL INSTRUMENTS

PART THREE

PROTOTYPE INSTRUMENTS

VOLUME X

PART ONE

BILATERAL INSTRUMENTS

PART TWO

PROTOTYPE INSTRUMENTS

VOLUME XI

PART ONE

MULTILATERAL INSTRUMENTS

PART TWO

REGIONAL AND INTERREGIONAL INSTRUMENTS

PART THREE

BILATERAL INSTRUMENTS

PART ONE

BILATERAL INSTRUMENTS

ASSOCIATION AGREEMENT BETWEEN THE EUROPEAN UNION AND CHILE[*]
[excerpts]

The association agreement between the European Union and Chile was signed on 18 November 2002. It entered into force on 1 February 2003.

TITLE III

TRADE IN SERVICES AND ESTABLISHMENT

Article 94
Objectives

1.   The Parties shall reciprocally liberalise trade in services, in accordance with the provisions of this Title and in conformity with Article V of the GATS.

2.   The aim of Chapter 3 is the improvement of the investment environment, and in particular the conditions of establishment between the Parties, on the basis of the principle of non-discrimination.

CHAPTER I
SERVICES

Section 1
General Provisions

Article 95
Scope

1.   For the purposes of this Chapter, trade in services is defined as the supply of a service through the following modes:

   (a)   from the territory of a Party into the territory of the other Party (mode 1);

   (b)   in the territory of a Party to the service consumer of the other Party (mode 2);

   (c)   by a service supplier of a Party, through commercial presence in the territory of the other Party (mode 3);

   (d)   by a service supplier of a Party, through presence of natural persons in the territory of the other Party (mode 4).

[*] *Source*: The Organization of American States (OAS) (2002). "Association Agreement Between the European Union and Chile", available on the Internet (http://www.sice.oas.org/Trade/chieu_e/cheuin_e.asp). [Note added by the editor.]

2.   This Chapter applies to trade in all service sectors with the exception of:

(a)   financial services, which is subject to Chapter 2;

(b)   audio-visual services;

(c)   national maritime cabotage; and

(d)   air transport services, including domestic and international air transportation services, whether scheduled or non-scheduled, and services directly related to the exercise of traffic rights, other than:

      (i)   aircraft repair and maintenance services during which an aircraft is withdrawn from service;

      (ii)   the selling and marketing of air transport services; and

      (iii)   computer reservation system (CRS) services.

3.   Nothing in this Chapter shall be construed to impose any obligation with respect to government procurement, which is subject to Title IV of this Part of the Agreement.

4.   The provisions of this Chapter shall not apply to subsidies granted by the Parties. The Parties shall review the issue of disciplines on subsidies related to trade in services in the context of the review of this Chapter, as provided in Article 100, with a view to incorporating any disciplines agreed under Article XV of the GATS.

5.   Section 1 applies to international maritime transport and telecommunication services subject to the provisions laid down in sections 2 and 3.

Article 96
Definitions

For the purposes of this Chapter:

(a)   "measure" means any measure by a Party, whether in the form of a law, regulation, rule, procedure, decision, administrative action, or any other form;

(b)   "measure adopted or maintained by a Party" means measures taken by:

      (i)   central, regional or local governments and authorities; and

      (ii)   non-governmental bodies in the exercise of powers delegated by central, regional or local governments or authorities;

(c)   "service supplier" means any legal or natural person that seeks to supply or supplies a service;

(d)   "commercial presence" means any type of business or professional establishment, including through:

      (i)   the constitution, acquisition or maintenance of a legal person, or

      (ii)   the creation or maintenance of a branch or a representative office, within the territory of a Party for the purpose of supplying a service;

(e)   "legal person" means any legal entity duly constituted or otherwise organised under applicable law, whether for profit or otherwise, and whether privately-owned or governmentally-owned, including any corporation, trust, partnership, joint venture, sole proprietorship or association;

(f)   "legal person of a Party" means a legal person constituted or otherwise organised under the law of the Community or its Member States or of Chile.

Should such a legal person have only its registered office or central administration in the territory of the Community or of Chile, it shall not be considered as a Community or a Chilean legal person respectively, unless it is engaged in substantive business operations in the territory of the Community or of Chile, respectively.

(g)   A "natural person" means a national of one of the Member States or of Chile according to their respective legislation.

Article 97
Market access

1.   With respect to market access through the modes of supply identified in Article 95, each Party shall accord services and service suppliers of the other Party treatment no less favourable than that provided for under the terms, limitations and conditions agreed and specified in its Schedule referred to in Article 99.

2.   In sectors where market-access commitments are undertaken, the measures which a Party shall not maintain or adopt either on the basis of a regional subdivision or on the basis of its entire territory, unless otherwise specified in its Schedule, are defined as:

      (a)   limitations on the number of services suppliers whether in the form of numerical quotas, monopolies, exclusive service suppliers or the requirements of an economic needs test;

      (b)   limitations on the total value of service transactions or assets in the form of numerical quotas or the requirement of an economic needs test;

      (c)   limitations on the total number of service operations or on the total quantity of service output expressed in terms of designated numerical units in the form of quotas or the requirement of an economic needs test;[5]

      (d)   limitations on the total number of natural persons that may be employed in a particular service sector or that a service supplier may employ and who are necessary for, and directly related to, the supply of a specific service in the form of numerical quotas or a requirement of an economic needs test;

---

[5] paragraph 2(c) does not cover measures of a Party which limit inputs for the supply of services.

   (e)   measures which restrict or require specific types of legal entities or joint ventures through which a service supplier of the other Party may supply a service; and

   (f)   limitations on the participation of foreign capital in terms of maximum percentage limit on foreign shareholding or the total value of individual or aggregate foreign investment.

Article 98
National treatment

1.   In the sectors inscribed in its Schedule, and subject to the conditions and qualifications set out therein, each Party shall grant to services and service suppliers of the other Party, in respect of all measures affecting the supply of services, treatment no less favourable than that it accords to its own like services and services suppliers.[6]

2.   A Party may meet the requirement of paragraph 1 by according to services and service suppliers of the other Party, either formally identical treatment or formally different treatment to that it accords to its own like services and service suppliers.

3.   Formally identical or formally different treatment shall be considered to be less favourable if it modifies the conditions of competition in favour of services or service suppliers of a Party compared to like services or service suppliers of the other Party.

Article 99
Schedule of specific commitments

1.   The specific commitments undertaken by each Party under Articles 97 and 98 are set out in the schedule included in Annex VII. With respect to sectors where such commitments are undertaken, each Schedule specifies:

   (a)   terms, limitations and conditions on market access;

   (b)   conditions and qualifications on national treatment;

   (c)   undertakings relating to additional commitments referred to in paragraph 3;

   (d)   where appropriate the time-frame for implementation of such commitments and the date of entry into force of such commitments.

2.   Measures inconsistent with both Articles 97 and 98 are inscribed in the column relating to Article 97. In this case the inscription is considered to provide a condition or qualification to Article 98 as well.

3.   Where a Party undertakes specific commitments on measures affecting trade in services not subject to scheduling under Articles 97 and 98, such commitments are inscribed in its Schedule as additional commitments.

---

[6] Specific commitments assumed under this Article shall not be construed to require the Parties to compensate for any inherent competitive disadvantages which result from the foreign character of the relevant services or service suppliers.

Article 100
Review

1.   The Parties shall review this Chapter three years after the entry into force of this Agreement, with a view to further deepening liberalisation and reducing or eliminating remaining restrictions on a mutually advantageous basis and ensuring an overall balance of rights and obligations.

2.   The Association Committee shall examine the operation of this Chapter every three years after the review undertaken under paragraph 1 and shall submit appropriate proposals to the Association Council.

Article 101
Movement of natural persons

Two years after the entry into force of this Agreement, the Parties shall review the rules and conditions applicable to movement of natural persons (mode 4) with a view to achieving further liberalisation. This review may also address the revision of the definition of natural person provided in Article 96(g).

Article 102
Domestic regulation

1.   In sectors where a Party has undertaken commitments in its Schedule, and with a view to ensuring that any measure relating to the requirements and procedures of licensing and certification of service suppliers of the other Party does not constitute an unnecessary barrier to trade, that Party shall endeavour to ensure that any such measure:

(a)   is based on objective and transparent criteria, such as, *inter alia*, competence and the ability to provide the service;

(b)   is not more trade-restrictive than necessary to ensure the achievement of a legitimate policy objective;

(c)   does not constitute a disguised restriction on the supply of a service.

2.   The disciplines of paragraph 1 may be reviewed within the framework of the procedure of Article 100 in order to take into account the disciplines agreed under Article VI of the GATS with a view to their incorporation into this Agreement.

3.   Where a Party recognises, unilaterally or by agreement, education, experience, licenses or certifications obtained in the territory of a third country, that Party shall afford the other Party an adequate opportunity to demonstrate that education, experience, licenses or certifications obtained in the other Party's territory should also be recognised or to conclude an agreement or arrangement of comparable effect.

4.   The Parties shall consult periodically with a view to determining the feasibility of removing any remaining citizenship or permanent residency requirement for the licensing or certification of each other's service suppliers.

Article 103
Mutual recognition

1.   Each Party shall ensure that its competent authorities, within a reasonable period of time after the submission by a services supplier of the other Party of an application for a licence or certification:

   (a)   where the application is complete, make a determination on the application and inform the applicant of that determination; or

   (b)   where the application is not complete, inform the applicant without undue delay of the status of the application and the additional information that is required under the Party's domestic law.

2.   The Parties shall encourage the relevant bodies in their respective territories to provide recommendations on mutual recognition, for the purpose of enabling service suppliers to fulfil, in whole or in part, the criteria applied by each Party for the authorisation, licensing, accreditation, operation and certification of service suppliers and in particular professional services.

3.   The Association Committee, within a reasonable period of time and considering the level of correspondence of the respective regulations, shall decide whether a recommendation referred to in paragraph 2 is consistent with this Chapter. If that is the case, such a recommendation shall be implemented through an agreement on mutual recognition of requirements, qualifications, licences and other regulations to be negotiated by the competent authorities.

4.   Any such agreement shall be in conformity with the relevant provisions of the WTO Agreement and, in particular, Article VII of the GATS.

5.   Where the Parties agree, each Party shall encourage its relevant bodies to develop procedures for the temporary licensing of professional service suppliers of the other Party.

6.   The Association Committee shall periodically, and at least once every three years, review the implementation of this Article.

Article 104
Electronic commerce[7]

The Parties, recognising that the use of electronic means increases trade opportunities in many sectors, agree to promote the development of electronic commerce between them, in particular by co-operating on the market access and regulatory issues raised by electronic commerce.

Article 105
Transparency

Each Party shall respond promptly to all requests by the other Party for specific information on any of its measures of general application or international agreements which pertain to or affect

---

[7] The inclusion of this provision in this Chapter is made without prejudice of the Chilean position on the question of whether or not electronic commerce should be considered as a supply of services.

this Chapter. The contact point referred to in Article 190 shall provide specific information on all such matters to service suppliers of the other Party upon request. Contact points need not be depositories of laws and regulations.

Section 2
International Maritime Transport

Article 106
Scope

1.   Notwithstanding Article 95(5), the provisions of this section shall apply with respect to shipping companies established outside the Community or Chile and controlled by nationals of a Member State or of Chile, respectively, if their vessels are registered in accordance with their respective legislation, in that Member State or in Chile and carry the flag of a Member State or Chile.

2.   This Article applies to international maritime transport, including door-to-door and intermodal transport operations involving a sea-leg.

Article 107
Definitions

For the purposes of this section:

(a)   "intermodal transport operations" is defined as the right to arrange door-to-door transport services of international cargo and to this effect directly contract with providers of other modes of transport;

(b)   "international maritime service suppliers" covers the suppliers of services relating to international cargo for maritime services, cargo handling, storage and warehousing services, customs clearance services, container station and depot services, agency services and freight forwarding services.

Article 108
Market access and national treatment

1.   In view of the existing levels of liberalisation between the Parties in international maritime transport:

(a)   the Parties shall continue to effectively apply the principle of unrestricted access to the international maritime market and traffic on a commercial and non-discriminatory basis;

(b)   each Party shall continue to grant to ships flying the flag of or operated by service suppliers of the other Party treatment no less favourable than that accorded to its own ships with regard to, inter alia, access to ports, use of infrastructure and auxiliary maritime services of the ports, and related fees and charges, customs facilities and the assignment of berths and facilities for loading and unloading.

2.   In applying the principles of paragraph 1, the Parties shall:

(a)   not introduce cargo-sharing clauses in future bilateral agreements with third countries, other than in those exceptional circumstances where liner shipping companies from the Party concerned would not otherwise have an effective opportunity to ply for trade to and from the third country concerned;

(b)   prohibit cargo-sharing arrangements in future bilateral agreements concerning dry and liquid bulk trade;

(c)   abolish, upon the entry into force of this Agreement, all unilateral measures and administrative, technical and other barriers which could have restrictive or discriminatory effects on the free supply of services in international maritime transport.

3.   Each Party shall permit international maritime service suppliers of the other Party to have a commercial presence in its territory under conditions of establishment and operation no less favourable than those accorded to its own service suppliers or those of any third country, whichever are the better, in accordance with the conditions inscribed in its Schedule.

Section 3
Telecommunications Services

Article 109
Definitions

For the purposes of this section:

(a)   "telecommunications services" means the transport of electro-magnetic signals - sound, data image and any combinations thereof, excluding broadcasting.[8] Therefore, commitments in this sector do not cover the economic activity consisting of content provision which require telecommunications services for its transport. The provision of that content, transported via a telecommunications service, is subject to the specific commitments undertaken by the Parties in other relevant sectors.

(b)   a "regulatory authority" means the body or bodies with any of the regulatory tasks assigned in relation to the issues mentioned in this section.

(c)   "essential telecommunications facilities" mean facilities of a public telecommunications transport network and service that:

(i)   are exclusively or predominantly provided by a single supplier or a limited number of suppliers; and

---

[8] Broadcasting is defined as the uninterrupted chain of transmission required for the distribution of TV and radio programme signals to the general public, but does not cover contribution links between operators.

(ii)   cannot feasibly be economically or technically substituted in order to provide a service.

Article 110
Regulatory authority

1.   Regulatory authorities for telecommunications services shall be separate from, and not accountable to, any supplier of basic telecommunications services.

2.   The decisions of and the procedures used by regulatory authorities shall be impartial with respect to all market participants.

3.   A supplier affected by the decision of a regulatory authority shall have a right to appeal against that decision.

Article 111
Supply of services

1.   Where a licence is required, the terms and conditions for such a license shall be made publicly available and the period of time normally required to reach a decision concerning an application for a licence shall be made publicly available.

2.   Where a licence is required, the reasons for the denial of a licence shall be made known to the applicant upon request.

Article 112
Major suppliers

1.   A major supplier is a supplier which has the ability to materially affect the terms of participation having regard to price and supply in the relevant market for basic telecommunications services as a result of:

(a)   control over essential facilities; or

(b)   the use of its position in the market.

2.   Appropriate measures shall be maintained for the purpose of preventing suppliers who, alone or together, are a major supplier from engaging in or continuing anti-competitive practices.

3.   The anti-competitive practices referred to above shall include in particular:

(a)   engaging in anti-competitive cross-subsidisation;

(b)   using information obtained from competitors with anti-competitive results; and

(c)   not making available to other services suppliers on a timely basis technical information about essential facilities and commercially relevant information which are necessary for them to supply services.

Article 113
Interconnection

1.   This section applies to linking with suppliers providing public telecommunications transport networks or services in order to allow the users of one supplier to communicate with users of another supplier and to access services provided by another supplier.

2.   Interconnection with a major supplier shall be ensured at any technically feasible point in the network. Such interconnection shall be provided:

(a)   under non-discriminatory terms, conditions (including technical standards and specifications) and rates and of a quality no less favourable than that provided for its own like services or for like services of non-affiliated service suppliers or for its subsidiaries or other affiliates;

(b)   in a timely fashion, on terms, conditions (including technical standards and specifications) and cost-oriented rates that are transparent, reasonable, having regard to economic feasibility, and sufficiently unbundled so that the supplier need not pay for network components or facilities that it does not require for the service to be provided; and

(c)   upon request, at points in addition to the network termination points offered to the majority of users, subject to charges that reflect the cost of construction of necessary additional facilities.

4.   The procedures applicable for interconnection to a major supplier shall be made publicly available.

5.   Major suppliers shall make interconnection agreements available to service suppliers of the Parties to ensure non-discrimination, and/or shall publish reference interconnection offers in advance, unless they are already available to the public.

Article 114
Scarce resources

Any procedures for the allocation and use of scarce resources, including frequencies, numbers and rights of way, shall be carried out in an objective, timely, transparent and non-discriminatory manner.

Article 115
Universal service

1.   Each Party has the right to define the kind of universal service obligation it wishes to maintain.

2.   The provisions governing universal service shall be transparent, objective and non-discriminatory. They shall also be neutral with respect to competition and be no more burdensome than necessary.

CHAPTER II
FINANCIAL SERVICES

Article 116
Scope

1.   This Chapter applies to measures adopted or maintained by the Parties affecting trade in financial services.

2.   For the purposes of this Chapter, trade in financial services is defined as the supply of a financial service through the following modes:

(a)   from the territory of a Party into the territory of the other Party (mode 1);

(b)   in the territory of a Party to the financial service consumer of the other Party (mode 2);

(c)   by a financial service supplier of a Party, through commercial presence in the territory of the other Party (mode 3);

(d)   by a financial service supplier of a Party, through presence of natural persons in the territory of the other Party (mode 4).

3.   Nothing in this Chapter shall be construed to impose any obligation with respect to government procurement, which is subject to Title IV of this Part of the Agreement.

4.   The provisions of this Chapter shall not apply to subsidies granted by the Parties. The Parties shall review the issue of disciplines on subsidies related to trade in financial services, with a view to incorporating in this Agreement any disciplines agreed under Article XV of GATS.

5.   This Chapter does not apply to:

(i)   activities conducted by a central bank or monetary authority or by any other public entity in pursuit of monetary or exchange rate policies;

(ii)   activities forming part of a statutory system of social security or public retirement plans; and

(iii)   other activities conducted by a public entity for the account or with the guarantee or using the financial resources of the Government.

6.   For the purposes of paragraph 5, if a Party allows any of the activities referred to in paragraph 5(ii) or (iii) to be conducted by its financial service suppliers in competition with a public entity or a financial service supplier, this Chapter applies to such activities.

Article 117
Definitions

For the purposes of this Chapter:

1.   "measure" means any measure by a Party, whether in the form of a law, regulation, rule, procedure, decision, administrative action, or any other form;

2.   "measures adopted or maintained by a Party" means measures taken by:

(i)   central, regional or local governments and authorities; and

(ii)   non-governmental bodies in the exercise of powers delegated by central, regional or local governments or authorities;

3.   "financial service supplier" means any natural or legal person that seeks to supply or supplies financial services but the term "financial service supplier" does not include a public entity;

4.   "public entity" means:

(i)   a government, a central bank or a monetary authority of a Party, or an entity owned or controlled by a Party, that is principally engaged in carrying out governmental functions or activities for governmental purposes, not including an entity principally engaged in supplying financial services on commercial terms; or

(ii)   a private entity, performing functions normally performed by a central bank or monetary authority, when exercising those functions;

5.   "commercial presence" means any type of business or professional establishment, including through:

(i)   the constitution, acquisition or maintenance of a legal person, or

(ii)   the creation or maintenance of a branch or a representative office, within the territory of a Party for the purpose of supplying a financial service;

6.   "legal person" means any legal entity duly constituted or otherwise organized under applicable law, whether for profit or otherwise, and whether privately-owned or governmentally-owned, including any corporation, trust, partnership, joint venture, sole proprietorship or association;

7.   "legal person of a Party" means a legal person constituted or otherwise organised under the law of the Community or its Member States or of Chile. Should such a legal person have only its registered office or central administration in the territory of the Community or Chile, it shall not be considered as a Community or a Chilean legal person respectively, unless it is engaged in substantive business operations in the territory of the Community or Chile, respectively.

8.   "natural person" means a national of one of the Member States or of Chile according to their respective legislation.

9.   "financial service" means any service of a financial nature offered by a financial service supplier of a Party. Financial services comprise the following activities:

Insurance and insurance-related services

    (i)   direct insurance (including co-insurance):

          (A)   life
          (B)   non-life

    (ii)   reinsurance and retrocession;

    (iii)   insurance intermediation, such as brokerage and agency;

    (iv)   services auxiliary to insurance, such as consultancy, actuarial, risk assessment and claim settlement services.

Banking and other financial services (excluding insurance)

    (v)   acceptance of deposits and other repayable funds from the public;

    (vi)   lending of all types, including consumer credit, mortgage credit, factoring and financing of commercial transactions;

    (vii)   financial leasing;

    (viii) all payment and money transmission services, including credit, charge and debit cards, travellers cheques and bankers drafts;

    (ix)   guarantees and commitments;

    (x)   trading for own account or for account of customers, whether on an exchange, in an over-the-counter market or otherwise, the following:

          (A)   money market instruments, including cheques, bills, certificates of deposits;

          (B)   foreign exchange;

          (C)   derivative products including, but not limited to, futures and options;

          (D)   exchange rate and interest rate instruments, including products such as swaps, forward rate agreements;

          (E)   transferable securities;

          (F)   other negotiable instruments and financial assets, including bullion.

    (xi)   participation in issues of all kinds of securities, including underwriting and placement as agent (whether publicly or privately) and provision of services related to such issues;

    (xii)   money broking;

(xiii) asset management, such as cash or portfolio management, all forms of collective investment management, pension fund management, custodial, depository and trust services;

(xiv) settlement and clearing services for financial assets, including securities, derivative products, and other negotiable instruments;

(xv) provision and transfer of financial information, and financial data processing and related software by suppliers of other financial services;

(xvi) advisory, intermediation and other auxiliary financial services on all the activities listed in subparagraphs (v) through (xv), including credit reference and analysis, investment and portfolio research and advice, advice on acquisitions and on corporate restructuring and strategy.

10.   "new financial service" means a service of a financial nature, including services related to existing and new products or the manner in which a product is delivered, that is not supplied by any financial service supplier in the territory of a Party but which is supplied in the territory of the other Party.

Article 118
Market access

1.   With respect to market access through the modes of supply identified in Article 116, each Party shall accord financial services and financial service suppliers of the other Party treatment no less favourable than that provided for under the terms, limitations and conditions agreed and specified in its Schedule referred to in Article 120.

2.   In sectors where market-access commitments are undertaken, the measures which a Party shall not maintain or adopt either on the basis of a regional subdivision or on the basis of its entire territory, unless otherwise specified in its Schedule, are defined as:

(a) limitations on the number of financial services suppliers whether in the form of numerical quotas, monopolies, exclusive service suppliers or the requirements of an economic needs test;

(b) limitations on the total value of financial service transactions or assets in the form of numerical quotas or the requirement of an economic needs test;

(c) limitations on the total number of financial service operations or on the total quantity of service output expressed in terms of designated numerical units in the form of quotas or the requirement of an economic needs test;[9]

(d) limitations on the total number of natural persons that may be employed in a particular financial service sector or that a financial service supplier may employ and who are necessary for, and directly related to, the supply of a specific

---

[9] Paragraph 2(c) does not cover measures of a Party which limit inputs for the supply of financial services.

financial service in the form of numerical quotas or a requirement of an economic needs test;

(e)   measures which restrict or require specific types of legal entities or joint ventures through which a financial service supplier of the other Party may supply a financial service; and

(f)   limitations on the participation of foreign capital in terms of maximum percentage limit on foreign shareholding or the total value of individual or aggregate foreign investment.

Article 119
National treatment

1.   In the sectors inscribed in its Schedule, and subject to the conditions and qualifications set out therein, each Party shall accord to financial services and financial service suppliers of the other Party, in respect of all measures affecting the supply of financial services, treatment no less favourable than that it accords to its own like financial services and financial service suppliers.[10]

2.   A Party may meet the requirement of paragraph 1 by according to financial services and financial service suppliers of the other Party, either formally identical treatment or formally different treatment to that it accords to its own like financial services and financial service suppliers.

3.   Formally identical or formally different treatment shall be considered to be less favourable if it modifies the conditions of competition in favour of financial services or financial service suppliers of a Party compared to like financial services or financial service suppliers of the other Party.

Article 120
Schedule of specific commitments

1.   The specific commitment undertaken by each Party under Articles 118 and 119 are set out in the Schedule included in Annex VIII. With respect to sectors where such commitments are undertaken, each Schedule specifies:

(a)   terms, limitations and conditions on market access;

(b)   conditions and qualifications on national treatment;

(c)   undertakings relating to additional commitments referred to in paragraph 3;

(d)   where appropriate the time-frame for implementation of such commitments and the date of entry into force of such commitments.

---

[10] Specific commitments assumed under this Article shall not be construed to require the Parties to compensate for any inherent competitive disadvantages which result from the foreign character of the relevant financial services or financial service suppliers.

2.   Measures inconsistent with both Articles 118 and 119 are inscribed in the column relating to Article 118. In this case, the inscription is considered to provide a condition or qualification to Article 119 as well.

3.   Where a Party undertakes specific commitments on measures affecting trade in financial services not subject to scheduling under Articles 118 and 119, such commitments are inscribed in its Schedule as additional commitments.

Article 121
New financial services

1.   A Party shall permit financial service suppliers of the other Party established in its territory to offer in its territory any new financial service within the scope of the subsectors and financial services committed in its Schedule and subject to the terms, limitations, conditions and qualifications established in that Schedule and provided that the introduction of this new financial service does not require a new law or the modification of an existing law.

2.   A Party may determine the legal form through which the service may be provided and may require authorisation for the provision of the financial service. Where such authorisation is required, a decision shall be taken within a reasonable period of time and the authorisation may only be refused for prudential reasons.

Article 122
Data processing in the financial services sector

1.   Each Party shall permit a financial service supplier of the other Party to transfer information in electronic or other form, into and out of its territory, for data processing where such processing is required in the ordinary course of business of such financial service supplier.

2.   Where the information referred to in paragraph 1 consists of or contains personal data, the transfer of such information from the territory of one Party to the territory of the other Party shall take place in accordance with the domestic law regulating the protection of individuals with respect to the transferring and processing of personal data of the Party out of whose territory the information is transferred.

Article 123
Effective and transparent regulation in the financial services sector

1.   Each Party shall, to the extent practicable, provide in advance to all interested persons any measure of general application that the Party proposes to adopt in order to allow an opportunity for such persons to comment on the measure. Such measure shall be provided:

(a)   by means of an official publication; or

(b)   in other written or electronic form.

2.   Each Party's appropriate financial authority shall make available to interested persons its requirements for completing applications relating to the supply of financial services.

3.   On the request of an applicant, the appropriate financial authority shall inform the applicant of the status of its application. If such authority requires additional information from the applicant, it shall notify the applicant without undue delay.

4.   Each Party shall make its best endeavours to implement and apply in its territory internationally agreed standards for regulation and supervision in the financial services sector and for the fight against money laundering. For this purpose, the Parties shall cooperate and exchange information and experience within the Special Committee on Financial Services referred to in Article 127.

Article 124
Confidential information

Nothing in this Chapter:

(a)   shall require any of the Parties to provide confidential information, the disclosure of which would impede law enforcement, or otherwise be contrary to the public interest, or which would prejudice legitimate commercial interests of particular enterprises, public or private.

(b)   shall be construed to require a Party to disclose information relating to the financial affairs and accounts of individual customers of financial service suppliers, or any confidential or proprietary information in the possession of public entities.

Article 125
Prudential carve out

1.   Nothing in this Chapter shall be construed to prevent a Party from adopting or maintaining reasonable measures for prudential reasons, such as:

(a)   the protection of investors, depositors, financial market participants, policy-holders, or persons to whom a fiduciary duty is owed by a financial services supplier;

(b)   the maintenance of the safety, soundness, integrity or financial responsibility of financial services suppliers; and

(c)   ensuring the integrity and stability of a Party's financial system.

2.   Where such measures do not conform with the provisions of this Chapter, they shall not be used as a means of avoiding the Party's commitments or obligations under the Chapter.

Article 126
Recognition

1.   A Party may recognise prudential measures of the other Party in determining how the Party's measures relating to financial services shall be applied. Such recognition, which may be achieved through harmonisation or otherwise, may be based upon an agreement or arrangement or may be accorded autonomously.

2.   A Party that is a party to an agreement or arrangement with a third party such as those referred to in paragraph 1, whether future or existing, shall afford adequate opportunity for the other Party to negotiate its accession to such agreements or arrangements, or to negotiate comparable ones with it, under circumstances in which there would be equivalent regulation, oversight, implementation of such regulation, and, if appropriate, procedures concerning the sharing of information between the Parties to the agreement or arrangement. Where a Party accords recognition autonomously, it shall afford adequate opportunity for the other Party to demonstrate that such circumstances exist.

Article 127
Special Committee on Financial Services

1.   The Parties hereby establish a Special Committee on Financial Services. The Special Committee shall be composed of representatives of the Parties. The principal representative of each Party shall be an official of the Party's authority responsible for financial services set out in Annex IX.

2.   The functions of the Special Committee shall include:

(a)   supervising the implementation of this Chapter;

(b)   considering issues regarding financial services that are referred to it by a Party.

3.   The Special Committee shall meet upon request of one of the Parties on a date and with an agenda agreed in advance by the Parties. The office of chair person shall be held alternately. The Special Committee shall report to the Association Committee the results of its meetings.

4.   Three years after the entry into force of this Agreement the Special Committee on Financial Services will consider actions with the aim of facilitating and expanding trade in financial services and further contributing to the objectives of this Agreement, and shall report to the Association Committee.

Article 128
Consultations

1.   A Party may request consultations with the other Party regarding any matter arising under this Chapter. The other Party shall give sympathetic consideration to the request. The Parties shall report the results of their consultations to the Special Committee on Financial Services.

2.   Consultations under this Article shall include officials of the authorities specified in Annex IX.

3.   Nothing in this Article shall be construed to require financial authorities participating in consultations to disclose information or take any action that would interfere with individual regulatory, supervisory, administrative or enforcement matters.

4.   Where a financial authority of a Party requires information for supervisory purposes concerning a financial service supplier in the other Party's territory, such financial authority may approach the competent financial authority in the other Party's territory to seek the information. The provision of such information may be subject to the terms, conditions and limitations

contained in the other Party's relevant law or to the requirement of a prior agreement or arrangement between the respective financial authorities.

Article 129
Specific provisions on dispute settlement

1.   Except as otherwise provided in this Article, any disputes under this Chapter shall be settled in accordance with the provisions of Title VIII.

2.   For the purpose of Article 184, consultations held under Article 128 shall be deemed to constitute the consultations referred to in Article 183, unless the Parties otherwise agree.

Upon initiation of consultations, the Parties shall provide information to enable the examination of how a measure of a Party or any other matter may affect the operation and application of this Chapter, and give confidential treatment to the information exchanged during consultations. If the matter has not been resolved within 45 days after holding the consultations under Article 128 or 90 days after the delivery of the request for consultations under Article 128(1), whichever is earlier, the complaining Party may request in writing the establishment of an arbitration panel. The Parties shall report the results of their consultations directly to the Association Committee.

3.   For the purpose of Article 185:

   (a)   the chairperson of the arbitration panel shall be a financial expert;

   (b)   the Association Committee shall, no later than six months after the entry into force of this Agreement, establish a list of at least five individuals who are not nationals of either Party, and who are willing and able to serve as arbitrators and be identified as chairperson of arbitration panels in financial services. The Association Committee shall ensure that the list always contains five individuals at any point in time. Those individuals shall have expertise or experience in financial services law or practice, which may include the regulation of financial institutions, be independent, serve in their individual capacities and not be affiliated with, nor take instructions from, any Party or organisation and shall comply with the Code of Conduct set out in Annex XVI. Such list may be amended every three years;

   (c)   within three days of the request for establishment of the arbitration panel, the chair person of the arbitration panel shall be selected by lot by the chairperson of the Association Committee from the list referred to in paragraph (b). The other two arbitrators of the panel shall be selected by lot by the chairperson of the Association Committee from the list referred to in Article 185(2), one among the individuals proposed to the Association Committee by the complaining Party, and the other among the individuals proposed to the Association Committee by the Party complained against.

CHAPTER III
ESTABLISHMENT

Article 130
Scope

This Chapter shall apply to establishment in all sectors with the exception of all services sectors, including the financial services sector.

Article 131
Definitions

For the purposes of this Chapter,

(a)   "legal person" means any legal entity duly constituted or otherwise organised under applicable law, whether for profit or otherwise, and whether privately-owned or governmentally-owned, including any corporation, trust, partnership, joint venture, sole proprietorship or association;

(b)   "legal person of a Party" means a legal person constituted or otherwise organised under the law of the Community or its Member States or of Chile.

Should such a legal person have only its registered office or central administration in the territory of the Community or of Chile, it shall not be considered as a Community or a Chilean legal person respectively, unless it is engaged in substantive business operations in the territory of the Community or of Chile respectively.

(c)   "natural person" means a national of one of the Member States or of Chile according to their respective legislation.

(d)   "establishment" means:

(i)   the constitution, acquisition or maintenance of a legal person, or

(ii)   the creation or maintenance of a branch or a representative office, within the territory of a Party for the purpose of performing an economic activity.

As regards natural persons, this shall not extend to seeking or taking employment in the labour market or confer a right of access to the labour market of a Party.

Article 132
National treatment

In the sectors inscribed in Annex X, and subject to any conditions and qualifications set out therein, with respect to establishment, each Party shall grant to legal and natural persons of the other Party treatment no less favourable than that it accords to its own legal and natural persons performing a like economic activity.

Article 133
Right to regulate

Subject to the provisions of Article 132, each Party may regulate the establishment of legal and natural persons.

Article 134
Final provisions

1. With respect to this Chapter, the Parties confirm their rights and obligations existing under any bilateral or multilateral agreements to which they are parties.

2. With the objective of progressive liberalisation of investment conditions, the Parties affirm their commitment to review the investment legal framework, the investment environment and the flow of investment between them consistent with their commitments in international investment agreements, no later than three years after the entry into force of this Agreement.

CHAPTER 4
EXCEPTIONS

Article 135
Exceptions

1. Subject to the requirement that such measures are not applied in a manner which would constitute a means of arbitrary or unjustifiable discrimination between the Parties where like conditions prevail, or a disguised restriction on trade in services, financial services or establishment, nothing in this Title shall be construed to prevent the adoption or enforcement by either Party of measures:

(a) necessary to protect public morals or to maintain public order and public security;

(b) necessary to protect human, animal or plant life or health;

(c) relating to the conservation of exhaustible natural resources if such measures are applied in conjunction with restrictions on the domestic supply or consumption of services or on domestic investments;

(d) necessary for the protection of national treasures of artistic, historic or archaeological value;

(e) necessary to secure compliance with laws or regulations which are not inconsistent with the provisions of this Title including those relating to:

(i) the prevention of deceptive and fraudulent practices or to deal with the effects of a default on services contracts;

(ii) the protection of the privacy of individuals in relation to the processing and dissemination of personal data and the protection of confidentiality of individual records and accounts; or

(iii)   safety.

2.   The provisions of this Title shall not apply to the Parties respective social security systems or to activities in the territory of each Party which are connected, even occasionally, with the exercise of official authority.

3.   Nothing in this Title shall prevent a Party from applying its laws, regulations and requirements regarding entry and stay, work, labour conditions, and establishment of natural persons[11] provided that, in so doing, it does not apply to them in such a manner as to nullify or impair the benefits accruing to the other Party under the terms of a specific provision of this Title.

TITLE IV
GOVERNMENT PROCUREMENT

Article 136
Objective

In accordance with the provisions of this Title, the Parties shall ensure the effective and reciprocal opening of their government procurement markets.

Article 137
Scope and coverage

1.   This Title applies to any law, regulation, procedure or practice regarding any procurement, by the entities of the Parties, of goods and services including works, subject to the conditions specified by each Party in Annexes XI, XII and XIII.

2.   This Title shall not be applicable to:

(a)   contracts awarded pursuant to:

   (i)   an international agreement and intended for the joint implementation or exploitation of a project by the contracting Parties;

   (ii)   an international agreement relating to the stationing of troops; and

   (iii)   the particular procedure of an international organisation.

(b)   non-contractual agreements or any form of government assistance and procurement made in the framework of assistance or cooperation programmes.

(c)   contracts for :

   (i)   the acquisition or rental of land, existing buildings, or other immovable property or concerning rights thereon;

---

[11] In particular, a Party may require that natural persons must possess the necessary academic qualifications and/or

(ii)   the acquisition, development, production or co-production of programme material by broadcasters and contracts for broadcasting time.

(iii)   arbitration and conciliation services;

(iv)   employment contracts; and

(v)   research and development services other than those where the benefits accrue exclusively to the entity for its use in the conduct of its own affairs, on condition that the service is wholly remunerated by the entity.

(d)   financial services.

3.   Public works concessions, as defined in Article 138(i), shall also be subject to this Title, as specified in Annexes XI, XII and XIII.

4.   Neither Party may prepare, design or otherwise structure any procurement contract in order to avoid the obligations under this Title.

Article 138
Definitions

For the purpose of this Title, the following definitions shall apply:

(a)   "government procurement" means any type of procurement of goods, services or a combination thereof, including works carried out by public entities of the Parties for governmental purposes and not with a view to commercial resale or with a view to use in the production of goods or the supply of services for commercial sale, unless otherwise specified. It includes procurement by such methods as purchase or lease, or rental or hire purchase, with or without an option to buy;

(b)   "entities" means the public entities of the Parties, such as central, sub-central or local government entities, municipalities, public undertakings and all other entities that procure in accordance with the provisions of this Title, as set out in Annexes XI, XII and XIII;

(c)   "public undertakings" means any undertaking over which the public authorities may exercise directly or indirectly a dominant influence by virtue of their ownership of it, their financial participation therein, or the rules which govern it. A dominant influence on the part of the public authorities shall be presumed when these authorities, directly or indirectly, in relation to an undertaking:

(i)   hold the majority of the undertaking's subscribed capital;

(ii)   control the majority of the votes attaching to shares issued by the undertaking; or

(iii)   can appoint more than half of the members of the undertaking's administrative, managerial or supervisory body.

(d)   "supplier of the Parties" means any natural or legal person or public body or group of such persons of a Party and/or bodies of a Party which can provide goods, services or the execution of works. The term shall cover equally a supplier of goods, a service provider or a contractor;

(e)   "legal person" means any legal entity duly constituted or otherwise organised under applicable law, whether for profit or otherwise, and whether privately-owned or governmentally-owned, including any corporation, trust, partnership, joint venture, sole proprietorship or association;

(f)   "legal person of a Party" means a legal person constituted or otherwise organised under the law of the Community or its Member States or of Chile;

Should such a legal person have only its registered office or central administration in the territory of the Community or Chile, it shall not be considered as a Community or a Chilean legal person respectively, unless it is engaged in substantive business operations in the territory of the Community or Chile respectively.

(g)   a natural person means a national of one of the Member States or of Chile according to their respective legislation;

(h)   "tenderer" means a supplier who has submitted a tender;

(i)   "public" works concessions means a contract of the same type as public works procurement contracts, except for the fact that the remuneration for the works to be carried out consists either solely in the right to exploit the construction or in this right together with a payment;

(j)   "offsets" means those conditions imposed or considered by an entity prior to, or in the course of its procurement process, that encourage local development or improve its Party's balance of payments accounts by means of requirements of local content, licensing of technology, investment, counter-trade or similar requirements;

(k)   "in writing or written" means any expression of information in words, numbers or other symbols, including electronic means, that can be read, reproduced and stored;

(l)   "technical specifications" means a specification which lays down the characteristics of the products or services to be procured, such as quality, performance, safety and dimensions, symbols, terminology, packaging, marking and labelling, or the processes and methods for their production and requirements relating to conformity assessment procedures prescribed by procuring entities;

(m)   "privatisation" means a process by means of which government control over an entity is effectively eliminated and is transferred to the private sector;

(n)   "liberalisation" means a process as a result of which an entity enjoys no exclusive or special rights and is exclusively engaged in the provision of goods or services on markets that are subject to effective competition.

Article 139
National treatment and non-discrimination

1.   Each Party shall ensure that the procurement of its entities covered by this Title takes place in a transparent, reasonable and non-discriminatory manner, treating any supplier of either Party equally and ensuring the principle of open and effective competition.

2.   With respect to any laws, regulations, procedures and practices regarding government procurement covered by this Title, each Party shall grant the goods, services and suppliers of the other Party a treatment no less favourable than that accorded by it to domestic goods, services and suppliers.

3.   With respect to any laws, regulations, procedures and practices regarding government procurement covered by this Title, each Party shall ensure:

   (a)   that its entities do not treat a locally-established supplier less favourably than another locally-established supplier on the basis of the degree of foreign affiliation to, or ownership by, a person of the other Party; and

   (b)   that its entities do not discriminate against a locally-established supplier on the basis that the goods or services offered by that supplier for a particular procurement are goods or services of the other Party.

4.   This Article shall not apply to measures concerning customs duties or other charges of any kind imposed on or in connection with importation, the method of levying such duties and charges, other import regulations, including restrictions and formalities, nor to measures affecting trade in services other than measures specifically governing procurement covered by this Title.

Article 140
Prohibition of offsets and national preferences

Each Party shall ensure that its entities do not, in the qualification and selection of suppliers, goods or services, in the evaluation of bids or in the award of contracts, consider, seek or impose offsets, nor conditions regarding national preferences such as margins allowing price preference.

Article 141
Valuation rules

1.   Entities shall not split up a procurement, nor use any other method of contract valuation with the intention of evading the application of this Title when determining whether a contract is covered by the disciplines of thereof, subject to the conditions set out in Annexes XI and XII, Appendices 1 to 3.

2.   In calculating the value of a contract, an entity shall take into account all forms of remuneration, such as premiums, fees, commissions and interests, as well as the maximum permitted total amount, including option clauses, provided for by the contract.

3.   When, due to the nature of the contract, it is not possible to calculate in advance its precise value, entities shall estimate this value on the basis of objective criteria.

Article 142
Transparency

1.   Each Party shall promptly publish any law, regulation, judicial decision and administrative ruling of general application and procedure, including standard contract clauses, regarding procurement covered by this Title in the appropriate publications referred to in Annex XIII, Appendix 2, including officially designated electronic media.

2.   Each Party shall promptly publish in the same manner all modifications to such measures.

Article 143
Tendering procedures

1.   Entities shall award their public contracts by open or selective tendering procedures according to their national procedures, in compliance with this Title and in a non-discriminatory manner.

2.   For the purposes of this Title:

   (a)   open tendering procedures are those procedures whereby any interested supplier may submit a tender.

   (b)   selective tendering procedures are those procedures whereby, consistent with Article 144 and other relevant provisions of this Title, only suppliers satisfying qualification requirements established by the entities are invited to submit a tender.

3.   However, in the specific cases and only under the conditions laid down in Article 145, entities may use a procedure other than the open or selective tendering procedures referred to in paragraph 1 of that Article, in which case the entities may choose not to publish a notice of intended procurement, and may consult the suppliers of their choice and negotiate the terms of contract with one or more of these.

4.   Entities shall treat tenders in confidence. In particular, they shall not provide information intended to assist particular participants to bring their tenders up to the level of other participants.

Article 144
Selective tendering

1.   In selective tendering, entities may limit the number of qualified suppliers they will invite to tender, consistent with the efficient operation of the procurement process, provided that they select the maximum number of domestic suppliers and suppliers of the other Party, and that they make the selection in a fair and non-discriminatory manner and on the basis of the criteria indicated in the notice of intended procurement or in tender documents.

2.   Entities maintaining permanent lists of qualified suppliers may select suppliers to be invited to tender from among those listed, under the conditions foreseen in Article 146(7). Any selection shall allow for equitable opportunities for suppliers on the lists.

Article 145
Other procedures

1.   Provided that the tendering procedure is not used to avoid maximum possible competition or to protect domestic suppliers, entities shall be allowed to award contracts by means other than an open or selective tendering procedure in the following circumstances and subject to the following conditions, where applicable:

(a)   when no suitable tenders or request to participate have been submitted in response to a prior procurement, on condition that the requirements of the initial procurement are not substantially modified;

(b)   when, for technical or artistic reasons, or for reasons connected with protection of exclusive rights, the contract may be performed only by a particular supplier and no reasonable alternative or substitute exists;

(c)   for reasons of extreme urgency brought about by events unforeseeable by the entity, the products or services could not be obtained in time by means of open or selective tendering procedures;

(d)   for additional deliveries of goods or services by the original supplier where a change of supplier would compel the entity to procure equipment or services not meeting requirements of interchangeability with already existing equipment, software or services;

(e)   when an entity procures prototypes or a first product or service which are developed at its request in the course of, and for, a particular contract for research, experiment, study or original development;

(f)   when additional services which were not included in the initial contract but which were within the objectives of the original tender documentation have, through unforeseeable circumstances, become necessary to complete the services described therein. However, the total value of contracts awarded for the additional construction services may not exceed 50 per cent of the amount of the main contract;

(g)   for new services consisting of the repetition of similar services and for which the entity has indicated, in the notice concerning the initial service, that tendering procedures other than open or selective might be used in awarding contracts for such new services;

(h)   in the case of contracts awarded to the winner of a design contest, provided that the contest has been organised in a manner which is consistent with the principles of this Title; in case of several successful candidates, all successful candidates shall be invited to participate in the negotiations; and

(i)   for quoted goods purchased on a commodity market and for purchases of goods made under exceptionally advantageous conditions which only arise in the very short term in the case of unusual disposals and not for routine purchases from regular suppliers.

2.   The Parties shall ensure that, whenever it is necessary for entities to resort to a procedure other than the open or selective tendering procedures based on the circumstances set forth in paragraph 1, the entities shall maintain a record or prepare a written report providing specific justification for the contract awarded under that paragraph.

Article 146
Qualification of suppliers

1.   Any conditions for participation in procurement shall be limited to those that are essential to ensure that the potential supplier has the capability to fulfil the requirements of the procurement and the ability to execute the contract in question.

2.   In the process of qualifying suppliers, entities shall not discriminate between domestic suppliers and suppliers of the other Party.

3.   A Party shall not impose the condition that, in order for a supplier to participate in a procurement, the supplier has previously been awarded one or more contracts by an entity of that Party or that the supplier has prior work experience in the territory of that Party.

4.   Entities shall recognise as qualified suppliers all suppliers who meet the conditions for participation in a particular intended procurement. Entities shall base their qualification decisions solely on the conditions for participation that have been specified in advance in notices or tender documentation.

5.   Nothing in this Title shall preclude the exclusion of any supplier on grounds such as bankruptcy or false declarations or conviction for serious crime such as participation in criminal organisations.

6.   Entities shall promptly communicate to suppliers that have applied for qualification their decision on whether or not they qualify.

Permanent lists of qualified suppliers

7.   Entities may establish permanent lists of qualified suppliers provided that the following rules are respected :

(a)   entities establishing permanent lists shall ensure that suppliers may apply for qualification at any time.

(b)   any supplier having requested to become a qualified supplier shall be notified by the entities concerned of the decision in this regard.

(c)   suppliers requesting to participate in a given intended procurement who are not on the permanent list of qualified suppliers shall be given the possibility to participate in the procurement by presenting the equivalent certifications and other means of proof requested from suppliers who are on the list.

(d) when an entity operating in the utilities sector uses a notice on the existence of a permanent list as a notice of intended procurement, as provided in Article 147(7), suppliers requesting to participate who are not on the permanent list of qualified suppliers shall also be considered for the procurement, provided there is sufficient time to complete the qualification procedure; in this event, the procuring entity shall promptly start procedures for qualification and the process of, and the time required for, qualifying suppliers shall not be used in order to keep suppliers of other Parties off the suppliers list.

Article 147
Publication of notices

General provisions

1. Each Party shall ensure that its entities provide for effective dissemination of the tendering opportunities generated by the relevant government procurement processes, providing suppliers of the other Party with all the information required to take part in such procurement.

2. For each contract covered by this Title, except as set out in Articles 143(3) and 145, entities shall publish in advance a notice inviting interested suppliers to submit tenders, or where appropriate, requests for participation for that contract.

3. The information in each notice of intended procurement shall include at least the following.

(a) name, address, telefax number, electronic address of the entity and, if different, the address where all documents relating to the procurement may be obtained;

(b) the tendering procedure chosen and the form of the contract;

(c) a description of the intended procurement, as well as essential contract requirements to be fulfilled;

(d) any conditions that suppliers must fulfil to participate in the procurement;

(e) time-limits for submission of tenders and, where appropriate, other time limits;

(f) main criteria to be used for award of the contract; and

(g) if possible, terms of payment and any other terms.

Notice of planned procurement

4. Each Party shall encourage its entities to publish as early as possible in each fiscal year, a notice of planned procurement containing information regarding entities future procurement plans. Such notice should include the subject matter of the procurement and the planned date of the publication of the notice of intended procurement.

5.   Entities operating in the utilities sector may use a notice of planned procurement as a notice of intended procurement, under the condition that such notice contains as much of the information referred to in paragraph 3 as is available, and that it explicitly invites interested suppliers to express their interest in the procurement to the entity.

6.   Entities having used a notice of planned procurement as a notice of intended procurement shall subsequently communicate to all suppliers who have expressed an initial interest further information that shall include, at least, the information referred to in paragraph 3 and ask them to confirm their interest on that basis.

Notice regarding permanent lists of qualified suppliers

7.   Entities which intend to maintain permanent lists shall, consistently with paragraph 2, publish a notice which shall identify the entity, and indicate the purpose of the permanent list and the availability of the rules concerning its operation, including criteria for qualification and disqualification, as well as its duration.

8.   Where the permanent list is of a duration greater than three years, the notice shall be published annually.

9.   Entities operating in the utilities sector may use a notice on the existence of permanent lists of qualified suppliers as a notice of intended procurement. In that case, they shall provide, in a timely manner, information which allows all those who have expressed an interest to assess their interest in participating in the procurement. This information shall include the information contained in the notice referred to in paragraph 3, to the extent that such information is available. Information provided to one interested supplier shall be provided in a non-discriminatory manner to the other interested suppliers.

Common provisions

10.   Each notice referred to in this Article shall be accessible during the entire time period established for tendering for the relevant procurement.

11.   Entities shall publish the notices in a timely manner through means which offer the widest possible and non-discriminatory access to the interested suppliers of the Parties. These means shall be accessible free of charge through a single point of access specified in Annex XIII, Appendix 2.

Article 148
Tender documentation

1.   Tender documentation provided to suppliers shall contain all information necessary to permit them to submit responsive tenders.

2.   Where contracting entities do not offer free direct access to the entire tender documents and any supporting documents by electronic means, entities shall make promptly available the tender documentation at the request of any supplier of the Parties.

3.   Entities shall promptly reply to any reasonable request for relevant information relating to the intended procurement, on condition that such information does not give that supplier an advantage over its competitors.

Article 149
Technical specifications

1.   Technical specifications shall be set out in the notices, tender documents or additional documents.

2.   Each Party shall ensure that its entities do not prepare, adopt or apply any technical specifications with a view to, or with the effect of, creating unnecessary barriers to trade between the Parties.

3.   Technical specifications prescribed by entities shall

   (a)   be in terms of performance and functional requirements rather than design or descriptive characteristics; and

   (b)   be based on international standards, where these exist or, in their absence, on national technical regulations[12], recognised national standards[13], or building codes.

4.   The provisions of paragraph 3 do not apply when the entity can objectively demonstrate that the use of technical specifications referred to in that paragraph would be ineffective or inappropriate for the fulfilment of the legitimate objectives pursued.

5.   In all cases, entities shall consider bids which do not comply with the technical specifications but meet the essential requirements thereof and are fit for the purpose intended. The reference to technical specifications in the tender documents must include words such as or equivalent.

6.   There shall be no requirement for or reference to a particular trademark or trade name, patent, design or type, specific origin, producer or supplier, unless there is no other sufficiently precise or intelligible way of describing the procurement requirements and provided that words, such as "or equivalent", are included in the tender documentation.

7.   The tenderer shall have the burden of proving that his bid meets the essential requirements.

---

[12] For the purpose of this Title, a technical regulation is a document which lays down characteristics of a product or a service or their related processes and production methods, including the applicable administrative provisions, with which compliance is mandatory. It may also include or deal exclusively with terminology, symbols, packaging, marking or labelling requirements as they apply to a product, service, process or production method.

[13] For the purpose of this Title, a standard is a document approved by a recognised body, that provides, for common and repeated use, rules, guidelines or characteristics for products or services or related processes and production methods, with which compliance is not mandatory. It may also include or deal exclusively with terminology, symbols, packaging, marking or labeling requirements as they apply to a product, service, process or production method.

Article 150
Time-limits

1.   All time-limits established by the entities for the receipt of tenders and requests to participate shall be adequate to allow suppliers of the other Party, as well as domestic suppliers, to prepare and to submit tenders, and where appropriate, requests for participation or applications for qualifying. In determining any such time-limit, entities shall, consistent with their own reasonable needs, take into account such factors as the complexity of the intended procurement and the normal time for transmitting tenders from foreign as well as domestic points.

2.   Each Party shall ensure that its entities shall take due account of publication delays when setting the final date for receipt of tenders or of request for participation or for qualifying for the supplier's list.

3.   The minimum time-limits for the receipt of tenders are specified in Annex XIII, Appendix 3.

Article 151
Negotiations

1.   A Party may provide for its entities to conduct negotiations:

(a)   in the context of procurements in which they have indicated such intent in the notice of intended procurement; or

(b)   when it appears from evaluation that no one tender is obviously the most advantageous in terms of the specific evaluation criteria set forth in the notices or tender documentation.

2.   Negotiations shall primarily be used to identify the strengths and weaknesses in tenders.

3.   Entities shall not, in the course of negotiations, discriminate between tenderers. In particular, they shall ensure that:

(a)   any elimination of participants is carried out in accordance with the criteria set forth in the notices and tender documentation;

(b)   all modifications to the criteria and to the technical requirements are transmitted in writing to all remaining participants in the negotiations;

(c)   on the basis of the revised requirements and/or when negotiations are concluded, all remaining participants are afforded an opportunity to submit new or amended tenders in accordance with a common deadline.

Article 152
Submission, receipt and opening of tenders

1.   Tenders and requests to participate in procedures shall be submitted in writing.

2.   Entities shall receive and open bids from tenderers under procedures and conditions guaranteeing the respect of the principles of transparency and non-discrimination.

Article 153
Awarding of contracts

1.   To be considered for award, a tender must, at the time of opening, conform to the essential requirements of the notices or tender documentation and be submitted by a supplier which complies with the conditions for participation.

2.   Entities shall make the award to the tenderer whose tender is either the lowest tender or the tender which, in terms of the specific objective evaluation criteria previously set forth in the notices or tender documentation, is determined to be the most advantageous.

Article 154
Information on contract award

1.   Each Party shall ensure that its entities provide for effective dissemination of the results of government procurement processes.

2.   Entities shall promptly inform tenderers of decisions regarding the award of the contract and of the characteristics and relative advantages of the selected tender. Upon request, entities shall inform any eliminated tenderer of the reasons for the rejection of its tender.

3.   Entities may decide to withhold certain information on the contract award where release of such information would prevent law enforcement or otherwise be contrary to the public interest, would prejudice the legitimate commercial interests of suppliers, or might prejudice fair competition between them.

Article 155
Bid challenges

1.   Entities shall accord impartial and timely consideration to any complaints from suppliers regarding an alleged breach of this Title in the context of a procurement procedure.

2.   Each Party shall provide non-discriminatory, timely, transparent and effective procedures enabling suppliers to challenge alleged breaches of this Title arising in the context of procurements in which they have, or have had, an interest.

3.   Challenges shall be heard by an impartial and independent reviewing authority. A reviewing authority which is not a court shall either be subject to judicial review or shall have procedural guarantees similar to those of a court.

4.   Challenge procedures shall provide for:

(a)   rapid interim measures to correct breaches of this Title and to preserve commercial opportunities. Such action may result in suspension of the procurement process. However, procedures may provide that overriding adverse consequences for the interests concerned, including the public interest, may be taken into account in deciding whether such measures should be applied; and

(b)   if appropriate, correction of the breach of this Title or, in the absence of such correction, compensation for the loss or damages suffered, which may be limited to costs for tender preparation and protest.

Article 156
Information technology

1.   The Parties shall, to the extent possible, endeavour to use electronic means of communication to permit efficient dissemination of information on government procurement, particularly as regards tender opportunities offered by entities, while respecting the principles of transparency and non-discrimination.

2.   With a view to improving access to government procurement markets, each Party shall endeavour to implement an electronic information system, which is compulsory for their respective entities.

3.   The Parties shall encourage the use of electronic means for the transmission of offers.

Article 157
Cooperation and assistance

The Parties shall endeavour to provide each other with technical cooperation and assistance through the development of training programs with a view to achieving a better understanding of their respective government procurement systems and statistics and better access to their respective markets.

Article 158
Statistical reports

Where a Party does not ensure an acceptable level of compliance with Article 147(11), it shall, upon request of the other Party, collect and provide to the other Party on an annual basis statistics on its procurements covered by this Title. Such reports shall contain the information established in Annex XIII, Appendix 4.

Article 159
Modifications to coverage

1.   A Party may modify its coverage under this Title, provided that it:

(a)   notifies the other Party of the modification; and

(b)   provides the other Party, within 30 days following the date of such notification, appropriate compensatory adjustments to its coverage in order to maintain a level of coverage comparable to that existing prior to the modification.

2.   Notwithstanding paragraph 1(b), no compensatory adjustments shall be provided to the other Party where the modification by a Party of its coverage under this Title concerns:

(a)   rectifications of a purely formal nature and minor amendments to Annexes XI and XII;

(b)   one or more covered entities on which government control or influence has been effectively eliminated as a result of privatisation or liberalisation.

3.   Where appropriate, the Association Committee shall by decision modify the relevant Annex to reflect the modification notified by the Party concerned.

Article 160
Further negotiations

If either Party should offer in the future a third party additional advantages with regard to access to their respective procurement markets beyond what has been agreed under this Title, it shall agree to enter into negotiations with the other Party with a view to extending these advantages to it on a reciprocal basis by means of a decision of the Association Committee.

Article 161
Exceptions

Provided that such measures are not applied in a manner that would constitute a means of arbitrary or unjustifiable discrimination between the Parties or a disguised restriction on trade between them, nothing in this Title shall be construed to prevent any Party from adopting or maintaining measures:

(a)   necessary to protect public morals, order or safety;

(b)   necessary to protect human life, health or security;

(c)   necessary to protect animal or plant life or health;

(d)   necessary to protect intellectual property; or

(e)   relating to goods or services of handicapped persons, of philanthropic institutions or of prison labour.

Article 162
Review and implementation

The Association Committee shall review the implementation of this Title every two years, unless otherwise agreed by the Parties; it shall consider any issue arising from it, and take appropriate action in the exercise of its functions. It shall, in particular, fulfil the following tasks:

(a)   coordinate exchanges between the Parties regarding the development and implementation of information technology systems in the field of public procurement;

(b)   make appropriate recommendations regarding the cooperation between the Parties; and

(c)   adopt decisions where provided for under this Title.

TITLE V
CURRENT PAYMENTS AND CAPITAL MOVEMENTS

Article 163
Objective and scope

1.   The Parties shall aim at the liberalisation of current payments and capital movements between them, in conformity with the commitments undertaken in the framework of the international financial institutions and with due consideration to each Party's currency stability.

2.   This Title applies to all current payments and capital movements between the Parties.

Article 164
Current Account

The Parties shall allow, in freely convertible currency and in accordance with the Articles of Agreement of the International Monetary Fund, any payments and transfers of the Current Account between the Parties.

Article 165
Capital Account

With regard to movement of capital of the Balance of Payments, from the entry into force of this Agreement, the Parties shall allow the free movements of capital relating to direct investments made in accordance with the laws of the host country and investments established in accordance with the provisions of Title III of this Part of the Agreement, and the liquidation or repatriation of these capitals and of any profit stemming therefrom.

Article 166
Exceptions and safeguard measures

1.   Where, in exceptional circumstances, payments and capital movements between the Parties cause or threaten to cause serious difficulties for the operation of monetary policy or exchange rate policy in either Party, the Party concerned may take safeguard measures with regard to capital movements that are strictly necessary for a period not exceeding one year.

The application of safeguard measures may be extended through their formal reintroduction.

2.   The Party adopting the safeguard measures shall inform the other Party forthwith and present, as soon as possible, a time schedule for their removal.

Article 167
Final provisions

1.   With respect to this Title, the Parties confirm the rights and obligations existing under any bilateral or multilateral agreements to which they are parties.

2.   The Parties shall consult each other with a view to facilitating the movement of capital between them in order to promote the objectives of this Agreement.

TITLE VI
INTELLECTUAL PROPERTY RIGHTS

Article 168
Objective

The Parties shall grant and ensure adequate and effective protection of intellectual property rights in accordance with the highest international standards, including effective means of enforcing such rights provided for in international treaties.

Article 169
Scope

For the purposes of this Agreement, intellectual property rights embodies copyright including copyright in computer programs and in databases - and related rights, the rights related to patents, industrial designs, geographical indications including appellation of origins, trademarks, layout-designs (topographies) of integrated circuits, as well as protection of undisclosed information and protection against unfair competition as referred to in Article 10 bis of the Paris Convention for the Protection of Industrial Property (Stockholm Act 1967).

Article 170
Protection of intellectual property rights

In pursuance of the objectives set out in Article 168, the Parties shall:

(a)   continue to ensure an adequate and effective implementation of the obligations arising from the following conventions:

  (i)   Agreement on Trade-related Aspects of Intellectual Property, Annex 1C to the Agreement establishing the World Trade Organisation ("the TRIPs");

  (ii)   Paris Convention for the Protection of Industrial Property (Stockholm Act, 1967);

  (iii)   Berne Convention for the Protection of Literary and Artistic Works (Paris Act, 1971);

  (iv)   Rome Convention for the Protection of Performers, Producers of Phonograms and Broadcasting Organisations (Rome, 1961); and

  (v)   International Convention for the Protection of New Varieties of Plants 1978 ("1978 UPOV Convention"), or the International Convention for the Protection of New Varieties of Plants 1991 ("1991 UPOV Convention");

(b)   by 1 January 2007 acceed to and ensure an adequate and effective implementation of the obligations arising from the following multilateral conventions:

  (i)   Nice Agreement Concerning the International Classification of Goods and Services for the Purposes of Registration of Marks (Geneva Act, 1977, amended in 1979);

(ii)   World Intellectual Property Organization Copyright Treaty (Geneva, 1996);

(iii)   World Intellectual Property Organization Performances and Phonograms Treaty (Geneva, 1996);

(iv)   Patent Co-operation Treaty (Washington, 1970, amended in 1979 and modified in 1984); and

(v)   The 1971 Strasbourg Agreement Concerning the International Patent Classification (Strasbourg 1971, amended in 1979)

(c)   by 1 January 2009 acceed to and ensure an adequate and effective implementation of the obligations arising from the following multilateral conventions:

(i)   Convention for the Protection of Producers of Phonograms against the Unauthorised Reproduction of their Phonograms (Geneva 1971);

(ii)   Locarno Agreement establishing an International Classification for Industrial Designs (Locarno Union 1968, amended in 1979);

(iii)   Budapest Treaty on the International Recognition of the Deposit of Micro-organisms for the Purposes of Patent Procedure (1977, amended in 1980); and

(iv)   Trademark Law Treaty (Geneva, 1994);

(d)   make every effort to ratify and ensure an adequate and effective implementation of the obligations arising from the following multilateral conventions at the earliest possible opportunity:

(i)   Protocol to the Madrid Agreement concerning the International Registration of Marks (1989);

(ii)   Madrid Agreement concerning the International Registration of Marks (Stockholm Act 1967, amended in 1979); and

(iii)   The Vienna Agreement establishing an International Classification of Figurative Elements of Marks (Vienna 1973, amended in 1985).

Article 171
Review

While the Parties express their attachment to observing the obligations deriving from the above multilateral conventions, the Association Council may decide to include in Article 170 other multilateral conventions in this field.

*

SINGAPORE-AUSTRALIA FREE TRADE AGREEMENT (SAFTA)[*]
[CONSOLIDATED TEXT]
[excerpts]

The free trade agreement between the Government of Singapore and the Government of Australia was signed on 17 February 2003. It entered into force on 28 July 2003.

PREAMBLE

Singapore and Australia ("the Parties")

Conscious of their longstanding friendship and growing trade and investment relationship;

Desiring to improve the efficiency and competitiveness of their goods and services sectors and expand trade and investment between them;

Recognising that strengthening of their closer economic partnership will bring economic and social benefits and improve the living standards of their people;

Building on their rights, obligations and undertakings under the World Trade Organization, and other multilateral, regional and bilateral agreements and arrangements;

Recognising their commitment to securing trade liberalisation and an outward looking approach to trade and investment;

Mindful of the Asia-Pacific Economic Cooperation goals of free and open trade and investment;

Conscious that a framework of rules for trade in goods and services, and investment will contribute to the promotion of closer links with other economies, especially in the Asia-Pacific region;

Recognising the need for good corporate governance and a predictable, transparent and consistent business environment to enable businesses to conduct transactions freely, use resources efficiently and take investment and planning decisions with certainty; and

Believing that their cooperative framework could be a dynamic one that also covers newer areas of economic cooperation;

Have agreed as follows:

---

[*] *Source*: The Government of Australia and the Government of Singapore (2003). "Singapore-Australia Free Trade Agreement (SAFTA) Consolidated Text", available on the Internet (http://www.mti.gov.sg/Public/PDF/CMT/FTA_SAFTA_Agreement.pdf). [Note added by the editor.]

01 OBJECTIVES AND GENERAL DEFINITIONS

ARTICLE 1
Objectives

The objectives of the Parties in concluding this Agreement are:

(a)   to strengthen the relationship between them;

(b)   to liberalise trade in goods and services between them and to establish a framework conducive for bilateral investments;

(c)   to support the wider liberalisation process in the Asia-Pacific Economic Cooperation consistent with its goals of free and open trade and investment;

(d)   to build upon their commitments at the World Trade Organization, and to support its efforts to create a predictable, and more free and open global trading environment;

(e)   to improve the efficiency and competitiveness of their goods and services sectors and expand trade and investment between them;

(f)   to establish a framework of transparent rules to govern trade and investment between them; and

(g)   to explore newer areas of economic cooperation.

06 GOVERNMENT PROCUREMENT

ARTICLE 1
Definitions

1.   For the purposes of this Chapter:

(a)   "confidential information" includes: trade secrets; know-how; privileged information; or any other information that is expressed to be confidential or sensitive by the person disclosing the information or is disclosed in circumstances importing, either expressly or implicitly, an obligation of confidence as recognised by the laws, regulations, procedures and practices of the Party concerned;

(b)   "entities" means:

(i)   for Australia, those entities listed at Annex 3A and their successors other than those subsequently commercialised or privatised; and

(ii)   for Singapore, those entities listed at Annex 3B and their successors other than those subsequently commercialised or privatised;

(b)   "limited tendering procedures" means those tendering procedures in which the procuring entity directly invites one or more suppliers to submit tenders;

(c)   "open tendering procedures" means those tendering procedures in which the procuring entity issues a public call for tenders; and

(d)   "tender process" includes all activities directly related to the process of procuring goods or services conducted by a Party or its entities which is open to participation by persons of the other Party before a contract for the supply of those goods or services is concluded.

ARTICLE 2
Scope and Coverage

1.   This Chapter shall apply to:

(a)   any law, regulation, procedure or practice regarding any procurement by entities; and

(b)   procurement of goods and services[1] by any contractual means, including through such methods as purchase or as lease, rental or hire purchase, with or without an option to buy, including any combination of goods and services.

2.   This Chapter shall not apply to:

(a)   internal procurement of goods and services by a Party from its own entities where no other supplier has been asked to tender. However, where such an entity submits a tender in an open tendering procedure, this Chapter shall apply;

(b)   procurement of proprietary items required to ensure the integrity of machinery, equipment or systems. However, where such items are available from a number of sources and an open tendering procedure is used, this Chapter shall apply;

(c)   procurement of proprietary equipment of a work, health or safety nature specified in industrial agreements. However, where such items are available from a number of sources and an open tendering procedure is used, this Chapter shall apply;

(d)   procurement for the purposes of overseas development assistance;

(e)   procurement of goods and services outside the territory of the procuring Party, for consumption outside the territory of the procuring Party; or

(f)   procurement of asset management and financial advisory services pertaining to reserves held by each Party's Government or its entities.

---

[1] For the purposes of this Chapter, "goods and services" includes construction.

ARTICLE 3
National Treatment

1.   With respect to all laws, regulations, procedures and practices regarding government procurement covered by this Chapter, each Party shall provide immediately and unconditionally to the goods, services and suppliers of the other Party offering goods or services of the other Party, treatment no less favourable than that accorded to domestic goods, services and suppliers.

2.   With respect to all laws, regulations, procedures and practices regarding government procurement covered by this Chapter, each Party shall ensure:

(a)   that its entities shall not treat a locally-established supplier less favourably than another locally-established supplier on the basis of degree of foreign affiliation or ownership; and

(b)   that its entities shall not discriminate against a locally-established supplier on the basis that it is a supplier of a good or service of the other Party.

3.   The provisions of paragraphs 1 and 2 shall not apply to customs duties and charges of any kind imposed on or in connection with importation, the method of levying such duties and charges, other import regulations and formalities, and measures affecting trade in services other than laws, regulations, procedures and practices regarding government procurement covered by this Chapter.

4.   A Party shall not discriminate in favour of corporate bodies in which that Party is a shareholder.

ARTICLE 4
Rules of Origin

A Party shall not apply rules of origin to goods or services imported or supplied for purposes of government procurement covered by this Chapter from the other Party, which are different from the rules of origin applied in the normal course of trade and at the time of the transaction in question to imports or supplies of the same goods or services from that other Party.

ARTICLE 5
Technical Specifications

Technical specifications laying down the characteristics of the goods or services to be procured shall not be prepared, adopted or applied with a view to, or with the effect of, creating unnecessary obstacles to trade between the Parties.

ARTICLE 6
Tendering Principles

1.   Entities may use open tendering procedures or limited tendering procedures.

2.   Each Party shall ensure that the tendering procedures of its entities are consistent with the provisions of this Chapter, provide for mechanisms to eliminate conflict of interest between

persons administering a tendering procedure and potential suppliers, achieve value for money outcomes and are conducted in a fair and non-discriminatory manner.

3.   In an open tendering procedure, entities shall publish an invitation to participate in such a way as to be readily accessible to any interested supplier of the other Party. In particular, entities shall make tender notices accessible to suppliers. Where a deadline has been specified for the close of tenders, the existence of such a deadline shall be made known in the same medium as used to publish tender notices.

4.   Any conditions for participation in open tendering procedures shall be published in adequate time to enable interested suppliers of the other Party to initiate and, to the extent that it is compatible with the efficient operation of the procurement process, complete the registration and/or qualification procedures.

5.   Entities shall not provide to any tenderer information with regard to a specific procurement in a manner which would have the effect of giving that tenderer an advantage over other tenderers.

6.   The tender evaluation process shall be fair and non-discriminatory and shall have a mechanism to eliminate potential conflict of interest between persons administering the process and suppliers participating in the process.

7.   Entities shall, on request from an unsuccessful supplier of the other Party which participated in the relevant tender, promptly provide pertinent information concerning reasons for the rejection of its tender, unless the release of such information would impede law enforcement or otherwise be contrary to the public interest or would prejudice the legitimate commercial interest of particular enterprises, public or private, or might prejudice fair competition between suppliers.

ARTICLE 7
Registration and Qualification of Suppliers

1.   In the process of registering and/or qualifying suppliers, the entities of a Party shall not discriminate between domestic suppliers and suppliers of the other Party.

2.   Any conditions for participation in open tendering procedures shall be no less favourable to suppliers of the other Party than to domestic suppliers.

3.   The process of, and the time required for, registering and/or qualifying suppliers shall not be used in order to keep suppliers of the other Party off a list of suppliers or from being considered for a particular procurement.

4.   Entities maintaining permanent lists of registered and/or qualified suppliers shall ensure that suppliers may apply for registration or qualification at any time, and that all registered and qualified suppliers are included in the lists within a reasonably short time.

ARTICLE 8
Protection and Proper Use of Confidential Information

1.   When a person of a Party discloses confidential information to the other Party or its entities, the latter Party shall ensure that such information is kept confidential and is not used for a purpose other than that for which it was disclosed, except where disclosure is required:

    (a)   by an order of a court or tribunal;

    (b)   by a House of Parliament or its Committees, however the relevant Party or entity may resist such an order by a claim of public interest immunity; or

    (c)   under legislation governing access to government information, unless an exception or exemption under such legislation is successfully invoked in relation to the information.

2.   Before any confidential information is disclosed pursuant to Article 8.1, reasonable notice in writing shall be given to the person of a Party who provided the information.

ARTICLE 9
Protection of Intellectual Property in a Tender Process
and the Resulting Contracts

1.   Material protected by intellectual property rights as defined in Chapter 13 (Intellectual Property) that is supplied by a person of a Party in a tender process shall not lose that protection on the sole basis that it is so supplied.

2.   Ownership of intellectual property specifically produced under a contract for the procurement of goods and services concluded between a person of one Party and the other Party or its entities shall be as determined by the contract.

3.   The contract for the procurement of goods or services shall not affect intellectual property rights in material that existed prior to the date of the contract unless the contracting Parties expressly agree otherwise in the contract.

4.   Where the contract for goods or services includes the provision of licensed software, the procuring Party or procuring entities, may not reverse assemble or reverse compile the licensed software except to the extent permitted under its copyright law.

ARTICLE 10
Application of provisions of other Chapters to this Chapter

The provisions of Article 4 (Competitive Neutrality) of Chapter 12 (Competition Policy) shall apply, *mutatis mutandis*, to procurements within the scope of this Chapter.

ARTICLE 11
Electronic Procurement

1.   The Parties shall, within the context of their commitment to promote electronic commerce, seek to provide opportunities for government procurement to be undertaken through electronic means, hereafter referred to as "e-procurement".

2.   Each Party shall work toward a single entry point for the purpose of enabling suppliers to access information on procurement opportunities in its territory.

3.   To facilitate access of suppliers of one Party to e-procurement opportunities of the other Party, the Parties shall, to the extent possible, cooperate to ensure policies and procedures are adopted that:

(a)   promote equitable access for all potential suppliers of the other Party;

(b)   promote the use of systems that are the most cost-effective for potential suppliers, where the Parties utilise authentication systems;

(c)   provide for the least cost to potential suppliers, where the Parties elect to procure goods or services through online or reverse auctions;

(d)   protect documentation from unauthorised and undetected alteration; and

(e)   provide appropriate levels of security for data on, and passing through, the procuring entity's network.

4.   Each Party shall, to the extent possible, make procurement opportunities that are available to the public accessible to suppliers via the Internet or any publicly available electronic medium. To the extent possible, each Party shall make available relevant documentation by the same means.

ARTICLE 12
Review of tender process

1.   In the event of a complaint by a supplier that there has been a breach of the procuring Party's laws, regulations, procedures or practices regarding procurement in the context of a procurement in which they have, or have had, an interest, each Party shall encourage the supplier to seek resolution of its complaint in consultation with the procuring entity. In such instances the procuring entity shall accord timely and impartial consideration to any such complaint.

2.   Each Party shall provide suppliers of the other Party with non-discriminatory, timely, transparent and effective access to an administrative or judicial body competent to hear or review complaints of alleged breaches of the procuring Party's laws, regulations, procedures and practices regarding procurement in the context of procurements in which they have, or have had, an interest.

3.   Each Party shall make information on complaint mechanisms generally available.

ARTICLE 13
Transparency

1.   The Parties shall apply all procurement laws, regulations, procedures and practices consistently, fairly and equitably so that their corporate governance structures provide transparency to potential suppliers.

2.   The Parties shall publish and make accessible information relating to government procurement, and any changes or additions to this information, in a consistent and timely manner. Information relating to government procurement includes:

      (a)   procurement laws, regulations, and policy guidelines;

      (b)   open tendering opportunities and the conditions for participation;

      (c)   supplier qualification mechanisms and criteria for qualification; and

      (d)   decisions on contract awards.

ARTICLE 14
Exceptions

1.   Nothing in this Chapter shall be construed to prevent either Party from taking any action or not disclosing any information which it considers necessary for the protection of its essential security interests relating to the procurement of arms, ammunition or war materials, or to procurement indispensable for national security or for national defence purposes.

2   Subject to the requirement that such measures are not applied in a manner which would constitute a means of arbitrary or unjustifiable discrimination between countries where the same conditions prevail or a disguised restriction on international trade, nothing in this Chapter shall be construed to prevent either Party from imposing or enforcing measures:

      (a)   necessary to protect public morals, order or safety, human, animal or plant life or health or intellectual property;

      (b)   relating to the goods or services of handicapped persons, of philanthropic institutions or of prison labour; or

      (c)   relating to the conservation of exhaustible natural resources.

ARTICLE 15
Opportunities for indigenous persons

Subject to the requirement that such measures are not applied in a manner which would constitute a means of arbitrary or unjustifiable discrimination between countries where the same conditions prevail or a disguised restriction on international trade, nothing in this Chapter shall prevent Australia from promoting employment and training opportunities for its indigenous people in regions where significant indigenous populations exist.

ARTICLE 16
Industry Development

Nothing in this Chapter shall prevent the Parties from using government procurement to promote industry development including measures to assist small and medium enterprises (SMEs) within their territory to gain access to the government procurement market.

ARTICLE 17
Dispute Settlement

A Party may not initiate dispute settlement proceedings under Chapter 16 (Dispute Settlement) regarding its rights and obligations under this Chapter unless:

(a)   the matter giving rise to the dispute involves a pattern of practice; and

(b)   the suppliers affected have exhausted the available remedies regarding the particular matter.

ARTICLE 18
Review of Commitments

1.   If, after this Agreement enters into force, a Party enters into any agreement on government procurement with a non-Party, it shall give positive consideration to a request by the other Party for incorporation herein of treatment no less favourable than under the aforesaid agreement.   Any such incorporation should maintain the overall balance of commitments undertaken by each Party under this Agreement.

2.   Not later than 12 months from the date of entry into force of this Agreement and biennially thereafter, the Parties shall examine and, where appropriate, update the entities specified in Annexes 3A and 3B.

3.   As part of the examination referred to in Article 18.2, both Parties shall consider adding entities to their respective Annexes. This undertaking shall include Australia encouraging its State and Territory Governments to list their entities by the time of the first review, and Singapore considering adding entities not covered by the WTO Plurilateral Agreement on Government Procurement.

07 TRADE IN SERVICES

ARTICLE 1
Definitions

For the purposes of this Chapter:

(a)   "a service supplied in the exercise of governmental authority" means any service which is supplied neither on a commercial basis nor in competition with one or more service suppliers;

(b)   "commercial presence" means any type of business or professional establishment, including through:

(i)   the constitution, acquisition or maintenance of a legal person,
or
(ii)   the creation or maintenance of a branch or a representative office,

within the territory of a Party for the purpose of supplying a service;

(c) "direct taxes" comprise all taxes on total income, on total capital or on elements of income or of capital, including taxes on gains from the alienation of property, taxes on estates, inheritances and gifts, and taxes on the total amounts of wages or salaries paid by enterprises, as well as taxes on capital appreciation;

(d) "existing measures" means measures in force as of the date of entry into force of this Agreement;

(e) "legal person" means any legal entity duly constituted or otherwise organised under applicable law, whether for profit or otherwise, and whether privately-owned or governmentally-owned, including any corporation, trust, partnership, joint venture, sole proprietorship or association;

(f) "legal person of the other Party" means a legal person which is either:

(i)   constituted or otherwise organised under the law of the other Party; or

(ii)   in the case of the supply of a service through commercial presence, owned or controlled by:

(A)   natural persons of the other Party; or
(B)   legal persons of the other Party identified under Article 1 (f)(i);

(g) "measure" means any measure by a Party, whether in the form of a law, regulation, rule, procedure, decision, administrative action, or any other form;

(h) "measures by Parties" means measures taken by:

(i)   central, regional or local governments and authorities; and

(ii)   non-governmental bodies in the exercise of powers delegated by central, regional or local governments or authorities;

(i) "measures by Parties affecting trade in services "include measures in respect of:

(i)   the purchase, payment or use of a service;

(ii)   the access to and use of, in connection with the supply of a service, services which are required by the Parties to be offered to the public generally;

(iii) the presence, including commercial presence, of persons of a Party for the supply of a service in the territory of the other Party;

(j)   "monopoly supplier of a service" means any person, public or private, which in the relevant market of the territory of a Party is authorised or established formally or in effect by that Party as the sole supplier of that service;

(k)   "natural person of a Party" means a natural person who resides in the territory of the Party or elsewhere and who under the law of that Party:

       (i)   is a national of that Party; or

       (ii)   has the right of permanent residence in that Party;

(l)   "new measures" means measures adopted after the date of entry into force of this Agreement;

(m)   "person" means either a natural person or a legal person;

(n)   "services" means all services including new and variant services in any sector except services supplied in the exercise of governmental authority;

(o)   "service consumer" means any person that receives or uses a service;

(p)   "service of the other Party" means a service which is supplied:

       (i)   from or in the territory of the other Party, or in the case of maritime transport, by a vessel registered under the laws of the other Party, or by a person of the other Party which supplies the service through the operation of a vessel and/or its use in whole or in part; or

       (ii)   in the case of the supply of a service through commercial presence or through the presence of natural persons, by a service supplier of the other Party;

(q)   "service supplier" means any person that supplies a service;[1]

(r)   "supply of a service" includes the production, distribution, marketing, sale and delivery of a service; and

(s)   "trade in services" is defined as the supply of a service:

       (i)   from the territory of a Party into the territory of the other Party ("cross-border");

       (ii)   in the territory of a Party to the service consumer of the other Party ("consumption abroad");

       (iii)   by a service supplier of a Party, through commercial presence in the territory of the other Party ("commercial presence");

---

[1] Where the service is not supplied directly by a legal person but through other forms of commercial presence such as a branch or a representative office, the service supplier (i.e. the legal person) shall, nonetheless, through such presence be accorded the treatment provided for service suppliers under this Agreement. Such treatment shall be extended to the presence through which the service is supplied and need not be extended to any other parts of the supplier located outside the territory where the service is supplied.

    (iv)   by a service supplier of a Party, through presence of natural persons of a Party in the territory of the other Party ("presence of natural persons").

ARTICLE 2
Scope

1.   This Chapter applies to measures by a Party affecting trade in services by service suppliers of the other Party.

2.   This Chapter shall not apply to:

    (a)   subsidies or grants provided by a Party or to any conditions attached to the receipt or continued receipt of such subsidies or grants, whether or not such subsidies or grants are offered exclusively to domestic services, service consumers or service suppliers; or

    (b)   a service supplied in the exercise of governmental authority within the territory of each respective Party.

3.   This Chapter shall not apply to measures affecting natural persons seeking access to the employment market of a Party, nor shall it apply to measures regarding citizenship, residence or employment on a permanent basis.

4.   Nothing in this Chapter shall prevent a Party from applying measures to regulate the entry of natural persons of the other Party into, or their temporary stay in, its territory, including those measures necessary to protect the integrity of, and to ensure the orderly movement of natural persons across its borders, provided that such measures are not applied in such a manner as to nullify or impair the benefits accruing to the other Party under the terms of this Chapter.

ARTICLE 3
Market Access

Neither Party shall maintain or adopt, either on the basis of a regional subdivision or on the basis of its entire territory,[2]

(a)   limitations on the number of service suppliers whether in the form of numerical quotas, monopolies, exclusive service suppliers or the requirements of an economic needs test;

(b)   limitations on the total value of service transactions or assets in the form of numerical quotas or the requirement of an economic needs test;

(c)   limitations on the total number of service operations or on the total quantity of service output expressed in terms of designated numerical units in the form of quotas or the requirement of an economic needs test;[3]

---

[2] Subject to the reservations that a Party makes in respect of market access pursuant to Article 5 (Reservations), where the cross-border movement of capital is an essential part of a service supplied through the mode of supply referred to in Article 1(s)(i), that Party is hereby committed to allow such movement of capital. Subject to the reservations that a Party makes in respect of market access pursuant to Article 5 (Reservations), where a service is supplied through the mode of supply referred to in Article 1(s)(iii) that Party is hereby committed to allow related transfers of capital into its territory.

(d)   limitations on the total number of natural persons that may be employed in a particular service sector or that a service supplier may employ and who are necessary for, and directly related to, the supply of a specific service in the form of numerical quotas or the requirement of an economic needs test;

(e)   measures which restrict or require specific types of legal entity or joint venture through which a service supplier may supply a service; and

(f)   limitations on the participation of foreign capital in terms of maximum percentage limit on foreign shareholding or the total value of individual or aggregate foreign investment.

ARTICLE 4
National Treatment

1.   Each Party shall accord to services and service suppliers of the other Party, in respect of all measures affecting the supply of services, treatment no less favourable than that it accords to its own like services and service suppliers.

2.   A Party may meet the requirement of Article 4.1 by according to services and service suppliers of the other Party, either formally identical treatment or formally different treatment to that it accords to its own like services and service suppliers.

3.   Formally identical or formally different treatment shall be considered to be less favourable if it modifies the conditions of competition in favour of services or service suppliers of the Party compared to like services or service suppliers of the other Party.

4.   This Article shall not be construed to require any Party to compensate for any inherent competitive disadvantages which result from the foreign character of the relevant services or service suppliers.

ARTICLE 5
Reservations

1.   Articles 3 (Market Access) and 4 (National Treatment) shall not apply to:

   (a)   any existing non-conforming measure that is maintained by a Party at:

      (i)   the central or regional level, as set out in Annex 4-I; or
      (ii)   the local level; or

   (b)   the continuation or prompt renewal of any non-conforming measure referred to in Article 5.1(a).

2.   Articles 3 (Market Access) and 4 (National Treatment) shall not apply to any existing or new measure that a Party adopts or maintains with respect to sectors, subsectors or activities as set out in Annex 4-II.

3.   Article 11 (Domestic Regulation) shall not apply to:

---

[3] Article 3(c) does not cover measures of a Party which limit inputs for the supply of services.

(a)   any existing non-conforming measure that is maintained by a Party as set out in Annex 4-I; or

(b)   any existing or new   measure that a Party adopts or maintains with respect to sectors, subsectors or activities as set out in Annex 4-II.

4.   Each Party shall set out its reservations through a description of:

(a)   with respect to Annex 4-I, the non-conforming measure to which the reservation applies; and

(b)   with respect to Annex 4-II, the sectors, subsectors or activities to which the reservation applies.

ARTICLE 6
Transitional Provisions on Regional Government Measures

1.   Articles 3 (Market Access) and 4 (National Treatment) shall not apply to measures maintained by a Party at the regional level until the first review of this Agreement under Article 3   (Review) of Chapter 17 (Final Provisions), when modifications or additions may be incorporated into the reservations in Annex 4-I and Annex 4-II to extend the coverage of Articles 3 (Market Access) and 4 (National Treatment) to these measures. Following the first review, Articles 3 (Market Access) and 4 (National Treatment) shall apply, at the regional level, unless the non-conforming measures maintained at the regional level are covered by the reservations in Annexes 4-I and 4-II.

2.   A Party shall enter into consultations at the request of the other Party with a view to ensuring that modifications or additions incorporated into the reservations in accordance with Article 6.1 are consistent with the overall balance of benefits under the Agreement, and deciding whether any necessary adjustment in the commitments of the Parties is required to preserve this balance. Article 7 (Modification or Addition of Reservations) and Chapter 16   (Dispute Settlement) shall not apply to any such adjustments. The Parties shall not apply any measure affecting trade in services at the regional level in such a manner as would improve their negotiating position and leverage.

ARTICLE 7
Modification or Addition of Reservations

1.   By giving three months written notification to the other Party, a Party may modify or add to its non-conforming measures as set out in Annex 4-I and add new sectors, subsectors or activities to its reservations set out in Annex 4-II. At the request of the other Party, it shall hold consultations with a view to reaching agreement on any necessary adjustment required to maintain the overall balance of commitments undertaken by each Party under this Agreement. If agreement is not reached between the Parties on any necessary adjustment, the matter may be referred to arbitration in accordance with Chapter 16 (Dispute Settlement).

2.   Article 7.1 shall not be construed to prejudice the right of both Parties to maintain any existing measures or adopt new measures consistent with the reservations set out in Annexes 4-I and 4-II.

ARTICLE 8
Additional Commitments

1.   The Parties shall set out their respective additional commitments in Annex 4-III of this Agreement with respect to measures affecting trade in services not covered by Articles 3 (Market Access) and 4 (National Treatment), including those regarding qualifications, standards or licensing matters and any other matters as may be mutually agreed.

ARTICLE 9
Transparency

1.   Each Party shall publish promptly and, except in emergency situations, at the latest by the time of their entry into force, all relevant measures of general application which pertain to or affect the operation of this Chapter. International agreements pertaining to or affecting trade in services to which a Party is a signatory shall also be published.

2.   Where publication as referred to in Article 9.1 is not practicable, such information shall be made otherwise publicly available.

3.   Each Party shall respond promptly to all requests by the other Party for specific information on any of its measures of general application or international agreements within the meaning of Article 9.1. Each Party shall also establish one or more enquiry points to provide specific information to the other Party, upon request, on all such matters.

ARTICLE 10
Disclosure of Confidential Information

Nothing in this Chapter shall require any Party to provide confidential information, the disclosure of which would impede law enforcement, or otherwise be contrary to the public interest, or which would prejudice legitimate commercial interests of particular enterprises, public or private.

ARTICLE 11
Domestic Regulation

1.   Each Party shall ensure that all measures of general application affecting trade in services are administered in a reasonable, objective and impartial manner.

2.   Each Party shall ensure that its judicial, arbitral or administrative tribunals or procedures which provide for the prompt review of, and where justified, appropriate remedies for, administrative decisions affecting trade in services are open on a non-discriminatory basis to service suppliers of the other Party. Where such procedures are not independent of the agency entrusted with the administrative decision concerned, the Party shall ensure that the procedures in fact provide for an objective and impartial review.

3.   Article 11.2 shall not be construed to require a Party to institute such tribunals or procedures where this would be inconsistent with its constitutional structure or the nature of its legal system.

4.   Where authorisation is required for the supply of a service, the competent authorities of a Party shall promptly, after the submission of an application considered complete under domestic laws and regulations, inform the applicant of the decision concerning the application. At the request of the applicant, the competent authorities of the Party shall provide, without undue delay, information concerning the status of the application.

5.   With the objective of ensuring that domestic regulation, including measures relating to qualification requirements and procedures, technical standards and licensing requirements, do not constitute unnecessary barriers to trade in services, the Parties shall jointly review the results of the negotiations on disciplines on these measures, pursuant to Article VI.4 of the WTO General Agreement on Trade in Services (GATS), with a view to their incorporation into this Agreement. The Parties note that such disciplines aim to ensure that such requirements are *inter alia*:

   (a)   based on objective and transparent criteria, such as competence and the ability to supply the service;

   (b)   not more burdensome than necessary to ensure the quality of the service;

   (c)   in the case of licensing procedures, not in themselves a restriction on the supply of the service.

6.   Pending the incorporation of disciplines pursuant to Article 11.5, a Party shall not apply licensing and qualification requirements and technical standards that nullify or impair its obligations under this Chapter in a manner which:

   (a)   does not comply with the criteria outlined in Articles 11.5(a), 11.5(b) or 11.5(c); and

   (b)   could not reasonably have been expected of that Party at the time the obligations were undertaken.

7.   In determining whether a Party is in conformity with its obligations under Article 11.6, account shall be taken of international standards of relevant international organisations[4] applied by that Party.

8.   Pending the incorporation of disciplines pursuant to Article 11.5, each Party or its competent authorities shall endeavour to:

   (a)   make publicly available:

      (i)   information on requirements and procedures to obtain, renew or retain any licences or professional qualifications; and

      (ii)   information on technical standards;

---

[4] The term "relevant international organisations" refers to international bodies whose membership is open to relevant bodies of both Parties.

(b)   explain, on request, the policy rationale of a measure, particularly of a new measure; and

(c)   provide opportunity for comment, and give consideration to such comments, before their adoption, when introducing measures which significantly affect trade in services.

ARTICLE 12
Monopoly and Exclusive Service Suppliers

1.   Each Party shall ensure that any monopoly supplier of a service in its territory does not, in the supply of the monopoly service in the relevant market, act in a manner inconsistent with the Party's obligations under Articles 3 (Market Access) and 4 (National Treatment).

2.   Where a Party's monopoly supplier competes, either directly or through an affiliated company, in the supply of a service outside the scope of its monopoly rights and which is subject to that Party's obligations under Articles 3 (Market Access) and 4 (National Treatment), the Party shall ensure that such a supplier does not abuse its monopoly position to act in its territory in a manner inconsistent with such commitments.

3.   If a Party has reason to believe that a monopoly supplier of a service of the other Party is acting in a manner inconsistent with paragraph 1 or 2, it may request the other Party establishing, maintaining or authorising such supplier to provide specific information concerning the relevant operations in its territory.

4.   The provisions of this Article shall also apply to cases of exclusive service suppliers, where a Party, formally or in effect, (a) authorises or establishes a small number of service suppliers and (b) substantially prevents competition among those suppliers in its territory.

ARTICLE 13
Safeguard Measures

Neither Party shall take safeguard action against services and service suppliers of the other Party from the date of entry into force of this Agreement. Neither Party shall initiate or continue any safeguard investigations in respect of services and service suppliers of the other Party.

ARTICLE 14
Payments and Transfers

1.   Subject to its reservations pursuant to Article 5 (Reservations) and except under the circumstances envisaged in Article 15 (Restrictions to Safeguard the Balance of Payments), a Party shall not apply restrictions on international transfers and payments for current transactions.

2.   Nothing in this Chapter shall affect the rights and obligations of the Parties as members of the International Monetary Fund under the Articles of Agreement of the Fund, including the use of exchange actions which are in conformity with the Articles of Agreement, provided that a Party shall not impose restrictions on any capital transactions inconsistently with its obligations under this Chapter regarding such transactions, except under Article 15 (Restrictions to Safeguard the Balance of Payments) or at the request of the Fund.

ARTICLE 15
Restrictions to Safeguard the Balance of Payments

1.   In the event of serious balance of payments and external financial difficulties or threat thereof, a Party may adopt or maintain restrictions on trade in services in respect of which it has obligations under Articles 3 (Market Access) and 4 (National Treatment), including on payments or transfers for transactions relating to such obligations. It is recognized that particular pressures on the balance of payments of a Party in the process of economic development may necessitate the use of restrictions to ensure, *inter alia*, the maintenance of a level of financial reserves adequate for the implementation of its programme of economic development.

2.   The restrictions referred to in Article 15.1 shall:

   (a)   be consistent with the Articles of Agreement of the International Monetary Fund;

   (b)   avoid unnecessary damage to the commercial, economic and financial interests of the other Party;

   (c)   not exceed those necessary to deal with the circumstances described in Article 15.1;

   (d)   be temporary and be phased out progressively as the situation specified in Article 15.1 improves;

   (e)   be applied on a national treatment basis and such that the other Party is treated no less favourably than any non-Party.

3.   Any restrictions adopted or maintained under Article 15.1, or any changes therein, shall be promptly notified to the other Party.

4.   The Party adopting any restrictions under Article 15.1 shall commence consultations with the other Party in order to review the restrictions adopted by it.

ARTICLE 16
Government Procurement

Articles 3 (Market Access) and 4 (National Treatment) shall not apply to laws, regulations or requirements governing the procurement by governmental agencies of services purchased for governmental purposes and not with a view to commercial resale or with a view to use in the supply of services for commercial sale.

ARTICLE 17
Denial of Benefit

Subject to prior notification and consultation, a Party may deny the benefits of this Chapter to a service supplier of the other Party where the Party establishes that the service supplier is owned or controlled by persons of a non-Party and that it has no substantive business operations in the territory of the other Party.

ARTICLE 18
General Exceptions

Subject to the requirement that such measures are not applied in a manner which would constitute a means of arbitrary or unjustifiable discrimination between the Parties where like conditions prevail, or a disguised restriction on trade in services, nothing in this Chapter shall be construed to prevent the adoption or enforcement by a Party of measures:

(a)   necessary to protect public morals or to maintain public order;[5]

(b)   necessary to protect human, animal or plant life or health;

(c)   necessary to secure compliance with laws or regulations which are not inconsistent with the provisions of this Chapter including those relating to:

(i)   the prevention of deceptive and fraudulent practices or to deal with the effects of a default on services contracts;

(ii)   the protection of the privacy of individuals in relation to the processing and dissemination of personal data and the protection of confidentiality of individual records and accounts;

(iii)   safety;

(d)   inconsistent with Article 4 (National Treatment), provided that the difference in treatment is aimed at ensuring the equitable or effective[6] imposition or collection of direct taxes in respect of services or service suppliers of the other Party.

---

[5] The public order exception may be invoked only where a genuine and sufficiently serious threat is posed to one of the fundamental interests of society.

[6] Measures that are aimed at ensuring the equitable or effective imposition or collection of direct taxes include measures taken by a Party under its taxation system which:

(i)   apply to non-resident service suppliers in recognition of the fact that the tax obligation of non-residents is determined with respect to taxable items sourced or located in the Party's territory; or

(ii)   apply to non-residents in order to ensure the imposition or collection of taxes in the Party's territory; or

(iii)   apply to non-residents or residents in order to prevent the avoidance or evasion of taxes, including compliance measures; or

(iv)   apply to consumers of services supplied in or from the territory of the other Party in order to ensure the imposition or collection of taxes on such consumers derived from sources in the Party's territory; or

(v)   distinguish service suppliers subject to tax on worldwide taxable items from other service suppliers, in recognition of the difference in the nature of the tax base between them; or

(vi)   determine, allocate or apportion income, profit, gain, loss, deduction or credit of resident persons or branches, or between related persons or branches of the same person, in order to safeguard the Party's tax base.

Tax terms or concepts in Article 18(d) and in this footnote are determined according to tax definitions and concepts, or equivalent or similar definitions and concepts, under the domestic law of the Party taking the measure.

ARTICLE 19
Security Exceptions

Nothing in this Chapter shall be construed:

(a)   to require a Party to furnish any information, the disclosure of which it considers contrary to its essential security interests; or

(b)   to prevent a Party from taking any action which it considers necessary for the protection of its essential security interests:

> (i)   relating to the supply of services as carried out directly or indirectly for the purpose of provisioning a military establishment;

> (ii)   relating to fissionable and fusionable materials or the materials from which they are derived;

> (iii)   taken in time of war or other emergency in international relations; or

(c)   to prevent a Party from taking any action in pursuance of its obligations under the United Nations Charter for the maintenance of international peace and security.

ARTICLE 20
Review of Commitments

1.   If, after this Agreement enters into force, a Party enters into any agreement on trade in services with a non-Party, it shall give positive consideration to a request by the other Party for the incorporation herein of treatment no less favourable than that provided under the aforesaid agreement.   Any such incorporation should maintain the overall balance of commitments undertaken by each Party under this Agreement.

2.   If, after this Agreement enters into force, a Party further liberalizes any of its non-conforming measures in Annex 4-I or sectors, subsectors, or activities in Annex 4-II unilaterally, it shall give positive consideration to a request by the other Party for the incorporation herein of the unilateral liberalisation.   Any such incorporation should maintain the overall balance of commitments undertaken by each Party under this Agreement.

3.   If, after this Agreement enters into force, a service previously supplied in the exercise of governmental authority is subsequently supplied on a commercial basis or in competition with one or more service suppliers, the Party concerned may modify or add to its reservations in respect of that service. At the request of the other Party, the Party concerned shall enter into consultations with a view to ensuring the maintenance of the overall balance of commitments undertaken by each Party under this Agreement.

ARTICLE 21
Review of Subsidies

1.   The Parties shall review the treatment of subsidies in the context of developments in international fora of which both Parties are Members.

2.   The Parties shall consult on appropriate steps in regard to subsidies related to trade in services where any subsidies issues arise under this Chapter.

ARTICLE 22
Air Transport Services

1.   For the purposes of this Article:

   (a)   "aircraft repair and maintenance services" mean such activities when undertaken on an aircraft or a part thereof while it is withdrawn from service and do not include so-called line maintenance;

   (b)   "air transport" means the public carriage by aircraft of passengers, baggage, cargo or mail, separately or in combination, for remuneration or hire; and

   (c)   "computer reservation system (CRS) services" mean services provided by computerised systems that contain information about air carriers' schedules, availability, fares and fare rules, through which reservations can be made or tickets may be issued.

2.   This Chapter and Chapter 16 (Dispute Settlement), shall not apply to measures affecting:

   (a)   rights in relation to air transport, however granted; or

   (b)   services directly related to the exercise of rights in relation to air transport, except as provided in paragraph 3 of this Article.

3.   This Chapter shall apply to measures affecting:

   (a)   aircraft repair and maintenance services; and

   (b)   computer reservation system services (CRS).

4.   Both Parties agree to review developments in the air transport sector at the first review of this Agreement under Article 3 (Review) of Chapter 17 (Final Provisions), or at any other time agreed between the Parties, with a view to including these developments in this Agreement.

5.   While both Parties affirm their rights and obligations under the Agreement between the Government of the Commonwealth of Australia and the Government of the Republic of Singapore relating to Air Services, signed on 3 November 1967 and any subsequent amendments thereto, both Parties agree to work towards an Open Skies Air Services Agreement and to review that work in accordance with the provisions of Article 22.4.

6.   The Parties affirm, *mutatis mutandis*, their rights and obligations under the GATS, including the Annex on Air Transport Services.

ARTICLE 23
Recognition

1.   For the purposes of the fulfilment of its standards or criteria for the authorisation, licensing or certification of services suppliers, a Party may recognise the education or experience obtained, requirements met, or licenses or certifications granted in the other Party.

2.   The Parties shall encourage their relevant competent bodies to enter into negotiations on recognition of professional qualifications and/or registration procedures with a view to the achievement of early outcomes.

08 INVESTMENT

ARTICLE 1
Definitions

1.   For the purposes of this Chapter:

(a)   "enterprise" means any corporation, company, association, partnership, trust, joint venture, sole-proprietorship or other legally recognised entity that is duly incorporated, constituted, set up, or otherwise duly organised under the law of a Party, including branches, regardless of whether or not the entity is organised for pecuniary gain, privately or otherwise owned, or organised with limited or unlimited liability;

(b)   "freely useable currency" means a currency widely used to make payments for international transactions as classified by the International Monetary Fund;

(c)   "investment" means every kind of asset, owned or controlled, directly or indirectly, by an investor, including but not limited to the following:

(i)   movable and immovable property and other property rights such as mortgages, liens or pledges;

(ii)   shares, stocks, bonds and debentures of an enterprise;

(iii)   claims to money or to any contractual performance related to a business and having an economic value;

(iv)   intellectual property rights and goodwill; and

(v)   business concessions or similar rights required to conduct economic activity and having economic value conferred by law or under a contract, including any concession to search for, cultivate, extract or exploit natural resources;

(d)   "investor" means:

(i)   an enterprise of a Party; or

    (ii)   a natural person who resides in the territory of a Party or elsewhere and who under the law of that Party:

        (A)   is a citizen of that Party; or

        (B)   has the right of permanent residence in that Party;

        that has made, is in the process of making, or is seeking to make an investment;

(e)   "measure" means any measure by a Party, whether in the form of a law, regulation, rule, procedure, decision, administrative action, or any other form, and includes measures taken by:

    (i)   central, regional or local governments and authorities; and

    (ii)   non-governmental bodies in the exercise of powers delegated by central, regional or local governments or authorities; and

(f)   "return" means an amount yielded by or derived from an investment, including profits, dividends, interest, capital gains, royalty payments, payments in connection with intellectual property rights, and all other lawful income.

2.   For the purposes of Article 1.1(c), returns that are invested shall be treated as investments and any alteration of the form in which assets are invested or reinvested shall not affect their character as investments.

3.   An investment may be owned or controlled by an investor of a Party, notwithstanding the fact that the investment was made through an enterprise duly incorporated, constituted, set up or otherwise duly organised under the law of a non-Party.

ARTICLE 2
Scope of Application

1.   This Chapter shall apply to investments made, in the process of being made, or sought to be made, by an investor of a Party in the territory of the other Party.

2.   This Chapter shall not apply to:

(a)   subsidies or grants provided by a Party or to any conditions attached to the receipt or continued receipt of such subsidies or grants, whether or not such subsidies or grants are offered exclusively to domestic investors and investments; or

(b)   a natural person who is a permanent resident but not a citizen of a Party where:

    (i)   the provisions of an investment protection agreement between the other Party and the country of which the person is a citizen have already been invoked in respect of the same matter; or

    (ii)   the person is a citizen of the other Party.

3.   Unless otherwise provided, this Chapter shall not apply to any taxation measure.

4.   An enterprise of a Party shall not be treated as an investor of the other Party, but any investments in that enterprise by investors of that other Party shall be protected by this Chapter.

5.   Nothing in this Chapter shall be construed to impose an obligation on a Party to privatise.

ARTICLE 3
National Treatment

Each Party shall accord to investors of the other Party, and investments of investors of the other Party, in relation to the establishment, acquisition, expansion, management, conduct, operation, liquidation, sale, transfer (or other disposition) and expropriation (including any compensation) of investments in its territory, treatment that is no less favourable than that which it accords in like circumstances to its own investors and investments.

ARTICLE 4
Transparency

Each Party shall promptly make public its laws, regulations and investment policies, and any amendments thereto, of general application that pertain to or affect investments in its territory by investors of the other Party.

ARTICLE 5
Reservations

1.   Article 3 (National Treatment) shall not apply to:

    (a)   any existing non-conforming measure that is maintained by a Party at:

        (i)   the central or regional level, as set out in Annex 4-I; or

        (ii)   the local level; or

    (b)   the continuation or prompt renewal of any non-conforming measure referred to in Article 5.1(a)

2.   Article 3 (National Treatment) shall not apply to any existing or new measure that a Party adopts or maintains with respect to sectors, subsectors or activities as set out in Annex 4-II.

3.   Each Party shall set out its reservation through a description of:

    (a)   with respect to Annex 4-I, the non-conforming measure to which the reservation applies; and

    (b)   with respect to Annex 4-II, the sectors, subsectors or activities to which the reservation applies.

4.   If a Party undertakes any privatisation measure, that Party shall include in Annex 4-I or Annex 4-II any non-conforming measure relating to that privatisation. For the purpose of this

paragraph, "privatisation measure" means the divestment by either Party of its equity interests in an enterprise where it has a controlling ownership interest. Article 14 (Settlement of Disputes between a Party and an Investor of the other Party) shall not apply to this paragraph.

ARTICLE 6
Transitional Provision on Regional Government Measures

1.   Articles 3 (National Treatment) shall not apply to measures maintained by a Party at the regional level until the first review of this Agreement under Article 3 (Review) of Chapter 17 (Final Provisions), when modifications or additions may be incorporated into the reservations in Annex 4-I and Annex 4-II to extend the coverage of Article 3 (National Treatment) to these measures. Following the first review, Article 3 (National Treatment) shall apply, at the regional level, unless the non-conforming measures maintained at the regional level are covered by the reservations in Annexes 4-I and 4-II by a Party.

2.   A Party shall enter into consultations at the request of the other Party with a view to ensuring that modifications or additions incorporated into the reservations in accordance with Article 6.1 are consistent with the overall balance of benefits under the Agreement, and deciding whether any necessary adjustment in the commitments of the Parties is required to preserve this balance.   Article 7 (Modification or Addition of Reservations) and Chapter 16 (Dispute Settlement) shall not apply to any such adjustments. The Parties shall not apply any measure affecting investment at the regional level in such a manner as would improve their negotiating position and leverage.

ARTICLE 7
Modification or Addition of Reservations

1.   By giving three months written notification to the other Party, a Party may modify or add to its non-conforming measures as set out in Annex 4-I and add new sectors, subsectors or activities to its reservations set out in Annex 4-II. At the request of the other Party, it shall hold consultations with a view to reaching agreement on any necessary adjustment required to maintain the overall balance of commitments undertaken by each Party under this Agreement. If agreement is not reached between the Parties on any necessary adjustment, the matter may be referred to arbitration in accordance with Chapter 16 (Dispute Settlement).

2.   Article 7.1 shall not be construed to prejudice the right of both Parties to maintain any existing measures or adopt any new measures consistent with the reservations set out in Annexes 4-I and 4-II.

ARTICLE 8
Additional Commitments

1.   The Parties shall set out their respective additional commitments in Annex 4-III of this Agreement with respect to investment matters not covered by Article 3 (National Treatment).

2.   Article 14 (Settlement of Disputes between a Party and an Investor of the other Party) shall not apply to these additional commitments.

ARTICLE 9
Expropriation and Nationalisation

1.   Neither Party shall nationalise, expropriate or subject to measures having effect equivalent to nationalisation or expropriation (hereinafter referred to as "expropriation") the investments of investors of the other Party unless such a measure is taken on a non-discriminatory basis, for a public purpose, in accordance with due process of law, and upon payment of compensation in accordance with this Article.

2.   The expropriation shall be accompanied by the payment of prompt, adequate and effective compensation. Compensation shall be equivalent to the fair market value of the expropriated investment immediately before the expropriation or impending expropriation became public knowledge. Compensation shall carry an appropriate interest, taking into account the length of time from the time of expropriation until the time of payment. Such compensation shall be effectively realisable, freely transferable in accordance with Article 11 (Transfers) and made without delay.

3.   Notwithstanding Articles 9.1 and 9.2, any measure of expropriation relating to land, which shall be as defined in the existing domestic legislation of the expropriating Party on the date of entry into force of this Agreement, shall be for a purpose and upon payment of compensation in accordance with the aforesaid legislation and any subsequent amendments thereto relating to the amount of compensation where such amendments follow the general trends in the market value of the land.

4.   This Article does not apply to the issuance of compulsory licenses granted in relation to intellectual property rights, or to the revocation, limitation or creation of intellectual property rights, to the extent that such issuance, revocation, limitation or creation is consistent with the WTO Agreement on Trade-Related Aspects of Intellectual Property Rights and Chapter 13 (Intellectual Property).

ARTICLE 10
Compensation for Losses

A Party shall accord to investors of the other Party whose investments in the territory of the former Party have suffered losses owing to war or other armed conflict or civil strife in that territory, treatment, as regards restitution, indemnification, compensation, or other settlement or measures it adopts or maintains relating to such losses, no less favourable than that which it accords to its own investors and investors of any non-Party.

ARTICLE 11
Transfers

1.   Each Party shall permit, on a non-discriminatory basis, all funds of an investor of the other Party related to an investment in its territory to be transferred freely and without undue delay. Such funds include the following:

    (a)   the initial capital plus any additional capital used to maintain or expand the investment;

    (b)   returns;

(c)   proceeds from the sale or partial sale or liquidation of the investment;

(d)   loan payments in connection with the investment;

(e)   unspent earnings and other remuneration of personnel engaged from abroad in connection with that investment; and

(f)   compensation paid pursuant to Article 10 (Compensation for Losses).

2.   Each Party shall permit such transfers to be made in the currency of the other Party or any freely useable currency at the prevailing rate of exchange on the date of transfer.

3.   Notwithstanding Article 11.1, a Party may prevent a transfer through the equitable, non-discriminatory and good faith application of its laws relating to:

(a)   bankruptcy, insolvency or the protection of the rights of creditors;

(b)   issuing, trading or dealing in securities, futures, options, or derivatives;

(c)   criminal or penal offences, and the recovery of proceeds of crime;

(d)   ensuring the satisfaction of judgements, orders or awards in adjudicatory proceedings; or

(e)   social security, public retirement or compulsory savings schemes.

4.   Nothing in this Chapter shall affect the rights and obligations of the members of the International Monetary Fund under the Articles of Agreement of the Fund, including the use of exchange actions which are in conformity with the Articles of Agreement, provided that a Party shall not impose restrictions on any capital transactions inconsistently with its obligations under this Chapter regarding such transactions, except under Article 12 (Restrictions to Safeguard the Balance of Payments) or at the request of the Fund.

ARTICLE 12
Restrictions to Safeguard the Balance of Payments

1.   In the event of serious balance of payments and external financial difficulties or threat thereof, a Party may adopt or maintain restrictions on payments or transfers related to investments. It is recognized that particular pressures on the balance of payments of a Party in the process of economic development may necessitate the use of restrictions to ensure, *inter alia*, the maintenance of a level of financial reserves adequate for the implementation of its programme of economic development.

2.   The restrictions referred to in Article 12.1 shall:

(a)   be consistent with the Articles of Agreement of the International Monetary Fund;

(b)   avoid unnecessary damage to the commercial, economic and financial interests of the other Party;

(c)   not exceed those necessary to deal with the circumstances described in Article 12.1;

(d)   be temporary and be phased out progressively as the situation specified in Article 12.1 improves;

(e)   be applied on a national treatment basis and such that the other Party is treated no less favourably than any non-Party.

3.   Any restrictions adopted or maintained under Article 12.1, or any changes therein, shall be promptly notified to the other Party.

4.   The Party adopting any restrictions under Article 12.1 shall commence consultations with the other Party in order to review the restrictions adopted by it.

ARTICLE 13
Subrogation

1.   If a Party or a designated agency of a Party makes a payment to any of its investors under a guarantee, a contract of insurance or other form of indemnity it has granted in respect of an investment of an investor of that Party, the other Party shall recognise the subrogation or transfer of any right or title in respect of such investment.

The subrogated or transferred right or claim shall not be greater than the original right or claim of the investor.

2.   Where a Party or a designated agency of a Party has made a payment to an investor of that Party and has taken over rights and claims of the investor, that investor shall not, unless authorised to act on behalf of the Party or the designated agency of the Party making the payment, pursue those rights and claims against the other Party.

ARTICLE 14
Settlement of Disputes between a Party and an Investor of the other Party

1.   This Article shall apply to disputes between a Party and an investor of the other Party concerning an alleged breach of an obligation of the former under this Chapter which causes loss or damage to the investor or its investment.

2.   The parties to the dispute shall initially seek to resolve the dispute by consultations and negotiations.

3.   Where the dispute cannot be resolved as provided for under Article 14.2 within 6 months from the date of a request for consultations and negotiations, then unless the disputing investor and the disputing Party agree otherwise or either of them has already submitted the dispute to the courts or administrative tribunals of the disputing Party (excluding proceedings for interim measures of protection referred to in Article 14.5), the dispute may be submitted by either party to the dispute to:

(a)   the courts or administrative tribunals of the disputing Party;

(b)   the International Centre for Settlement of Investment Disputes (ICSID) for conciliation or arbitration pursuant to Articles 28 or 36 of the Convention on the Settlement of Investment Disputes between States and Nationals of Other States, done at Washington on 18 March 1965; or

(c)   arbitration under the rules of the United Nations Commission on International Trade Law (UNCITRAL).

4.   Each Party hereby consents to the submission of a dispute to conciliation or arbitration under Articles 14.3(b) and 14.3(c) in accordance with the provisions of this Article, conditional upon:

(a)   the submission of the dispute to such conciliation or arbitration taking place within three years of the time at which the disputing investor became aware, or should reasonably have become aware, of a breach of an obligation under this Chapter causing loss or damage to the investor or its investment; and

(b)   the disputing investor providing written notice, which shall be submitted at least 30 days before the claim is submitted, to the disputing Party of his or her intent to submit the dispute to such conciliation or arbitration and which:

(i)   nominates either Article 14.3(b) or Article 14.3(c) as the forum for dispute settlement (and, in the case of Article 14.3(b), nominates whether conciliation or arbitration is being sought);

(ii)   waives its right to initiate or continue any proceedings (excluding proceedings for interim measures of protection referred to in Article 14.5) before any of the other dispute settlement fora referred to in Article 14.3 in relation to the matter under dispute; and

(iii)   briefly summarises the alleged breach of the disputing Party under this Chapter (including the articles alleged to have been breached) and the loss or damage allegedly caused to the investor or its investment.

5.   Neither Party shall prevent the disputing investor from seeking interim measures of protection, not involving the payment of damages or resolution of the substance of the matter in dispute before the courts or administrative tribunals of the disputing Party, prior to the institution of proceedings before any of the dispute settlement fora referred to in Article 14.3, for the preservation of its rights and interests.

6.   Neither Party shall give diplomatic protection, or bring an international claim, in respect of a dispute which one of its investors and the other Party shall have consented to submit or have submitted to conciliation or arbitration under this Article, unless such other Party has failed to abide by and comply with the award rendered in such dispute. Diplomatic protection, for the purposes of this paragraph, shall not include informal diplomatic exchanges for the sole purpose of facilitating a settlement of the dispute.

ARTICLE 15
Review of Commitments

1.   If, after this Agreement enters into force, a Party enters into any agreement on investment with a non-Party, it shall give positive consideration to a request by the other Party for the incorporation herein of treatment no less favourable than that provided under the aforesaid agreement.   Any such incorporation should maintain the overall balance of commitments undertaken by each Party under this Agreement.

2.   If, after this Agreement enters into force, a Party further liberalises any of its non-conforming measures in Annex 4-I or sectors, subsectors or activities in Annex 4- II unilaterally, it shall give positive consideration to a request by the other Party for the incorporation herein of the unilateral liberalisation.   Any such incorporation should maintain the overall balance of commitments undertaken by each Party under this Agreement.

ARTICLE 16
Review of Subsidies

1.   The Parties shall review the treatment of subsidies in the context of developments at international fora to which both Parties are Members.

2.   The Parties shall consult on appropriate steps in regard to subsidies related to investments or investors where any subsidies issues arise under this Chapter.

ARTICLE 17
Government Procurement

Article 3 (National Treatment) shall not apply to laws, regulations or requirements governing the procurement by governmental agencies of goods and services purchased for governmental purposes and not with a view to commercial resale or with a view to use in the production of goods or the supply of services for commercial sale.

ARTICLE 18
Denial of Benefits

Subject to prior notification and consultation, a Party may deny the benefits of this Chapter to an investor of the other Party that is an enterprise of such Party and to investments of such an investor where the Party establishes that the enterprise is owned or controlled by persons of a non-Party and has no substantive business operations in the territory of the other Party.

ARTICLE 19
General Exceptions

Subject to the requirement that such measures are not applied in a manner which would constitute a means of arbitrary or unjustifiable discrimination between the Parties where like conditions prevail, or a disguised restriction on investments in the territory of a Party by investors of the other Party, nothing in this Chapter shall be construed to prevent the adoption or enforcement by a Party of measures:

(a)   necessary to protect public morals or to maintain public order;[1]

(b)   necessary to protect human, animal or plant life or health;

(c)   necessary to secure compliance with laws or regulations which are not inconsistent with the provisions of this Chapter including those relating to:

> (i)   the prevention of deceptive and fraudulent practices or to deal with the effects of a default on a contract;

> (ii)   the protection of the privacy of individuals in relation to the processing and dissemination of personal data and the protection of confidentiality of individual records and accounts;

> (iii)   safety;

(d)   imposed for the protection of national treasures of artistic, historic or archaeological value;

(e)   relating to the conservation of exhaustible natural resources if such measures are made effective in conjunction with restrictions on domestic production or consumption.

ARTICLE 20
Security Exceptions

Nothing in this Chapter shall be construed:

(a)   to require a Party to furnish any information, the disclosure of which it considers contrary to its essential security interests; or

(b)   to prevent a Party from taking any action which it considers necessary for the protection of its essential security interests:

> (i)   relating to fissionable and fusionable materials or the materials from which they are derived;

> (ii)   taken in time of war or other emergency in international relations;

> (iii)   relating to the production or supply of arms and ammunition; or

(c)   to prevent a Party from taking any action in pursuance of its obligations under the United Nations Charter for the maintenance of international peace and security.

---

[1] The public order exception may be invoked only where a genuine and sufficiently serious threat is posed to one of the fundamental interests of society.

ARTICLE 21
Disclosure of Confidential Information

Nothing in this Chapter shall require any Party to provide confidential information, the disclosure of which would impede law enforcement, or otherwise be contrary to the public interest, or which would prejudice legitimate commercial interests of particular enterprises, public or private.

09 FINANCIAL SERVICES

ARTICLE 1
Definitions and Scope

1.   The purpose of this Chapter is to provide for commitments additional to Chapter 7 (Trade in Services) and Chapter 8 (Investment) in relation to financial services to ensure that the market access treatment of financial services is based on transparent principles that are applied in a non-discriminatory manner. In the event of any inconsistency between the former provisions and the provisions of this Chapter, the latter shall prevail to the extent of such inconsistency.

2.   For the purposes of this Chapter:

    (a)   "financial service" means a service of a financial nature, including insurance, and a service incidental or auxiliary to a service of a financial nature. Financial services shall include the activities as stated in Appendix 1;

    (b)   "financial service supplier" means any natural or legal person authorised by the law of a Party to supply financial services;

    (c)   "new financial service" means a financial service, including services related to existing and new products or the manner in which a product is delivered, that is not supplied by any financial service supplier in the territory of a Party but which is supplied in the territory of the other Party; and

    (d)   "public entity" means:

        (i)   a government, a central bank or a monetary authority, of a Party, or an entity owned or controlled by a Party, that is principally engaged in carrying out governmental functions or activities for governmental purposes, not including an entity principally engaged in supplying financial services on commercial terms; or

        (ii)   a private entity, performing functions normally performed by a central bank or monetary authority, when exercising those functions.

3.   For the purposes of Articles 1(a) and 2.2(b) of Chapter 7 (Trade in Services), .a service supplied in the exercise of governmental authority. means the following:

(a)   activities conducted by a central bank or monetary authority or by any other public entity, including the management of official   foreign reserves, in pursuit of monetary or exchange rate policies;

(b)   activities forming part of a statutory system of social security or public retirement plans; and

(c)   other activities conducted by a public entity for the account or with the guarantee or using the financial resources of the Government.

4.   If a Party allows any of the activities referred to in Articles 1.3(b) or 1.3(c) to be conducted by its financial service suppliers in competition with a public entity or a financial service supplier, measures affecting such activities shall not be excluded from this Chapter and Chapter 7 (Trade in Services).

ARTICLE 2
New Financial Services

Each Party shall permit a financial service supplier of the other Party established in its territory to supply any new financial service of a type similar to those services that a Party would permit its own financial service suppliers, in like circumstances, to supply under its domestic law. A Party may however determine the institutional and juridical form through which the new financial service may be supplied and may require authorisation for the supply of the service. Where such authorisation is required, a decision shall be made within a reasonable time and the authorisation may only be refused for prudential reasons.

ARTICLE 3
Prudential and Regulatory Supervision

1.   Nothing in this Agreement shall be construed to prevent a Party from taking measures for prudential reasons, including measures for the protection of investors, depositors, policy holders or persons to whom a fiduciary duty is owed by a financial service supplier, or to ensure the integrity and stability of a Party's financial system. Where such measures do not conform with the provisions of this Agreement, they shall not be used as a means of avoiding the Party's commitments or obligations under this Agreement.

2.   These measures shall not constitute a means of arbitrary or unjustifiable discrimination against financial service suppliers of the other Party in comparison to its own like financial service suppliers, or a disguised restriction on trade in services.
Each Party shall endeavour to ensure that these measures are not more burdensome than necessary to achieve their aim.

3.   Nothing in this Agreement shall be construed to require a Party to disclose information relating to the affairs and accounts of individual customers or any confidential or proprietary information in the possession of public entities.

ARTICLE 4
Transfers of Information and Processing of Information

Neither Party shall take measures that prevent transfers of information or the processing of financial information, including transfers of data by electronic means, or that, subject to importation rules consistent with international agreements, prevent transfers of equipment, where such transfers of information, processing of financial information or transfers of equipment are necessary for the conduct of the ordinary business of a financial service supplier. Nothing in this paragraph restricts the right of a Party to protect personal data, personal privacy and the confidentiality of individual records and accounts so long as such right is not used to circumvent the provisions of this Agreement.

ARTICLE 5
Exceptions

For the avoidance of doubt, this Chapter shall be subject to the general and security exceptions listed in Articles 18 and 19 of Chapter 7 (Trade in Services) and Articles 19 and 20 of Chapter 8 (Investment).

ARTICLE 6
Dispute Settlement

Arbitral tribunals agreed between or appointed by the Parties under Chapter 16 (Dispute Settlement) to adjudicate disputes on prudential issues and other financial matters, and any procedures agreed for good offices, conciliation or mediation on such matters, shall have or provide for the necessary expertise relevant to the specific financial service and dispute.

APPENDIX 1

Insurance and insurance-related services

(i)   Direct insurance (including co-insurance):

    (A)   life
    (B)   non-life;

(ii)   Reinsurance and retrocession;

(iii)   Insurance intermediation, such as brokerage and agency;

(iv)   Services auxiliary to insurance, such as consultancy, actuarial, risk assessment and claim settlement services.

Banking and other financial services (excluding insurance)

(v)   Acceptance of deposits and other repayable funds from the public;

(vi)   Lending of all types, including consumer credit, mortgage credit, factoring and financing of commercial transaction;

(vii)   Financial leasing;

(viii)   All payment and money transmission services, including credit, charge and debit cards, travellers cheques and bankers drafts;

(ix)   Guarantees and commitments;

(x)   Trading for own account or for account of customers, whether on an exchange, in an over-the-counter market or otherwise, the following:

    (A)   money market instruments (including cheques, bills, certificates of deposits);
    (B)   foreign exchange;
    (C)   derivative products including, but not limited to, futures and options;
    (D)   exchange rate and interest rate instruments, including products such as swaps, forward rate agreements;
    (E)   transferable securities;
    (F)   other negotiable instruments and financial assets, including bullion;

(xi)   Participation in issues of all kinds of securities, including underwriting and placement as agent (whether publicly or privately) and provision of services related to such issues;

(xii)   Money broking;

(xiii)   Asset management, such as cash or portfolio management, all forms of collective investment management, pension fund management, custodial, depository and trust services;

(xiv)   Settlement and clearing services for financial assets, including securities, derivative products, and other negotiable instruments;

(xv)   Provision and transfer of financial information, and financial data processing and related software by suppliers of other financial services;

(xvi)   Advisory, intermediation and other auxiliary financial services on all the activities listed in subparagraphs (v) through (xv), including credit reference and analysis, investment and portfolio research and advice, advice on acquisitions and on corporate restructuring and strategy.

10 TELECOMMUNICATIONS SERVICES

ARTICLE 1
Purpose and Definitions

1.   The purpose of this Chapter is to provide for commitments additional to Chapters 7 (Trade in Services) and 8 (Investment) in relation to telecommunication services.

2.   For the purpose of this Chapter:

    (a) .   "end user" means a person (including a service consumer and a service supplier) to whom a public telecommunications network or service is supplied, other than for use in the further supply of a public telecommunications network or service;

(b)   "essential facilities" means facilities of a public telecommunications network or service that:

    (i)   are exclusively or predominantly provided by a single or limited number of suppliers; and

    (ii)   cannot feasibly be economically or technically substituted in order to provide a service;

(c)   "facilities-based suppliers" means suppliers of public telecommunications networks or services that are:

    (i)   licensed carriers in Australia; or

    (ii)   facilities-based operators in Singapore;

(d)   "leased circuits" means telecommunications facilities between two or more designated points which are set aside for the dedicated use of or availability to a particular user;

(e)   a "major supplier" is a supplier of public telecommunications networks or services that has the ability to materially affect the terms of participation (having regard to price and supply) in the relevant market[1] for public telecommunications networks or services as a result of:

    (i)   control over essential facilities; or

    (ii)   use of its position in the market;

(f)   "network element" means facilities or equipment used in the provision of a public telecommunications service, including features, functions, and capabilities that are provided by means of such facilities or equipment, which may include local loops, sub-loops and line sharing;

(g)   "number portability" means the ability of service consumers of public telecommunications networks or services to retain existing telephone numbers when switching between suppliers of like public telecommunications networks or services;

(h)   "public telecommunications service" means any telecommunications service required, explicitly or in effect, by a Party to be offered to the public generally;[2]

---

[1] For the avoidance of doubt, "relevant market" may refer to a market for the supply of public telecommunications networks or services (or parts thereof) provided by any supplier of public telecommunications networks or services, that give this supplier the ability to materially affect the terms of participation in the market (having regard to price and supply).

[2] "Public telecommunications service" includes Internet routing and connectivity services.

(i)   "public telecommunications network" means the telecommunications infrastructure authorised by a Party to be used to provide public telecommunications services between defined network termination points;

(j)   "regulator" means any person authorised or designated to have responsibility for the regulation of telecommunications;

(k)   "regulatory decisions" means decisions by regulators made pursuant to authority conferred under domestic law in relation to:

(i)   the making of rules for the telecommunications industry excluding legislation and statutory rules;

(ii)   the approval of terms and conditions, standards and codes to apply in the telecommunications industry;

(iii)   the adjudication or other resolution of disputes between suppliers of public telecommunications networks or services; and

(iv)   licensing;

(l)   a "supplier of public telecommunications networks or services" means a supplier of public telecommunications networks and/or public telecommunications services to users;

(m)   "telecommunications" means the transmission and reception of signals by any electromagnetic means; and

(n)   "user" means an end-user or a supplier of public telecommunications network or services.

ARTICLE 2
Scope

1.   This Chapter shall apply to measures by a Party affecting trade in telecommunications services.

2.   This Chapter shall not apply to measures by a Party affecting the distribution of broadcasting and audio-visual services, as defined in each Party's domestic law and regulations.

ARTICLE 3
Access to and Use of Public Telecommunications Networks or Services[3]

1.   Each Party shall ensure that all service suppliers of the other Party have access to and use of any public telecommunications network or service, including leased circuits, offered in its

---

[3] For avoidance of doubt, access to unbundled network elements is addressed in Article 9.3.

territory or across its borders in a timely fashion, on reasonable, transparent, and non-discriminatory terms and conditions, including as set out in Article 3.2 to Article 3.6.[4]

2.   Each Party shall ensure that such service suppliers are permitted to:

(a)   purchase or lease and attach terminal or other equipment that interfaces with the public telecommunications network and which is necessary to supply a supplier's services;

(b)   provide services to individual or multiple service consumers over any leased or owned circuits;

(c)   interconnect leased or owned circuits with public telecommunications networks or services in the territory or across the borders of that Party or with circuits leased or owned by another service supplier;

(d)   perform switching, signalling, processing and conversion functions; and

(e)   use operating protocols of their choice in the supply of any service, other than as necessary to ensure the availability of telecommunications networks and services to the public generally.

3.   Each Party shall ensure that all service suppliers of the other Party may use public telecommunications networks or services for the movement of information in its territory or across its borders and for access to information contained in the databases or otherwise stored in machine-readable form in the territory of either Party.

4.   Notwithstanding the preceding paragraph, a Party may take such measures as are necessary to:

(a)   ensure the security and confidentiality of messages; or

(b)   protect the privacy of personal data of end users of public telecommunications networks or services

subject to the requirement that such measures are not applied in a manner that would constitute a means of arbitrary or unjustifiable discrimination or a disguised restriction on trade in services.

5.   Each Party shall ensure that no condition is imposed on access to and use of public telecommunications networks or services other than as necessary:

(a)   to safeguard the public service responsibilities of suppliers of public telecommunications networks or services, in particular their ability to make their networks or services available to the public generally; or

---

[4] For avoidance of doubt, each Party may fulfil the obligations in this Article by any measure it considers necessary or appropriate, within the context of domestic law and regulation.

(b)   to protect the technical integrity of public telecommunications networks or services.

6.   Provided that they satisfy the criteria set out in Article 3.5, conditions for access to and use of public telecommunications networks or services may include:

(a)   a requirement to use specified technical interfaces, including interface protocols, for interconnection with such networks and services;

(b)   requirements, where necessary, for the inter-operability of such services;

(c)   type approval of terminal or other equipment which interfaces with the network and technical requirements relating to the attachment of such equipment to such networks; or

(d)   notification, registration and licensing.

ARTICLE 4
Transparency

1.   The Parties shall apply the measures referred to in Article 2.1 in a transparent manner, which:

(a)   provides suppliers of public telecommunications networks or services of the other Party who are likely to be affected by regulatory decisions with a fair and reasonable opportunity to obtain sufficient information to enable them to form informed views on proposed regulatory decisions and to provide these views to regulators;

(b)   requires regulators to take into account views provided by such suppliers pursuant to Article 4.1(a); and

(c)   ensures that regulators make available to such suppliers their regulatory decisions and an explanation of their reasons for those regulatory decisions.

2.   At the request of a supplier of public telecommunications networks or services who is likely to be affected by regulatory decisions, regulators may, where necessary to avoid causing prejudice to the legitimate commercial interests of that supplier, impose reasonable limitations on the requirement to provide the information referred to in Article 4.1(a) and Article 4.1(c) provided that such limitations:

(a)   are applied only to the extent necessary to protect such commercial interests; and

(b)   do not deprive suppliers of public telecommunications networks or services of the other Party of their right under Article 4.1(a) to provide their views to regulators.

3.   Where a licence is required, the following shall be made publicly available:

(a)   all the licensing criteria, any terms and conditions of the licence, and the period of time normally required to reach a decision concerning an application for a licence; and

(b)   the terms and conditions of individual licences.

4.   The reasons for the denial of a licence shall be made known to the applicant upon request.

ARTICLE 5
Independent Regulators

1.   Regulators shall be independent of any supplier of public telecommunications networks or services.

2.   The decisions of, and the procedures used by, regulators shall be fair and impartial and shall be made and implemented without undue delay.

ARTICLE 6
Dispute Settlement and Appeal

1.   Each Party shall ensure that suppliers of public telecommunications networks or services of the other Party have timely recourse to a regulator to consider and, to the extent provided for in domestic law, to resolve disputes regarding compliance with domestic measures relating to the obligations contained in this Chapter.

2.   Each Party shall ensure that any supplier of public telecommunications networks or services of the other Party aggrieved by a regulatory decision has the opportunity to appeal such regulatory decision to an independent judicial or administrative authority. Such an appeal shall not constitute grounds for non-compliance by that supplier with the regulatory decision unless an appropriate authority stays such decision.

3.   Each Party shall ensure that, in the hearing of appeals by an administrative authority referred to in Article 6.2:[5]

(a)   suppliers of public telecommunications networks or services of the other Party which are party to the appeal have a fair and reasonable opportunity to obtain sufficient information to enable them to form informed views on the issues to be determined in the appeal and to provide these views to the administrative authority;

(b)   the administrative authority takes into account views provided by such suppliers pursuant to Article 6.3(a); and

(c)   the administrative authority makes available to such suppliers its decision and an explanation of the reasons for its decision.

4.   At the request of a supplier of public telecommunications networks or services which is a party to an appeal referred to in Article 6.3, an administrative authority may, where necessary to

---

[5] For the avoidance of doubt, this paragraph does not apply to judicial authorities of either Party.

avoid causing prejudice to the legitimate commercial interests of that supplier, impose reasonable limitations on the requirement to provide the information referred to in Article 6.3(a) and Article 6.3(c) provided that such limitations:

(a)   are applied only to the extent necessary to protect such commercial interests; and

(b)   do not deprive suppliers of public telecommunications networks or services of the other Party which are party to an appeal referred to in Article 6.3 of their right under Article 6.3(a) to provide their views to the administrative authority.

ARTICLE 7
General Competitive Safeguards

1.   Each Party shall maintain appropriate measures[6] for the purpose of preventing suppliers of public telecommunications networks or services in its territory from engaging in or continuing anti-competitive practices.

2.   The anti-competitive practices referred to in Article 7.1 shall be defined in each Party's sectoral or generic competition regime, as the case may be, and shall include:

(a)   anti-competitive horizontal arrangements;

(b)   misuse of market power;

(c)   anti-competitive vertical arrangements; and

(d)   anti-competitive mergers and acquisitions.

ARTICLE 8
Interconnection between Suppliers of Public Telecommunications Networks

Each Party shall maintain appropriate measures to achieve connectivity between public telecommunications networks in order to ensure that end-users of telecommunications services can communicate with each other including, where that Party considers it necessary, by requiring facilities-based suppliers to interconnect with one another.

ARTICLE 9
Additional Obligations Relating to Major Suppliers[7]

1.   Non-discrimination

(a)   Each Party shall ensure that major suppliers in its territory accord suppliers of public telecommunications networks or services of the other Party treatment no less favourable than such major supplier accords to itself, its subsidiaries, its affiliates, or any non-affiliated supplier of public telecommunications networks or services regarding:

---

[6] The maintenance of appropriate measures includes the effective enforcement of such measures.

[7] For the avoidance of doubt, the obligations imposed under this Article only apply with respect to those public telecommunications networks or services, or parts thereof, that result in a supplier of public telecommunications networks or services being a major supplier.

       (i)   availability, provisioning, rates,[8] or quality of like public telecommunications networks or services; and

       (ii)   availability of technical interfaces

where such suppliers of public telecommunications networks or services and subsidiaries, affiliates and non-affiliates of the major supplier are in like circumstances.

2.   Competitive Safeguards

   (a)   Each Party shall maintain appropriate measures[9] for the purpose of preventing major suppliers in its territory from engaging in or continuing anti-competitive practices.

   (b)   The anti-competitive practices referred to in Article 9.2(a) shall include:

       (i)   engaging in anti-competitive cross-subsidisation;

       (ii)   using information obtained from competitors with anti-competitive results;

       (iii)   not making available, on a timely basis, to suppliers of public telecommunications networks or services of the other Party, technical information about essential facilities and commercially relevant information which is necessary for them to provide services; and

       (iv)   pricing services in a manner that is likely to unreasonably restrict competition, such as predatory pricing.

3.   Unbundled Network Elements

   (a)   Each Party shall ensure that major suppliers in its territory provide to facilities-based suppliers of the other Party access to network elements for the provision of public telecommunications services at any technically feasible point, on an unbundled basis, in a timely fashion; and on terms, conditions, and cost-oriented rates that are reasonable, transparent, and non-discriminatory.

   (b)   Each Party may determine, in accordance with its domestic laws and regulations, which network elements it requires major suppliers in its territory to provide access to in accordance with Article 9.3(a) on the basis of the technical feasibility of unbundling and the state of competition in the relevant market.

---

[8] The costs incurred by a major supplier in supplying public telecommunications networks or services to itself may be determined in accordance with any cost-oriented costing methodology considered appropriate by a Party. Treatment that is no less favourable regarding rates for like public telecommunications networks or services may take into account the legitimate transaction costs which the major supplier incurs in supplying such public telecommunications networks or services to suppliers of public telecommunications networks or services of the other Party.

[9] The maintenance of appropriate measures includes the effective enforcement of such measures. technical feasibility of unbundling and the state of competition in the relevant market.

4.   Co-Location

(a)   Each Party shall ensure that major suppliers in its territory provide to facilities-based suppliers of the other Party physical co-location of equipment necessary for interconnection or access to unbundled network elements in a timely fashion and on terms, conditions, and cost-oriented rates that are reasonable, transparent, and non-discriminatory.

(b)   Where physical co-location under Article 9.4(a) is not practical for technical reasons or because of space limitations, each Party shall ensure that major suppliers co-operate with facilities-based suppliers to find and implement the most feasible alternative solution in a timely fashion and on terms, conditions, and cost-oriented rates that are reasonable, transparent, and non-discriminatory. Such solutions may include:

(i)   permitting facilities-based suppliers to locate equipment in a nearby building and to connect such equipment to the major supplier's network;

(ii)   conditioning additional equipment space;

(iii)   optimizing the use of existing space; or

(iv)   finding adjacent space.

(c)   Each Party may determine in accordance with its domestic laws and regulations the locations at which it requires major suppliers in its territory to provide co-location under Article 9.4(a) on the basis of the state of competition in the relevant market.

5.   Resale

(a)   Each Party shall ensure that major suppliers in its territory:

(i)   allow suppliers of public telecommunications networks or services of the other Party to purchase at reasonable rates, for the purpose of resale, specific public telecommunications services supplied by the major suppliers at retail that are designated by the first Party; and

(ii)   do not impose unreasonable or discriminatory conditions or limitations on the resale of such public telecommunications services.

6.   Rights of Way

(a)   Each Party shall ensure that major suppliers in its territory provide access to poles, ducts, conduits, or any other structures deemed necessary by the Party, which are owned or controlled by such major suppliers to facilities-based suppliers of the other Party:

(i)   in a timely fashion; and

(ii)   on terms, conditions, and cost-oriented rates that are reasonable, transparent, and non-discriminatory.

(b)   Each Party may determine in accordance with its domestic laws and regulations the poles, ducts, conduits or other structures to which it requires major suppliers in its territory to provide access under Article 9.6(a) on the basis of the state of competition in the relevant market.

7.   Interconnection with a Major Supplier[10]

(a)   Each Party shall ensure that major suppliers in its territory provide interconnection to facilities-based suppliers of the other Party:

(i)   at any technically feasible point in the major supplier's network;

(ii)   under non-discriminatory terms, conditions (including technical standards and specifications) and rates;[11]

(ii)   of a quality no less favourable than that provided by such major supplier for its own like services or for like services of non-affiliated service suppliers or for its subsidiaries or other affiliates;

(iv)   in a timely fashion, on terms, conditions (including technical standards and specifications) and cost-oriented rates[12] 12 that are transparent, reasonable, having regard to economic feasibility, and sufficiently unbundled so that the supplier need not pay for network components or facilities that it does not require for the service to be provided; and

(v)   upon request, at points in addition to the network termination points offered to the majority of facilities-based suppliers, subject to charges that reflect the cost of construction of necessary additional facilities.

(b)   Each Party shall ensure that suppliers of public telecommunications networks or services of the other Party may interconnect with major suppliers in its territory pursuant to at least one of the following options:

(i)   a publicly available reference interconnection offer;

(ii)   any existing interconnection agreement between the major supplier and any similarly situated supplier of public telecommunications networks or services;

---

[10] Australia's interconnection regime provides access on terms and conditions which are fair and reasonable to all parties and which do not unfairly discriminate between users. Access rights are guaranteed by legislation and the terms and conditions of access are established primarily through processes of commercial negotiation or by reference to access undertakings given by suppliers of public telecommunications networks or services which may draw upon an industry code of practice. Any code of practice and each supplier's undertaking will be subject to approval by the regulator.

[11] In Australia, the rate at which interconnection is provided is determined by negotiation. Both negotiating parties have recourse to the regulator which will make a decision based on transparent criteria to ensure that rates are fair and reasonable in the circumstances.

[12] The regulator may resolve any dispute on what costs are relevant in determining rates.

      (iii)   an individualised agreement between the major supplier and the supplier of public telecommunications networks or services that seeks to interconnect with it; or

      (iv)   binding arbitration.

   c)   Each Party shall ensure that the applicable procedures for interconnection negotiations with major suppliers in its territory are made publicly available.

   (d)   Each Party shall ensure that major suppliers in its territory make publicly available either their interconnection agreements or a reference interconnection offer.

8.   Resolution of Interconnection Disputes

   (a)   When facilities-based suppliers are unable to resolve disputes regarding the terms, conditions and rates on which interconnection is to be provided by a major supplier, they shall have recourse to the regulator, which shall aim to resolve the disputes within 180 days of the referral to it, provided that the resolution of complex disputes may take longer than 180 days.

   (b)   Where the regulator is unable to resolve the disputes referred to in Article 9.8(a) within 180 days, each Party shall ensure that the regulator endeavours to provide interim determinations on the disputes where necessary to ensure that facilities-based suppliers of the other Party are able to interconnect with a major supplier.

ARTICLE 10
Number Portability

Each Party shall ensure that suppliers of public telecommunications services in its territory provide number portability, for those services designated by that Party, to the extent technically feasible, on a timely basis and on reasonable terms and conditions.

ARTICLE 11
Access to Buildings[13]

Each Party shall ensure that facilities-based suppliers may install, maintain and have access to their equipment in buildings or on land that the Party considers is necessary to enable public telecommunications services to be supplied to end users who are customers of the facilities-based supplier.

---

[13] To the extent of any inconsistency between this Article and Article 9, the latter shall prevail.

ARTICLE 12
Allocation and Use of Scarce Resources[14]

Any procedures for the allocation and use of scarce resources, including frequencies, numbers and rights of way, shall be carried out in an objective, timely, transparent and non-discriminatory manner. The current state of allocated frequency bands shall be made publicly available, but detailed identification of frequencies allocated for specific government use shall not be required.

ARTICLE 13
Industry Participation

1.   Each Party shall, through any forum or other mechanism it considers appropriate:

    (a)   facilitate the involvement of suppliers of public telecommunications networks or services of the other Party operating in its territory in the development of industry standards and, where it considers appropriate, in the regulation of the telecommunications industry; and

    (b)   encourage suppliers of public telecommunications networks or services of the other Party operating in its territory to provide feedback to regulators on the regulation of the telecommunications industry.

ARTICLE 14
Enforcement

Each Party shall adopt or maintain timely, proportionate and effective sanctions for the purpose of enforcing domestic measures relating to the obligations contained in this Chapter. Such sanctions may include financial penalties, injunctions, orders to cease and desist (on an interim or final basis), and/or the ability to suspend, modify or revoke licences.

ARTICLE 15
Exceptions

For the avoidance of doubt, this Chapter shall be subject to the general and security exceptions listed in Articles 18 and 19 of Chapter 7 (Trade in Services) and Articles 19 and 20 of Chapter 8 (Investment).

---

[14] Decisions on the allocation and assignment of spectrum and frequency management are not measures that are per se inconsistent with Article 3 (Market Access) of Chapter 7 (Trade in Services). Accordingly, each Party retains the ability to exe rcise its spectrum and frequency management policies, which may affect the number of service suppliers, provided that this is done in a manner that is consistent with the provisions of this Agreement. The Parties also retain the right to allocate frequency bands taking into account existing and future needs.

11 MOVEMENT OF BUSINESS PERSONS

ARTICLE 1
Purpose

The purposes of this Chapter are to:

(a)   provide for rights and obligations additional to those set out in Chapters 7 (Trade in Services) and 8 (Investment) in relation to the movement of natural persons between the Parties; and

(b)   enhance the mobility of business persons of either Party engaged in the conduct of trade and investment between the Parties, by facilitating temporary business entry and establishing streamlined, transparent immigration clearance procedures for business persons.

ARTICLE 2
Scope and Definitions

1.   This Chapter applies to measures affecting the movement of natural persons of a Party into the territory of the other Party where such persons are:

(a)   service suppliers of the first Party;

(b)   service sellers of the first Party;

(c)   investors of the first Party in respect of an investment of that investor in the territory of the other Party; or

(d)   employed by an investor of the frst Party in respect of an investment of that investor in the territory of the other Party.

2.   For the purposes of this Chapter, the following definitions shall apply:

(a)   "business visitors" means natural persons of either Party who are:

(i)   service sellers;

(ii)   short-term service suppliers;

(iii)   investors of a Party or employees of an investor (who are managers, executives or specialists as defined under Article 2.2(c) seeking temporary entry to establish an investment; or

(iv)   seeking temporary entry for the purposes of negotiating the sale of goods where such negotiations do not involve direct sales to the general public;

(b)   "immigration formality" means a visa, employment pass, or other document or electronic authority granting a natural person of one Party the right to reside or work in the territory of the other Party;

(c)   "intra-corporate transferee" means an employee of a service supplier, investor or enterprise of a Party established in the territory of the other Party through a branch, subsidiary or affiliate, who has been so employed for a period of not less than one year immediately preceding the date of the application for temporary entry, and who is:

    (i)   a manager - a business person within an organisation who primarily directs the organisation or a department or sub-division of the organisation, supervises and controls the work of other supervisory, professional or managerial employees, has the authority to hire and fire or take other personnel actions (such as promotion or leave authorisation), and exercises discretionary authority over day-to-day operations. This does not include a first-line supervisor, unless the employees supervised are professionals, nor does this include an employee who primarily performs tasks necessary for the provision of the service or operation of an investment;

    (ii)   an executive - a business person within an organisation who primarily directs the management of the organisation, exercises wide latitude in decision-making, and receives only general supervision or direction from higher level executives, the board of directors, or stockholders of the business. An executive would not directly perform tasks related to the actual provision of the service or the operation of an investment; or

    (iii)   a specialist - a business person within an organisation who possesses knowledge at an advanced level of expertise and who possesses proprietary knowledge of the organisation's service, research equipment, techniques, or management (A specialist may include, but is not limited to, members of a licensed profession.);

(d)   "service seller" means a natural person of a Party who is a sales representative of a service supplier of that Party and is seeking temporary entry to the other Party for the purpose of negotiating the sale of services for that service supplier, where such a representative will not be engaged in making direct sales to the general public or in supplying services directly;

(e)   "short-term service suppliers" means persons who:

    (i)   are employees of a service supplier or an enterprise of a Party not having a commercial presence or investment in the other, which has concluded a service contract with a service supplier or an enterprise engaged in substantive business operations in the other Party; and

    (ii)   have been employees of the service supplier or enterprise for a time period of not less than one year immediately preceding an application for admission for temporary entry; and

    (iii)   are managers, executives or specialists as defined under Article 2.2(c) and

(iv)   are seeking temporary entry to the other Party for the purpose of providing a service as a professional in the following service sectors on behalf of the service supplier or enterprise which employs them:

(A)   professional services;
(B)   computer and related services;
(C)   telecommunication services; or
(D)   financial services; and

(v)   satisfy any other requirements under the domestic laws and regulations of the other Party to provide such services in the territory of that Party; and

(f)   "temporary entry" means entry by a business visitor or an intra-corporate transferee, as the case may be, without the intent to establish permanent residence and for the purpose of engaging in activities which are clearly related to their respective business purposes. Additionally, in the case of a business visitor, the salaries of and any related payments to such a visitor should be paid entirely by the service supplier or enterprise which employs that visitor in the visitor's home country.

3.   Nothing in this Chapter shall apply to measures affecting natural persons seeking access to the employment market of a Party, nor shall it apply to measures regarding citizenship, residence or employment on a permanent basis.

ARTICLE 3
Short-Term Temporary Entry

A Party shall, upon application by a business visitor of the other Party who otherwise meets its criteria for the grant of an immigration formality, grant that business visitor, through the issue of a single immigration formality, the right to temporary entry in the granting Party's territory for a period of up to three months.

ARTICLE 4
Long-Term Temporary Entry

A Party shall grant temporary entry to an intra-corporate transferee of the other Party who otherwise meets its criteria for the grant of an immigration formality unless there has been a breach of any of the conditions governing temporary entry, or an application for an extension of an immigration formality has been refused on such grounds of national security or public order by the granting Party as it deems fit:

(a)   in the case of Singapore, for an initial period of up to two years which may be extended for periods of up to three years at a time for a total term not exceeding 14 years; and

(b)   in the case of Australia, for an initial period of up to four years which may be extended for further periods of up to four years at a time for a total term not exceeding 14 years.

ARTICLE 5
Provision of Information

A Party shall:

(a)   publish or otherwise make available to the other Party such information as will enable the other Party to become acquainted with its measures relating to this Chapter; and

(b)   no later than six months after the date of entry into force of this Agreement, prepare, publish or otherwise make available in its own territory, and in the territory of the other Party, explanatory material regarding the requirements for temporary entry under this Chapter in such a manner as will enable business persons of the other Party to become acquainted with them.

ARTICLE 6
Dispute Settlement

1.   A Party may not initiate proceedings under Chapter 16 (Dispute Settlement) regarding a refusal to grant temporary entry under this Chapter unless:

   (a)   the matter involves a pattern of practice; and

   (b)   its natural persons affected have exhausted the available domestic administrative remedies regarding the particular matter.

2.   The remedies referred to in Article 6.1(b) shall be deemed to be exhausted if a final determination in the matter has not been issued by the competent authority within one year of the institution of proceedings for domestic administrative remedies, including proceedings by way of review, and the failure to issue a determination is not attributable to delays caused by the natural person.

ARTICLE 7
Immigration Measures

Nothing in this Chapter shall prevent a Party from applying measures to regulate the entry of natural persons of the other Party into, or their temporary stay in, its territory, including those measures necessary to protect the integrity of, and to ensure the orderly movement of natural persons across its borders, provided that such measures are not applied in such a manner as to nullify or impair the benefits accruing to the other Party under the terms of this Chapter.

ARTICLE 8
Expeditious Application Procedures

A Party shall process expeditiously applications for immigration formalities from natural persons of the other Party, including further immigration formality requests or extensions thereof, particularly applications from members of professions for which mutual recognition arrangements have been concluded.

ARTICLE 9
Notification of Outcome of Application

A Party shall notify the applicants for temporary entry, either directly or through their prospective employers, of the outcome of their applications, including the period of stay and other conditions.

ARTICLE 10
Online Lodgement and Processing

As soon as possible after the date of entry into force of this Agreement, Parties shall provide facilities for online lodgement and processing:

(a)   in the case of Australia, of immigration formalities; and

(b)   in the case of Singapore, of employment passes which shall be applied for by the prospective employers.

ARTICLE 11
Resolution of Problems

The relevant authorities of both Parties shall endeavour to favourably resolve any specific or general problems (within the framework of their domestic laws, regulations and other similar measures governing the temporary entry of natural persons) which may arise from the implementation and administration of this Chapter.

ARTICLE 12
Labour Market Testing

Neither Party shall require labour market testing, labour certification tests or other procedures of similar effect as a condition for temporary entry in respect of natural persons on whom the benefits of this Chapter are conferred.

ARTICLE 13
Immigration Formality Requirements

1.   Australia shall accord to natural persons of Singapore conditions of entry and processing requirements relating to its Electronic Travel Authority ("ETA") no less favourable than those accorded to natural persons of any other country eligible under the ETA or equivalent processing system for immigration formalities.

2.   Singapore shall waive visa requirements for nationals of Australia, provided that such persons are not nationals of a non-Party for which visa-requirements are imposed for entry into Singapore.

ARTICLE 14
Inclusion of Permanent Residents

A Party shall grant the benefits of this Chapter, other than those accorded by Article 13 (Immigration Formality Requirements), to natural persons who have the right of permanent residence in the territory of the other Party, provided that these natural persons satisfy all the administrative, legal, repatriation and other requirements as may be imposed by the granting Party.

ARTICLE 15
Employment of Spouses and Dependants

For natural persons who have been granted the right to long-term temporary entry and who have been allowed to bring in their spouses or dependants, a Party shall, upon application, grant the accompanying spouses or dependants the right to work as managers, executives or specialists (as defined in Article 2.2(c)(i)-(iii)), or as office administrators in its territory, subject to the relevant licensing, administrative and registration requirements of the granting Party.

ARTICLE 16
Reservations

The commitments made by each Party under this Chapter shall be subject to any reservations it has taken in its Annex 4-I (Reservations to Chapter 7 (Trade in Services) and Chapter 8 (Investment)) and Annex 4-II (Reservations to Chapter 7 (Trade in Services) and Chapter 8 (Investment)).

13 INTELLECTUAL PROPERTY

ARTICLE 1
Purpose and Definitions

1.   The purpose of this Chapter is to increase the benefits from trade and investment through the protection and enforcement of intellectual property rights.

2.   For the purposes of this Chapter:

(a)   "intellectual property rights" refers to copyright and related rights; rights in trade marks, geographical indications, industrial designs, patents, and layout-designs (topographies) of integrated circuits; rights in plant varieties; and rights in undisclosed information; as defined and described in the WTO TRIPS Agreement;

(b)   "WIPO" means the World Intellectual Property Organisation; and

(c)   "WTO TRIPS Agreement" means the WTO Agreement on Trade-Related Aspects of Intellectual Property Rights.

ARTICLE 2
Adherence to International Instruments

1.   Each Party reaffirms its commitment to the provisions of the WTO TRIPS Agreement.

2.   The Parties shall accede to or ratify the WIPO Copyright Treaty concluded at Geneva on 20 December 1996 within four years of the date of entry into force of this Agreement, subject to completion of the necessary legislative and consultative processes required in each Party before formal accession to, or ratification of, that Treaty.

3.   The Parties shall accede to or ratify the WIPO Performances and Phonograms Treaty concluded at Geneva on 20 December 1996 within four years of the date of entry into force of this Agreement, subject to the completion of the necessary legislative and consultative processes required in each Party before formal accession to, or ratification of, that Treaty.

4.   The Parties agree to comply with the provisions of the Geneva Act of the Hague Agreement Concerning the International Registration of Industrial Designs concluded at Geneva on 2 July 1999, subject to the enactment of laws necessary to apply those provisions in their respective territories.

ARTICLE 3
Storage of Intellectual Property in Electronic Media

Copies of copyright material to which the right of reproduction applies shall include electronic copies of works, sound recordings, and cinematographic films. This is subject to limitations or exceptions as permitted under the laws of the Parties.

ARTICLE 4
Measures to Prevent the Export of Goods
that Infringe Copyright or Trade Marks

Each Party, on receipt of information or complaints, shall take measures to prevent the export of goods that infringe copyright or trade marks, in accordance with its laws, rules, regulations, directives or policies.

ARTICLE 5
Cooperation on Enforcement

The Parties agree to cooperate with a view to eliminating trade in goods infringing intellectual property rights, subject to their respective laws, rules, regulations, directives or policies. Such cooperation shall include:

(a)   the notification of contact points for the enforcement of intellectual property rights;

(b)   the exchange, between respective agencies responsible for the enforcement of intellectual property rights, of information concerning infringement of intellectual property rights;

(c)   policy dialogue on initiatives for the enforcement of intellectual property rights in multilateral and regional fora; and

(d)   such other activities and initiatives for the enforcement of intellectual property rights as may be mutually agreed between the Parties.

ARTICLE 6
Cooperation on Education and Exchange of Information on Protection, Management and
Exploitation of Intellectual Property Rights

The Parties, through their competent agencies, agree to:

(a)   exchange information and material on programmes pertaining to intellectual property rights education and awareness, and to commercialisation of intellectual property, to the extent permissible under their respective laws, rules, regulations and directives; and

(b)   encourage and facilitate the development of contacts and cooperation between their respective government agencies, educational institutions, organisations and other entities in the field of intellectual property rights protection and development, including in the education and training of patent agents.

ARTICLE 7
Settlement of Disputes relating to Domain Names and Trade Marks

Both Parties shall continue to monitor and support, where appropriate, endeavours to develop international policy or guidelines governing the resolution of disputes relating to domain names and trade marks.

*

FREE TRADE AGREEMENT BETWEEN THE GOVERNMENT OF THE REPUBLIC OF KOREA AND THE GOVERNMENT OF THE REPUBLIC OF CHILE*
[excerpts]

The free trade agreement between the Government of the Republic of Korea and the Government of the Republic of Chile was signed on 15 February 2003.

Article 1.2: Objectives

1. The objectives of this Agreement, as elaborated more specifically through its principles and rules, including national treatment, most-favoured-nation treatment and transparency, are to:

(a) encourage expansion and diversification of reciprocal trade between the Parties;

(b) eliminate barriers to trade in, and facilitate the cross-border movement of, goods and services between the territories of the Parties;

(c) promote conditions of fair competition in the free trade area;

(d) substantially increase investment opportunities between the territories of the Parties;

(e) provide adequate and effective protection and enforcement of intellectual property rights in each Party's territory;

(f) create effective procedures for the implementation and application of this Agreement, for its joint administration, and for the resolution of disputes; and

(g) establish a framework for further bilateral and multilateral cooperation in order to expand and enhance the benefits of this Agreement.

2. The Parties shall interpret and apply the provisions of this Agreement in the light of the objectives set out in paragraph 1 and in accordance with the applicable rules of international law.

* *Source*: The Government of Chile and the Government of Korea (2003). "Free Trade Agreement Between the Government of the Republic of Korea and the Government of the Republic of Chile", available on the Internet (http://www.mofat.go.kr/ko/division/data/Text.pdf). [Note added by the editor.]

PART III
INVESTMENT, SERVICES AND RELATED MATTERS

CHAPTER 10

INVESTMENT

Section A - Definitions

Article 10.1: Definitions

For purposes of this Chapter:

disputing investor means an investor that makes a claim under Section C;

disputing parties means the disputing investor and the disputing Party;

disputing Party means a Party against which a claim is made under Section C;

disputing party means the disputing investor or the disputing Party;

enterprise means an "enterprise" as defined in Article 2.1, and a branch of an enterprise;

enterprise of a Party means an enterprise constituted or organized under the law of a Party and a branch, located in the territory of a Party and carrying out business activities there;

financial institution means any natural person or enterprise of a Party wishing to supply or supplying financial services under the law of the Party in whose territory it is located;

G7 currency means the currency of Canada, France, Germany, Italy, Japan, the United Kingdom of Great Britain and Northern Ireland or the United States of America;

ICSID means the International Center for Settlement of Investment Disputes;

ICSID Convention means the Convention on the Settlement of Investment Disputes between States and Nationals of other States, done at Washington, March 18, 1965;

investment means every kind of asset that an investor owns or controls, directly or indirectly, and that has the characteristics of an investment, such as the commitment of capital or other resources, the expectation of gains or profits and the assumption of risk. Forms that an investment may take include, but are not limited to:

(a) an enterprise;

(b) shares, stocks, and other forms of equity participation in an enterprise;

(c) bonds, debentures, loans, and other debt instruments of an enterprise;

(d) rights under contracts, including turnkey, construction, management, production, concession or revenue-sharing contracts;

(e)   claims to money established and maintained in connection with the conduct of commercial activities;

(f)   intellectual property rights;

(g)   rights conferred pursuant to domestic law or contract such as concessions, licenses, authorizations and permits, except for those that do not create any rights protected by domestic law; and

(h)   other tangible or intangible, movable or immovable property, and related property rights, such as leases, mortgages, liens and pledges;

but **investment** does not mean,

(i)   claims to money that arise solely from:

        (i)   commercial contracts for the sale of goods or services by a national or enterprise in the territory of a Party to an enterprise in the territory of the other Party; or

        (ii)   the extension of credit in connection with a commercial transaction, such as trade financing; and

(j)   an order entered in a judicial or administrative action.

investment of an investor of a Party means an investment owned or controlled, directly or indirectly, by an investor of such a Party;

investor of a Party means a Party or state enterprise thereof, or a national or an enterprise of such a Party, that makes a juridical act in the territory of the other Party, towards materializing an investment within it, that submits capital or, when applicable, is making or has made an investment;

investor of a non-Party means an investor other than an investor of a Party;

New York Convention means the United Nations Convention on the Recognition and Enforcement of Foreign Arbitral Awards, done in New York on June 10, 1958;

Secretary-General means the Secretary-General of ICSID;

transfers means transfers and international payments;

Tribunal means an arbitration tribunal established under Article 10.24 or 10.30;

TRIMS Agreement means Agreement on Trade-Related Investment Measures, which is part of the WTO Agreement; and

UNCITRAL Arbitration Rules means the arbitration rules of the United Nations Commission on International Trade Law, approved by the United Nations General Assembly on December 15, 1976.

Section B

Investment

Article 10.2: Scope and Coverage

1.   This Chapter applies to measures adopted or maintained by a Party relating to:

   (a)   investors of the other Party;

   (b)   investments of investors of the other Party in the territory of the Party; and

   (c)   with respect to Articles 10.7 and 10.18, all investments in the territory of the Party.

2.   This Chapter applies to the existing investments at the date of the entry into force of this Agreement, as well as to the investments made or acquired after this date.

3.   This Chapter does not apply to:

   (a)   measures adopted or maintained by a Party relating to investors of the other Party, and investments of such investors, in financial institutions in the Party's territory; and

   (b)   claims arising out of events which occurred, or claims which had been raised, prior to the entry into force of this Agreement.

4.   Nothing in this Chapter shall be construed to prevent a Party from providing a service or performing a function such as law enforcement, correctional services, income security or insurance, social security or insurance, social welfare, public education, public training, health and child care.

5.   Notwithstanding paragraph 4, if services provided in the exercise of governmental authority are provided in the territory of a Party such as law enforcement, correctional services, income security or insurance, social security or insurance, social welfare, public education, public training, health, and child care on a commercial basis or in competition with one or more service providers, those services are covered by the provisions of this Chapter.

Article 10.3: National Treatment

1.   Each Party shall accord to investors of the other Party treatment no less favourable than that it accords, in like circumstances, to its own investors with respect to the establishment, acquisition, expansion, management, conduct, operation, and sale or other disposition of investments.

2.   Each Party shall accord to investments of investors of the other Party treatment no less favourable than that it accords, in like circumstances, to investments of its own investors with respect to the establishment, acquisition, expansion, management, conduct, operation, and sale or other disposition of investments.

Article 10.4: Most-Favoured-Nation Treatment

1.   Each Party shall accord to investments of investors of the other Party made or materialized in accordance with the laws and regulations of the other Party, and investors of the other Party who have made or materialized such investments, treatment no less favorable than it accords, in like circumstances, to investments made or materialized by investors of any non-Party or investors of such investments.

2.   If a Party accords more favorable treatment to investments of investors of a non- Party or investors of a non-Party by an agreement establishing, *inter alia*, a free trade area, a customs union, a common market, an economic union or any other form of regional economic organization to which the Party is a member, it shall not be obliged to accord such treatment to investments of the investors of the other Party or the investors of the other Party.

3.   Notwithstanding paragraph 2, if a Party makes any further liberalization, in conformity with Articles 10.9.1 and 10.9.2 by an agreement with a non-Party, it shall afford adequate opportunity to the other Party to negotiate treatment granted therein on a mutually advantageous basis with a view to securing an overall balance of rights and obligations.

Article 10.5: Minimum Standard of Treatment

1.   Each Party shall accord to investments of investors of the other Party treatment in accordance with the customary international law minimum standard of treatment of aliens, including fair and equitable treatment and full protection and security.

2.   The concepts of "fair and equitable treatment" and "full protection and security" in paragraph 1 do not require treatment in addition to or beyond that which is required by the customary international law minimum standard of treatment of aliens.

3.   A determination that there has been a breach of another provision of this Agreement, or of a separate international agreement, does not establish that there has been a breach of this Article.

Article 10.6: Losses and Compensation

Investors of a Party whose investments suffer losses owing to war or other armed conflict, a state of national emergency, revolt, insurrection, riot or other similar situations, and such losses as ones resulting from requisition or destruction of property, which was not caused in combat action or was not required by the necessity of the situation, in the territory of the other Party, shall be accorded by the latter Party treatment, as regards restitution, indemnification, compensation or other forms of settlement, no less favorable than that which the latter Party accords to its own investors or to investors of any non-Party, whichever is more favourable to the investors concerned.

Article 10.7: Performance Requirements

1.   Neither Party may impose or enforce any of the following requirements, or enforce any commitment or undertaking, in connection with the establishment, acquisition, expansion, management, conduct or operation of an investment of an investor of a Party or of a non-Party in its territory:

(a)   to export a given level or percentage of goods or services;

(b)   to achieve a given level or percentage of domestic content;

(c)   to purchase, use or accord a preference to goods produced or services provided in its territory, or to purchase goods or services from persons in its territory;

(d)   to relate in any way the volume or value of imports to the volume or value of exports or to the amount of foreign exchange inflows associated with such investment;

(e)   to restrict sales of goods or services in its territory that such investment produces or provides by relating such sales in any way to the volume or value of its exports or foreign exchange earnings;

(f)   to transfer technology, a production process or other proprietary knowledge to a person in its territory, except when the requirement is imposed or the commitment or undertaking is enforced by a court, administrative tribunal or competition authority to remedy an alleged violation of competition law or to act in a manner not inconsistent with other provisions of this Agreement; or

(g)   to act as the exclusive supplier of the goods it produces or services it provides to a specific region or world market.

2.   A measure that requires an investment to use a technology to meet generally applicable health, safety or environmental requirements shall not be construed to be inconsistent with subparagraph 1(f). For greater certainty, Articles 10.3 and 10.4 apply to the measure.

3.   Neither Party may condition the receipt or continued receipt of an advantage, in connection with an investment in its territory of an investor of a Party or of a non-Party, in compliance with any of the following requirements:

(a)   to achieve a given level or percentage of domestic content;

(b)   to purchase, use or accord a preference to goods produced in its territory, or to purchase goods from producers in its territory;

(c)   to relate in any way the volume or value of imports to the volume or value of exports or to the amount of foreign exchange inflows associated with such investment; or

(d)   to restrict sales of goods or services in its territory that such investment produces or provides by relating such sales in any way to the volume or value of its exports or foreign exchange earnings.

4.   Nothing in paragraph 3 shall be construed to prevent a Party from conditioning the receipt or continued receipt of an advantage, in connection with an investment in its territory of an investor of a Party or of a non-Party, in compliance with a requirement to locate production, provide a service, train or employ workers, construct or expand particular facilities, or carry out

research and development, in its territory. In the event of any inconsistency between this paragraph and the TRIMS Agreement, the latter shall prevail to the extent of the inconsistency.

5.   Paragraphs 1 and 3 do not apply to any requirement other than the requirements set out in those paragraphs.

6.   Provided that such measures are not applied in an arbitrary or unjustifiable manner, or do not constitute a disguised restriction on international trade or investment, nothing in subparagraphs 1(b) or (c) or 3(a) or (b) shall be construed to prevent a Party from adopting or maintaining measures, including environmental measures:

   (a)   necessary to secure compliance with laws and regulations that are not inconsistent with the provisions of this Agreement;

   (b)   necessary to protect human, animal or plant life or health; or

   (c)   necessary for the conservation of living or non-living exhaustible natural resources.

7.   The provisions of:

   (a)   subparagraphs 1(a), (b) and (c), and 3(a) and (b) shall not apply to qualification requirements for goods or services with respect to export promotion and foreign aid programs;

   (b)   subparagraphs 1(b), (c), (f) and (g), and 3(a) and (b) shall not apply to procurement by a Party or a state enterprise; and

   (c)   subparagraphs 3(a) and (b) shall not apply to requirements imposed by the importing Party relating to the content of goods necessary to qualify for preferential tariff or preferential quotas.

8.   This Article does not preclude the application of any commitment, obligation or requisite between private parties.

Article 10.8: Senior Management and Boards of Directors

1.   Neither Party may require that an enterprise of a Party that is an investment of an investor of the other Party appoint to senior management positions individuals of any particular nationality.

2.   A Party may require that a majority of the board of directors, or any committee thereof, of an enterprise of that Party that is an investment of an investor of the other Party, be of a particular nationality, or resident in the territory of the Party, provided that the requirement does not materially impair the ability of the investor to exercise control over its investment.

Article 10.9: Reservations and Exceptions

1.   Articles 10.3, 10.7 and 10.8 shall not apply to:

    (a)   any existing nonconforming measure that is maintained by:

        (i)   a Party at the national level, as set out in its Schedule to Annex I; or

        (ii)   a local government;

    (b)   the continuation or prompt renewal of any nonconforming measure referred to in subparagraph (a); or

    (c)   an amendment to any nonconforming measure referred to in subparagraph (a) to the extent that the amendment does not decrease the conformity of the measure, as it existed immediately before the amendment, with Articles 10.3, 10.7 and 10.8.

2.   Articles 10.3, 10.7 and 10.8 shall not apply to any measure that a Party adopts or maintains with respect to sectors, subsectors or activities, as set out in its Schedule to Annex II.

3.   Neither Party shall, under any measure adopted after the date of entry into force of this Agreement and covered by its Schedule to Annex II, require an investor of the other Party, by reason of its nationality, to sell or otherwise dispose of an investment existing at the time the measure becomes effective.

4.   Nothing in this Chapter shall be construed so as to derogate from rights and obligations under international agreements in respect of protection of intellectual property rights to which both Parties are party, including TRIPS Agreement and other treaties concluded under the auspices of the World Intellectual Property Organization.

5.   Articles 10.3 and 10.8 shall not apply to:

    (a)   procurement by a Party or a state enterprise; or

    (b)   subsidies or grants provided by a Party or a state enterprise, including government supported loans, guarantees and insurance.

6.   Articles 10.3, 10.7 and 10.8 shall not apply to any voluntary and special investment regime, as is established in Annex 10.9.6.

Article 10.10: Future Liberalization

Through future negotiations, to be scheduled every two years by the Commission after the date of entry into force of this Agreement, the Parties will engage in further liberalisation with a view to reaching the reduction or elimination of the remaining restrictions scheduled in conformity with paragraphs 1 and 2 of Article 10.9 on a mutually advantageous basis and securing an overall balance of rights and obligations.

Article 10.11: Transfers

1.   Except as provided in Annex 10.11, each Party shall permit all transfers relating to an investment of an investor of the other Party in the territory of the Party to be made freely and without delay. Such transfers include:

      (a)   the initial capital and additional amount to maintain or increase an investment;

      (b)   profits, dividends, interest, capital gains, royalty payments, management fees, technical assistance and other fees, returns in kind and other amounts derived from the investment;

      (c)   proceeds from the sale of all or any part of the investment or from the partial or complete liquidation of the investment;

      (d)   payments made under a contract entered into by the investor, or its investment, including payments made pursuant to a loan agreement;

      (e)   payments made pursuant to Article 10.13; and

      (f)   payments arising under Section C.

2.   Each Party shall permit transfers to be made in a freely usable or convertible currency at the market rate of exchange prevailing on the date of transfer.

3.   Neither Party may require its investors to transfer, or penalize its investors that fail to transfer, the income, earnings, profits or other amounts derived from, or attributable to, investments in the territory of the other Party.

4.   Notwithstanding paragraphs 1 and 2, a Party may prevent a transfer through the equitable, non-discriminatory and good faith application of its laws relating to:

      (a)   bankruptcy, insolvency or the protection of the rights of creditors;

      (b)   issuing, trading or dealing in securities;

      (c)   criminal or penal offenses;

      (d)   reports of transfers of currency or other monetary instruments; or

      (e)   ensuring the satisfaction of judgments in adjudicatory proceedings.

5.   Paragraph 3 shall not be construed to prevent a Party from imposing any measure through the equitable, non-discriminatory and good faith application of its laws relating to the matters set out in subparagraphs (a) through (e) of paragraph 4.

6.   Notwithstanding paragraph 1, a Party may restrict transfers of returns in kind in circumstances where it could otherwise restrict such transfers under this Agreement, including as set out in paragraph 4.

Article 10.12: Exceptions and Safeguard Measures

1.   Where, in exceptional circumstances, payments and capital movements between the Parties cause or threaten to cause serious difficulties for the operation of monetary policy or exchange rate policy in either Party, the Party concerned may take safeguard measures with

regard to capital movements that are strictly necessary for a period not exceeding one year. The application of safeguard measures may be extended through their formal reintroduction.

2.   The Party adopting the safeguard measures shall inform the other Party forthwith and present, as soon as possible, a time schedule for their removal.

Article 10.13: Expropriation and Compensation

1.   Neither Party may, directly or indirectly, nationalize or expropriate an investment of an investor of the other Party in its territory, except:

(a)   for a public purpose;

(b)   on a non-discriminatory basis;

(c)   in accordance with due process of law and Article 10.5(1); and

(d)   on payment of compensation in accordance with paragraphs 2 through 6.

2.   Compensation shall be equivalent to the fair market value of the expropriated investment immediately before the expropriation took place ("date of expropriation"), and shall not reflect any change in value occurring because the intended expropriation had become known earlier.

Valuation criteria shall include going concern value, asset value including declared tax value of tangible property, and other criteria, as appropriate, to determine fair market value.

3.   Compensation shall be paid without delay and be fully realizable.

4.   If payment is made in a G7 currency, compensation shall include interest at a commercially reasonable rate for that currency from the date of expropriation until the date of actual payment.

5.   If a Party elects to pay in a currency other than a G7 currency, the amount paid on the date of payment, if converted into a G7 currency at the market rate of exchange prevailing on that date, shall be no less than that if the amount of compensation owed on the date of expropriation had been converted into that G7 currency at the market rate of exchange prevailing on that date, and interest had accrued at a commercially reasonable rate for that G7 currency from the date of expropriation until the date of payment.

6.   On payment, compensation shall be freely transferable as provided in Article 10.11.

7.   This Article does not apply to the issuance of compulsory licenses granted in relation to intellectual property rights, or to the revocation, limitation or creation of intellectual property rights, to the extent that such issuance, revocation, limitation or creation is consistent with the TRIPS Agreement.

Article 10.14: Subrogation

1.   Where a Party or an agency authorized by that Party has granted a contract of insurance or any form of financial guarantee against non-commercial risks with regard to an investment by

one of its investors in the territory of the other Party and when payment has been made under this contract or financial guarantee by the former Party or the agency authorized by it, the latter Party shall recognize the rights of the former Party or the agency authorized by the Party by virtue of the principle of subrogation to the rights of the investor.

2.   Where a Party or the agency authorized by the Party has made a payment to its investor and has taken over rights and claims of the investor, that investor shall not, unless authorized to act on behalf of the Party making the payment, pursue those rights and claims against the other Party.

Article 10.15: Special Formalities and Information Requirements

1.   Nothing in Article 10.3 shall be construed to prevent a Party from adopting or maintaining a measure that prescribes special formalities in connection with the establishment of investments by investors of the other Party, such as the requirement that investments be legally constituted under the laws or regulations of the Party, provided that such formalities do not materially impair the protections afforded by a Party to investors of the other Party and investments of investors of the other Party pursuant to this Chapter.

2.   Notwithstanding Article 10.3 or 10.4, a Party may require an investor of the other Party, or its investment in its territory, to provide routine information concerning that investment solely for informational or statistical purposes. The Party shall protect such business information that is confidential from any disclosure that would prejudice the competitive position of the investor or the investment. Nothing in this paragraph shall be construed to prevent a Party from otherwise obtaining or disclosing information in connection with the equitable and good faith application of its law.

Article 10.16: Relation to Other Chapters

1.   In the event of any inconsistency between this Chapter and another Chapter in this Agreement, the other Chapter shall prevail to the extent of the inconsistency.

2.   The requirement by a Party that a service provider of the other Party post a bond or other form of financial security as a condition of providing a service into its territory does not of itself make this Chapter applicable to the provision of that cross-border service. This Chapter applies to that Party's treatment of the posted bond or financial security.

Article 10.17: Denial of Benefits

1.   A Party may deny the benefits of this Chapter to an investor of the other Party that is an enterprise of such Party and to investments of such investor, if investors of a non-Party own or control the enterprise and the denying Party:

    (a)   does not maintain diplomatic relations with the non-Party; or

    (b)   adopts or maintains measures with respect to the non-Party that prohibit transactions with the enterprise or that would be violated or circumvented if the benefits of this Chapter were accorded to the enterprise or to its investments.

2.   Subject to prior notification and consultation in accordance with Articles 17.4 and 19.4, a Party may deny the benefits of this Chapter to an investor of the other Party that is an enterprise of such Party and to investments of such investors if investors of a non-Party own or control the enterprise and the enterprise has no substantial business activities in the territory of the Party under whose law it is constituted or organized.

Article 10.18: Environmental Measures

1.   Nothing in this Chapter shall be construed to prevent a Party from adopting, maintaining or enforcing any measure otherwise consistent with this Chapter that it considers appropriate to ensure that an investment activity in its territory is undertaken in a manner sensitive to environmental concerns.

2.   The Parties recognize that it is inappropriate to encourage investment by relaxing domestic health, safety or environmental measures. Accordingly, a Party should not waive or otherwise derogate from, or offer to waive or otherwise derogate from, such measures as an encouragement for the establishment, acquisition, expansion or retention in its territory of an investment of an investor. If a Party considers that the other Party has offered such an encouragement, it may request consultations with the other Party and the Parties shall consult with a view to avoiding any such encouragement.

Section C

Settlement of Disputes between a Party and an Investor of the Other Party

Article 10.19: Purpose

Without prejudice to the rights and obligations of the Parties under Chapter 19, this Section establishes a mechanism for the settlement of investment disputes that assures both equal treatment among investors of the Parties in accordance with the principle of international reciprocity and due process before an impartial tribunal.

Article 10.20: Claim by an Investor of a Party on Its Own Behalf

1.   Subject to Annex 10.20, an investor of a Party may submit to arbitration under this Section a claim that the other Party has breached an obligation under Section B or Article 14.8, and that the investor has incurred loss or damage by reason of, or arising out of, that breach.

2.   An investor may not make a claim if more than three years have elapsed from the date on which the investor first acquired, or should have first acquired, knowledge of the alleged breach and knowledge that the investor has incurred loss or damage.

Article 10.21: Claim by an Investor of a Party on Behalf of an Enterprise

1.   Subject to Annex 10.20, an investor of a Party, on behalf of an enterprise of the other Party that is a juridical person that the investor owns or controls, directly or indirectly, may submit to arbitration under this Section a claim that the other Party has breached an obligation under Section B or Article 14.8, and that the enterprise has incurred loss or damage by reason of, or arising out of, that breach.

2.   An investor may not make a claim on behalf of an enterprise described in paragraph 1 if more than three years have elapsed from the date on which the enterprise first acquired, or should have first acquired, knowledge of the alleged breach and knowledge that the enterprise has incurred loss or damage.

3.   Where an investor makes a claim under this Article and the investor or a non-controlling investor in the enterprise makes a claim under Article 10.20 arising out of the same events that gave rise to the claim under this Article, and two or more of the claims are submitted to arbitration under Article 10.24, the claims should be heard together by a Tribunal established under Article 10.30, unless the Tribunal finds that the interests of a disputing party would be prejudiced thereby.

4.   An investment may not make a claim under this Section.

Article 10.22: Settlement of a Claim through Consultation and Negotiation

The disputing parties should first attempt to settle a claim through consultation or negotiation.

Article 10.23: Notice of Intent to Submit a Claim to Arbitration

The disputing investor shall deliver to the disputing Party written notice of its intention to submit a claim to arbitration at least 90 days before the claim is submitted, which notice shall specify:

  (a)   the name and address of the disputing investor and, where a claim is made under Article 10.21, the name and address of the enterprise;

  (b)   the provisions of this Agreement alleged to have been breached and any other relevant provisions;

  (c)   the issues and the factual basis for the claim; and

  (d)   the relief sought and the approximate amount of damages claimed.

Article 10.24: Submission of a Claim to Arbitration

1.   Provided that six months have elapsed since the events giving rise to a claim, a disputing investor may submit the claim to arbitration under:

  (a)   the ICSID Convention, provided that both the disputing Party and the Party of the investor are parties to the Convention;

  (b)   the Additional Facility Rules of ICSID, provided that either the disputing Party or the Party of the investor, but not both, is a party to the ICSID Convention; or

  (c)   the UNCITRAL Arbitration Rules.

2.   The applicable arbitration rules shall govern the arbitration except to the extent modified by this Section.

Article 10.25: Conditions Precedent to Submission of a Claim to Arbitration

1.   A disputing investor may submit a claim under Article 10.20 to arbitration only if:

  (a)   the investor and the enterprise, that is a juridical person that the investor owns or controls, directly or indirectly, have not submitted the same claim before any administrative tribunal or court of the disputing Party;

  (b)   the investor consents to arbitration in accordance with the procedures set out in this Agreement; and

  (c)   the investor and, where the claim is for loss or damage to an interest in an enterprise of the other Party that is a juridical person that the investor owns or controls, directly or indirectly, the enterprise, waive their right to initiate before any administrative tribunal or court under the law of a Party, or other dispute settlement procedures, any proceedings with respect to the measure of the disputing Party that is alleged to be a breach referred to in Article 10.20, except for proceedings for injunctive, declaratory or other extraordinary relief, not involving the payment of damages, before an administrative tribunal or court under the law of the disputing Party.

2.   A disputing investor may submit a claim under Article 10.21 to arbitration only if:

  (a)   both the investor and the enterprise that is a juridical person that the investor owns or controls, directly or indirectly, have not submitted the same claim before any administrative tribunal or court of the disputing Party;

  (b)   both the investor and the enterprise consent to arbitration in accordance with the procedures set out in this Agreement; and

  (c)   both the investor and the enterprise waive their rights to initiate before any administrative tribunal or court under the law of a Party, or other dispute settlement procedures, any proceedings with respect to the measure of the disputing Party that is alleged to be a breach referred to in Article 10.21, except for proceedings for injunctive, declaratory or other extraordinary relief, not involving the payment of damages, before an administrative tribunal or court under the law of the disputing Party.

3.   Once a disputing investor concerned submits the dispute for resolution before any administrative tribunal or court under the law of a Party, the investor may not thereafter allege the measure to be such a breach referred to in Article 10.20 or 10.21 in an arbitration under this Section.

4.   A consent and waiver required by this Article shall be in writing, shall be delivered to the disputing Party and shall be included in the submission of a claim to arbitration.

5.   Only where a disputing Party has deprived a disputing investor of control of an enterprise:

(a)   a waiver from the enterprise under subparagraph 1(c) or 2(c) shall not be required; and

(b)   Article 10.24.1(b) shall not be applicable.

Article 10.26: Consent to Arbitration

1.   Each Party consents to the submission of a claim to arbitration in accordance with the procedures set out in this Agreement.

2.   The consent given under paragraph 1 and the submission by a disputing investor of a claim to arbitration shall satisfy the requirements of:

(a)   Chapter II of the ICSID Convention (Jurisdiction of the Centre) and the Additional Facility Rules for written consent of the parties; and

(b)   Article II of the New York Convention for an agreement in writing.

Article 10.27: Number of Arbitrators and Method of Appointment

Except in respect of a Tribunal established under Article 10.30, and unless the disputing parties otherwise agree, the Tribunal shall comprise three arbitrators, one arbitrator appointed by each of the disputing parties and the third, who shall be the presiding arbitrator, appointed by agreement between the disputing parties.

Article 10.28: Constitution of a Tribunal When a Party Fails to Appoint an Arbitrator or the Disputing Parties are Unable to Agree on a Presiding Arbitrator

1.   The Secretary-General shall serve as appointing authority for an arbitration under this Section.

2.   If a Tribunal, other than a Tribunal established under Article 10.30, has not been constituted within 90 days from the date that a claim is submitted to arbitration, the Secretary-General, on the request of either disputing party, shall appoint, in his or her discretion, the arbitrator or arbitrators not yet appointed, except that the presiding arbitrator shall be appointed in accordance with paragraph 3.

3.   The Secretary-General shall appoint the presiding arbitrator from the roster of presiding arbitrators referred to in paragraph 4, provided that the presiding arbitrator shall not be a national of the disputing Party or a national of the Party of the disputing investor. In the event that no such presiding arbitrator is available to serve, the Secretary-General shall appoint, from the ICSID Panel of Arbitrators, a presiding arbitrator who is not a national of either of the Parties.

4.   On the date of entry into force of this Agreement, the Parties shall establish, and thereafter maintain, a roster of 30 presiding arbitrators, none of whom may be a national of a Party, meeting the qualifications of the Convention and rules referred to in Article 10.24 and experienced in international law and investment matters. The roster members shall be appointed by mutual agreement.

Article 10.29: Agreement to Appointment of Arbitrators

For purposes of Article 39 of the ICSID Convention and Article 7 of Schedule C to the ICSID Additional Facility Rules, and without prejudice to an objection to an arbitrator based on Article 10.28.3 or on a ground other than nationality:

(a)   the disputing Party agrees to the appointment of each individual member of a Tribunal established under the ICSID Convention or the ICSID Additional Facility Rules;

(b)   a disputing investor referred to in Article 10.20 may submit a claim to arbitration, or continue a claim, under the ICSID Convention or the ICSID Additional Facility Rules, only on condition that the disputing investor agrees in writing to the appointment of each individual member of the Tribunal; and

(c)   a disputing investor referred to in Article 10.21.1 may submit a claim to arbitration, or continue a claim, under the ICSID Convention or the ICSID Additional Facility Rules, only on condition that the disputing investor and the enterprise agree in writing to the appointment of each individual member of the Tribunal.

Article 10.30: Consolidation

1.   A Tribunal established under this Article shall be established under the UNCITRAL Arbitration Rules and shall conduct its proceedings in accordance with those Rules, except as modified by this Section.

2.   Where a Tribunal established under this Article is satisfied that claims have been submitted to arbitration under Article 10.24 that have a question of law or fact in common, the Tribunal may, in the interests of fair and efficient resolution of the claims, and after hearing the disputing parties, by order:

(a)   assume jurisdiction over, and hear and determine together, all or part of the claims; or

(b)   assume jurisdiction over, and hear and determine one or more of the claims, the determination of which it believes would assist in the resolution of the others.

3.   A disputing party that seeks an order under paragraph 2 shall request the Secretary-General to establish a Tribunal and shall specify in the request:

(a)   the name of the disputing Party or disputing investors against which the order is sought;

(b)   the nature of the order sought; and

(c)   the grounds on which the order is sought.

4.   The disputing party shall deliver to the disputing Party or disputing investors against which the order is sought a copy of the request.

5.   Within 60 days of receipt of the request, the Secretary-General shall establish a Tribunal comprising three arbitrators. The Secretary-General shall appoint the presiding arbitrator from the roster referred to in paragraph 4 of Article 10.28. In the event that no such presiding arbitrator is available to serve, the Secretary-General shall appoint, from the ICSID Panel of Arbitrators, a presiding arbitrator who is not a national of either Party. The Secretary-General shall appoint the two other members from the roster referred to in paragraph 4 of Article 10.28 and to the extent not available from that roster, from the ICSID Panel of Arbitrators, and to the extent not available from that Panel, in the discretion of the Secretary-General. One member shall be a national of the disputing Party and one member shall be a national of the Party of the disputing investors.

6.   Where a Tribunal has been established under this Article, a disputing investor that has submitted a claim to arbitration under Article 10.20 or 10.21 and that has not been named in a request made under paragraph 3 may make a written request to the Tribunal that it be included in an order made under paragraph 2, and shall specify in the request:

(a)   the name and address of the disputing investor;

(b)   the nature of the order sought; and

(c)   the grounds on which the order is sought.

7.   A disputing investor referred to in paragraph 6 shall deliver a copy of its request to the disputing parties named in a request made under paragraph 3.

8.   A Tribunal established under Article 10.24 shall not have jurisdiction to decide a claim, or a part of a claim, over which a Tribunal established under this Article has assumed jurisdiction.

9.   On application of a disputing party, a Tribunal established under this Article, pending its decision under paragraph 2, may order that the proceedings of a Tribunal established under Article 10.24 be stayed, unless the latter Tribunal has already adjourned its proceedings.

Article 10.31: Notice

1.   A disputing Party shall deliver to the Secretariat, within 15 days of receipt by the disputing Party, a copy of:

(a)   a request for arbitration made under paragraph (1) of Article 36 of the ICSID Convention;

(b)   a notice of arbitration made under Article 2 of Schedule C of the ICSID Additional Facility Rules; or

(c)   a notice of arbitration given under the UNCITRAL Arbitration Rules.

2.   A disputing Party shall deliver to the Secretariat a copy of a request made under paragraph 3 of Article 10.30:

    (a)   within 15 days of receipt of the request, in the case of a request made by a disputing investor; or

    (b)   within 15 days of making the request, in the case of a request made by the disputing Party.

3.   A disputing Party shall deliver to the Secretariat a copy of a request made under paragraph 6 of Article 10.30 within 15 days of receipt of the request.

4.   The Secretariat shall maintain a public register of the documents referred to in paragraphs 1, 2 and 3.

5.   A disputing Party shall deliver to the other Party:

    (a)   written notice of a claim that has been submitted to arbitration no later than 30 days after the date that the claim is submitted; and

    (b)   copies of all pleadings filed in the arbitration.

Article 10.32: Participation by a Party

Upon written notice to the disputing parties, a Party may make submissions to a Tribunal on a question of interpretation of this Agreement.

Article 10.33: Documents

1.   A Party shall be entitled to receive from the disputing Party, at the cost of the requesting Party, a copy of:

    (a)   the evidence that has been tendered to the Tribunal; and

    (b)   the written argument of the disputing parties.

2.   A Party receiving information pursuant to paragraph 1 shall treat the information as if it were a disputing Party.

Article 10.34: Place of Arbitration

Unless the disputing parties agree otherwise, a Tribunal shall hold an arbitration in the territory of a Party that is party to the New York Convention, selected in accordance with:

(a)   the ICSID Additional Facility Rules if the arbitration is under those Rules or the ICSID Convention; or

(b)   the UNCITRAL Arbitration Rules if the arbitration is under those Rules.

Article 10.35: Governing Law

1.   A Tribunal established under this Section shall decide the issues in dispute in accordance with this Agreement and applicable rules of international law.

2.   An interpretation by the Commission of a provision of this Agreement shall be binding on a Tribunal established under this Section.

Article 10.36: Interpretation of Annexes

1.   Where a disputing Party asserts as a defense that the measure alleged to be a breach is within the scope of a reservation or exception set out in Annex I or Annex II, upon request of the disputing Party, the Tribunal shall request the interpretation of the Commission on the issue. The Commission, within 60 days of delivery of the request, shall submit in writing its interpretation to the Tribunal.

2.   Further to paragraph 2 of Article 10.35, a Commission interpretation submitted under paragraph 1 shall be binding on the Tribunal. If the Commission fails to submit an interpretation within 60 days, the Tribunal shall decide the issue.

Article 10.37: Expert Reports

Without prejudice to the appointment of other kinds of experts where authorized by the applicable arbitration rules, a Tribunal, at the request of a disputing party or, unless the disputing parties disapprove, on its own initiative, may appoint one or more experts to report to it in writing on any factual issue concerning environmental, health, safety or other scientific matters raised by a disputing party in a proceeding, subject to such terms and conditions as the disputing parties may agree.

Article 10.38: Interim Measures of Protection

A Tribunal may order an interim measure of protection to preserve the rights of a disputing party, or to ensure that the Tribunal's jurisdiction is made fully effective, including an order to preserve evidence in the possession or control of a disputing party or to protect the Tribunal's jurisdiction. A Tribunal may not order attachment or enjoin the application of the measure alleged to constitute a breach referred to in Article 10.20 or 10.21. For purposes of this paragraph, an order includes a recommendation.

Article 10.39: Final Award

1.   Where a Tribunal makes a final award against a Party, the Tribunal may award, separately or in combination, only:

(a)   monetary damages and any applicable interest; and

(b)   restitution of property, in which case the award shall provide that the disputing Party may pay monetary damages and any applicable interest in lieu of restitution.

2.   A Tribunal may also award costs in accordance with the applicable arbitration rules.

3.   Subject to paragraphs 1 and 2, where a claim is made under Article 10.21.1:

(a)   an award of restitution of property shall provide that restitution be made to the enterprise;

(b)   an award of monetary damages and any applicable interest shall provide that the sum be paid to the enterprise; and

(c)   the award shall provide that it is made without prejudice to any right that any person may have in the relief under applicable domestic law.

4.   A Tribunal may not order a Party to pay punitive damages.

Article 10.40: Finality and Enforcement of an Award

1.   An award made by a Tribunal shall have no binding force except between the disputing parties and in respect of the particular case.

2.   Subject to paragraph 3 and the applicable review procedure for an interim award, a disputing party shall abide by and comply with an award without delay.

3.   A disputing party may not seek enforcement of a final award until:

(a)   in the case of a final award made under the ICSID Convention:

(i)   120 days have elapsed from the date the award was rendered and no disputing party has requested revision or annulment of the award; or

(ii)   revision or annulment proceedings have been completed; and

(b)   in the case of a final award under the ICSID Additional Facility Rules or the UNCITRAL Arbitration Rules:

(i)   three months have elapsed from the date the award was rendered and no disputing party has commenced a proceeding to revise, set aside or annul the award; or

(ii)   a court has dismissed or allowed an application to revise, set aside or annul the award and there is no further appeal.

4.   Each Party shall provide for the enforcement of an award in its territory.

5.   If a disputing Party fails to abide by or comply with a final award, the Commission, on delivery of a request by a Party whose investor was a party to the arbitration, shall establish a panel under Article 19.6. The requesting Party may seek in such proceedings:

(a)   a determination that the failure to abide by or comply with the final award is inconsistent with the obligations of this Agreement; and

(b)   a recommendation that the Party abide by or comply with the final award.

6.   A disputing investor may seek enforcement of an arbitration award under the ICSID Convention or the New York Convention regardless of whether proceedings have been taken under paragraph 5.

7.   A claim that is submitted to arbitration under this Section shall be considered to arise out of a commercial relationship or transaction for purposes of Article I of the New York Convention.

Article 10.41: General Provision

Time when a Claim is Submitted to Arbitration

1.   A claim is submitted to arbitration under this Section when:

(a)   the request for arbitration under paragraph 1 of Article 36 of the ICSID Convention has been received by the Secretary-General;

(b)   the notice of arbitration under Article 2 of Schedule C of the ICSID Additional Facility Rules has been received by the Secretary-General; or

(c)   the notice of arbitration given under the UNCITRAL Arbitration Rules is received by the disputing Party.

Service of Documents

2.   Delivery of notice and other documents on a Party shall be made to the place named for that Party in Annex 10.41.2.

Receipts under Insurance or Guarantee Contracts

3.   In an arbitration under this Section, a Party shall not assert, as a defense, counterclaim, right of setoff or otherwise, that the disputing investor has received or will receive, pursuant to an insurance or guarantee contract, indemnification or other compensation for all or part of its alleged damages.

Publication of an Award

4.   Annex 10.41.4 applies to the Parties specified in that Annex with respect to publication of an award.

Article 10.42: Exclusions

Without prejudice to the applicability or non-applicability of the dispute settlement provisions of this Section or of Chapter 19 to other actions taken by a Party pursuant to Article 20.2, a decision by a Party to prohibit or restrict the acquisition of an investment in its territory by an investor of the other Party, or investment of such an investor, pursuant to that Article shall not be subject to such provisions.

Section D

Investment and Cross-Border Trade in Services Committee

Article 10.43: Investment and Cross-Border Trade in Services Committee

1.   The Parties hereby establish an Investment and Cross-Border Trade in Services Committee, comprising representatives of each Party, in accordance with Annex 10.43.

2.   The Committee shall meet at least once a year, or in any time at request of a Party or the Commission.

3.   The Committee shall perform, *inter alia*, the following functions:

(a)   to overlook the execution and administration of this Chapter and Chapter 11;

(b)   to discuss the subjects of bilateral interest regarding investment and cross-border services; and

(c)   to examine subjects related to investment and cross-border services, which are being discussed at other international fora.

Annex 10.9.6

1.   Decree Law 600 (1974), the Foreign Investment Statute, is a voluntary and special investment regime for Chile.

2.   As an alternative to the common regime for the entry of capital into Chile, potential investors may apply to the Foreign Investment Committee to be subject to the regime set out in Decree Law 600.

3.   The obligations and commitments contained in this Chapter, do not apply to Decree Law 600, Foreign Investment Statute, to Law 18.657 Foreign Capital Investment Fund Law, to the continuation or prompt renewal of such laws, to amendments to those laws or to any special and/or voluntary investment regime that may be adopted in the future by Chile.

4.   For greater certainty, it is understood that the Foreign Investment Committee of Chile has the right to reject applications to invest through Decree Law 600 and Law 18.657. Additionally, the Foreign Investment Committee has the right to regulate the terms and conditions of foreign investment under Decree Law 600 and Law 18.657.

Annex 10.11

With respect to its obligations under Article 10.11, Chile reserves:

1.   The right, without prejudice to paragraph 3 of this Annex, to maintain existing requirements that transfers from Chile of proceeds from the sale of all or any part of an investment of an investor of Korea or from the partial or complete liquidation of the investment may not take place until a period not to exceed:

(a)   in the case of an investment made pursuant to Decree Law 600 Foreign Investment Statute (Decreto Ley 600, Estatuto de la Inversion Extranjera), one year has elapsed from the date of transfer to Chile; or

(b)   in the case of an investment made pursuant to Law 18657 Foreign Capital Investment Fund Law (Ley 18.657, Ley Sobre Fondo de Inversiones de Capitales Extranjeros), five years have elapsed from the date of transfer to Chile;

2.   The right to adopt measures, consistent with this Annex, establishing future special voluntary investment programs in addition to the general regime for foreign investment in Chile, except that any such measures may restrict transfers from Chile of proceeds from the sale of all or any part of an investment of an investor of Korea or from the partial or complete liquidation of the investment for a period not to exceed five years from the date of transfer to Chile; and

3.   The right of the Central Bank of Chile to maintain or adopt measures in conformity with the Constitutional Organic Law of the Central Bank of Chile "Ley Orgánica Constitucional del Banco Central de Chile, Ley 18.840" (hereinafter, Law 18.840) or other legislation, in order to ensure currency stability and the normal operation of domestic and foreign payments. For this purpose, the Central Bank of Chile is empowered to regulate the supply of money and credit in circulation and international credit and foreign exchange operations. The Central Bank of Chile is empowered as well to issue regulations governing monetary, credit, financial, and foreign exchange matters. Such measures include, *inter alia*, the establishment of restrictions or limitations on current payments and transfers (capital movements) to or from Chile, as well as transactions related to them, such as requiring that deposits, investments or credits from or to a foreign country, be subject to a reserve requirement ("encaje").

Notwithstanding the above, the reserve requirement that the Central Bank of Chile can apply pursuant to Article 49 No. 2 of Law 18.840, shall not exceed 30 per cent of the amount transferred and shall not be imposed for a period which exceeds two years.

Annex 10.20

1.   An investor of a Party, on its own behalf or on behalf of an enterprise, may only make a claim under Section C of this Chapter, in relation to investments made and materialized in accordance with the laws and regulations of the other Party.

2.   Both Parties shall negotiate the coverage of Section C of this Chapter, as well as the modification of any other Articles in Section C they deem appropriate, taking into account the outcome of bilateral, regional or multilateral negotiations that address relevant issues, no later than one year after the entry into force of this Agreement.

Annex 10.41.2
Service of Documents

Chile

The place for the delivery of notice and other documents under Section C for Chile is:
Direccion de Asuntos Jurídicos del Ministerio de Relaciones Exteriores de la República de Chile
Morandé 441

Santiago, Chile

Korea

The place for the delivery of notice and other documents under Section C for Korea is:

Office of International Legal Affairs, Ministry of Justice of the
Republic of Korea
Government Complex, Kwacheon
Korea

Annex 10.41.4
Publication of an Award

Chile

Where Chile is the disputing Party, either Chile or a disputing investor that is a party to arbitration may make an award public.

Korea

Where Korea is the disputing Party, either Korea or a disputing investor that is a party to arbitration may make an award public.

Annex 10.43
Composition of the Investment and Cross-Border Trade in Services Committee

For purposes of Article 10.43, the Committee shall comprise:

(a)   in the case of Chile, the General Directorate of International Economic Affairs of the Ministry of Foreign Affairs, or its successor; and

(b)   in the case of Korea, the Director General of International Economic Cooperation Bureau of the Ministry of Finance and Economy, or its successor.

CHAPTER 11

CROSS-BORDER TRADE IN SERVICES

Article 11.1: Definitions

For purposes of this Chapter:

cross-border provision of a service or cross-border trade in services means the provision of a service:

(a)   from the territory of a Party into the territory of the other Party,

(b)   in the territory of a Party by a person of that Party to a person of the other Party, or

(c)   by a national of a Party in the territory of the other Party,

but does not include the provision of a service in the territory of a Party by an investment, as defined in Article 10.1, in that territory;

enterprise means an "enterprise" as defined in Article 2.1, and a branch of an enterprise;

enterprise of a Party means an enterprise constituted or organized under the law of a Party and a branch, located in the territory of a Party and carrying out business activities there;

financial services means any service of a financial nature including those defined in paragraph 5(a) on Annex of Financial Services of GATS;

professional services means services, the provision of which requires specialized postsecondary education, or equivalent training or experience, and for which the right to practice is granted or restricted by a Party, but does not include services provided by trades-persons or vessel and aircraft crew members;

quantitative restriction means a non-discriminatory measure that imposes limitations on:

(a)   the number of service providers, whether in the form of a quota, a monopoly or an economic needs test, or by any other quantitative means; or

(b)   the operations of any service provider, whether in the form of a quota or an economic needs test, or by any other quantitative means;

service provider of a Party means a person of a Party that seeks to provide or provides a service; and

specialty air services means aerial mapping, aerial surveying, aerial photography, forest fire management, fire fighting, aerial advertising, flight training, aerial inspection and surveillance, and aerial spraying services.

Article 11.2: Scope and Coverage

1.   This Chapter applies to measures adopted or maintained by a Party relating to cross-border trade in services by service providers of the other Party, including measures with respect to:

(a)   the production, distribution, marketing, sale and delivery of a service;

(b)   the purchase or use of, or payment for, a service;

(c)   the access to and use of distribution and transportation systems in connection with the provision of a service;

(d)   the presence in its territory of a service provider of the other Party; and

(e)   the provision of a bond or other form of financial security as a condition for the provision of a service.

2.   For purposes of this Chapter, measures adopted or maintained by a Party mean measures adopted or maintained by government or non-governmental bodies in the exercise of any regulatory, administrative or other governmental authority delegated to it by that government.

3.   This Chapter does not apply to:

(a)   cross-border trade in financial services;

(b)   air services, including domestic and international air transportation services, whether scheduled or non-scheduled, and related services in support of air services, other than:

(i)   aircraft repair and maintenance services during which an aircraft is withdrawn from service;

(ii)   specialty air services;

(iii)   glider towing, parachute jumping, aerial construction, heli-logging, aerial sightseeing; and

(iv)   computerized reservation system;

(c)   government procurement by a Party or a state enterprise;

(d)   subsidies or grants provided by a Party or a state enterprise, including government supported loans, guarantees and insurance; and

(e)   services provided in the exercise of governmental authority such as law enforcement, correctional services, income security or insurance, social security or insurance, social welfare, public education, public training, health, and child care.

4.   Notwithstanding subparagraph 3(e), if services provided in the exercise of governmental authority are provided in the territory of a Party such as law enforcement, correctional services, income security or insurance, social security or insurance, social welfare, public education, public training, health, and child care on a commercial basis or in competition with one or more service providers, such services shall be covered by the provisions of this Chapter.

5.   Nothing in this Chapter shall be construed to impose any obligation on a Party with respect to a national of the other Party seeking access to its employment market, or employed on a permanent basis in its territory, or to confer any right on that national with respect to such access or employment.

Article 11.3: National Treatment

Each Party shall accord to services and service providers of the other Party treatment no less favorable than that it accords, in like circumstances, to its own services and service providers.

Article 11.4: Local Presence

Neither Party may require a service provider of the other Party to establish or maintain a representative office or any form of enterprise, or to be resident, in its territory as a condition for the cross-border provision of a service.

Article 11.5: Reservations

1.   Articles 11.3 and 11.4 do not apply to:

(a)   any existing non-conforming measure that is maintained by:

(i)   a Party at the national level, as set out in its Schedule to Annex I; or

(ii)   a local government;

(b)   the continuation or prompt renewal of any non-conforming measure referred to in subparagraph (a); or

(c)   an amendment to any non-conforming measure referred to in subparagraph (a) to the extent that the amendment does not decrease the conformity of the measure, as it existed immediately before the amendment, with Articles 11.3 and 11.4.

2.   Articles 11.3 and 11.4 do not apply to any measure that a Party adopts or maintains with respect to sectors, subsectors or activities, as set out in its Schedule to Annex II.

Article 11.6: Quantitative Restrictions

1.   Each Party shall set out in its Schedule to Annex III any quantitative restriction that it maintains at the national level.

2.   Each Party shall notify the other Party of any quantitative restriction that it adopts, other than at the local government level, after the date of entry into force of this Agreement and shall set out the restriction in its Schedule to Annex III.

3.   The Parties shall periodically, but in any event at least every two years, endeavor to negotiate the liberalization or removal of the quantitative restrictions set out in Annex III pursuant to paragraphs 1 and 2.

Article 11.7: Future Liberalization

1.   Through future negotiations, to be scheduled every two years by the Commission after the date of entry into force of this Agreement, the Parties will further deepen liberalization with a view to reaching the reduction or elimination of the remaining restrictions scheduled in conformity with Article 11.5, on a mutually advantageous basis and ensuring an overall balance of rights and obligations.

2.   If a Party makes any further liberalization, in conformity with Article 11.5 by an agreement with a non-Party, it shall afford adequate opportunity to the other Party to negotiate

treatment granted therein on a mutually advantageous basis and with a view to securing an overall balance of rights and obligations.

Article 11.8: Liberalization of Non-Discriminatory Measures

Each Party shall set out in its Schedule to Annex IV its commitments to liberalize quantitative restrictions, licensing requirements, performance requirements or other non discriminatory measures.

Article 11.9: Procedures

The Commission shall establish procedures for:

(a)   a Party to notify and include in its relevant Schedule:

   (i)   quantitative restrictions in accordance with Article 11.6.2;

   (ii)   commitments pursuant to Article 11.8; and

   (iii)   amendments of measures referred to in Article 11.5.1(c); and

(b)   consultations on reservations, quantitative restrictions or commitments with a view to further liberalization.

Article 11.10: Licensing and Certification

1.   With a view to ensuring that any measure adopted or maintained by a Party related to requirements and procedures to the licensing or certification of nationals of the other Party does not constitute an unnecessary barrier to cross-border trade in services, each Party shall endeavor to ensure that any such measure:

   (a)   s based on objective and transparent criteria, such as competence and the ability to provide a service;

   (b)   is not more burdensome than necessary to ensure the quality of a service; and

   (c)   does not constitute a disguised restriction on the cross-border provision of a service.

2.   Where a Party recognizes, unilaterally or by an agreement or arrangement, education, experience, licenses or certifications obtained in the territory of a non-Party, the Party shall afford the other Party an adequate opportunity to demonstrate that education, experience, licenses or certifications obtained in the other Party's territory should also be recognized or to conclude an agreement or arrangement of comparable effect.

3.   Annex 11.10 applies to measures adopted or maintained by a Party relating to the licensing or certification of professional service providers.

Article 11.11: Denial of Benefits

Subject to prior notification and consultation in accordance with Articles 17.4 and 19.4, a Party may deny the benefits of this Chapter to a service provider of the other Party where the Party establishes that the service is being provided by an enterprise that is owned or controlled by persons of a non-Party and that has no substantive business activities in the territory of the other Party.

Annex 11.10
Professional Services

Objectives

1.   The objective of this Annex is the establishment of rules to be followed by the Parties in the reduction and gradual elimination, within their territories of the barriers in the rendering of professional services.

Processing of Applications for Licenses and Certifications

2.   Each Party shall ensure that its competent authorities, within a reasonable time after the submission by a national of the other Party of an application for a license or certification:

(a)   where the application is complete, make a determination on the application and inform the applicant of that determination; or

(b)   where the application is not complete, inform the applicant, without undue delay, of the status of the application and the additional information that is required under the Party's law.

Development of Professional Standards

3.   The Parties shall encourage the relevant bodies in their respective territories to develop mutually acceptable standards and criteria for licensing and certification of professional service providers and to provide recommendations on mutual recognition to the Commission.

4.   The standards and criteria referred to in paragraph 3 may be developed with regard to the following matters:

(a)   education - accreditation of schools or academic programs;

(b)   examinations - qualifying examinations for licensing, including alternative methods of assessment such as oral examinations and interviews;

(c)   experience - length and nature of experience required for licensing;

(d)   conduct and ethics - standards of professional conduct and the nature of disciplinary action for non-conformity with those standards;

(e)   professional development and re-certification - continuing education and ongoing requirements to maintain professional certification;

(f)   scope of practice - extent of, or limitations on, permissible activities;

(g)   local knowledge - requirements for knowledge of such matters as local laws, regulations, language, geography or climate; and

(h)   consumer protection - alternatives to residency requirements, including bonding, professional liability insurance and client restitution funds, to provide for the protection of consumers.

5.   Upon receipt of a recommendation referred to in paragraph 3, the Commission shall review the recommendation within a reasonable time to determine whether it is consistent with this Agreement. Based on the Commission's review, each Party shall encourage its respective competent authorities, where appropriate, to implement the recommendation within a mutually agreed time.

Temporary Licensing

6.   Where the Parties agree, each Party shall encourage the relevant bodies in its territory to develop procedures for the temporary licensing of professional service providers of the other Party.

Review

7.   The Commission shall periodically, at least once every three years, review the implementation of this Section.

CHAPTER 12

TELECOMMUNICATIONS

Article 12.1: Definitions

For purposes of this Chapter:

authorized equipment means terminal or other equipment that has been approved for attachment to the public telecommunications transport network in accordance with the conformity assessment procedures of a Party;

conformity assessment procedures means "conformity assessment procedures" as defined in Article 9.1 and includes the procedures established in Annex 12.1;

enhanced or value-added services means telecommunications services employing computer processing applications that:

(a)   act on the format, content, code, protocol or similar aspects of a customer's transmitted information;

(b)   provide a customer with additional, different or restructured information; or

(c)   involve customer interaction with stored information;

intracorporate communications means telecommunications through which an enterprise communicates:

(a)   internally or with or among its subsidiaries, branches or affiliates, as defined by each Party, or

(b)   on a non-commercial basis with other persons that are fundamental to the economic activity of the enterprise and that have a continuing contractual relationship with it,

but does not include telecommunications services provided to persons other than those described herein;

monopoly means an entity, including a consortium or government agency, that in any relevant market in the territory of a Party is maintained or designated as the sole provider of a public telecommunication transport network or service;

network termination point means the final demarcation of the public telecommunications transport network at the customer's premises;

non-discriminatory means on terms and conditions no less favorable than those accorded to any other customer, user or potential customer or user of like public telecommunications transport networks or services or enhanced or value added services in like circumstances;

private network means a telecommunications transport network that is used exclusively for intracorporate communications or among pre-defined persons;

protocol means a set of rules and formats that govern the exchange of information between two peer entities for purposes of transferring signaling and/or data information;

public telecommunications transport network means public telecommunications infrastructure that permits telecommunications between defined network termination points;

public telecommunications transport networks or services means public telecommunications transport networks or public telecommunications transport services;

public telecommunications transport service means any telecommunications transport service required by a Party, explicitly or in effect, to be offered to the public generally, including telegraph, telephone, telex and data transmission, that typically involves the real-time transmission of customer-supplied information between two or more points without any end-to end change in the form or content of the customer's information;

standard means a document, approved by a recognized body, that provides, for common and repeated use, rules, guidelines or characteristics for goods or related processes and production methods, or for services or related operating methods, with which compliance is not mandatory. It may also include or deal exclusively with terminology, symbols, packaging, marking or labelling requirements as they apply to a good, process, or production or operating method;

telecommunications means the transmission and reception of signals by any electromagnetic means;

technical regulation means a document which lays down goods' characteristics or their related processes and production methods, or services' characteristics or their related operating methods, including the applicable administrative provisions, with which compliance is mandatory. It may also include or deal exclusively with terminology, symbols, packaging, marking or labelling requirements as they apply to a good, process, or production or operating method;

telecommunications service means a service provided by means of the transmission and reception of signals by any electromagnetic means, but does not mean the cable, broadcast or other electromagnetic distribution of radio or television programming to the public generally; and

terminal equipment means any digital or analog device capable of processing, receiving, switching, signaling or transmitting signals by electromagnetic means and that is connected by radio or wire to a public telecommunications transport network at a termination point.

Article 12.2: Scope and Coverage

1.   This Chapter applies to:

   (a)   measures adopted or maintained by a Party relating to access to and use of public telecommunications transport networks or services by persons of the other Party, including access and use by such persons operating private networks;

   (b)   measures adopted or maintained by a Party relating to the provision of enhanced or value-added services by persons of the other Party in the territory, or across the borders, of a Party; and

   (c)   standards-related measures relating to attachment of terminal or other equipment to public telecommunications transport networks.[2]

2.   Except to ensure that persons operating broadcast stations and cable systems have continued access to and use of public telecommunications transport networks and services, this Chapter shall not apply to any measure adopted or maintained by a Party relating to broadcast or cable distribution of radio or television programming.

3.   Nothing in this Chapter shall be construed to:

   (a)   require a Party to authorize a person of the other Party to establish, construct, acquire, lease, operate or provide telecommunications transport networks or telecommunications transport services;

   (b)   require a Party, or require a Party to compel any person, to establish, construct, acquire, lease, operate or provide telecommunications transport networks or telecommunications transport services not offered to the public generally;

---

[2] For equipment that is not connected to the public telecommunications transport network or not referred to in this Agreement, the Parties shall abide by the standard-related provisions of Chapter 9.

(c)   prevent a Party from prohibiting persons operating private networks from using their networks to provide public telecommunications transport networks or services to third persons; or

(d)   require a Party to compel any person engaged in the broadcast or cable distribution of radio or television programming to make available its cable or broadcast facilities as a public telecommunications transport network.

Article 12.3: Access to and Use of Public Telecommunications Transport Networks and Services

1.   Each Party shall ensure that persons of the other Party have access to and use of any public telecommunications transport network or service, including private leased circuits, offered in its territory or across its borders for the conduct of their business, on reasonable and non-discriminatory terms and conditions, including as those set out in paragraphs 2 through 8.

2.   Subject to paragraphs 6 and 7, each Party shall ensure that persons of the other Party are permitted to:

(a)   purchase or lease, and attach terminal or other equipment that interfaces with the public telecommunications transport network;

(b)   interconnect private leased or owned circuits with public telecommunications transport networks in the territory, or across the borders, of that Party, including those for use in providing dial-up access to and from their customers or users, or with circuits leased or owned by another person on terms and conditions mutually agreed by those persons;

(c)   perform switching, signaling and processing functions; and

(d)   use operating protocols of their choice.

3.   Each Party shall ensure that the pricing of public telecommunications transport services reflects economic costs directly related to providing the services.

4.   Each Party shall ensure that persons of the other Party may use public telecommunications transport networks or services for the movement of information in its territory or across its borders, including for intracorporate communications, and for access to information contained in data bases or otherwise stored in machine-readable form in the territory of the other Party.

5.   Further to Article 20.1, nothing in this Chapter shall be construed to prevent a Party from adopting or enforcing any measure necessary to:

(a)   ensure the security and confidentiality of messages; or

(b)   protect the privacy of subscribers to public telecommunications transport networks or services.

6.   Each Party shall ensure that, further to Article 12.5, no condition is imposed on access to and use of public telecommunications transport networks or services, other than that necessary to:

(a)   safeguard the public service responsibilities of providers of public telecommunications transport networks or services, in particular their ability to make their networks or services available to the public generally; or

(b)   protect the technical integrity of public telecommunications transport networks or services.

7.   Provided that conditions for access to and use of public telecommunications transport networks or services satisfy the criteria set out in paragraph 6, such conditions may include:

(a)   a restriction on resale or shared use of such services;

(b)   a requirement to use specified technical interfaces, including interface protocols, for interconnection with such networks or services;

(c)   a restriction on interconnection of private leased or owned circuits with such networks or services or with circuits leased or owned by another person; and

(d)   a licensing, permit, registration or notification procedure which, if adopted or maintained, is transparent and applications filed thereunder are processed expeditiously.

Article 12.4: Conditions for the Provision of Enhanced or Value-Added Services

1.   Each Party shall ensure that:

(a)   any licensing, permit, registration or notification procedure that it adopts or maintains relating to the provision of enhanced or value-added services is transparent and non-discriminatory, and that applications filed thereunder are processed expeditiously; and

(b)   information required under such procedures is limited to that necessary to demonstrate that the applicant has the financial solvency to begin providing services or to assess conformity of the applicant's terminal or other equipment with the applicable standards or technical regulations of the Party.

2.   Neither Party may require a person providing enhanced or value-added services to:

(a)   provide those services to the public generally;
(b)   cost-justify its rates;
(c)   file a tariff;
(d)   interconnect its networks with any particular customer or network; or
(e)   conform with any particular standard or technical regulation for interconnection other than for interconnection to a public telecommunications transport network.

3.   Notwithstanding paragraph 2(c), a Party may require the filing of a tariff by:

(a)   such a provider to remedy a practice of that provider that the Party has found in a particular case to be anti-competitive under its law; or

(b)   a monopoly to which Article 12.6 applies.

Article 12.5: Standards-Related Measures

1.   Further to the TBT Agreement, each Party shall ensure that its standards-related measures relating to the attachment of terminal or other equipment to the public telecommunications transport networks, including those measures relating to the use of testing and measuring equipment for conformity assessment procedures, are adopted or maintained only to the extent necessary to:

(a)   prevent technical damage to public telecommunications transport networks;

(b)   prevent technical interference with, or degradation of, public telecommunications transport services;

(c)   prevent electromagnetic interference, and ensure compatibility, with other uses of the electromagnetic spectrum;

(d)   prevent billing equipment malfunction;

(e)   ensure users' safety and access to public telecommunications transport networks or services;

(f)   ensure the electrical safety of communication equipment; or

(g)   facilitate the efficient utilization of radio spectrum resources.

2.   A Party may require, before an unauthorized terminal or other equipment may be marketed, an approval for the attachment to the public telecommunications transport network, provided that the criteria for that approval are consistent with paragraph 1.

3.   Each Party shall ensure that the network termination points for its public telecommunications transport networks are defined on a reasonable and transparent basis.

4.   Neither Party may require separate authorization for equipment that is connected on the customer's side of authorized equipment that serves as a protective device fulfilling the criteria of paragraph 1.

5.   Further to the TBT Agreement, each Party shall:

(a)   ensure that its conformity assessment procedures are transparent and non-discriminatory and that applications filed thereunder are processed expeditiously;

(b)   permit any technically qualified entity to perform the testing required under the Party's conformity assessment procedures for terminal or other equipment to be attached to the public telecommunications transport network, subject to the Party's right to review the accuracy and completeness of the test results; and

(c)   ensure that any measure that it adopts or maintains requiring persons to be authorized to act as agents for suppliers of telecommunications equipment before the Party's relevant conformity assessment bodies is non-discriminatory.

6.   No later than one year after the date of entry into force of this Agreement, each Party shall adopt, as part of its conformity assessment procedures, provisions necessary to accept the test results from laboratories or testing facilities in the territory of the other Party for tests performed in accordance with the accepting Party's standards-related measures and procedures. For the detailed procedures and methods for mutual recognition of testing laboratories and mutual acceptance of test reports, follows the procedures and methods as prescribed in the "Asia-Pacific Economic Cooperation (APEC) Mutual Recognition Arrangement for Conformity Assessment of Telecommunications Equipment (adopted on May 8, 1998)" shall be taken into consideration by the Telecommunication Committee.

7.   The Parties hereby establish a Committee on Telecommunications Standards, comprising representatives of each Party.

8.   The Committee on Telecommunications Standards shall perform the functions set out in Annex 12.5.8.

Article 12.6: Monopolies

1.   Where a Party maintains or designates a monopoly to provide public telecommunications transport networks or services, and the monopoly, directly or through an affiliate, competes in the provision of enhanced or value-added services or other telecommunications-related services or telecommunications-related goods, the Party shall ensure that the monopoly does not use its monopoly position to engage in anti-competitive conduct in those markets, either directly or through its dealings with its affiliates, in such a manner as to affect adversely a person of the other Party. Such conduct may include cross-subsidization, predatory conduct and the discriminatory provision of access to public telecommunications transport networks or services.

2.   To prevent such anti-competitive conduct, each Party shall adopt or maintain, as stated in paragraph 1, effective measures, such as:

(a)   accounting requirements;

(b)   requirements for structural separation;

(c)   rules to ensure that the monopoly accords its competitors access to and use of its public telecommunications transport networks or services on terms and conditions no less favorable than those it accords to itself or its affiliates; and

(d)   rules to ensure the timely disclosure of technical changes to public telecommunications transport networks and their interfaces.

Article 12.7: Transparency

Further to Article 17.3, each Party shall make publicly available its measures relating to access to and use of public telecommunications transport networks or services, including measures relating to:

(a)   tariffs and other terms and conditions of service;

(b)   specifications of technical interfaces with the networks or services;

(c)   information on bodies responsible for the preparation and adoption of standards related measures affecting such access and use;

(d)   conditions applying to attachment of terminal or other equipment to the networks; and

(e)   notification, permit, registration, or licensing or concession requirements.

Article 12.8: Relation to Other Chapters

In the event of any inconsistency between this Chapter and another Chapter in this Agreement, this Chapter shall prevail to the extent of the inconsistency.

Article 12.9: Relation to International Organizations and Agreements

The Parties recognize the importance of international standards for global compatibility and interoperability of telecommunication networks or services and undertake to promote those standards through the work of relevant international bodies, including the International Telecommunication Union and the International Organization for Standardization.

Article 12.10: Technical Cooperation and Other Consultations

1.   To encourage the development of interoperable telecommunications transport services infrastructure, the Parties shall cooperate in the exchange of technical information, the development of government-to-government training programs and other related activities. In implementing this obligation, the Parties shall give special emphasis to existing exchange programs.

2.   The Parties shall consult with a view to determining the feasibility of further liberalizing trade in all telecommunications services, including public telecommunications transport networks and services.

Annex 12.1
Conformity Assessment Procedures

For Chile:

1.   The competent institution responsible for the adoption of conformity assessment procedures is the Undersecretary of Telecommunications, Ministry of Transport and Telecommunications, or its successor.

2.   The existing measures are the following:

(a)   Law 18.168, Official Gazette, October 2, 1982, General Law of Telecommunications ("Ley 18.168, Diario Oficial, octubre 2, 1982, Ley General de Telecomunicaciones")

(b)   Supreme Decree 220 of the Ministry of Transport and Telecommunications, Official Gazette, January 8, 1981

(c)   Regulation on the Homologation of Telephone Equipment (Decreto 220 de Ministerio de Transportes y Telecomunicaciones, Diario Oficial, enero 8, 1981, "Reglamento de Homologación de Aparatos Telefónicos")

For Korea:

1.   The competent institution responsible for the adoption of conformity assessment procedures is the Ministry of Information and Communication, or its successor.

2.   The existing measures are the following:

(a)   Areas of Type Approval

•   Telecommunications Basic Act (Act No. 5454, Dec. 13, 1997)

-     Enforcement Decree of Telecommunications Basic Act (Presidential Decree No. 15282, Feb. 22, 1997)

-     Enforcement Regulations of Telecommunications Basic Act (Ordinance of the Ministry of Information and Communication No. 64, Feb. 26, 1999): definitions of the type approval items, and application and process procedures

-     Regulations on the Technical Standards of Telecommunications Facilities (Ordinance of the Ministry of Information and Communication No. 58, Dec. 1, 1998)

-     Terminal-installment Technical Regulations (Ministry of Information and Communication Announcement No. 1998-18, Feb. 21, 1998): definitions of the technical regulations of terminal-installment equipment

(b)   Areas of Type Verification and Type Registration of Wireless Equipment

•   Radio Waves Act (Act No. 5637, Jan. 18, 1999)

-     Enforcement Decree of the Radio Waves Act (Presidential Decree No.16158, March 3, 1999)

-     Enforcement Regulations of the Radio Waves Act (Ordinance of the Ministry of Information and Communication No. 53, July 31, 1998)

-     Confirmation Regulations on Type Verification, Type Registration and Technical Standard Certification for Wireless Facility (Ordinance of the Ministry of Information and Communication No. 52, July 16, 1998): definitions of the object of verification or registration, and the application and process procedure

- Regulations on Wireless Facilities (Ordinance of the Ministry of Information and Communication No. 45, Jan. 31, 1998): definitions of the technical regulations

(c)   Areas of Electromagnetic Compatibility Registration

•   Radio Waves Act (Act No. 5637, Jan.18, 1999)

- Regulations on Electromagnetic Compatibility Registration (Act No. 39, May 8, 1997): definitions of the registration items, application and process procedures, and relevant technical regulations

Annex 12.5.8
Committee on Telecommunications Standards

1.   The Committee on Telecommunications Standards, established under Article 12.5.7, shall comprise representatives of each Party.

2.   The Committee shall, within six months of the date of entry into force of this Agreement, develop a work program, including a timetable, for making compatible to the greatest extent possible, the standards-related measures of the Parties for authorized equipment as defined in this Chapter.

3.   The Committee may address other appropriate standards-related matters regarding telecommunications equipment or services and such other matters as it considers appropriate.

4.   The Committee shall take into account relevant work carried out by the Parties in other fora, and that of non-governmental standardizing bodies.

CHAPTER 13

TEMPORARY ENTRY FOR BUSINESS PERSONS

Article 13.1: Definitions

For purposes of this Chapter:

business person means a citizen of a Party who is engaged in trade in goods, the provision of services or the conduct of investment activities; and

temporary entry means entry into the territory of a Party by a business person of the other Party without the intent to establish permanent residence.

Article 13.2: General Principles

1.   Further to Article 1.2, this Chapter reflects the preferential trading relationship between the Parties, the desirability of facilitating temporary entry on a reciprocal basis and of establishing transparent criteria and procedures for temporary entry, and the need to ensure

border security and to protect the domestic labour force and permanent employment in their respective territories.

2.   The Parties reconfirm their voluntary commitments established in the APEC Business Travel Card "Operating Framework". This recognition shall be understood to be under the APEC general principles.

Article 13.3: General Obligations

1.   Each Party shall apply its measures relating to the provisions of this Chapter in accordance with Article 13.2 and, in particular, shall apply expeditiously those measures so as to avoid unduly impairing or delaying trade in goods or services or conduct of investment activities under this Agreement.

2.   The Parties shall endeavour to develop and adopt common criteria, definitions and interpretations for the implementation of this Chapter.

Article 13.4: Grant of Temporary Entry

1.   In accordance with this Chapter and subject to the provisions of Annex 13.4 and Annex 13.4.1, each Party shall grant temporary entry to business persons who are otherwise qualified for entry under applicable measures relating to public health and safety and national security.

2.   A Party may refuse to issue an immigration document authorizing employment to a business person where the temporary entry of that person might affect adversely:

  (a)   the settlement of any labour dispute that is in progress at the place or intended place of employment; or

  (b)   the employment of any person who is involved in such dispute.

3.   When a Party refuses pursuant to paragraph 2 to issue an immigration document authorizing employment, it shall:

  (a)   inform in writing the business person of the reasons for the refusal; and

  (b)   promptly notify the other Party in writing of the reasons for the refusal.

4.   Each Party shall limit any fees for processing applications for temporary entry of business persons to the approximate cost of services rendered.

Article 13.5: Provision of Information

1.   Further to Article 17.3, each Party shall:

  (a)   provide to the other Party such materials as will enable the latter Party to become acquainted with its own measures relating to this Chapter; and

  (b)   no later than six months after the date of entry into force of this Agreement, prepare, publish and make available in its own territory, and in the territory of the other Party, explanatory material in a consolidated document regarding the requirements for temporary entry under this Chapter in such a manner as will enable business persons of the other Party to become acquainted with them.

2.   Each Party shall collect and maintain, and make available to the other Party in accordance with its domestic law, data regarding the granting of temporary entry under this Chapter to business persons of the other Party who have been issued immigration documentation, including data specific to each occupation, profession or activity.

Article 13.6: Working Group

The Parties hereby establish a Temporary Entry Working Group, comprising representatives of each Party, including immigration officials, to consider the implementation and administration of this Chapter and any measures of mutual interest.

Article 13.7: Dispute Settlement

1.   A Party may not initiate proceedings under Article 19.6 regarding a refusal to grant temporary entry under this Chapter or a particular case arising under Article 13.2 unless:

   (a)   the matter involves a pattern of practice; and

   (b)   the business person has exhausted the available administrative remedies regarding the particular matter.

2.   The remedies referred to in subparagraph 1(b) shall be deemed to be exhausted if a final determination in the matter has not been issued by the competent authority within six months of the institution of an administrative proceeding, and the failure to issue a determination is not attributable to delay caused by the business person.

Article 13.8: Relation to Other Chapters

Except for this Chapter, Chapters 1, 2, 18, 19 and 21 and Articles 17.2, 17.3, 17.4 and 17.6, no provision of this Agreement shall impose any obligation on a Party regarding its immigration measures.

Annex 13.4
Temporary Entry for Business Persons

Section I - Business Visitors

1. Each Party shall grant temporary entry to a business person seeking to engage in a business activity set out in Appendix 13.4.I.1, without requiring that person to obtain an employment authorization, provided that the business person otherwise complies with existing immigration measures applicable to temporary entry, on presentation of:

   (a)   proof of citizenship of a Party;

   (b)   documentation demonstrating that the business person will be so engaged and describing the purpose of entry; and

    (c)   evidence demonstrating that the proposed business activity is international in scope and the business person is not seeking to enter the local labour market.

2.   Each Party shall provide that a business person may satisfy the requirements of subparagraph 1(c) by demonstrating that:

    (a)   the primary source of remuneration for the proposed business activity is outside the territory of the Party granting temporary entry; and

    (b)   the business person's principal place of business and the actual place of accrual of profits, at least, predominantly, remain outside such a territory.

3.   Each Party shall grant temporary entry to a business person seeking to engage in a business activity other than those set out in Appendix 13.4.I.1, without requiring that person to obtain an employment authorization, on a basis no less favourable than that provided under the existing provisions of the measures set out in Appendix 13.4.I.3, provided that the business person otherwise complies with existing immigration measures applicable to temporary entry.

4.   Neither Party may:

    (a)   as a condition for temporary entry under paragraph 1 or 3, require prior approval procedures, petitions, labour certification tests or other procedures of similar effect;

or

    (b)   impose or maintain any numerical restriction relating to temporary entry under paragraph 1 or 3.

5.   Notwithstanding paragraph 4, a Party may require a business person seeking temporary entry under this Section to obtain a visa or its equivalent in accordance with its domestic immigration law prior to entry. Before imposing the visa requirement, the Party shall consult with the other Party with a view to avoiding the imposition of the requirement. With respect to an existing visa requirement, a Party shall consult, upon request, with the other Party with a view to its removal.

Section II - Traders and Investors

1.   Each Party shall grant temporary entry and provide confirming documentation to a business person seeking to:

    (a)   carry on substantial trade in goods or services principally between the territory of the Party of which the business person is a citizen and the territory of the other Party into which entry is sought, or

    (b)   establish, develop, administer or provide advice or key technical services to the operation of an investment to which the business person or the business person's enterprise has committed, or is in the process of committing, a substantial amount of capital, in a capacity that is supervisory or executive, or involves essential skills, provided that the business person otherwise complies with existing immigration measures applicable to temporary entry.

2.   Neither Party may:

(a)   as a condition for temporary entry under paragraph 1, require labour certification tests or other procedures of similar effect; or

(b)   impose or maintain any numerical restriction relating to temporary entry under paragraph 1.

3.   Notwithstanding paragraph 2, a Party may require a business person seeking temporary entry under this Section to obtain a visa or its equivalent in accordance with its domestic immigration law prior to entry. Before imposing the visa requirement, the Party shall consult with the other Party with a view to avoiding the imposition of the requirement. With respect to an existing visa requirement, a Party shall consult, upon request, with the other Party with a view to its removal.

Section III - Intra-Company Transferees

1.   Each Party shall grant temporary entry and provide confirming documentation to a business person employed by an enterprise who seeks to render services to that enterprise of a Party or a subsidiary or affiliate thereof, in a capacity that is managerial, executive or involves specialised knowledge, provided that the business person otherwise complies with existing immigration measures applicable to temporary entry. A Party may require the business person to have been employed continuously by the enterprise for one year within the three-year period immediately preceding the date of the application for admission.

2.   Neither Party may:

(a)   as a condition for temporary entry under paragraph 1, require labour certification tests or other procedures of similar effect; or

(b)   impose or maintain any numerical restriction relating to temporary entry under paragraph 1.

3.   Notwithstanding paragraph 2, a Party may require a business person seeking temporary entry under this Section to obtain a visa or its equivalent in accordance with its domestic immigration law prior to entry. Before imposing visa requirement, the Party shall consult with the other Party with a view to avoiding the imposition of the requirement. With respect to an existing visa requirement, a Party shall consult, upon request, with the other Party with a view to its removal.

Annex 13.4.1

In the case of Chile:

1.   Business persons who enter Chile under any of the categories set out in Annex 13.4 shall be deemed to be engaged in activities which are in the country's interest.

2.   Business persons who enter Chile under any of the categories set out in Annex 13.4 are issued with a temporary resident visa for a period up to one year. Such a temporary visa may be

extended for subsequent periods, provided the conditions on which it is based remain in effect, without requiring that person to apply for permanent residence.

3.   Business persons who enter Chile may also obtain an identity card for foreigners.

4.   Business persons who enter Chile under any of the categories set out in Annex 13.4 may freely enter and leave Chile without re-entry permission during the validity of their visas on the basis of reciprocity.

In the case of Korea:

1.   Business visitors who enter Korea under Section I of Annex 13.4 are issued with a short term business visa (C-2) for a period of up to six months. A change of visa status to that of an intra-company transferee visa (D-7), investment visa (D-8) or trade management visa (D-9), may be permitted, if the activities of the business visitors satisfy the conditions under Sections II and III of Annex 13.4.

2.   Investors and traders who enter Korea under Section II of Annex 13.4 are issued with an investment visa (D-8) or a trade and management visa (D-9), respectively, for a period of up to one year. These visas may be extended for subsequent periods provided the conditions on which they are based remain in effect.

3.   Intra-company transferees who enter Korea under Section III of Annex 13.4 are issued with an intra-company transferee visa (D-7) for a period of up to one year. This visa may be extended for subsequent periods provided the conditions on which it is based remain in effect.

4.   Business persons who enter Korea under any of the categories set out in Annex 13.4 may freely enter and leave Korea without re-entry permission during the validity of their visa on the basis of the reciprocity.

5.   Business persons who intend to stay over 90 days in Korea shall register the aliens registration at the competent immigration office.

Appendix 13.4.I.1
Business Visitors

1.   For purposes of this Appendix, "territory of the other Party" means the territory of the Party other than the territory of the Party into which temporary entry is sought.

2.   Business activities referred to in Section I.1 of Annex 13.4 are:

Research and Design

*   Technical, scientific and statistical researchers conducting research for an enterprise located in the territory of the other Party.

Growth, Manufacture and Production

*   Purchasing and production management personnel conducting commercial transactions for an enterprise located in the territory of the other Party.

Marketing

- Market researchers and analysts conducting analysis or research for an enterprise located in the territory of the other Party.

- Trade fair and promotional personnel attending a trade convention.

Sales

- Sales representatives and agents taking orders or negotiating contracts for goods or services for an enterprise located in the territory of the other Party but not delivering goods or providing services.

- Buyers purchasing for an enterprise located in the territory of the other Party.

Distribution

- Customs brokers providing consulting services regarding the facilitation of the import or export of goods.

After-Sales Service

- Installers, repair and maintenance personnel, and supervisors, possessing specialised knowledge essential to a seller's contractual obligation, performing services or training workers to perform services, pursuant to a warranty or other service contract incidental to the sale of commercial or industrial equipment or machinery, including computer software, purchased from an enterprise located outside the territory of the Party into which temporary entry is sought, during the life of the warranty or service agreement.

General Service

- Consultants engaging in a business activity at the cross-border services provision level.

- Management and supervisory personnel engaging in a commercial transaction for an enterprise located in the territory of the other Party.

- Financial services personnel (insurers, bankers or investment brokers) engaging in commercial transactions for an enterprise located in the territory of the other Party.

- Public relations and advertising personnel consulting with business associates, or attending or participating in conventions.

- Tourism personnel (tour and travel agents, tour guides or tour operators) attending or participating in conventions or conducting a tour that has begun in the territory of the other Party.

- Translators or interpreters performing services as employees of an enterprise located in the territory of the other Party.

Appendix 13.4.I.3
Existing Immigration Measures

1.   In the case of Chile, Title I, paragraph 6 of Decree Law 1094, Official Gazette, July 19, 1975, Immigration Law ("Decreto Ley 1094, Diario Oficial, julio 19, 1975, Ley de Extranjería"), and Title III of Immigration Regulation ("Decreto Supremo 597 del Ministerio del Interior, Diario Oficial noviembre 24, 1984, Reglamento de Extranjería").

2.   In the case of Korea, Immigration Law Article 7 and Article 8 (amended February 5, 1999), Immigration Law Enforcement Ordinance Article 7, Article 11 and Article 12 (amended November 27, 1999), Immigration Law Enforcement Regulations Article 8, Article 9, Article 10, Article 13, Article 18, Article 71 and Article 76 (amended December 2, 1999), Visa Issuance Procedure for Short-Term Business (C-2), Short-Term Visitors (C-3).

PART IV

GOVERNMENT PROCUREMENT

CHAPTER 15

GOVERNMENT PROCUREMENT

Article 15.1: Definitions

For purposes of this Chapter:

entity means an entity of a Party covered in Annex 15.1;

government procurement means the process by which a government, through any contractual means, obtains the use of or acquires goods or services, or any combination thereof, for governmental purposes and not with a view to commercial sale or resale, or use in the production or supply of goods or services for commercial sale or resale;

offsets means those conditions imposed or considered by an entity prior to, or in the course of its procurement process, that encourage local development or improve its Party's balance of payments accounts by means of requirements of local content, licensing of technology,investment, counter-trade or similar requirements;

open tendering procedures means those procedures whereby any interested supplier may submit a tender;

privatisation means a process by means of which a public entity is no longer subject to government control, whether by public tender of the shares of that entity or otherwise, as contemplated in the respective Party's legislation in force;

public works concession and build-operate-transfer contract means a contract of the same type as the public works procurement contract, except for the fact that the remuneration for the works to be carried out consists either solely of the right to exploit the construction or in such a right together with a payment;

supplier means a natural or legal person that provides or could provide goods or services to an entity;

technical specifications means a specification, which lays down the characteristics of the products or services to be procured, such as quality, performance, safety and dimensions, symbols, terminology, packaging, marking and labelling, or the processes and methods for their production and requirements relating to conformity assessment procedures prescribed by procuring entities; and

tenderer means a supplier who has submitted a tender.

Article 15.2: Scope and Coverage

1.   This Chapter applies to measures adopted or maintained by a Party relating to procurement by an entity, by any contractual means, including purchase and rental or lease, with or without an option to buy, subject to the conditions specified in Annexes 15.1 and 15.2. For purposes of this Chapter, public works concession and build-operate-transfer contracts shall be considered as procurement.

2.   This Chapter does not apply to:

   (a)   non-contractual agreements or any form of assistance provided by a Party or a state enterprise, including grants, loans, fiscal incentives, subsidies, guarantees, cooperative agreements, government provision of goods and services to persons or to state, regional or local governments, and purchases for the direct purpose of providing foreign assistance;

   (b)   purchases funded by international grants, loans or other assistance, where the provision of such assistance is subject to conditions inconsistent with the provisions of this Chapter;

   (c)   hiring of government employees and hiring of entities' other long-term staff and personnel, and related employment measures; and

   (d)   financial services.

3.   Neither Party may prepare, design or otherwise structure any procurement contract in order to avoid the obligations under this Chapter.

Article 15.3: National Treatment and Non-Discrimination

1.   Each Party shall ensure that the procurement of its entities covered by this Chapter takes place in a transparent, reasonable and non-discriminatory manner, treating any supplier of either Party equally and ensuring the principle of open and effective competition.

2.   With respect to any laws, regulations, procedures and practices regarding government procurement covered by this Chapter, each Party shall grant the goods, services and suppliers of

the other Party a treatment no less favourable than that accorded by it to domestic goods, services and suppliers.

3.   With respect to any laws, regulations, procedures and practices regarding government procurement covered by this Chapter, each Party shall ensure:

(a)   that its entities do not treat a locally-established supplier less favourably than any other locally-established supplier on the basis of the degree of foreign affiliation to, or ownership by, a person of the other Party; and

(b)   that its entities do not discriminate against a locally-established supplier on the basis that the goods or services offered by that supplier for a particular procurement are goods or services of the other Party.

4.   This Article shall not apply to measures concerning customs duties or other charges of any kind imposed on, or in connection with importation, the method of levying such duties and charges, other import regulations, including restrictions and formalities, nor to measures affecting trade in services other than measures specifically governing procurement covered by this Chapter.

Article 15.4: Prohibition of Offsets

Each Party shall ensure that its entities do not, in the qualification and selection of suppliers, goods or services, in the evaluation of bids or in the award of contracts, consider, seek or impose offsets.

Article 15.5: Transparency

1.   Each Party shall promptly publish any law, regulation, judicial decision and administrative ruling of general application and procedure, including standard contract clauses, regarding procurement covered by this Chapter, in the appropriate publications, including officially designated electronic media.

2.   Each Party shall promptly publish in the same manner as in paragraph 1 any modification to such measures therein.

Article 15.6: Tendering Procedures

1.   Entities shall award their public contracts by open tendering procedures according to their respective domestic procedures, in compliance with this Chapter and in a non-discriminatory manner.

2.   Provided that the tendering procedure is not used to avoid competition or to protect domestic suppliers, entities shall be allowed to award contracts by means other than an open tendering procedure in the following circumstances and subject to the following conditions, where applicable:

(a)   in the absence of tenders that conform to the essential requirements in the tender documentation provided in a prior tendering procedure, including any conditions for participation, provided that the requirements of the initial procurement are not substantially modified in the contract as awarded;

(b)   where, for works of art, or for reasons connected with the protection of exclusive rights, such as patents, copyrights or proprietary information or in the absence of competition for technical reasons, the goods or services can be supplied only by a particular supplier and no reasonable alternative or substitute exists;

(c)   for additional deliveries by the original supplier that are intended either as replacement parts, extensions, or continuing services for existing equipment, software, services or installations, where a change of supplier would compel the entity to procure goods or services not meeting requirements of interchangeability with existing equipment, software, services, or installations;

(d)   for quoted goods purchased on a commodity market and for purchases of goods made under exceptionally advantageous conditions, which only arise in the very short term in the case of unusual disposals, and not for routine purchases from regular suppliers;

(e)   when an entity procures prototypes or a first good or service which are developed at its request in the course of, and for, a particular contract for research, experiment, study or original development;

(f)   when additional construction services which were not included in the initial contract but which were within the objectives of the original tender documentation have, due to unforeseeable circumstances, become necessary to complete the construction services described therein, provided that the total value of contracts awarded for additional construction services does not exceed 50 per cent of the amount of the main contract; or

(g)   insofar as it is strictly necessary where, for reasons of extreme urgency brought about by events unforeseeable by the entity, the goods or services could not be obtained in time under an open tendering procedure and the use of such procedure would result in serious injury to the entity, the entity's program responsibilities or the responsible Party. This exception may not be used as a result of a lack of advance planning or concerns relating to the amount of funds available to an entity within a particular period of time.

3.   The Parties shall ensure that, whenever it is necessary for entities to resort to a procedure other than open tendering procedures based on the circumstances set forth in paragraph 2, the entities shall maintain a record or prepare a written report providing specific justification for the contract.

Article 15.7: Conditions for Suppliers' Participation in Procurement

1.   Where an entity requires suppliers to satisfy registration, qualification, or any other requirements or conditions before being permitted to participate in a procurement, each Party shall ensure that a notice inviting suppliers to apply for registration, qualification or demonstration of the suppliers' satisfaction of any other conditions for participation is published

sufficiently in advance for interested suppliers to prepare and submit responsive applications and for entities to evaluate and make their determinations based on such applications.

2.   Each Party shall ensure that any conditions for participation in a procurement are limited to those that are essential to ensure that the potential supplier has the legal, technical and financial abilities to fulfil the requirements and technical specifications of the procurement and that qualification decisions are based solely on the conditions for participation that have been specified in advance in notices or tender documentation.

3.   Entities shall be allowed to establish a publicly available list of suppliers qualified to participate in procurements. Where an entity requires suppliers to qualify for such a list before being permitted to participate in a procurement, and a supplier that has not previously satisfied such requirements or conditions submits an application, the entity shall promptly start the relevant procedures and shall allow such supplier to participate in the procurement, provided there is sufficient time to complete the procedures within the time period established for tendering.

4.   Entities shall not impose the condition that, in order for a supplier to participate in a procurement, the supplier has previously been awarded one or more contracts by an entity of that Party or that the supplier has prior work experience in the territory of that Party.

Article 15.8: Publication of Advance Notices

1.   For each contract covered by this Chapter, entities shall publish in advance a notice inviting interested suppliers to submit tenders for that contract, except as provided for in Article 15.6.2.

2.   The information in each advance notice of intended procurement shall include a description of the intended procurement, any conditions that suppliers must fulfil to participate in the procurement, the name of the entity, the address where all documents relating to the procurement may be obtained and the time limits for submission of tenders.

3.   Entities shall publish the notices in a timely manner through means which offer the widest possible and non-discriminatory access to the interested suppliers of the Parties. These means shall be accessible free of charge through a single point of access specified in Annex 15.2.

Article 15.9: Tender Documentation

1.   Tender documentation provided to suppliers shall contain all information necessary to permit them to submit responsive tenders.

2.   Where contracting entities do not offer free direct access to the entire tender documents and any supporting documents by electronic means, entities shall make promptly available the tender documentation at the request of any supplier of the Parties.

Article 15.10: Time-Limits

1.   Time-limits established by the entities during a procurement process shall be sufficiently long to enable suppliers to prepare and submit responsive tenders, in relation to the nature and complexity of the procurement.

2.   Notwithstanding paragraph 1, entities shall establish no less than ten days between the date on which the advance notice of intended procurement is published and the final date for the submission of tenders.

Article 15.11: Technical Specifications

1.   Technical specifications shall be set out in the notices, tender documents or additional documents.

2.   Each Party shall ensure that its entities do not prepare, adopt or apply any technical specifications with a view to, or with the effect of, creating unnecessary obstacles to trade between the Parties.

3.   Technical specifications prescribed by entities shall:

(a)   be in terms of performance and functional requirements, rather than design or descriptive characteristics; and

(b)   be based on international standards, where they exist or, in absence of such standards, on national technical regulations[3], recognised national standards[4] or building codes.

4.   Paragraph 3 does not apply when the entity may objectively demonstrate that the use of technical specifications referred to in that paragraph would be ineffective or inappropriate for the fulfilment of the legitimate objectives pursued.

5.   In all cases, entities shall consider bids which do not comply with the technical specifications but meet the essential requirements thereof and are fit for the purpose intended. The reference to technical specifications in the tender documents must include words such as "or equivalent".

6.   There shall be no requirement or reference to a particular trademark or trade name, patent, design or type, specific origin, producer or supplier, unless there is no sufficiently precise or intelligible way of describing the procurement requirements and provided that words, such as "or equivalent", are included in the tender documentation.

7.   The tenderer shall have the burden of proof to demonstrate that its bid meets the essential requirements.

---

[3] For the purpose of this Chapter, a technical regulation is a document, which lays down characteristics of a product or a service or their related processes and production methods, including the applicable administrative provisions, with which compliance is mandatory. It may also include or deal exclusively with terminology, symbols, packaging, marking or labelling requirements as they apply to a product, service, process or production method.

[4] For the purpose of this Chapter, a standard is a document approved by a recognised body, that provides, for common and repeated use, rules, guidelines or characteristics for products or services or related processes and production methods, with which compliance is not mandatory. It may also include or deal exclusively with terminology, symbols, packaging, marking or labelling requirements as they apply to a product, service, process or production method.

Article 15.12: Awarding of Contracts

1.   To be considered for award, a tender must, at the time of opening, conform to the essential requirements of the notices or tender documentation and be submitted by a tenderer who complies with the conditions for participation.

2.   Unless an entity determines that it is not in the public interest to award a contract, entities shall award the contract to the tenderer who has been determined to be fully capable of undertaking the contract and whose tender is determined to be the most advantageous in terms of the requirements and evaluation criteria set forth in the tender documentation.

3.   Each Party shall ensure that its entities provide for effective dissemination of the results of government procurement processes.

Article 15.13: Bid Challenges

1.   Entities shall accord impartial and timely consideration to any complaints from suppliers regarding an alleged breach of this Chapter in the context of a procurement procedure.

2.   Each Party shall provide non-discriminatory, timely, transparent and effective procedures enabling suppliers to challenge alleged breaches of this Chapter, arising in the context of procurements in which they have, or have had, an interest.

3.   Challenges shall be heard by an impartial and independent reviewing authority. A reviewing authority which is not a court shall either be subject to judicial review or shall have procedural guarantees similar to those of a court.

4.   Challenge procedures shall provide for, if appropriate, correction of the breach of this Chapter or, in the absence of such correction, compensation for the loss or damages suffered, which may be limited to costs for tender preparation and protest.

Article 15.14: Information Technology and Cooperation

1.   The Parties shall, to the extent possible, endeavour to use electronic means of communication to permit efficient dissemination of information on government procurement, particularly as regards tender opportunities offered by entities, while respecting the principles of transparency and non-discrimination.

2.   The Parties shall endeavour to provide each other with technical cooperation and assistance through the development of training programs with a view to achieving a better understanding of their respective government procurement systems and statistics, as well as a better access to their respective markets.

Article 15.15: Modifications to Coverage

1.   A Party may modify its coverage under this Chapter, provided that it:

   (a)   notifies the other Party of the modification; and

(b)   provides the other Party, within 30 days following the date of such notification, appropriate compensatory adjustments to its coverage in order to maintain a level of coverage comparable to that existing prior to the modification.

2.   Notwithstanding subparagraph 1(b), no compensatory adjustments shall be provided to the other Party where the modification by a Party of its coverage under this Chapter concerns:

(a)   rectifications of a purely formal nature and minor amendments to Annex 15.1; or

(b)   one or more covered entities on which government control or influence has been effectively eliminated as a result of privatisation.

3.   Where appropriate, the Commission shall by decision modify the relevant Annex to reflect the modification notified by the Party concerned.

Article 15.16: Further Negotiations

In the case that either Party offers, in the future, a non-Party additional advantages with regard to the government procurement market access coverage agreed under this Chapter, it shall agree, upon request of the other Party, to enter into negotiations with a view to extending coverage under this Chapter on a reciprocal basis.

Article 15.17: Government Procurement Working Group

Upon request of a Party, the Parties shall convene a Government Procurement Working Group to address issues related to the implementation of this Chapter. Such issues may include:

(a)   bilateral cooperation relating to the development and use of electronic communications in government procurement systems;

(b)   exchange of statistics and other information needed for monitoring procurement conducted by the Parties and the results of the application of this Chapter; and

(c)   exploration of potential interest in further negotiations aimed at further broadening of the scope of market access commitments under this Chapter.

PART V

INTELLECTUAL PROPERTY RIGHTS

CHAPTER 16

INTELLECTUAL PROPERTY RIGHTS

Article 16.1: Obligations

1.   Each Party shall provide, in its territory, to the nationals of the other Party adequate and effective protection and enforcement of intellectual property rights, while ensuring that measures

to enforce intellectual property rights do not themselves become unnecessary barriers to legitimate trade.

2.   To provide adequate and effective protection and enforcement of intellectual property rights, each Party shall faithfully implement the international conventions it has acceded to, including the TRIPS Agreement.

Article 16.2: More Extensive Protection

A Party may implement in its domestic law more extensive protection of intellectual property rights than is required under this Agreement, provided that such protection is not inconsistent with this Agreement and the TRIPS Agreement.

Article 16.3: Protection of Trademarks

1.   Article 6 bis of the Paris Convention shall apply, *mutatis mutandis*, to services. In determining whether a trademark is well known, the Parties shall take account of the knowledge of the trademark in the relevant sector of the public, including knowledge in the Party concerned, obtained as a result of the promotion of the trademark.

2.   If the use of a trademark is required by the legislation of a Party to maintain registration, the registration may be cancelled only after an uninterrupted period of at least three years of nonuse, unless valid reasons based on the existence of obstacles to such use are shown by the trademark owner.

3.   When subject to the control of its owner, use of a trademark by another person shall be recognized as use of the trademark for the purpose of maintaining the registration.

Article 16.4: Protection of Geographical Indications

1.   For the purpose of this Agreement, geographical indications are indications, which identify a good as originating in the territory of a Party, or a region or locality in that territory, where a given quality, reputation or other characteristic of the good is essentially attributable to its geographical origin.

2.   With the recognition of the importance of the protection of geographical indications, both Parties shall protect, in compliance with their respective domestic legislation, the geographical indications of the other Party registered and/or protected by that other Party, that fall within the scope of protection stated in Articles 22, 23 and 24 of the TRIPS Agreement. Further to the acceptance of this obligation, both Parties shall not permit the importation, manufacture and sale of products, in compliance with their respective domestic legislation, which use such geographical indications of the other Party, unless such products have been produced in that other Party.

3.   Chile shall protect the geographical indications listed in Annex 16.4.3 for their exclusive use in products originating in Korea. Chile shall prohibit the importation, manufacture and sale of products with such geographical indications, unless they have been produced in Korea, in accordance with the applicable Korean law.

4.   Korea shall protect the geographical indications listed in Annex 16.4.4 for their exclusive use in products originating in Chile. Korea shall prohibit the importation, manufacture and sale of products with such geographical indications, unless they have been produced in Chile, in accordance with the applicable Chilean law. This shall in no way prejudice the rights that Korea may recognize, in addition to Chile, exclusively to Peru with respect to "Pisco".

5.   Within two years from the entry into force of this Agreement, both Parties shall enter into consultations to protect additional geographical indications. As a result of these consultations, both Parties shall protect and/or recognize, under the terms stated in this Agreement, the geographical indications listed in Annex 16.4.5 and any additional geographical indications submitted by the Parties that fall within the scope of protection of geographical indications set out in Articles 22, 23 and 24 of the TRIPS Agreement.

Article 16.5: Enforcement

The Parties shall provide in their respective laws for the enforcement of intellectual property rights consistent with the TRIPS Agreement, in particular, Articles 41 to 61 thereof.

Article 16.6: Consultative Mechanism

Any consultations between the Parties with respect to the implementation or interpretation of this Chapter shall be carried out under the dispute settlement procedures referred to in Chapter 19.

*

FREE TRADE AGREEMENT BETWEEN THE GOVERNMENT OF THE UNITED STATES OF AMERICA AND THE GOVERNMENT OF THE REPUBLIC OF CHILE*
[excerpts]

The free trade agreement between the Government of the United States of America and the Government of the Republic of Chile was signed on 6 June 2003.

Chapter Nine

Government Procurement

Objectives

The objectives of this Chapter are to recognize the importance of conducting government procurement in accordance with the fundamental principles of openness, transparency, and due process; and to strive to provide comprehensive coverage of procurement markets by eliminating market access barriers to the supply of goods and services, including construction services.

Article 9.1: Scope and Coverage

1.   This Chapter applies to any measure adopted or maintained by a Party relating to procurement by an entity listed in Annex 9.1:

   (a)   by any contractual means, including purchase and rental or lease, with or without an option to buy, build-operate-transfer contracts, and public works concession contracts; and

   (b)   subject to the conditions specified in Annex 9.1.

2.   This Chapter does not apply to:

   (a)   non-contractual agreements or any form of assistance provided by a Party or a state enterprise, including grants, loans, equity infusions, fiscal incentives, subsidies, guarantees, cooperative agreements, government provision of goods and services to persons or to a regional or local level of government, and purchases for the direct purpose of providing foreign assistance;

   (b)   purchases funded by international grants, loans, or other assistance, where the provision of such assistance is subject to conditions inconsistent with the provisions of this Chapter;

---

* *Source*: The Government of the Republic of Chile and the Government of the United States of America (2003). "Free Trade Agreement Between the Government of the United States of America and the Government of the Republic of Chile", available on the Internet (http://www.sice.oas.org/Trade/chiusa_e/chiusaind_e.asp). [Note added by the editor.]

(c)   hiring of government employees and related employment measures; and

(d)   acquisition of fiscal agency or depository services, liquidation and management services for regulated financial institutions, and sale and distribution services for government debt.

3.   Each Party shall ensure that its procuring entities listed in Annex 9.1 comply with this Chapter in conducting procurement covered by this Chapter.

4.   Where an entity awards a contract that is not covered by this Chapter, nothing in this Chapter shall be construed to cover any good or service component of that contract.

5.   No entity may prepare, design, or otherwise structure or divide, in any stage of the procurement, any procurement in order to avoid the obligations of this Chapter.

6.   Nothing in this Chapter shall prevent either Party from developing new procurement policies, procedures, or contractual means, provided they are not inconsistent with this Chapter.

Article 9.2: General Principles

National Treatment and Non-Discrimination

1.   With respect to any measure governing procurement covered by this Chapter, each Party shall accord to the goods and services of the other Party, and to the suppliers of the other Party of such goods and services, treatment no less favorable than the most favorable treatment the Party accords to its own goods, services, and suppliers.

2.   With respect to any measure governing procurement covered by this Chapter, neither Party may:

(a)   treat a locally established supplier less favorably than another locally established supplier on the basis of degree of foreign affiliation or ownership; or

(b)   discriminate against a locally established supplier on the basis that the goods or services offered by that supplier for a particular procurement are goods or services of the other Party.

Determination of Origin

3.   For purposes of paragraphs 1 and 2, determination of the origin of goods shall be made on a non-preferential basis.

Offsets

4.   An entity shall not consider, seek, or impose offsets at any stage of a procurement.

Measures Not Specific to Procurement

5.   Paragraphs 1 and 2 do not apply to measures respecting customs duties or other charges of any kind imposed on or in connection with importation, the method of levying such duties and

charges or other import regulations, including restrictions and formalities, or measures affecting trade in services other than measures specifically governing procurement covered by this Chapter.

Article 9.3: Publication of Procurement Measures

Each Party shall promptly publish:

(a)   its measures of general application specifically governing procurement covered by this Chapter; and

(b)   any changes in such measures in the same manner as the original publication.

Article 9.4: Publication of Notice of Intended Procurement

1.   For each procurement covered by this Chapter, an entity shall publish in advance a notice inviting interested suppliers to submit tenders for that procurement ("notice of intended procurement"), except as provided in Article 9.9(2). Each such notice shall be accessible during the entire period established for tendering for the relevant procurement.

2.   Each notice of intended procurement shall include a description of the intended procurement, any conditions that suppliers must fulfil to participate in the procurement, the name of the entity issuing the notice, the address where suppliers may obtain all documents relating to the procurement, the time limits for submission of tenders, and the dates for delivery of the goods or services to be procured.

Article 9.5: Time Limits for the Tendering Process

1.   An entity shall prescribe time limits for the tendering process that allow sufficient time for suppliers to prepare and submit responsive tenders, taking into account the nature and complexity of the procurement. An entity shall provide no less than 30 days between the date on which it publishes the notice of intended procurement and the deadline for submitting tenders.

2.   Notwithstanding paragraph 1, where there are no qualification requirements for suppliers, entities may establish a time limit of less than 30 days, but in no case less than 10 days, in the following circumstances:

(a)   where the entity has published a notice containing the information specified in Article 9.4(2) at least 30 days and not more than 12 months in advance;

(b)   in the case of the second or subsequent publications of notices for procurement of a recurring nature;

(c)   where an entity procures commercial goods or services that are sold or offered for sale to, and customarily purchased and used by, non-governmental buyers for non-governmental purposes; or

(d)   where an unforeseen state of urgency duly substantiated by the entity renders impracticable the time limits specified in paragraph 1.

Article 9.6: Information on Intended Procurements

1.   An entity shall provide interested suppliers tender documentation that includes all the information necessary to permit suppliers to prepare and submit responsive tenders. The documentation shall include all criteria that the entity will consider in awarding the contract, including all cost factors, and the weights or, where appropriate, the relative values, that the entity will assign to these criteria in evaluating tenders.

2.   Where an entity does not publish all the tender documentation by electronic means, the entity shall, on request of any supplier, promptly make the documentation available in written form to the supplier.

3.   Where an entity, during the course of a procurement, modifies the criteria referred to in paragraph 1, it shall transmit all such modifications in writing:

    (a)   to all suppliers that are participating in the procurement at the time the criteria are modified, if the identities of such suppliers are known, and in all other cases, in the same manner as the original information was transmitted; and

    (b)   in adequate time to allow such suppliers to modify and re-submit their tenders, as appropriate.

Article 9.7: Technical Specifications

1.   An entity shall not prepare, adopt, or apply any technical specification with the purpose or the effect of creating unnecessary obstacles to trade between the Parties.

2.   Any technical specification prescribed by an entity shall be, where appropriate:

    (a)   specified in terms of performance requirements rather than design or descriptive characteristics; and

    (b)   based on international standards, where applicable, otherwise on national technical regulations, recognized national standards, or building codes.

3.   An entity shall not prescribe technical specifications that require or refer to a particular trademark or trade name, patent, design or type, specific origin or producer or supplier unless there is no sufficiently precise or intelligible way of otherwise describing the procurement requirements and provided that, in such cases, words such as "or equivalent" are included in the tender documentation.

4.   An entity shall not seek or accept, in a manner that would have the effect of precluding competition, advice that may be used in the preparation or adoption of any technical specification for a specific procurement from a person that may have a commercial interest in that procurement.

5.   For greater certainty, this Article is not intended to preclude a Party from preparing, adopting, or applying technical specifications to promote the conservation of natural resources.

Article 9.8: Conditions for Participation

1.   Where an entity requires suppliers to satisfy registration, qualification, or any other requirements or conditions for participation ("conditions for participation") in order to participate in a procurement, the entity shall publish a notice inviting suppliers to apply for participation. The entity shall publish the notice sufficiently in advance to provide interested suppliers sufficient time to prepare and submit applications and for the entity to evaluate and make its determinations based on such applications.

2.   Each entity shall:

(a)   limit any conditions for participation in a procurement to those that are essential to ensure that the potential supplier has the legal, technical, and financial capacity to fulfil the requirements and technical specifications of the procurement;

(b)   base qualification decisions solely on the conditions for participation that it has specified in advance in notices or tender documentation; and

(c)   recognize as qualified all suppliers of the other Party that meet the requisite conditions for participation in a procurement covered by this Chapter.

3.   Entities may establish publicly available lists of suppliers qualified to participate in procurements. Where an entity requires suppliers to qualify for such a list in order to participate in a procurement, and a supplier that has not yet qualified applies to be included on the list, the entity shall promptly start the qualification procedures for the supplier and shall allow the supplier to participate in the procurement, provided there is sufficient time to complete the procedures within the time period established for tendering.

4.   No entity may impose the condition that, in order for a supplier to participate in a procurement, the supplier has previously been awarded one or more contracts by an entity of that Party or that the supplier has prior work experience in the territory of that Party. An entity shall judge a supplier's financial and technical capacities on the basis of its global business activities including both its activity in the territory of the Party of the supplier, and its activity, if any, in the territory of the Party of the entity.

5.   An entity shall promptly communicate to any supplier that has applied for qualification its decision on whether that supplier is qualified. Where an entity rejects an application for qualification or ceases to recognize a supplier as qualified, that entity shall, on request of the supplier, promptly provide it a written explanation of the reasons for its decision.

6.   Nothing in this Article shall preclude an entity from excluding a supplier from a procurement on grounds such as bankruptcy or false declarations.

Article 9.9: Tendering Procedures

1.   Entities shall award contracts by means of open tendering procedures, in the course of which any interested supplier may submit a tender.

2.   Provided that the tendering procedure is not used to avoid competition or to protect domestic suppliers, entities may award contracts by means other than open tendering procedures in the following circumstances, where applicable:

(a)   in the absence of tenders that conform to the essential requirements in the tender documentation provided in a prior invitation to tender, including any conditions for participation, on condition that the requirements of the initial procurement are not substantially modified in the contract as awarded;

(b)   where, for works of art, or for reasons connected with the protection of exclusive rights, such as patents or copyrights, or proprietary information, or where there is an absence of competition for technical reasons, the goods or services can be supplied only by a particular supplier and no reasonable alternative or substitute exists;

(c)   for additional deliveries by the original supplier that are intended either as replacement parts, extensions, or continuing services for existing equipment, software, services or installations, where a change of supplier would compel the entity to procure goods or services not meeting requirements of interchangeability with existing equipment, software, services, or installations;

(d)   for goods purchased on a commodity market;

(e)   where an entity procures a prototype or a first good or service that is developed at its request in the course of, and for, a particular contract for research, experiment, study, or original development. When such contracts have been fulfilled, subsequent procurements of such goods or services shall be subject to Articles 9.2 through 9.8 and Article 9.17;

(f)   where additional construction services that were not included in the initial contract but that were within the objectives of the original tender documentation have, due to unforeseeable circumstances, become necessary to complete the construction services described therein. However, the total value of contracts awarded for additional construction services may not exceed 50 percent of the amount of the initial contract; or

(g)   in so far as is strictly necessary where, for reasons of extreme urgency brought about by events unforeseeable by the entity, the goods or services could not be obtained in time by means of an open tendering procedure and the use of an open tendering procedure would result in serious injury to the entity, or the entity's program responsibilities, or the Party. For purposes of this subparagraph, lack of advance planning by an entity or its concerns relating to the amount of funds available to it within a particular period do not constitute unforeseeable events.

3.   An entity shall maintain a record or prepare a written report providing specific justification for any contract awarded by means other than open tendering procedures, as provided in paragraph 2.

Article 9.10: Awarding of Contracts

1.   An entity shall require that in order to be considered for award, a tender must be submitted in writing and must, at the time it is submitted:

>   (a)   conform to the essential requirements of the tender documentation; and

>   (b)   be submitted by a supplier that has satisfied the conditions for participation that the entity has provided to all participating suppliers.

2.   Unless an entity determines that it is not in the public interest to award a contract, it shall award the contract to the supplier that the entity has determined to be fully capable of undertaking the contract and whose tender is determined to be the most advantageous in terms of the requirements and evaluation criteria set out in the tender documentation.

3.   No entity may cancel a procurement, or terminate or modify awarded contracts, in order to avoid the obligations of this Chapter.

Article 9.11: Information on Awards

Information Provided to Suppliers

1.   Subject to Article 9.15, an entity shall promptly inform suppliers participating in a tendering procedure of its contract award decision. On request, an entity shall provide a supplier whose tender was not selected for award the reasons for not selecting its tender and the relative advantages of the tender the entity selected.

Publication of Award Information

2.   After awarding a contract covered by this Chapter, an entity shall promptly publish a notice that includes at least the following information about the award:

>   (a)   the name of the entity;

>   (b)   a description of the goods or services procured;

>   (c)   the name of the winning supplier;

>   (d)   the value of the contract award; and

>   (e)   where the entity has not used open tendering procedures, an indication of the circumstances justifying the procedures used.

Maintenance of Records

3.   An entity shall maintain records and reports relating to tendering procedures and contract awards covered by this Chapter, including the records and reports provided for in Article 9.9(3), for a period of at least three years.

Article 9.12: Ensuring Integrity in Procurement Practices

Each Party shall adopt the necessary legislative or other measures to establish that it is a criminal offense under its law for:

(a)   a procurement official of that Party to solicit or accept, directly or indirectly, any article of monetary value or other benefit, for that procurement official or for another person, in exchange for any act or omission in the performance of that procurement official's procurement functions;

(b)   any person to offer or grant, directly or indirectly, to a procurement official of that Party, any article of monetary value or other benefit, for that procurement official or for another person, in exchange for any act or omission in the performance of that procurement official's procurement functions; and

(c)   any person intentionally to offer, promise or give any undue pecuniary or other advantage, whether directly or through intermediaries, to a foreign procurement official, for that foreign procurement official or for a third party, in order that the foreign procurement official act or refrain from acting in relation to the performance of procurement duties, in order to obtain or retain business or other improper advantage.

Article 9.13: Domestic Review of Supplier Challenges

Independent Review Authorities

1.   Each Party shall establish or designate at least one impartial administrative or judicial authority that is independent from its entities to receive and review challenges that suppliers submit relating to the Party's measures implementing this Chapter in connection with a procurement covered by this Chapter and make appropriate findings and recommendations. Where a challenge by a supplier is initially reviewed by a body other than such an impartial authority, the Party shall ensure that the supplier may appeal the initial decision to an impartial administrative or judicial authority that is independent of the entity that is the subject of the challenge.

2.   Each Party shall provide that an authority it establishes or designates under paragraph 1 has authority to take prompt interim measures pending the resolution of a challenge to preserve the supplier's opportunity to participate in the procurement and to ensure that the Party complies with its measures implementing this Chapter, including by suspending the contract award or the performance of a contract that has already been awarded.

3.   Each Party shall ensure that its review procedures are published and are timely, transparent, effective, and consistent with due process principles.

4.   Each Party shall ensure that all documents related to a challenge to a procurement covered by this Chapter are made available to any authority it establishes or designates under paragraph 1.

5.   Notwithstanding other review procedures provided for or developed by each of the Parties, each Party shall ensure that any authority it establishes or designates under paragraph 1 provides at least the following:

(a)   an opportunity for the supplier to review relevant documents and to be heard by the authority in a timely manner;

(b)   sufficient time for the supplier to prepare and submit written challenges, which in no case shall be less than 10 days from the time when the basis of the complaint became known or reasonably should have become known to the supplier;

(c)   a requirement that the entity respond in writing to the supplier's challenge;

(d)   an opportunity for the supplier to reply to the entity's response to the challenge; and

(e)   prompt delivery in writing of the decisions relating to the challenge, with an explanation of the grounds for each decision.

6.   Each Party shall ensure that a supplier's submission of a challenge will not prejudice the supplier's participation in ongoing or future procurements.

Article 9.14: Modifications and Rectifications

1.   Either Party may modify its coverage under this Chapter provided that it:

(a)   notifies the other Party in writing and the other Party does not object in writing within 30 days of the notification; and

(b)   offers within 30 days acceptable compensatory adjustments to the other Party to maintain a level of coverage comparable to that existing prior to the modification, except as provided in paragraphs 2 and 3.

2.   Either Party may make rectifications of a purely formal nature to its coverage under this Chapter, or minor amendments to its Schedules to Annex 9.1, Sections (A) through (C), provided that it notifies the other Party in writing and the other Party does not object in writing within 30 days of the notification. A Party that makes such a rectification or minor amendment shall not be required to provide compensatory adjustments.

3.   A Party need not provide compensatory adjustments in those circumstances where the Parties agree that the proposed modification covers an entity over which a Party has effectively eliminated its control or influence. Where the Parties do not agree that such government control or influence has been effectively eliminated, the objecting Party may request further information or consultations with a view to clarifying the nature of any government control or influence and reaching agreement on the entity's continued coverage under this Chapter.

4.   Where the Parties are in agreement on the proposed modification, rectification, or minor amendment, including where a Party has not objected within 30 days under paragraph 1 or 2, the Commission shall give effect to the agreement by modifying forthwith the relevant Section of Annex 9.1.

Article 9.15: Non-Disclosure of Information

1.   The Parties, their entities, and their review authorities shall not disclose confidential information the disclosure of which would prejudice legitimate commercial interests of a particular person or might prejudice fair competition between suppliers, without the formal authorization of the person that provided the information to the Party.

2.   Nothing in this Chapter shall be construed as requiring a Party or its entities to disclose confidential information the disclosure of which would impede law enforcement or otherwise be contrary to the public interest.

Article 9.16: Exceptions

Provided that such measures are not applied in a manner that would constitute a means of arbitrary or unjustifiable discrimination between Parties where the same conditions prevail or a disguised restriction on trade between the Parties, nothing in this Chapter shall be construed to prevent a Party from adopting or maintaining measures:

   (a)   necessary to protect public morals, order, or safety;

   (b)   necessary to protect human, animal, or plant life or health;

   (c)   necessary to protect intellectual property; or

   (d)   relating to goods or services of handicapped persons, of philanthropic institutions, or of prison labor.

The Parties understand that subparagraph (b) includes environmental measures necessary to protect human, animal, or plant life or health.

Article 9.17: Public Information

1.   In order to facilitate access to information on commercial opportunities under this Chapter, each Party shall ensure that electronic databases that provide current information on all procurements covered by this Chapter that are conducted by entities listed in Annex 9.1(A), including information that can be disaggregated by detailed categories of goods and services, are made available to interested suppliers of the other Party, through the Internet or a comparable computer-based telecommunications network. Each Party shall, on request of the other Party, provide information on:

   (a)   the classification system used to disaggregate information on procurement of different goods and services in such databases; and

   (b)   the procedures for obtaining access to such databases. 2. Entities listed in Annex 9.1(A) shall publish notices of intended procurement in a government-wide, single point of entry electronic publication that is accessible through the Internet or a comparable computer-based telecommunications network. For entities listed in Annex 9.1(B), each Party shall facilitate a reasonable means for suppliers of the other Party to easily identify procurement opportunities, which should include a single point of entry.

3.   Each Party shall encourage its entities to publish, as early as possible in the fiscal year, information regarding the entity's procurement plans.

Article 9.18: Committee on Procurement

The Parties hereby establish a Committee on Procurement comprising representatives of each Party. On request, the Committee shall meet to address matters related to the implementation of this Chapter, such as:

(a)   bilateral cooperation relating to the development and use of electronic communications in government procurement systems, including developments that may lead to reducing the time limits for tendering set out in Article 9.5;

(b)   exchange of statistics and other information to assist the Parties in monitoring the implementation and operation of this Chapter;

(c)   consideration of further negotiations aimed at broadening the coverage of this Chapter, including with respect to sub-federal or sub-central entities and state-owned enterprises; and

(d)   efforts to increase understanding of their respective government procurement systems, with a view to maximizing access to government procurement opportunities for small business suppliers. To that end, either Party may request the other to provide trade-related technical assistance, including training of government personnel or interested suppliers on specific elements of each Party's government procurement system.

Article 9.19: Further Negotiations

On request of either Party, the Parties shall enter into negotiations with a view to extending coverage under this Chapter on a reciprocal basis, if a Party provides, through an international agreement entered into after entry into force of this Agreement, access to its procurement market for suppliers of a non-Party beyond what it provides under this Agreement to suppliers of the other Party.

Article 9.20: Definitions

For purposes of this Chapter:

build-operate-transfer contract and public works concession contract mean any contractual arrangement, the primary purpose of which is to provide for the construction or rehabilitation of physical infrastructure, plant, buildings, facilities, or other government owned works and under which, as consideration for a supplier's execution of a contractual arrangement, the entity grants to the supplier, for a specified period of time, temporary ownership or a right to control and operate, and demand payment for the use of, such works for the duration of the contract;

entity means an entity listed in Annex 9.1;

in writing or written means any expression of information in words, numbers, or other symbols, including electronic expressions, that can be read, reproduced, and stored;

international standard means a standard that has been developed in conformity with the document referenced in Article 7.3 (International Standards);

offsets means conditions imposed or considered by an entity prior to, or in the course of, its procurement process that encourage local development or improve a Party's balance of payments accounts by means of requirements of local content, licensing of technology, investment, counter-trade, or similar requirements;

procurement official means a person who performs procurement functions;

publish means to disseminate information in an electronic or paper medium that is distributed widely and is readily accessible to the general public;

supplier means a person that provides or could provide goods or services to an entity; and

technical specification means a specification that lays down the characteristics of goods to be procured or their related processes and production methods, or the characteristics of services to be procured or their related operating methods, including the applicable administrative provisions, and a requirement relating to conformity assessment procedures that an entity prescribes. A technical specification may also include or deal exclusively with terminology, symbols, packaging, marking or labeling requirements, as they apply to a good, process, service or production or operating method.

Annex 9.1

Section A - Central Level of Government Entities

This Agreement applies to procurement by the Central Level of Government Entities listed in this Section where the value of the procurement is estimated, in accordance with Section G, to equal or exceed the following relevant threshold. Unless otherwise specified within this Section, all agencies subordinate to those listed are covered by this Agreement.

Thresholds:

For procurement of goods and services

(To be adjusted according to the formula in Section G, paragraph 2): $56,190

For procurement of construction services

(To be adjusted according to the formula in Section G, paragraph 3): $6,481,000

Schedule of Chile

1. Presidencia de la República
2. Ministerio de Interior
3. Ministerio de Relaciones Exteriores
4. Ministerio de Defensa Nacional
5. Ministerio de Hacienda
6. Ministerio Secretaría General de la Presidencia

7. Ministerio Secretaría General de Gobierno
8. Ministerio de Economía, Fomento, Reconstrucción y Energía
9. Ministerio de Minería
10. Ministerio de Planificación y Cooperación
11. Ministerio de Educación
12. Ministerio de Justicia
13. Ministerio de Trabajo y Previsión Social
14. Ministerio de Obras Públicas
15. Ministerio de Transporte y Telecomunicaciones
16. Ministerio de Salud
17. Ministerio de la Vivienda y Urbanismo
18. Ministerio de Bienes Nacionales
19. Ministerio de Agricultura
20. Ministerio Servicio Nacional de la Mujer

Gobiernos Regionales

Intendencia I Región
Gobernación de Arica
Gobernación de Parinacota
Gobernación de Iquique

Intendencia II Región
Gobernación de Antofagasta
Gobernación de El Loa
Gobernación de Tocopilla

Intendencia III Región
Gobernación de Chañaral
Gobernación de Copiapó

Intendencia IV Región
Gobernación de Huasco
Gobernación de El Elqui
Gobernación de Limarí
Gobernación de Choapa

Intendencia V Región
Gobernación de Petorca
Gobernación de Valparaíso
Gobernación de San Felipe de Aconcagua
Gobernación de Los Andes
Gobernación de Quillota
Gobernación de San Antonio
Gobernación de Isla de Pascua

Intendencia VI Región
Gobernación de Cachapoal

Gobernación de Colchagua
Gobernación de Cardenal Caro

Intendencia VII Región
Gobernación de Curicó
Gobernación de Talca
Gobernación de Linares
Gobernación de Cauquenes

Intendencia VIII Región
Gobernación de Ñuble
Gobernación de Bío-Bío
Gobernación de Concepción
Gobernación de Arauco

Intendencia IX Región
Gobernación de Malleco
Gobernación de Cautín

Intendencia X Región
Gobernación de Valdivia
Gobernación de Osorno
Gobernación de Llanquihue
Gobernación de Chiloé
Gobernación de Palena

Intendencia XI Región
Gobernación de Coihaique
Gobernación de Aysén
Gobernación de General Carrera

Intendencia XII Región
Gobernación de Capitán Prat
Gobernación de Ultima Esperanza
Gobernación de Magallanes
Gobernación de Tierra del Fuego
Gobernación de Antártica Chilena

Intendencia Región Metropolitana
Gobernación de Chacabuco
Gobernación de Cordillera
Gobernación de Maipo
Gobernación de Talagante
Gobernación de Melipilla
Gobernación de Santiago

Schedule of the United States

1.   Advisory Commission on Intergovernmental Relations
2.   African Development Foundation
3.   Alaska Natural Gas Transportation System
4.   American Battle Monuments Commission
5.   Appalachian Regional Commission
6.   Broadcasting Board of Governors
7.   Commission of Fine Arts
8.   Commission on Civil Rights
9.   Commodity Futures Trading Commission
10.   Consumer Product Safety Commission
11.   Corporation for National and Community Service
12.   Delaware River Basin Commission
13.   Department of Agriculture (Not including procurement of agricultural goods made in furtherance of agricultural support programs or human feeding programs)
14.   Department of Commerce (Not including shipbuilding activities of NOAA)
15.   Department of Defense (Not including the procurement of the following goods:

   (a)   Federal Supply Classification (FSC) 83 - all elements of this classification other than pins, needles, sewing kits, flag staffs, flagpoles, and flagstaff trucks;
   (b)   FSC 84 - all elements other than sub-class 8460 (luggage);
   (c)   FSC 89 - all elements other than sub-class 8975 (tobacco products);
   (d)   FSC 2310 - (buses only);
   (e)   Specialty metals, defined as steels melted in steel manufacturing facilities located in the United States or its possessions, where the maximum alloy content exceeds one or more of the following limits, must be used in products purchased by DOD: (1) manganese, 1.65 per cent; silicon, 0.60 per cent; or copper, 0.06 per cent; or which contains more than 0.25 per cent of any of the following elements: aluminium, chromium, cobalt, columbium, molybdenum, nickel, titanium, tungsten, or vanadium; (2) metal alloys consisting of nickel, iron-nickel and cobalt base alloys containing a total of other alloying metals (except iron) in excess of 10 per cent; (3) titanium and titanium alloys; or (4) zirconium base alloys;
   (f)   FSC 19 and 20 - that part of these classifications defined as naval vessels or major components of the hull or superstructure thereof;
   (g)   FSC 51 and 52;
   (h)   The following FSC categories are not generally covered due to application of Article 17: 10, 12, 13, 14, 15,16, 17, 19, 20, 28, 31, 58, 59, 95. For detailed listing of the Federal Supply Classifications (FSC), see www.scrantonrtg.com/secrc/fsccodes/ fsc.htlm.

16.   Department of Education
17.   Department of Energy (Not including national security procurements made in support of safeguarding nuclear materials or technology and entered into under the authority of the Atomic Energy Act, and oil purchases related to the Strategic Petroleum Reserve)
18.   Department of Health and Human Services
19.   Department of Housing and Urban Development
20.   Department of the Interior, including the Bureau of Reclamation
21.   Department of Justice
22.   Department of Labor

23.   Department of State
24.   Department of Transportation (Not including the Federal Aviation Administration)
25.   Department of the Treasury
26.   Department of Veterans Affairs
27.   Environmental Protection Agency
28.   Equal Employment Opportunity Commission
29.   Executive Office of the President
30.   Export-Import Bank of the United States
31.   Farm Credit Administration
32.   Federal Communications Commission
33.   Federal Crop Insurance Corporation
34.   Federal Deposit Insurance Corporation
35.   Federal Election Commission
36.   Federal Emergency Management Agency
37.   Federal Home Loan Mortgage Corporation
38.   Federal Housing Finance Board
39.   Federal Maritime Commission
40.   Federal Mediation and Conciliation Service
41.   Federal Mine Safety and Health Review Commission
42.   Federal Prison Industries, Inc.
43.   Federal Reserve System
44.   Federal Retirement Thrift Investment Board
45.   Federal Trade Commission
46.   General Services Administration (Not including Federal Supply Groups 51 and 52 and Federal Supply Class 7340). For detailed listing of the Federal Supply Classifications (FSC), see www.scrantonrtg.com/secrc/fsc-codes/fsc.htlm.
47.   Government National Mortgage Association
48.   Holocaust Memorial Council
49.   Inter-American Foundation
50.   Merit Systems Protection Board
51.   National Aeronautics and Space Administration (NASA)
52.   National Archives and Records Administration
53.   National Capital Planning Commission
54.   National Commission on Libraries and Information Science
55.   National Council on Disability
56.   National Credit Union Administration
57.   National Foundation on the Arts and the Humanities
58.   National Labor Relations Board
59.   National Mediation Board
60.   Nuclear Regulatory Commission
61.   National Science Foundation
62.   National Transportation Safety Board
63.   Occupational Safety and Health Review Commission
64.   Office of Government Ethics
65.   Office of the Nuclear Waste Negotiator
66.   Office of Personnel Management
67.   Office of Special Counsel
68.   Office of Thrift Supervision
69.   Overseas Private Investment Corporation
70.   Peace Corps

71. Pennsylvania Avenue Development Corporation
72. Railroad Retirement Board
73. Securities and Exchange Commission
74. Selective Service System
75. Small Business Administration
76. Smithsonian Institution
77. Susquehanna River Basin Commission
78. United States Agency for International Development
79. United States International Trade Commission

Section B - Sub-Central Level Government Entities

This Agreement applies to procurement by the Sub-Central Level Government Entities listed in this Section where the value of the procurement is estimated, in accordance with Section G, to equal or exceed the following relevant threshold.

Thresholds:

(To be adjusted according to the formula in Section G, paragraph 3)

For procurement of goods and services: $460,000

For procurement of construction services: $6,481,000

Schedule of Chile

1. Municipalidad de Arica
2. Municipalidad de Iquique
3. Municipalidad de Pozo Almonte
4. Municipalidad de Pica
5. Municipalidad de Huara
6. Municipalidad de Camarones
7. Municipalidad de Putre
8. Municipalidad de General Lagos
9. Municipalidad de Camiña
10. Municipalidad de Colchane
11. Municipalidad de Tocopilla
12. Municipalidad de Antofagasta
13. Municipalidad de Mejillones
14. Municipalidad de Taltal
15. Municipalidad de Calama
16. Municipalidad de Ollagüe
17. Municipalidad de Maria Elena
18. Municipalidad de San Pedro De Atacama
19. Municipalidad de Sierra Gorda
20. Municipalidad de Copiapó
21. Municipalidad de Caldera

22. Municipalidad de Tierra Amarilla
23. Municipalidad de Chañaral
24. Municipalidad de Diego De Almagro
25. Municipalidad de Vallenar
26. Municipalidad de Freirina
27. Municipalidad de Huasco
28. Municipalidad de Alto Del Carmen
29. Municipalidad de La Serena
30. Municipalidad de La Higuera
31. Municipalidad de Vicuña
32. Municipalidad de Paihuano
33. Municipalidad de Coquimbo
34. Municipalidad de Andacollo
35. Municipalidad de Ovalle
36. Municipalidad de Río Hurtado
37. Municipalidad de Monte Patria
38. Municipalidad de Punitaqui
39. Municipalidad de Combarbalá
40. Municipalidad de Illapel
41. Municipalidad de Salamanca
42. Municipalidad de Los Vilos
43. Municipalidad de Canela
44. Municipalidad de Valparaíso
45. Municipalidad de Viña Del Mar
46. Municipalidad de Quilpue
47. Municipalidad de Villa Alemana
48. Municipalidad de Casablanca
49. Municipalidad de Quintero
50. Municipalidad de Puchuncaví
51. Municipalidad de Quillota
52. Municipalidad de La Calera
53. Municipalidad de La Cruz
54. Municipalidad de Hijuelas
55. Municipalidad de Nogales
56. Municipalidad de Limache
57. Municipalidad de Olmué
58. Municipalidad de Isla De Pascua
59. Municipalidad de San Antonio
60. Municipalidad de Santo Domingo
61. Municipalidad de Cartagena
62. Municipalidad de El Tabo
63. Municipalidad de El Quisco
64. Municipalidad de Algarrobo
65. Municipalidad de San Felipe
66. Municipalidad de Santa María
67. Municipalidad de Putaendo
68. Municipalidad de Catemu
69. Municipalidad de Panquehue
70. Municipalidad de Llay - Llay
71. Municipalidad de Los Andes

72.	Municipalidad de San Esteban
73.	Municipalidad de Calle Larga
74.	Municipalidad de Rinconada
75.	Municipalidad de La Ligua
76.	Municipalidad de Cabildo
77.	Municipalidad de Petorca
78.	Municipalidad de Papudo
79.	Municipalidad de Zapallar
80.	Municipalidad de Juan Fernández
81.	Municipalidad de Con - Con
82.	Municipalidad de Buin
83.	Municipalidad de Calera De Tango
84.	Municipalidad de Colina
85.	Municipalidad de Curacaví
86.	Municipalidad de El Monte
87.	Municipalidad de Isla De Maipo
88.	Municipalidad de Pudahuel
89.	Municipalidad de La Cisterna
90.	Municipalidad de Las Condes
91.	Municipalidad de La Florida
92.	Municipalidad de La Granja
93.	Municipalidad de Lampa
94.	Municipalidad de Conchalí
95.	Municipalidad de La Reina
96.	Municipalidad de Maipú
97.	Municipalidad de Estación Central
98.	Municipalidad de Melipilla
99.	Municipalidad de Ñuñoa
100.	Municipalidad de Paine
101.	Municipalidad de Peñaflor
102.	Municipalidad de Pirque
103.	Municipalidad de Providencia
104.	Municipalidad de Puente Alto
105.	Municipalidad de Quilicura
106.	Municipalidad de Quinta Normal
107.	Municipalidad de Renca
108.	Municipalidad de San Bernardo
109.	Municipalidad de San José De Maipo
110.	Municipalidad de San Miguel
111.	Municipalidad de Santiago
112.	Municipalidad de Talagante
113.	Municipalidad de Til Til
114.	Municipalidad de Alhué
115.	Municipalidad de San Pedro
116.	Municipalidad de Maria Pinto
117.	Municipalidad de San Ramón
118.	Municipalidad de La Pintana
119.	Municipalidad de Macul
120.	Municipalidad de Peñalolen
121.	Municipalidad de Lo Prado

122.   Municipalidad de Cerro Navia
123.   Municipalidad de San Joaquín
124.   Municipalidad de Cerrillos
125.   Municipalidad de El Bosque
126.   Municipalidad de Recoleta
127.   Municipalidad de Vitacura
128.   Municipalidad de Lo Espejo
129.   Municipalidad de Lo Barnechea
130.   Municipalidad de Independencia
131.   Municipalidad de Pedro Aguirre Cerda
132.   Municipalidad de Huechuraba
133.   Municipalidad de Padre Hurtado
134.   Municipalidad de Rancagua
135.   Municipalidad de Machalí
136.   Municipalidad de Graneros
137.   Municipalidad de Codegua
138.   Municipalidad de Mostazal
139.   Municipalidad de Peumo
140.   Municipalidad de Las Cabras
141.   Municipalidad de San Vicente
142.   Municipalidad de Pichidegua
143.   Municipalidad de Doñihue
144.   Municipalidad de Coltauco
145.   Municipalidad de Rengo
146.   Municipalidad de Quinta De Tilcoco
147.   Municipalidad de Requínoa
148.   Municipalidad de Olivar
149.   Municipalidad de Coinco
150.   Municipalidad de Malloa
151.   Municipalidad de San Fernando
152.   Municipalidad de Chimbarongo
153.   Municipalidad de Nancagua
154.   Municipalidad de Placilla
155.   Municipalidad de Santa Cruz
156.   Municipalidad de Lolol
157.   Municipalidad de Chépica
158.   Municipalidad de Pumanque
159.   Municipalidad de Paredones
160.   Municipalidad de Palmilla
161.   Municipalidad de Litueche
162.   Municipalidad de Pichilemu
163.   Municipalidad de Marchihue
164.   Municipalidad de La Estrella
165.   Municipalidad de Navidad
166.   Municipalidad de Peralillo
167.   Municipalidad de Curicó
168.   Municipalidad de Romeral
169.   Municipalidad de Teno
170.   Municipalidad de Rauco
171.   Municipalidad de Licantén

172.	Municipalidad de Vichuquén
173.	Municipalidad de Hualañé
174.	Municipalidad de Molina
175.	Municipalidad de Sagrada Familia
176.	Municipalidad de Talca
177.	Municipalidad de San Clemente
178.	Municipalidad de Pelarco
179.	Municipalidad de Río Claro
180.	Municipalidad de Pencahue
181.	Municipalidad de Maule
182.	Municipalidad de Curepto
183.	Municipalidad de Constitución
184.	Municipalidad de Empedrado
185.	Municipalidad de San Javier
186.	Municipalidad de Linares
187.	Municipalidad de Yerbas Buenas
188.	Municipalidad de Colbún
189.	Municipalidad de Longaví
190.	Municipalidad de Parral
191.	Municipalidad de Retiro
192.	Municipalidad de Chanco
193.	Municipalidad de Cauquenes
194.	Municipalidad de Villa Alegre
195.	Municipalidad de Pelluhue
196.	Municipalidad de San Rafael
197.	Municipalidad de Chillán
198.	Municipalidad de Pinto
199.	Municipalidad de Coihueco
200.	Municipalidad de Ranquil
201.	Municipalidad de Coelemu
202.	Municipalidad de Quirihue
203.	Municipalidad de Ninhue
204.	Municipalidad de Portezuelo
205.	Municipalidad de Trehuaco
206.	Municipalidad de Cobquecura
207.	Municipalidad de San Carlos
208.	Municipalidad de Ñiquén
209.	Municipalidad de San Fabián
210.	Municipalidad de San Nicolás
211.	Municipalidad de Bulnes
212.	Municipalidad de San Ignacio
213.	Municipalidad de Quillón
214.	Municipalidad de Yungay
215.	Municipalidad de Pemuco
216.	Municipalidad de El Carmen
217.	Municipalidad de Concepción
218.	Municipalidad de Penco
219.	Municipalidad de Hualqui
220.	Municipalidad de Florida
221.	Municipalidad de Tomé

222.   Municipalidad de Talcahuano
223.   Municipalidad de Coronel
224.   Municipalidad de Lota
225.   Municipalidad de Santa Juana
226.   Municipalidad de Lebu
227.   Municipalidad de Los Alamos
228.   Municipalidad de Arauco
229.   Municipalidad de Curanilahue
230.   Municipalidad de Cañete
231.   Municipalidad de Contulmo
232.   Municipalidad de Tirúa
233.   Municipalidad de Los Angeles
234.   Municipalidad de Santa Bárbara
235.   Municipalidad de Laja
236.   Municipalidad de Quilleco
237.   Municipalidad de Nacimiento
238.   Municipalidad de Negrete
239.   Municipalidad de Mulchén
240.   Municipalidad de Quilaco
241.   Municipalidad de Yumbel
242.   Municipalidad de Cabrero
243.   Municipalidad de San Rosendo
244.   Municipalidad de Tucapel
245.   Municipalidad de Antuco
246.   Municipalidad de Chillán Viejo
247.   Municipalidad de San Pedro De La Paz
248.   Municipalidad de Chiguayante
249.   Municipalidad de Angol
250.   Municipalidad de Purén
251.   Municipalidad de Los Sauces
252.   Municipalidad de Renaico
253.   Municipalidad de Collipulli
254.   Municipalidad de Ercilla
255.   Municipalidad de Traiguén
256.   Municipalidad de Lumaco
257.   Municipalidad de Victoria
258.   Municipalidad de Curacautín
259.   Municipalidad de Lonquimay
260.   Municipalidad de Temuco
261.   Municipalidad de Vilcún
262.   Municipalidad de Freire
263.   Municipalidad de Cunco
264.   Municipalidad de Lautaro
265.   Municipalidad de Perquenco
266.   Municipalidad de Galvarino
267.   Municipalidad de Nueva Imperial
268.   Municipalidad de Carahue
269.   Municipalidad de Saavedra
270.   Municipalidad de Pitrufquén
271.   Municipalidad de Gorbea

272.	Municipalidad de Toltén
273.	Municipalidad de Loncoche
274.	Municipalidad de Villarrica
275.	Municipalidad de Pucón
276.	Municipalidad de Melipeuco
277.	Municipalidad de Curarrehue
278.	Municipalidad de Teodoro Schmidt
279.	Municipalidad de Padre De Las Casas
280.	Municipalidad de Valdivia
281.	Municipalidad de Corral
282.	Municipalidad de Mariquina
283.	Municipalidad de Mafil
284.	Municipalidad de Lanco
285.	Municipalidad de Los Lagos
286.	Municipalidad de Futrono
287.	Municipalidad de Panguipulli
288.	Municipalidad de La Unión
289.	Municipalidad de Paillaco
290.	Municipalidad de Río Bueno
291.	Municipalidad de Lago Ranco
292.	Municipalidad de Osorno
293.	Municipalidad de Puyehue
294.	Municipalidad de San Pablo
295.	Municipalidad de Puerto Octay
296.	Municipalidad de Río Negro
297.	Municipalidad de Purranque
298.	Municipalidad de Puerto Montt
299.	Municipalidad de Calbuco
300.	Municipalidad de Puerto Varas
301.	Municipalidad de Llanquihue
302.	Municipalidad de Fresia
303.	Municipalidad de Frutillar
304.	Municipalidad de Maullín
305.	Municipalidad de Los Muermos
306.	Municipalidad de Ancud
307.	Municipalidad de Quemchi
308.	Municipalidad de Dalcahue
309.	Municipalidad de Castro
310.	Municipalidad de Chonchi
311.	Municipalidad de Queilén
312.	Municipalidad de Quellón
313.	Municipalidad de Puqueldón
314.	Municipalidad de Quinchao
315.	Municipalidad de Curaco De Velez
316.	Municipalidad de Chaitén
317.	Municipalidad de Palena
318.	Municipalidad de Futaleufú
319.	Municipalidad de San Juan De La Costa
320.	Municipalidad de Cochamo
321.	Municipalidad de Hualaihue

322. Municipalidad de Aysén
323. Municipalidad de Cisnes
324. Municipalidad de Coyhaique
325. Municipalidad de Chile Chico
326. Municipalidad de Cochran
327. Municipalidad de Lago Verde
328. Municipalidad de Guaitecas
329. Municipalidad de Río Ibañez
330. Municipalidad de O'higgins
331. Municipalidad de Tortel
332. Municipalidad de Punta Arenas
333. Municipalidad de Puerto Natales
334. Municipalidad de Porvenir
335. Municipalidad de Torres Del Paine
336. Municipalidad de Rio Verde
337. Municipalidad de Laguna Blanca
338. Municipalidad de San Gregorio
339. Municipalidad de Primavera
340. Municipalidad de Timaukel
341. Municipalidad de Navarino

Schedule of the United States

Arizona
Executive branch agencies

Arkansas
Executive branch agencies, including universities but excluding the Office of Fish and Game and construction services

California
Executive branch agencies

Colorado
Executive branch agencies

Connecticut
Department of Administrative Services
Connecticut Department of Transportation
Connecticut Department of Public Works
Constituent Units of Higher Education

Delaware*
Administrative Services (Central Procurement Agency)
State Universities
State Colleges

Florida*
Executive branch agencies

Hawaii
Department of Accounting and General Services (with the exception of procurements of software developed in the state and construction)

Idaho
Central Procurement Agency (including all colleges and universities subject to central purchasing oversight)

Illinois*
Department of Central Management Services

Iowa*
Department of General Services
Department of Transportation
Board of Regents' Institutions (universities)

Kansas
Executive branch agencies, excluding construction services, automobiles and aircraft

Kentucky
Division of Purchases, Finance and Administration Cabinet, excluding construction projects

Louisiana
Executive branch agencies

Maine*
Department of Administrative and Financial Services
Bureau of General Services (covering state government agencies and school construction)
Maine Department of Transportation

Maryland*
Office of the Treasury
Department of the Environment
Department of General Services
Department of Housing and Community Development
Department of Human Resources
Department of Licensing and Regulation
Department of Natural Resources
Department of Public Safety and Correctional Services
Department of Personnel
Department of Transportation

Massachusetts
Executive Office for Administration and Finance
Executive Office of Communities and Development
Executive Office of Consumer Affairs
Executive Office of Economic Affairs
Executive Office of Education
Executive Office of Elder Affairs
Executive Office of Environmental Affairs

Executive Office of Health and Human Service
Executive Office of Labor
Executive Office of Public Safety
Executive Office of Transportation and Construction

Michigan*
Department of Management and Budget

Minnesota
Executive branch agencies

Mississippi
Department of Finance and Administration (does not include services)

Missouri
Office of Administration
Division of Purchasing and Materials Management

Montana
Executive branch agencies (only for services and construction)

Nebraska
Central Procurement Agency

New Hampshire*
Central Procurement Agency

New York*
State agencies
State university system
Public authorities and public benefit corporations, with the exception of those entities with multi-state mandates
In addition to the exceptions noted at the end of this Section, transit cars, buses and related equipment are not covered.

Oklahoma*
Office of Public Affairs and all state agencies and departments subject to the Oklahoma Central Purchasing Act, excluding construction services.

Oregon
Department of Administrative Services

Pennsylvania*
Executive branch agencies, including:
Governor's Office
Department of the Auditor General
Treasury Department
Department of Agriculture
Department of Banking
Pennsylvania Securities Commission

Department of Health
Department of Transportation
Insurance Department
Department of Aging
Department of Correction
Department of Labor and Industry
Department of Military Affairs
Office of Attorney General
Department of General Services
Department of Education
Public Utility Commission
Department of Revenue
Department of State
Pennsylvania State Police
Department of Public Welfare
Fish Commission
Game Commission
Department of Commerce
Board of Probation and Parole
Liquor Control Board
Milk Marketing Board
Lieutenant Governor's Office
Department of Community Affairs
Pennsylvania Historical and Museum Commission
Pennsylvania Emergency Management Agency
State Civil Service Commission
Pennsylvania Public Television Network
Department of Environmental Resources
State Tax Equalization Board
Department of Public Welfare
State Employees' Retirement System
Pennsylvania Municipal Retirement Board
Public School Employees' Retirement System
Pennsylvania Crime Commission
Executive Offices

Rhode Island
Executive branch agencies, excluding boats, automobiles, buses and related equipment

South Dakota
Central Procuring Agency (including universities and penal institutions)
In addition to the exceptions noted at the end of this Section, procurements of beef are not covered.

Tennessee
Executive branch agencies (excluding services and construction)

Texas
Texas Building and Procurement Commission

Utah
Executive branch agencies
Vermont
Executive branch agencies

Washington
Washington State executive branch agencies, including:

General Administration
Department of Transportation
State Universities
In addition to the exceptions noted at the end of this Section, procurements of fuel, paper products, boats, ships and vessels are not covered.

Wisconsin
Executive branch agencies, including:
Department of Administration
State Correctional Institutions
Department of Development
Educational Communications Board
Department of Employment Relations
State Historical Society
Department of Health and Social Services
Insurance Commissioner
Department of Justice
Lottery Board
Department of Natural Resources
Administration for Public Instruction
Racing Board
Department of Revenue
State Fair Park Board
Department of Transportation
State University System

Wyoming*
Procurement Services Division
Wyoming Department of Transportation
University of Wyoming

U.S. Notes

1.   For those states marked by an asterisk with pre-existing restrictions, the Chapter does not apply to procurement of construction-grade steel (including requirements on subcontracts), motor vehicles and coal.

2.   Nothing in this Section shall be construed to prevent any state entity from applying restrictions that promote the general environmental quality in that state, as long as such restrictions are not disguised barriers to international trade.

3.   This Chapter shall not apply to any procurement made by a covered entity on behalf of non-covered entities at a different level of government.

4.   This Chapter shall not apply to restrictions attached to Federal funds for mass transit and highway projects.

5.   This Chapter shall not apply to State Government Entities' procurements of printing services.

6.   This Chapter shall not apply to preferences or restrictions associated with programs administered by entities that promote the development of distressed areas and businesses owned by minorities, disabled veterans, and women.

Section C - Other Covered Entities

This Agreement applies to procurement by the Other Covered Entities listed in this Section where the value of the procurement is estimated, in accordance with Section G, to equal or exceed the following relevant threshold.

Thresholds:

For goods and services of List A Entities

(To be adjusted according to the formula in Section G, paragraph 2): $280,951

For goods and services of List B Entities

(To be adjusted according to the formula in Section G, paragraph 3): $518,000

For construction services of List A and List B Entities

(To be adjusted according to the formula in Section G, paragraph 3): $6,481,000

Schedule of Chile

List A:

1. Empresa Portuaria Arica
2. Empresa Portuaria Iquique
3. Empresa Portuaria Antofagasta
4. Empresa Portuaria Coquimbo
5. Empresa Portuaria Valparaíso
6. Empresa Portuaria San Antonio
7. Empresa Portuaria San Vicente-Talcahuano
8. Empresa Portuaria Puerto Montt
9. Empresa Portuaria Chacabuco
10. Empresa Portuaria Austral
11. Aeropuertos de propiedad del Estado, dependientes de la Dirección de Aeronáutica Civil

Schedule of the United States

List A:

1. Tennessee Valley Authority
2. Bonneville Power Administration
3. Western Area Power Administration
4. Southeastern Power Administration
5. Southwestern Power Administration
6. St. Lawrence Seaway Development Corporation

List B:

1.   The Port Authority of New York and New Jersey, with the following exceptions:

    (a)   maintenance, repair and operating materials and supplies (e.g., hardware, tools, lamps/lighting, plumbing);

    (b)   in exceptional cases, individual procurements may require certain regional production of goods if authorized by the Board of Directors; and,

    (c)   procurements pursuant to multi-jurisdictional agreement (i.e., for contracts which have initially been awarded by other jurisdictions).

2.   The Port of Baltimore (not including procurement of transit cars, buses and related equipment and subject to the conditions specified for the state of New York in Section B)

3.   The New York Power Authority (not including procurement of transit cars, buses and related equipment and subject to the conditions specified for the state of New York in Section B)

4.   Rural Utilities Service Financing:

    (a)   waiver of Buy American restriction on financing for all power generation projects (restrictions on financing for telecommunication projects) are excluded from the Chapter;

    (b)   application of WTO Government Procurement Agreement – equivalent procurement procedures and national treatment to funded projects exceeding the thresholds specified above.

U.S. Notes

1.   With respect to procurement by entities listed in this Section, this Chapter shall not apply to restrictions attached to Federal funds for airport projects.

Section D – Goods

This Chapter applies to all goods procured by the entities listed in Annex 9.1, Sections (A) through (C), subject to the Notes to the respective Sections and the General Notes. (For complete listing of U.S. Federal Supply Classification, see http://www.scrantonrtg.com/secrc/fsc-codes/fsc.html.)

Section E – Services

This Chapter applies to all services procured by the entities listed in Annex 9.1, Sections (A) through (C), subject to the Notes to the respective Sections, the General Notes, and the Notes to this Section, except for the services in the categories of the Common Classification System excluded in the Schedules of each Party. (For complete listing of the Common Classification System, see http://www.sice.oas.org/trade/nafta/chap-105.asp.)

Schedule of Chile

The following services, as elaborated in the Common Classification System, are excluded:

L.   Financial and Related Services

All classes

Schedule of the United States

The following services, as elaborated in the Common Classification System, are excluded:

A.   Research and Development

All classes

D.   Information Processing and Related Telecommunications Services

D304 ADP Telecommunications and Transmission Services, except for those services classified as "enhanced or value-added services." For purposes of this provision, the procurement of "ADP Telecommunications and Transmission services" does not include the ownership or furnishing of facilities for the transmission of voice or data services.
D305 ADP Teleprocessing and Timesharing Services
D316 Telecommunications Network Management Services
D317 Automated News Services, Data Services or Other Information Services
D399 Other ADP and Telecommunications Services

J.   Maintenance, Repair, Modification, Rebuilding and Installation of Equipment

J019 Maintenance, Repair, Modification, Rebuilding and Installation of Equipment Related to Ships

J998 Non-nuclear Ship Repair

M.   Operation of Government-Owned Facilities
All facilities operated by the Department of Defense, Department of Energy and the National Aeronautics and Space Administration; and for all entities:

M180 Research and Development

S.   Utilities

All Classes

V.   Transportation, Travel and Relocation Services

All Classes except V503 Travel Agent Services

U.S. Notes:

All services purchased in support of military forces overseas are excluded from coverage of this Chapter.

Section F – Construction Services

This Chapter applies to all construction services procured by the Entities listed in Annex 9.1, Sections (A) through (C), subject to the Notes to the respective sections, the General Notes, and the Notes to this Section, except for the construction services set out in the Schedules to this Annex.

Schedule of Chile

No construction services are excluded.

Schedule of the United States

The following construction services are excluded:

Dredging.

U.S. Notes:

In accordance with this Chapter, buy national requirements on articles, supplies and materials acquired for use in construction contracts covered by this Chapter shall not apply to goods of Chile.

Section G – Threshold Adjustment Formulas

1.   In calculating the value of a contract for the purpose of ascertaining whether the procurement is covered by this Chapter, an entity shall include the maximum total estimated value of the procurement over its entire duration, taking into account all options, premiums, fees, commissions, interest and other revenue streams or other forms of renumeration provided for in such contracts.

2.   The calculations referred to in Annex 9.1, Sections (A) through (C) that specifically referenced this paragraph shall be made in accordance with the following:

      (a)   the U.S. inflation rate shall be measured by the Producer Price Index for Finished Goods published by the U.S. Bureau of Labor Statistics;

(b) the first adjustment for inflation, to take effect on January 1, 2004, shall be calculated using the period from November 1, 2001 through October 31, 2003;

(c) all subsequent adjustments shall be calculated using two-year periods, each period beginning November 1, and shall take effect on January 1 of the year immediately following the end of the two-year period;

(d) the United States shall notify Chile of the adjusted threshold values no later than November 16 of the year before the adjustment takes effect;

(e) the inflationary adjustment shall be estimated according to the following formula:

$$T0 \times (1 + Pi) = T1$$

> $T0$ = threshold value at base period
> Pi = accumulated U.S. inflation rate for the ith two year-period
> $T1$ = new threshold value.

(f) Chile shall calculate and convert the value of the thresholds applicable to this paragraph into Chilean currency using the conversion formula set out in subparagraph (g). Chile shall notify the United States of the value in its currency of the newly calculated thresholds no later than one month before the thresholds take effect; and,

(g) Chile shall use for its calculation the official conversion rate of the Central Bank of Chile (Banco Central de Chile). Its conversion rate shall be the existing value of the Chilean currency in terms of U.S. dollars as of December 1 and June 1 of each year, or the first working day thereafter. The conversion rate as of December 1 shall apply from January 1 to June 30 of the following year, and as of June 1 shall apply from July 1 to December 31 of that year.

3.   The calculations referred to in Annex 9.1, Sections (A) through (C) that specifically referenced this paragraph shall be made in accordance with the following:

(a) Chile shall calculate and convert the value of the thresholds applicable to this paragraph into its national currency using the conversion rates published by the IMF in its monthly "International Financial Statistics". Chile shall notify the United States without delay of the methodology used and the results of its calculations;

(b) the conversion rates shall be the average of the daily values of the respective national currency in terms of the Standard Drawing Right (SDR) over the two-year period preceding October 1 or November 1 of the year prior to the thresholds in national currency becoming effective, which shall be from January 1;

(c) thresholds shall be fixed for two years, i.e. calendar years for all Parties where the fiscal year (1 April-31 March) will be used; and

(d) the Parties agree that if a major change in a national currency vis-a-vis the SDR during a year were to create a significant problem with regard to the application of the Chapter, they shall consult as to whether an interim adjustment is appropriate.

Section H - General Notes

Schedule of Chile

None.

Schedule of the United States

1.   This Chapter does not apply to set-asides on behalf of small and minority businesses.

2.   This Chapter does not apply to the procurement of transportation services that form a part of, or are incidental to, a procurement contract.

3.   Where a contract to be awarded by an entity is not covered by this Chapter, nothing in this Chapter shall be construed to cover any good or service component of that contract.

Chapter Ten

Investment

Section A - Investment

Article 10.1: Scope and Coverage[1]

1.   This Chapter applies to measures adopted or maintained by a Party relating to:

    (a)   investors of the other Party;

    (b)   covered investments; and

    (c)   with respect to Articles 10.5 and 10.12, all investments in the territory of the Party.

2.   In the event of any inconsistency between this Chapter and another Chapter, the other Chapter shall prevail to the extent of the inconsistency.

3.   A requirement by a Party that a service provider of the other Party post a bond or other form of financial security as a condition of providing a service into its territory does not of itself make this Chapter applicable to the provision of that cross-border service. This Chapter applies to that Party's treatment of the posted bond or financial security.

---

[1] For greater certainty, the provisions of this Chapter do not bind either Party in relation to any act or fact that took place or any situation that ceased to exist before the date of entry into force of this Agreement. Also, for greater certainty, this Chapter is subject to and shall be interpreted in accordance with Annexes 10-A through 10-H.

4.   This Chapter does not apply to measures adopted or maintained by a Party to the extent that they are covered by Chapter Twelve (Financial Services).

Article 10.2: National Treatment

1.   Each Party shall accord to investors of the other Party treatment no less favorable than that it accords, in like circumstances, to its own investors with respect to the establishment, acquisition, expansion, management, conduct, operation, and sale or other disposition of investments in its territory.

2.   Each Party shall accord to covered investments treatment no less favorable than that it accords, in like circumstances, to investments in its territory of its own investors with respect to the establishment, acquisition, expansion, management, conduct, operation, and sale or other disposition of investments.

3.   The treatment to be accorded by a Party under paragraphs 1 and 2 means, with respect to a regional level of government, treatment no less favorable than the most favorable treatment accorded, in like circumstances, by that regional level of government to investors, and to investments of investors, of the Party of which it forms a part.

Article 10.3: Most-Favored-Nation Treatment

1.   Each Party shall accord to investors of the other Party treatment no less favorable than that it accords, in like circumstances, to investors of any non-Party with respect to the establishment, acquisition, expansion, management, conduct, operation, and sale or other disposition of investments in its territory.

2.   Each Party shall accord to covered investments treatment no less favorable than that it accords, in like circumstances, to investments in its territory of investors of any non-Party with respect to the establishment, acquisition, expansion, management, conduct, operation, and sale or other disposition of investments.

Article 10.4: Minimum Standard of Treatment[2]

1.   Each Party shall accord to covered investments treatment in accordance with customary international law, including fair and equitable treatment and full protection and security.

2.   For greater certainty, paragraph 1 prescribes the customary international law minimum standard of treatment of aliens as the minimum standard of treatment to be afforded to covered investments. The concepts of "fair and equitable treatment" and "full protection and security" do not require treatment in addition to or beyond that which is required by that standard, and do not create additional substantive rights. The obligation in paragraph 1 to provide:

    (a)   "fair and equitable treatment" includes the obligation not to deny justice in criminal, civil, or administrative adjudicatory proceedings in accordance with the principle of due process embodied in the principal legal systems of the world; and

---

[2] For greater certainty, Article 10.4 shall be interpreted in accordance with Annex 10-A.

      (b)   "full protection and security" requires each Party to provide the level of police protection required under customary international law.

3.   A determination that there has been a breach of another provision of this Agreement, or of a separate international agreement, does not establish that there has been a breach of this Article.

4.   Notwithstanding Article 10.7(5)(b), each Party shall accord to investors of the other Party, and to covered investments, non-discriminatory treatment with respect to measures it adopts or maintains relating to losses suffered by investments in its territory owing to armed conflict or civil strife.

5.   Notwithstanding paragraph 4, if an investor of a Party, in the situations referred to in that paragraph, suffers a loss in the territory of the other Party resulting from:

      (a)   requisitioning of its covered investment or part thereof by the latter's forces or authorities; or

      (b)   destruction of its covered investment or part thereof by the latter's forces or authorities, which was not required by the necessity of the situation,

          the latter Party shall provide the investor restitution or compensation, which in either case shall be prompt, adequate, and effective, and, with respect to compensation, shall be in accordance with Article 10.9(2) through (4).

6.   Paragraph 4 does not apply to existing measures relating to subsidies or grants that would be inconsistent with Article 10.2 but for Article 10.7(5)(b).

Article 10.5: Performance Requirements

Mandatory Performance Requirements

1.   Neither Party may impose or enforce any of the following requirements, or enforce any commitment or undertaking, in connection with the establishment, acquisition, expansion, management, conduct, operation, or sale or other disposition of an investment of an investor of a Party or of a non-Party in its territory:

      (a)   to export a given level or percentage of goods or services;

      (b)   to achieve a given level or percentage of domestic content;

      (c)   to purchase, use, or accord a preference to goods produced in its territory, or to purchase goods from persons in its territory;

      (d)   to relate in any way the volume or value of imports to the volume or value of exports or to the amount of foreign exchange inflows associated with such investment;

(e) to restrict sales of goods or services in its territory that such investment produces or supplies by relating such sales in any way to the volume or value of its exports or foreign exchange earnings;

(f) to transfer a particular technology, a production process, or other proprietary knowledge to a person in its territory; or

(g) to supply exclusively from the territory of the Party the goods that it produces or the services that it supplies to a specific regional market or to the world market.

Advantages Subject to Performance Requirements

2. Neither Party may condition the receipt or continued receipt of an advantage, in connection with the establishment, acquisition, expansion, management, conduct, operation, or sale or other disposition of an investment in its territory of an investor of a Party or of a non-Party, on compliance with any of the following requirements:

(a) to achieve a given level or percentage of domestic content;

(b) to purchase, use, or accord a preference to goods produced in its territory, or to purchase goods from persons in its territory;

(c) to relate in any way the volume or value of imports to the volume or value of exports or to the amount of foreign exchange inflows associated with such investment; or

(d) to restrict sales of goods or services in its territory that such investment produces or supplies by relating such sales in any way to the volume or value of its exports or foreign exchange earnings.

Exceptions and Exclusions

3. (a) Nothing in paragraph 2 shall be construed to prevent a Party from conditioning the receipt or continued receipt of an advantage, in connection with an investment in its territory of an investor of a Party or of a non-Party, on compliance with a requirement to locate production, supply a service, train or employ workers, construct or expand particular facilities, or carry out research and development, in its territory.

(b) Paragraph 1(f) does not apply:

(i) when a Party authorizes use of an intellectual property right in accordance with Article 31[3] of the TRIPS Agreement, or to measures requiring the disclosure of proprietary information that fall within the scope of, and are consistent with, Article 39 of the TRIPS Agreement; or

(ii) when the requirement is imposed or the commitment or undertaking is enforced by a court, administrative tribunal, or competition authority to

---

[3] The reference to "Article 31" includes footnote 7 to Article 31.

remedy a practice determined after judicial or administrative process to be anticompetitive under the Party's competition laws.[4]

(c)   Provided that such measures are not applied in an arbitrary or unjustifiable manner, or do not constitute a disguised restriction on international trade or investment, paragraphs 1(b), (c), and (f), and 2(a) and (b), shall not be construed to prevent a Party from adopting or maintaining measures, including environmental measures:

   (i)   necessary to secure compliance with laws and regulations that are not inconsistent with this Agreement;

   (ii)   necessary to protect human, animal, or plant life or health; or

   (iii)   related to the conservation of living or non-living exhaustible natural resources.

(d)   Paragraphs 1(a), (b), and (c), and 2(a) and (b), do not apply to qualification requirements for goods or services with respect to export promotion and foreign aid programs.

(e)   Paragraphs 1(b), (c), (f), and (g), and 2(a) and (b), do not apply to procurement.

(f)   Paragraphs 2(a) and (b) do not apply to requirements imposed by an importing Party relating to the content of goods necessary to qualify for preferential tariffs or preferential quotas.

4.   For greater certainty, paragraphs 1 and 2 do not apply to any requirement other than the requirements set out in those paragraphs.

5.   This Article does not preclude enforcement of any commitment, undertaking, or requirement between private parties, where a Party did not impose or require the commitment, undertaking, or requirement.

Article 10.6: Senior Management and Boards of Directors

1.   Neither Party may require that an enterprise of that Party that is a covered investment appoint to senior management positions individuals of any particular nationality.

2.   A Party may require that a majority of the board of directors, or any committee thereof, of an enterprise of that Party that is a covered investment, be of a particular nationality, or resident in the territory of the Party, provided that the requirement does not materially impair the ability of the investor to exercise control over its investment.

Article 10.7: Non-Conforming Measures[5]

1.   Articles 10.2, 10.3, 10.5, and 10.6 do not apply to:

---

[4] The Parties recognize that a patent does not necessarily confer market power.
[5] For greater certainty, Article 10.7 is subject to Annex 10-B.

(a)   any existing non-conforming measure that is maintained by a Party at:

   (i)   the central level of government, as set out by that Party in its Schedule to Annex I,

   (ii)   a regional level of government, as set out by that Party in its Schedule to Annex I, or

   (iii)   a local level of government;

(b)   the continuation or prompt renewal of any non-conforming measure referred to in subparagraph (a); or

(c)   an amendment to any non-conforming measure referred to in subparagraph (a) to the extent that the amendment does not decrease the conformity of the measure, as it existed immediately before the amendment, with Articles 10.2, 10.3, 10.5, and 10.6.

2.   Articles 10.2, 10.3, 10.5, and 10.6 do not apply to any measure that a Party adopts or maintains with respect to sectors, subsectors, or activities, as set out in its Schedule to Annex II.

3.   Neither Party may, under any measure adopted after the date of entry into force of this Agreement and covered by its Schedule to Annex II, require an investor of the other Party, by reason of its nationality, to sell or otherwise dispose of an investment existing at the time the measure becomes effective.

4.   Articles 10.2 and 10.3 do not apply to any measure that is an exception to, or derogation from, the obligations under Article 17.1(6) (General Provisions) as specifically provided for in that Article.

5.   Articles 10.2, 10.3, and 10.6 do not apply to:

(a)   procurement; or

(b)   subsidies or grants provided by a Party, including government-supported loans, guarantees, and insurance.

Article 10.8: Transfers [6]

1.   Each Party shall permit all transfers relating to a covered investment to be made freely and without delay into and out of its territory. Such transfers include:

(a)   contributions to capital;

(b)   profits, dividends, interest, capital gains, royalty payments, management fees, and technical assistance and other fees;

---

[6] For greater certainty, Article 10.8 is subject to Annex 10-C.

    (c)   proceeds from the sale of all or any part of the covered investment or from the partial or complete liquidation of the covered investment;

    (d)   payments made under a contract entered into by the investor, or the covered investment, including payments made pursuant to a loan agreement;

    (e)   payments made pursuant to Article 10.4(4) and (5) and Article 10.9; and

    (f)   payments arising under Section B.

2.   Each Party shall permit returns in kind relating to a covered investment to be made as authorized or specified in an investment authorization or other written agreement[7] between the Party and a covered investment or an investor of the other Party.

3.   Each Party shall permit transfers relating to a covered investment to be made in a freely usable currency at the market rate of exchange prevailing on the date of transfer.

4.   Neither Party may require its investors to transfer, or penalize its investors that fail to transfer, the income, earnings, profits, or other amounts derived from, or attributable to, investments in the territory of the other Party.

5.   Notwithstanding paragraphs 1 through 3, a Party may prevent a transfer through the equitable, nondiscriminatory, and good faith application of its laws relating to:

    (a)   bankruptcy, insolvency, or the protection of the rights of creditors;

    (b)   issuing, trading, or dealing in securities, futures, or derivatives;

    (c)   criminal or penal offenses;

    (d)   financial reporting or record keeping of transfers when necessary to assist law enforcement or financial regulatory authorities; or

    (e)   ensuring compliance with orders or judgments in judicial or administrative proceedings.

6.   Notwithstanding paragraph 2, a Party may restrict transfers of returns in kind in circumstances where it could otherwise restrict such transfers under this Agreement, including as set out in paragraph 5.

Article 10.9: Expropriation and Compensation[8]

1.   Neither Party may expropriate or nationalize a covered investment either directly or indirectly through measures equivalent to expropriation or nationalization ("expropriation"), except:

    (a)   for a public purpose;

---

[7] Notwithstanding any other provision of this Chapter, this paragraph takes effect on the date of entry into force of this Agreement.

[8] For greater certainty, Article 10.9 shall be interpreted in accordance with Annex 10-A and Annex 10-D.

(b)   in a non-discriminatory manner;

(c)   on payment of prompt, adequate, and effective compensation in accordance with paragraphs 2 through 4; and

(d)   in accordance with due process of law and Article 10.4(1) through (3).

2.   Compensation shall:

(a)   be paid without delay;

(b)   be equivalent to the fair market value of the expropriated investment immediately before the expropriation took place ("the date of expropriation");

(c)   not reflect any change in value occurring because the intended expropriation had become known earlier; and

(d)   be fully realizable and freely transferable.

3.   If the fair market value is denominated in a freely usable currency, the compensation paid shall be no less than the fair market value on the date of expropriation, plus interest at a commercially reasonable rate for that currency, accrued from the date of expropriation until the date of payment.

4.   If the fair market value is denominated in a currency that is not freely usable, the compensation paid – converted into the currency of payment at the market rate of exchange prevailing on the date of payment – shall be no less than:

(a)   the fair market value on the date of expropriation, converted into a freely usable currency at the market rate of exchange prevailing on that date, plus

(b)   interest, at a commercially reasonable rate for that freely usable currency, accrued from the date of expropriation until the date of payment.

5.   This Article does not apply to the issuance of compulsory licenses granted in relation to intellectual property rights in accordance with the TRIPS Agreement, or to the revocation, limitation, or creation of intellectual property rights, to the extent that such revocation, limitation, or creation is consistent with Chapter Seventeen (Intellectual Property Rights).

Article 10.10: Special Formalities and Information Requirements

1.   Nothing in Article 10.2 shall be construed to prevent a Party from adopting or maintaining a measure that prescribes special formalities in connection with covered.10-10 investments, such as a requirement that investors be residents of the Party or that covered investments be legally constituted under the laws or regulations of the Party, provided that such formalities do not materially impair the protections afforded by a Party to investors of the other Party and covered investments pursuant to this Chapter.

2.   Notwithstanding Articles 10.2 and 10.3, a Party may require an investor of the other Party, or a covered investment, to provide information concerning that investment solely for informational or statistical purposes. The Party shall protect such information that is confidential

from any disclosure that would prejudice the competitive position of the investor or the covered investment. Nothing in this paragraph shall be construed to prevent a Party from otherwise obtaining or disclosing information in connection with the equitable and good faith application of its domestic law.

Article 10.11: Denial of Benefits

1.   A Party may deny the benefits of this Chapter to an investor of the other Party that is an enterprise of such other Party and to investments of that investor if an investor of a non-Party owns or controls the enterprise and the denying Party:

(a)   does not maintain diplomatic relations with the non-Party; or

(b)   adopts or maintains measures with respect to the non-Party or an investor of the non-Party that prohibit transactions with the enterprise or that would be violated or circumvented if the benefits of this Chapter were accorded to the enterprise or to its investments.

2.   Subject to Article 22.4 (Consultations), a Party may deny the benefits of this Chapter to:

(a)   an investor of the other Party that is an enterprise of such other Party and to investments of that investor if an investor of a non-Party owns or controls the enterprise and the enterprise has no substantial business activities in the territory of the other Party; or

(b)   an investor of the other Party that is an enterprise of such other Party and to investments of that investor if an investor of the denying Party owns or controls the enterprise and the enterprise has no substantial business activities in the territory of the other Party.

Article 10.12: Investment and Environment

Nothing in this Chapter shall be construed to prevent a Party from adopting, maintaining, or enforcing any measure otherwise consistent with this Chapter that it.10-11 considers appropriate to ensure that investment activity in its territory is undertaken in a manner sensitive to environmental concerns.

Article 10.13: Implementation

The Parties shall consult annually, or as otherwise agreed, to review the implementation of this Chapter and consider any investment matter of mutual interest, including consideration of the development of procedures that could contribute to greater transparency of measures described in Article 10.7(1)(c).

Section B - Investor-State Dispute Settlement Article

10.14: Consultation and Negotiation

In the event of an investment dispute, the claimant and the respondent should initially seek to resolve the dispute through consultation and negotiation, which may include the use of non-binding, third-party procedures.

Article 10.15: Submission of a Claim to Arbitration[9]

1.   In the event that a disputing party considers that an investment dispute cannot be settled by consultation and negotiation:

    (a)   the claimant, on its own behalf, may submit to arbitration under this Section a claim

        (i)   that the respondent has breached

            (A)   an obligation under Section A or Annex 10-F,

            (B)   an investment authorization, or

            (C)   an investment agreement; and

        (ii)   that the claimant has incurred loss or damage by reason of, or arising out of, that breach; and

    (b)   the claimant, on behalf of an enterprise of the respondent that is a juridical person that the claimant owns or controls directly or indirectly, may submit to arbitration under this Section a claim

        (i)   that the respondent has breached

            (A)   an obligation under Section A or Annex 10-F,

            (B)   an investment authorization, or

            (C)   an investment agreement; and

        (ii)   that the enterprise has incurred loss or damage by reason of, or arising out of, that breach.

2.   For greater certainty, a claimant may submit to arbitration under this Section a claim that the respondent has breached an obligation under Section A or Annex 10-F through the actions of a designated monopoly or a state enterprise exercising delegated government authority as described in Article 16.3(3)(a) (Designated Monopolies) and Article 16.4(2) (State Enterprises), respectively.

---

[9] For greater certainty, Article 10.15 is subject to Annex 10-E.

3.   Without prejudice to Article 12.1(2) (Scope and Coverage), no claim may be submitted under this Section that alleges a violation of any provision of this Agreement other than an obligation under Section A or Annex 10-F.

4.   At least 90 days before submitting any claim to arbitration under this Section, a claimant shall deliver to the respondent a written notice of its intention to submit the claim to arbitration ("notice of intent"). The notice shall specify:

(a)   the name and address of the claimant and, where a claim is submitted on behalf of an enterprise, the name, address, and place of incorporation of the enterprise;

(b)   for each claim, the provision of this Agreement, investment authorization, or investment agreement alleged to have been breached and any other relevant provisions;

(c)   the legal and factual basis for each claim; and

(d)   the relief sought and the approximate amount of damages claimed.

5.   Provided that six months have elapsed since the events giving rise to the claim, a claimant may submit a claim referred to in paragraph 1:

(a)   under the ICSID Convention, provided that both the non-disputing Party and the respondent are parties to the ICSID Convention;

(b)   under the ICSID Additional Facility Rules, provided that either the non-disputing Party or the respondent, but not both, is a party to the ICSID Convention;

(c)   under the UNCITRAL Arbitration Rules; or

(d)   if the disputing parties agree, to any other arbitration institution or under any other arbitration rules.

6.   A claim shall be deemed submitted to arbitration under this Section when the claimant's notice of or request for arbitration ("notice of arbitration"):

(a)   referred to in paragraph 1 of Article 36 of the ICSID Convention is received by the Secretary-General;

(b)   referred to in Article 2 of Schedule C of the ICSID Additional Facility Rules is received by the Secretary-General;

(c)   referred to in Article 3 of the UNCITRAL Arbitration Rules, together with the statement of claim referred to in Article 18 of the UNCITRAL Arbitration Rules, are received by the respondent; or

(d)   referred to under any other arbitral institution or arbitral rules selected under paragraph 5(d) is received by the respondent.

7.   The arbitration rules applicable under paragraph 5, and in effect on the date the claim or claims were submitted to arbitration under this Section, shall govern the arbitration except to the extent modified by this Agreement.

8.   The claimant shall provide with the notice of arbitration referred to in paragraph 6:

  (a)   the name of the arbitrator that the claimant appoints; or

  (b)   the claimant's written consent for the Secretary-General to appoint the claimant's arbitrator.

Article 10.16: Consent of Each Party to Arbitration

1.   Each Party consents to the submission of a claim to arbitration under this Section in accordance with this Agreement.

2.   The consent under paragraph 1 and the submission of a claim to arbitration under this Section shall satisfy the requirements of:

  (a)   Chapter II of the ICSID Convention (Jurisdiction of the Centre) and the ICSID Additional Facility Rules for written consent of the parties to the dispute;

  (b)   Article II of the New York Convention for an "agreement in writing;" and

  (c)   Article I of the Inter-American Convention for an "agreement."

Article 10.17: Conditions and Limitations on Consent of Each Party

1.   No claim may be submitted to arbitration under this Section if more than three years have elapsed from the date on which the claimant first acquired, or should have first acquired, knowledge of the breach alleged under Article 10.15(1) and knowledge that the claimant (for claims brought under Article 10.15(1)(a)) or the enterprise (for claims brought under Article 10.15(1)(b)) has incurred loss or damage.

2.   No claim may be submitted to arbitration under this Section unless:

  (a)   the claimant consents in writing to arbitration in accordance with the procedures set out in this Agreement; and

  (b)   the notice of arbitration referred to in Article 10.15(6) is accompanied,

    (i)   for claims submitted to arbitration under Article 10.15(1)(a), by the claimant's written waiver, and

    (ii)   for claims submitted to arbitration under Article 10.15(1)(b), by the claimant's and the enterprise's written waivers of any right to initiate or continue before any administrative tribunal or court under the law of either Party, or other dispute settlement procedures, any proceeding with respect to the events alleged to give rise to the claimed breach.

3.   Notwithstanding paragraph 2(b), the claimant (for claims brought under Article 10.15(1)(a)) and the claimant or the enterprise (for claims brought under Article 10.15(1)(b)) may initiate or continue an action that seeks interim injunctive relief and does not involve the payment of monetary damages before a judicial or administrative tribunal of the respondent, provided that the action is brought for the sole purpose of preserving the claimant's or the enterprise's rights and interests during the pendency of the arbitration.

Article 10.18: Selection of Arbitrators

1.   Unless the disputing parties otherwise agree, the tribunal shall comprise three arbitrators, one arbitrator appointed by each of the disputing parties and the third, who shall be the presiding arbitrator, appointed by agreement of the disputing parties.

2.   The Secretary-General shall serve as appointing authority for an arbitration under this Section.

3.   If a tribunal has not been constituted within 75 days from the date that a claim is submitted to arbitration under this Section, the Secretary-General, on the request of a disputing party, shall appoint, in his or her discretion, the arbitrator or arbitrators not yet appointed.

4.   For purposes of Article 39 of the ICSID Convention and Article 7 of Schedule C to the ICSID Additional Facility Rules, and without prejudice to an objection to an arbitrator on a ground other than nationality:

    (a)   the respondent agrees to the appointment of each individual member of a tribunal established under the ICSID Convention or the ICSID Additional Facility Rules;

    (b)   a claimant referred to in Article 10.15(1)(a) may submit a claim to arbitration under this Section, or continue a claim, under the ICSID Convention or the ICSID Additional Facility Rules, only on condition that the claimant agrees in writing to the appointment of each individual member of the tribunal; and

    (c)   a claimant referred to in Article 10.15(1)(b) may submit a claim to arbitration under this Section, or continue a claim, under the ICSID Convention or the ICSID Additional Facility Rules, only on condition that the claimant and the enterprise agree in writing to the appointment of each individual member of the tribunal.

Article 10.19: Conduct of the Arbitration

1.   The disputing parties may agree on the legal place of any arbitration under the arbitral rules applicable under Article 10.15(5)(b), (c), or (d). If the disputing parties fail to reach agreement, the tribunal shall determine the place in accordance with the applicable arbitral rules, provided that the place shall be in the territory of a State that is a party to the New York Convention.

2.   The non-disputing Party may make oral and written submissions to the tribunal regarding the interpretation of this Agreement.

3.   The tribunal shall have the authority to accept and consider amicus curiae submissions from a person or entity that is not a disputing party (the "submitter"). The submissions shall be

provided in both Spanish and English, and shall identify the submitter and any Party, other government, person, or organization, other than the submitter, that has provided, or will provide, any financial or other assistance in preparing the submission.

4.   Without prejudice to a tribunal's authority to address other objections as a preliminary question, such as an objection that a dispute is not within a tribunal's competence, a tribunal shall address and decide as a preliminary question any objection by the respondent that, as a matter of law, a claim submitted is not a claim for which an award in favor of the claimant may be made under Article 10.25.

> (a)   Such objection shall be submitted to the tribunal as soon as possible after the tribunal is constituted, and in no event later than the date the tribunal fixes for the respondent to submit its counter-memorial (or, in the case of an amendment to the notice of arbitration referred to in Article 10.15(6), the date the tribunal fixes for the respondent to submit its response to the amendment).

> (b)   On receipt of an objection under this paragraph, the tribunal shall suspend any proceedings on the merits, establish a schedule for considering the objection consistent with any schedule it has established for considering any other preliminary question, and issue a decision or award on the objection, stating the grounds therefor.

> (c)   In deciding an objection under this paragraph, the tribunal shall assume to be true claimant's factual allegations in support of any claim in the notice of arbitration (or any amendment thereof) and, in disputes brought under the UNCITRAL Arbitration Rules, the statement of claim referred to in Article 18 of the UNCITRAL Arbitration Rules. The tribunal may also consider any relevant facts not in dispute.

> (d)   The respondent does not waive any objection as to competence or any argument on the merits merely because the respondent did or did not raise an objection under this paragraph or make use of the expedited procedure set out in the following paragraph.

5.   In the event that the respondent so requests within 45 days after the tribunal is constituted, the tribunal shall decide on an expedited basis an objection under paragraph 4 or any objection that the dispute is not within the tribunal's competence. The tribunal shall suspend any proceedings on the merits and issue a decision or award on the objection(s), stating the grounds therefor, no later than 150 days after the date of the request. However, if a disputing party requests a hearing, the tribunal may take an additional 30 days to issue the decision or award. Regardless of whether a hearing is requested, a tribunal may, on a showing of extraordinary cause, delay issuing its decision or award by an additional brief period of time, which may not exceed 30 days.

6.   When it decides a respondent's objection under paragraph 4 or 5, the tribunal may, if warranted, award to the prevailing disputing party reasonable costs and attorneys' fees incurred in submitting or opposing the objection. In determining whether such an award is warranted, the tribunal shall consider whether either the claimant's claim or the respondent's objection was frivolous, and shall provide the disputing parties a reasonable opportunity to comment.

7.   A respondent may not assert as a defense, counterclaim, right of set-off, or for any other reason that the claimant has received or will receive indemnification or other compensation for all or part of the alleged damages pursuant to an insurance or guarantee contract.

8.   A tribunal may order an interim measure of protection to preserve the rights of a disputing party, or to ensure that the tribunal's jurisdiction is made fully effective, including an order to preserve evidence in the possession or control of a disputing party or to protect the tribunal's jurisdiction. A tribunal may not order attachment or enjoin the application of a measure alleged to constitute a breach referred to in Article 10.15. For purposes of this paragraph, an order includes a recommendation.

9.   (a)   At the request of a disputing party, a tribunal shall, before issuing an award on liability, transmit its proposed award to the disputing parties and to the non-disputing Party. Within 60 days after the tribunal transmits its proposed award, only the disputing parties may submit written comments to the tribunal concerning any aspect of its proposed award. The tribunal shall consider any such comments and issue its award not later than 45 days after the expiration of the 60-day comment period.

       (b)   Subparagraph (a) shall not apply in any arbitration for which an appeal has been made available pursuant to paragraph 10.

10.   If a separate multilateral agreement enters into force as between the Parties that establishes an appellate body for purposes of reviewing awards rendered by tribunals constituted pursuant to international trade or investment agreements to hear investment disputes, the Parties shall strive to reach an agreement that would have such appellate body review awards rendered under Article 10.25 in arbitrations commenced after the appellate body's establishment.

Article 10.20: Transparency of Arbitral Proceedings

1.   Subject to paragraphs 2 and 4, the respondent shall, after receiving the following documents, promptly transmit them to the non-disputing Party and make them available to the public:

       (a)   the notice of intent referred to in Article 10.15(4);

       (b)   the notice of arbitration referred to in Article 10.15(6);

       (c)   pleadings, memorials, and briefs submitted to the tribunal by a disputing party and any written submissions submitted pursuant to Article 10.19(2) and (3) and Article 10.24;

       (d)   minutes or transcripts of hearings of the tribunal, where available; and

       (e)   orders, awards, and decisions of the tribunal.

2.   The tribunal shall conduct hearings open to the public and shall determine, in consultation with the disputing parties, the appropriate logistical arrangements. However, any disputing party that intends to use information designated as confidential business information or information that is privileged or otherwise protected from disclosure under a Party's law in a

hearing shall so advise the tribunal. The tribunal shall make appropriate arrangements to protect the information from disclosure.

3.　　Nothing in this Section requires a respondent to disclose confidential business information or information that is privileged or otherwise protected from disclosure under a Party's law or to furnish or allow access to information that it may withhold in accordance with Article 23.2 (Essential Security) or Article 23.5 (Disclosure of Information).

4.　　Confidential business information or information that is privileged or otherwise protected from disclosure under a Party's law shall, if such information is submitted to the tribunal, be protected from disclosure in accordance with the following procedures:

(a)　　Subject to subparagraph (d), neither the disputing parties nor the tribunal shall disclose to the non-disputing Party or to the public any confidential business information or information that is privileged or otherwise protected from disclosure under a Party's law where the disputing party that provided the information clearly designates it in accordance with subparagraph (b);

(b)　　Any disputing party claiming that certain information constitutes confidential business information or information that is privileged or otherwise protected from disclosure under a Party's law shall clearly designate the information at the time it is submitted to the tribunal;

(c)　　A disputing party shall, at the same time that it submits a document containing information claimed to be confidential business information or information that is privileged or otherwise protected from disclosure under a Party's law, submit a redacted version of the document that does not contain the information. Only the redacted version shall be provided to the non-disputing Party and made public in accordance with paragraph 1; and

(d)　　The tribunal shall decide any objection regarding the designation of information claimed to be confidential business information or information that is privileged or otherwise protected from disclosure under a Party's law. If the tribunal determines that such information was not properly designated, the disputing party that submitted the information may:

(i)　　withdraw all or part of its submission containing such information; or

(ii)　　agree to resubmit complete and redacted documents with corrected designations in accordance with the tribunal's determination and subparagraph (c).

In either case, the other disputing party shall, whenever necessary, resubmit complete and redacted documents which either remove the information withdrawn under subparagraph (d)(i) by the disputing party that first submitted the information or redesignate the information consistent with the designation under subparagraph (d)(ii) of the disputing party that first submitted the information.

5.　　Nothing in this Section authorizes a respondent to withhold from the public information required to be disclosed by its laws.

Article 10.21: Governing Law

1.   Subject to paragraph 3, when a claim is submitted under Article 10.15(1)(a)(i)(A) or Article 10.15(1)(b)(i)(A), the tribunal shall decide the issues in dispute in accordance with this Agreement and applicable rules of international law.

2.   Subject to paragraph 3, when a claim is submitted under Article 10.15(1)(a)(i)(B) or (C), or Article 10.15(1)(b)(i)(B) or (C), the tribunal shall decide the issues in dispute in accordance with the rules of law specified in the pertinent investment agreement or investment authorization, or as the disputing parties may otherwise agree. If the rules of law have not been specified or otherwise agreed, the tribunal shall apply the law of the respondent (including its rules on the conflict of laws), the terms of the investment agreement or investment authorization, such rules of international law as may be applicable, and this Agreement.

3.   A decision of the Commission declaring its interpretation of a provision of this Agreement under Article 21.1 (Free Trade Commission) shall be binding on a tribunal established under this Section, and any award must be consistent with that decision.

Article 10.22: Interpretation of Annexes

1.   Where a respondent asserts as a defense that the measure alleged to be a breach is within the scope of a non-conforming measure set out in Annex I or Annex II, the tribunal shall, on request of the respondent, request the interpretation of the Commission on the issue. The Commission shall submit in writing any decision declaring its interpretation under Article 21.1 (Free Trade Commission) to the tribunal within 60 days of delivery of the request.

2.   A decision issued by the Commission under paragraph 1 shall be binding on the tribunal, and any award must be consistent with that decision. If the Commission fails to issue such a decision within 60 days, the tribunal shall decide the issue.

Article 10.23: Expert Reports

Without prejudice to the appointment of other kinds of experts where authorized by the applicable arbitration rules, a tribunal, at the request of a disputing party or, unless the disputing parties disapprove, on its own initiative, may appoint one or more experts to report to it in writing on any factual issue concerning environmental, health, safety, or other scientific matters raised by a disputing party in a proceeding, subject to such terms and conditions as the disputing parties may agree.

Article 10.24: Consolidation

1.   Where two or more claims have been submitted separately to arbitration under Article 10.15(1) and the claims have a question of law or fact in common and arise out of the same events or circumstances, any disputing party may seek a consolidation order in accordance with the agreement of all the disputing parties sought to be covered by the order or the terms of paragraphs 2 through 10.

2.   A disputing party that seeks a consolidation order under this Article shall deliver, in writing, a request to the Secretary-General and to all the disputing parties sought to be covered by the order and shall specify in the request:

(a)   the names and addresses of all the disputing parties sought to be covered by the order;

(b)   the nature of the order sought; and

(c)   the grounds on which the order is sought.

3.   Unless the Secretary-General finds within 30 days after receiving a request under paragraph 2 that the request is manifestly unfounded, a tribunal shall be established under this Article.

4.   Unless all the disputing parties sought to be covered by the order otherwise agree, a tribunal established under this Article shall comprise three arbitrators:

(a)   one arbitrator appointed by agreement of the claimants;

(b)   one arbitrator appointed by the respondent; and

(c)   the presiding arbitrator appointed by the Secretary-General, provided, however, that the presiding arbitrator shall not be a national of either Party.

5.   If, within 60 days after the Secretary-General receives a request made under paragraph 2, the respondent fails or the claimants fail to appoint an arbitrator in accordance with paragraph 4, the Secretary-General, on the request of any disputing party sought to be covered by the order, shall appoint the arbitrator or arbitrators not yet appointed. If the respondent fails to appoint an arbitrator, the Secretary-General shall appoint a national of the respondent, and if the claimants fail to appoint an arbitrator, the Secretary-General shall appoint a national of the non-disputing Party.

6.   Where a tribunal established under this Article is satisfied that two or more claims that have been submitted to arbitration under Article 10.15(1) have a question of law or fact in common, and arise out of the same events or circumstances, the tribunal may, in the interest of fair and efficient resolution of the claims, and after hearing the disputing parties, by order:

(a)   assume jurisdiction over, and hear and determine together, all or part of the claims;

(b)   assume jurisdiction over, and hear and determine one or more of the claims, the determination of which it believes would assist in the resolution of the others; or

(c)   instruct a tribunal previously established under Article 10.18 to assume jurisdiction over, and hear and determine together, all or part of the claims, provided that

(i)   that tribunal, at the request of any claimant not previously a disputing party before that tribunal, shall be reconstituted with its original members, except that the arbitrator for the claimants shall be appointed pursuant to paragraphs 4(a) and 5; and

(ii)   that tribunal shall decide whether any prior hearing shall be repeated.

7.   Where a tribunal has been established under this Article, a claimant that has submitted a claim to arbitration under Article 10.15(1) and that has not been named in a request made under paragraph 2 may make a written request to the tribunal that it be included in any order made under paragraph 6, and shall specify in the request:

(a)   the name and address of the claimant;

(b)   the nature of the order sought; and

(c)   the grounds on which the order is sought.

The claimant shall deliver a copy of its request to the Secretary-General.

8.   A tribunal established under this Article shall conduct its proceedings in accordance with the UNCITRAL Arbitration Rules, except as modified by this Section.

9.   A tribunal established under Article 10.18 shall not have jurisdiction to decide a claim, or a part of a claim, over which a tribunal established or instructed under this Article has assumed jurisdiction.

10.   On application of a disputing party, a tribunal established under this Article, pending its decision under paragraph 6, may order that the proceedings of a tribunal established under Article 10.18 be stayed, unless the latter tribunal has already adjourned its proceedings.

Article 10.25: Awards

1.   Where a tribunal makes a final award against a respondent, the tribunal may award, separately or in combination, only:

(a)   monetary damages and any applicable interest;

(b)   restitution of property, in which case the award shall provide that the respondent may pay monetary damages and any applicable interest in lieu of restitution. A tribunal may also award costs and attorneys' fees in accordance with this Section and the applicable arbitration rules.

2.   Subject to paragraph 1, where a claim is submitted to arbitration under Article 10.15(1)(b):

(a)   an award of restitution of property shall provide that restitution be made to the enterprise;

(b)   an award of monetary damages and any applicable interest shall provide that the sum be paid to the enterprise; and

(c)   the award shall provide that it is made without prejudice to any right that any person may have in the relief under applicable domestic law.

3.   A tribunal may not award punitive damages.

4.   An award made by a tribunal shall have no binding force except between the disputing parties and in respect of the particular case.

5.   Subject to paragraph 6 and the applicable review procedure for an interim award, a disputing party shall abide by and comply with an award without delay.

6.   A disputing party may not seek enforcement of a final award until:

(a)   in the case of a final award made under the ICSID Convention.10-24

  (i)   120 days have elapsed from the date the award was rendered and no disputing party has requested revision or annulment of the award; or

  (ii)   revision or annulment proceedings have been completed; and

(b)   in the case of a final award under the ICSID Additional Facility Rules, the UNCITRAL Arbitration Rules, or the rules selected pursuant to Article 10.15(5)(d)

  (i)   90 days have elapsed from the date the award was rendered and no disputing party has commenced a proceeding to revise, set aside, or annul the award, or

  (ii)   a court has dismissed or allowed an application to revise, set aside, or annul the award and there is no further appeal.

7.   Each Party shall provide for the enforcement of an award in its territory.

8.   If the respondent fails to abide by or comply with a final award, on delivery of a request by the non-disputing Party, a panel shall be established under Article 22.6 (Request for an Arbitral Panel). The requesting Party may seek in such proceedings:

(a)   a determination that the failure to abide by or comply with the final award is inconsistent with the obligations of this Agreement; and

(b)   if the Parties agree, a recommendation that the respondent abide by or comply with the final award.

9.   A disputing party may seek enforcement of an arbitration award under the ICSID Convention, the New York Convention, or the Inter-American Convention regardless of whether proceedings have been taken under paragraph 8.

10.   A claim that is submitted to arbitration under this Section shall be considered to arise out of a commercial relationship or transaction for purposes of Article I of the New York Convention and Article I of the Inter-American Convention.

Article 10.26: Service of Documents

Delivery of notice and other documents on a Party shall be made to the place named for that Party in Annex 10-G.

Section C - Definitions

Article 10.27: Definitions

For purposes of this Chapter:

Centre means the International Centre for Settlement of Investment Disputes (ICSID) established by the ICSID Convention;

claimant means an investor of a Party that is a party to an investment dispute with the other Party;

disputing parties means the claimant and the respondent;

disputing party means either the claimant or the respondent;

enterprise means an "enterprise" as defined in Article 2.1 (Definitions of General Application), and a branch of an enterprise;

enterprise of a Party means an enterprise constituted or organized under the law of a Party, and a branch located in the territory of a Party and carrying out business activities there;

freely usable currency means "freely usable currency" as determined by the International Monetary Fund under its Articles of Agreement;

ICSID Additional Facility Rules means the Rules Governing the Additional Facility for the Administration of Proceedings by the Secretariat of the International Centre for Settlement of Investment Disputes;

ICSID Convention means the Convention on the Settlement of Investment Disputes between States and Nationals of other States, done at Washington, March 18, 1965;

Inter-American Convention means the Inter-American Convention on International Commercial Arbitration, done at Panama, January 30, 1975;

investment means every asset that an investor owns or controls, directly or indirectly, that has the characteristics of an investment, including such characteristics as the commitment of capital or other resources, the expectation of gain or profit, or the assumption of risk. Forms that an investment may take include:

(a)   an enterprise;

(b)   shares, stock, and other forms of equity participation in an enterprise;

(c)   bonds, debentures, loans, and other debt instruments;[10]

(d)   futures, options, and other derivatives;

---

[10] Some forms of debt, such as bonds, debentures, and long-term notes, are more likely to have the characteristics of an investment, while other forms of debt, such as claims to payment that are immediately due and result from the sale of goods or services, are less likely to have such characteristics.

(e)   rights under contract, including turnkey, construction, management, production, concession, or revenue-sharing contracts;

(f)   intellectual property rights;

(g)   rights conferred pursuant to domestic law, such as concessions, licenses, authorizations, and permits;[11] and

(h)   other tangible or intangible, movable or immovable property, and related property rights, such as leases, mortgages, liens, and pledges;

but investment does not mean an order or judgment entered in a judicial or administrative action;

investment agreement means a written agreement[12] that takes effect at least two years after the date of entry into force of this Agreement between a national authority[13] of a Party and a covered investment or an investor of the other Party:

(a)   that grants rights with respect to natural resources or other assets that a national authority controls; and

(b)   that the covered investment or the investor relies on in establishing or acquiring a covered investment;

investment authorization means an authorization that the foreign investment authority of a Party grants to a covered investment or an investor of the other Party;[14]

investor of a non-Party means, with respect to a Party, an investor that attempts to make, is making, or has made an investment in the territory of that Party, that is not an investor of either Party;

investor of a Party means a Party or state enterprise thereof, or a national or an enterprise of a Party, that attempts to make, is making, or has made an investment in the territory of the other Party; provided, however, that a natural person who is a dual national shall be deemed to be exclusively a national of the State of his/her dominant and effective nationality;

monopoly means "monopoly" as defined in Article 16.9 (Definitions);

---

[11] Whether a particular right conferred pursuant to domestic law, as referred to in paragraph (g), has the characteristics of an investment depends on such factors as the nature and extent of the rights that the holder has under the domestic law of the Party. Among such rights that do not have the characteristics of an investment are those that do not create any rights protected under domestic law. For greater certainty, the foregoing is without prejudice to whether any asset associated with such right has the characteristics of an investment.

[12] For purposes of this definition, "written agreement" means an agreement in writing, executed and entered into by both parties or their representatives, which sets forth an exchange of rights and obligations, for value. Neither a unilateral act of an administrative or judicial authority, such as a decree, order, or judgment, nor a consent decree, shall be considered a written agreement.

[13] For purposes of this definition, "national authority" means (a) for the United States, an authority at the central level of government; and (b) for Chile, an authority at the ministerial level of government. "National authority" does not include state enterprises.

[14] The Parties recognize that neither Party has a foreign investment authority, as of the date this Agreement enters into force.

New York Convention means the United Nations Convention on the Recognition and Enforcement of Foreign Arbitral Awards, done at New York, June 10, 1958;
non-disputing Party means the Party that is not a party to an investment dispute;

respondent means the Party that is a party to an investment dispute; Secretary-General means the Secretary-General of ICSID;

tribunal means an arbitration tribunal established under Article 10.18 or 10.24; and

UNCITRAL Arbitration Rules means the arbitration rules of the United Nations Commission on International Trade Law.

Annex 10-A
Customary International Law

The Parties confirm their shared understanding that "customary international law" generally and as specifically referenced in Articles 10.4 and 10.9 results from a general and consistent practice of States that they follow from a sense of legal obligation. With regard to Article 10.4, the customary international law minimum standard of treatment of aliens refers to all customary international law principles that protect the economic rights and interests of aliens.

Annex 10-B
Public Debt Chile

The rescheduling of the debts of Chile, or of its appropriate institutions owned or controlled through ownership interests by Chile, owed to the United States and the rescheduling of its debts owed to creditors in general are not subject to any provision of Section A other than Articles 10.2 and 10.3.

Annex 10-C
Special Dispute Settlement Provisions

Chile

1.   Where a claimant submits a claim alleging that Chile has breached an obligation under Section A, other than Article 10.3, that arises from its imposition of restrictive measures with regard to payments and transfers, Section B shall apply except as modified below:

    (a)   A claimant may submit any such claim only after one year has elapsed since the events giving rise to the claim;

    (b)   If the claim is submitted under Article 10.15(1)(b), the claimant may, on behalf of the enterprise, only seek damages with respect to the shares of the enterprise for which the claimant has a beneficial interest;

    (c)   Loss or damages arising from restrictive measures on capital inflows shall be limited to the reduction in value of the transfers and shall exclude loss of profits or business and any similar consequential or incidental damages;

(d) Paragraph 1(a) shall not apply to claims that arise from restrictions on:

(i) transfers of proceeds of foreign direct investment by investors of the United States, excluding external debt financing covered in subparagraph (d)

(ii) and excluding investments designed with the purpose of gaining direct or indirect access to the financial market; or (ii) payments pursuant to a loan or bond issued in a foreign market, including inter- and intra-company debt financing between affiliated enterprises made exclusively for the conduct, operation, management, or expansion of such affiliated enterprises, provided that these payments are made in accordance with the maturity date agreed on in the loan or bond agreement;

(e) Excluding restrictive measures referred to in paragraph 1(d), Chile shall incur no liability, and shall not be subject to claims, for damages arising from its imposition of restrictive measures with regard to payments and transfers that were incurred within one year from the date on which the restrictions were imposed, provided that such restrictive measures do not substantially impede transfers;.

(f) A restrictive measure of Chile with regard to payments and transfers that is consistent with this Annex shall be deemed not to contravene Article 10.2 provided that, as required under existing Chilean law, it does not discriminate among investors that enter into transactions of the same nature; and

(g) Claims arising from Chile's imposition of restrictive measures with regard to payments and transfers shall not be subject to Article 10.24 unless Chile consents.

2. The United States may not request the establishment of an arbitral panel under Chapter Twenty-Two (Dispute Settlement) relating to Chile's imposition of restrictive measures with regard to payments and transfers until one year has elapsed since the events giving rise to the dispute.

3. Restrictive measures on payments and transfers related to claims under this Annex shall otherwise be subject to applicable domestic law.

Annex 10-D
Expropriation

The Parties confirm their shared understanding that:

1. Article 10.9(1) is intended to reflect customary international law concerning the obligation of States with respect to expropriation.

2. An action or a series of actions by a Party cannot constitute an expropriation unless it interferes with a tangible or intangible property right or property interest in an investment.

3.   Article 10.9(1) addresses two situations. The first is direct expropriation, where an investment is nationalized or otherwise directly expropriated through formal transfer of title or outright seizure.

4.   The second situation addressed by Article 10.9(1) is indirect expropriation, where an action or series of actions by a Party has an effect equivalent to direct expropriation without formal transfer of title or outright seizure.

    (a)   The determination of whether an action or series of actions by a Party, in a specific fact situation, constitutes an indirect expropriation, requires a case-by-case, fact-based inquiry that considers, among other factors:

        (i)   the economic impact of the government action, although the fact that an action or series of actions by a Party has an adverse effect on the economic value of an investment, standing alone, does not establish that an indirect expropriation has occurred;

        (ii)   the extent to which the government action interferes with distinct, reasonable investment-backed expectations; and

        (iii)   the character of the government action.

    (b)   Except in rare circumstances, nondiscriminatory regulatory actions by a Party that are designed and applied to protect legitimate public welfare objectives, such as public health, safety, and the environment, do not constitute indirect expropriations.

Annex 10-E
Submission of a Claim to Arbitration

Chile

1.   An investor of the United States may not submit to arbitration under Section B:

    (a)   a claim that Chile has breached an obligation under Section A or Annex 10-F either:

        (i)   on its own behalf under Article 10.15(1)(a), or

        (ii)   on behalf of an enterprise of Chile that is a juridical person that the investor owns or controls directly or indirectly under Article 10.15(1)(b),

        if the investor or the enterprise, respectively, has alleged that breach of an obligation under Section A or Annex 10-F in proceedings before a court or administrative tribunal of Chile; or

    (b)   a claim that Chile has breached an investment agreement or investment authorization either:

(i)   on its own behalf under Article 10.15(1)(a), or

(ii)   on behalf of an enterprise of Chile that is a juridical person that the investor owns or controls directly or indirectly under Article 10.15(1)(b),

if the investor or the enterprise, respectively, has alleged that breach of an investment agreement or investment authorization in proceedings before a court or administrative tribunal of Chile.

2.   For greater certainty, if an investor of the United States elects to submit a claim of the type described in this Annex to a court or administrative tribunal of Chile, that election shall be definitive and the investor may not thereafter submit the claim to arbitration under Section B.

Annex 10-F
DL 600

Chile

1.   Without prejudice to paragraphs 3 through 7, Chile shall accord to an investor of the United States or to a covered investment that is a party to an investment contract under Estatuto de la Inversión Extranjera, Decreto Ley 600 de 1974 (DL 600) the better of the treatment required under this Agreement or the treatment under the investment contract.

2.   Without prejudice to paragraphs 3 through 7, Chile shall permit an investor of the United States or a covered investment that has entered into an investment contract under DL 600 to amend the investment contract to make it consistent with Chile's obligations under this Agreement.

3.   Subject to paragraph 4, when an investor of the United States or a covered investment has entered into an investment contract under DL 600, an investor, on its own behalf or on behalf of the investment, may only submit a claim against Chile under Section B with regard to the contract if the investor alleges that Chile has breached an obligation under:

(a)   Section A in connection with the investment contract; or

(b)   this Annex; provided, however, that such an investor may not submit any claim under Section B on the basis of the equity/debt ratio requirement of an investment contract under DL 600 except for claims that Chile has accorded the investor or its covered investment treatment less favorable than Chile accords under DL 600 to an investor of a non-Party or its investment in like circumstances.

4.   When an investor of the United States or a covered investment has entered into an investment contract under DL 600, and the investor, on its own behalf or on behalf of the investment, claims that Chile has breached the tax provisions of that contract, it shall, with regard to that claim, only have recourse to the dispute settlement provisions of the investment contract or the dispute settlement provisions of this Agreement relevant to taxation measures.

5.   For greater certainty, execution of an investment contract under DL 600 by an investor of the United States or a covered investment does not create any right on the part of the investor or

covered investment to engage in particular activities in Chile.

6.   Nothing in this Agreement shall limit the right of Chile's Comite de Inversiones Extranjeras, its Vicepresidencia Ejecutiva, or their successors to decide whether to authorize an investor of the United States or a covered investment to enter into an investment contract under DL 600, or to establish conditions in such contract, provided that Chile does so in a manner that is not inconsistent with Chile's obligations under Section A.

7.   Notwithstanding any other provision in this Agreement, Chile may prohibit an investor of the United States or a covered investment from transferring from Chile proceeds of the sale of all or any part of an investment made pursuant to a contract under DL 600 for up to one year after the date that the investor or covered investment transferred funds to Chile to establish the investment.

Annex 10-G
Service of Documents on a Party Under Section B

Chile

Notices and other documents in disputes under Section B shall be served on Chile by delivery to:

Dirección de Asuntos Jurídicos del Ministerio de Relaciones
Exteriores de la República de Chile
Morandé 441 Santiago, Chile

United States

Notices and other documents in disputes under Section B shall be served on the United States by delivery to:

Executive Director (L/EX)
Office of the Legal Adviser
Department of State
Washington, D.C. 20520
United States of America

Annex 10-H
Possibility of a Bilateral Appellate Body/Mechanism

Within three years after the date of entry into force of this Agreement, the Parties shall consider whether to establish a bilateral appellate body or similar mechanism to review awards rendered under Article 10.25 in arbitrations commenced after they establish the appellate body or similar mechanism.

Chapter Eleven

Cross-Border Trade in Services

Article 11.1: Scope and Coverage

1.   This Chapter applies to measures adopted or maintained by a Party affecting cross-border trade in services by service suppliers of the other Party. Such measures include measures affecting:

(a)   the production, distribution, marketing, sale, and delivery of a service;

(b)   the purchase or use of, or payment for, a service;

(c)   the access to and use of distribution, transport, or telecommunications networks and services in connection with the supply of a service;

(d)   the presence in its territory of a service supplier of the other Party; and

(e)   the provision of a bond or other form of financial security as a condition for the supply of a service.

2.   For purposes of this Chapter, "measures adopted or maintained by a Party" means measures adopted or maintained by:

(a)   central, regional, or local governments and authorities; and

(b)   non-governmental bodies in the exercise of powers delegated by central, regional, or local governments or authorities.

3.   Articles 11.4, 11.7, and 11.8 also apply to measures by a Party affecting the supply of a service in its territory by an investor of the other Party as defined in Article 10.27 (Definitions) or a covered investment.[1]

4.   This Chapter does not apply to:

(a)   financial services, as defined in Article 12.19 (Definitions), except as provided in paragraph 3;

(b)   air services, including domestic and international air transportation services, whether scheduled or non-scheduled, and related services in support of air services, other than:

(i)   aircraft repair and maintenance services during which an aircraft is withdrawn from service, and

(ii)   specialty air services;

---

[1] The Parties understand that nothing in this Chapter, including this paragraph, is subject to investor-state dispute settlement pursuant to Section B of Chapter Ten (Investment).

(c)   procurement; or

(d)   subsidies or grants provided by a Party or a state enterprise, including government-supported loans, guarantees, and insurance.

5.   This Chapter does not impose any obligation on a Party with respect to a national of the other Party seeking access to its employment market, or employed on a permanent basis in its territory, and does not confer any right on that national with respect to that access or employment.

6.   This Chapter does not apply to services supplied in the exercise of governmental authority. A "service supplied in the exercise of governmental authority" means any service which is supplied neither on a commercial basis, nor in competition with one or more service suppliers.

Article 11.2: National Treatment

1.   Each Party shall accord to service suppliers[2] of the other Party treatment no less favorable than that it accords, in like circumstances, to its own service suppliers.

2.   The treatment to be accorded by a Party under paragraph 1 means, with respect to a regional level of government, treatment no less favorable than the most favorable treatment accorded, in like circumstances, by that regional level of government to service suppliers of the Party of which it forms a part.

Article 11.3: Most-Favored-Nation Treatment

Each Party shall accord to service suppliers[3] of the other Party treatment no less favorable than that it accords, in like circumstances, to service suppliers of a non-Party.

Article 11.4: Market Access

Neither Party may, either on the basis of a regional subdivision or on the basis of its entire territory, adopt or maintain measures that:

(a)   impose limitations on:

(i)   the number of service suppliers,[4] whether in the form of numerical quotas, monopolies, exclusive service suppliers, or the requirement of an economic needs test,

(ii)   the total value of service transactions or assets in the form of numerical quotas or the requirement of an economic needs test,

---

[2] The Parties understand that "service suppliers" has the same meaning as "services and service suppliers" in Article XVII:1 of GATS.

[3] The Parties understand that "service suppliers" has the same meaning as "services and service suppliers" in Article II:1 of GATS.

[4] The Parties understand that "service suppliers" has the same meaning as "service and service suppliers" in Article XVI of GATS.

     (iii)   the total number of service operations or on the total quantity of services output expressed in terms of designated numerical units in the form of quotas or the requirement of an economic needs test,[5] or

     (iv)   the total number of natural persons that may be employed in a particular service sector or that a service supplier may employ and who are necessary for, and directly related to, the supply of a specific service in the form of a numerical quotas or the requirement of an economic needs test; or

(b)   restrict or require specific types of legal entity or joint venture through which a service supplier may supply a service.

Article 11.5: Local Presence

Neither Party may require a service supplier of the other Party to establish or maintain a representative office or any form of enterprise, or to be resident, in its territory as a condition for the cross-border supply of a service.

Article 11.6: Non-conforming Measures

1.   Articles 11.2, 11.3, 11.4, and 11.5 do not apply to:

     (a)   any existing non-conforming measure that is maintained by a Party at:

          (i)   the central level of government, as set out by that Party in its Schedule to Annex I,

          (ii)   a regional level of government, as set out by that Party in its Schedule to Annex I, or

          (iii)   a local level of government;

     (b)   the continuation or prompt renewal of any non-conforming measure referred to in subparagraph (a); or

     (c)   an amendment to any non-conforming measure referred to in subparagraph (a) to the extent that the amendment does not decrease the conformity of the measure, as it existed immediately before the amendment, with Articles 11.2, 11.3 , 11.4, or 11.5.

2.   Articles 11.2, 11.3, 11.4, and 11.5 do not apply to any measure that a Party adopts or maintains with respect to sectors, sub-sectors, or activities, as set out in its Schedule to Annex II.

3.   Annex 11.6 sets out specific commitments by the Parties.

---

[5] This clause does not cover measures of a Party which limit inputs for the supply of services.

Article 11.7: Transparency in Development and Application of Regulations [6]

Further to Chapter Twenty (Transparency):

(a)   each Party shall maintain or establish appropriate mechanisms for responding to inquiries from interested persons regarding their regulations relating to the subject matter of this Chapter; [7]

(b)   at the time it adopts final regulations relating to the subject matter of this Chapter, each Party shall, to the extent possible, including upon request, address in writing substantive comments received from interested persons with respect to the proposed regulations; and

(c)   to the extent possible, each Party shall allow a reasonable period of time between publication of final regulations and their effective date.

Article 11.8: Domestic Regulation

1.   Where a Party requires authorization for the supply of a service, the competent authorities of that Party shall, within a reasonable period of time after the submission of an application considered complete under domestic laws and regulations, inform the applicant of the decision concerning the application. At the request of the applicant, the competent authorities of the Party shall provide, without undue delay, information concerning the status of the application. This obligation shall not apply to authorization requirements that are within the scope of Article 11.6(2).

2.   With a view to ensuring that measures relating to qualification requirements and procedures, technical standards, and licensing requirements do not constitute unnecessary barriers to trade in services, each Party shall endeavor to ensure, as appropriate for individual sectors, that any such measures that it adopts or maintains are:

(a)   based on objective and transparent criteria, such as competence and the ability to supply the service;

(b)   not more burdensome than necessary to ensure the quality of the service; and

(c)   in the case of licensing procedures, not in themselves a restriction on the supply of the service.

3.   If the results of the negotiations related to Article VI:4 of GATS (or the results of any similar negotiations undertaken in other multilateral fora in which both Parties participate) enter into effect, this Article shall be amended, as appropriate, after consultations between the Parties, to bring those results into effect under this Agreement. The Parties agree to coordinate on such negotiations as appropriate.

---

[6] For greater certainty, "regulations" includes regulations establishing or applying to licensing authorization or criteria.

[7] Chile's implementation of its obligation to establish appropriate mechanisms for small administrative agencies may need to take into account resource and budget constraints.

Article 11.9: Mutual Recognition

1.   For the purposes of the fulfillment, in whole or in part, of its standards or criteria for the authorization, licensing, or certification of services suppliers, and subject to the requirements of paragraph 4, a Party may recognize the education or experience obtained, requirements met, or licenses or certifications granted in a particular country. Such recognition, which may be achieved through harmonization or otherwise, may be based upon an agreement or arrangement with the country concerned or may be accorded autonomously.

2.   Where a Party recognizes, autonomously or by agreement or arrangement, the education or experience obtained, requirements met, or licenses or certifications granted in the territory of a non-Party, nothing in Article 11.3 shall be construed to require the Party to accord such recognition to the education or experience obtained, requirements met, or licenses or certifications granted in the territory of the other Party.

3.   A Party that is a party to an agreement or arrangement of the type referred to in paragraph 1, whether existing or future, shall afford adequate opportunity for the other Party, if the other Party is interested, to negotiate its accession to such an agreement or arrangement or to negotiate comparable ones with it. Where a Party accords recognition autonomously, it shall afford adequate opportunity for the other Party to demonstrate that education, experience, licenses, or certifications obtained or requirements met in that other Party's territory should be recognized.

4.   A Party shall not accord recognition in a manner which would constitute a means of discrimination between countries in the application of its standards or criteria for the authorization, licensing, or certification of services suppliers, or a disguised restriction on trade in services.

5.   Annex 11.9 applies to measures adopted or maintained by a Party relating to the licensing or certification of professional service suppliers as set out in the provisions of that Annex.

Article 11.10: Implementation

The Parties shall consult annually, or as otherwise agreed, to review the implementation of this Chapter and consider other trade in services issues of mutual interest. Among other issues, the Parties will consult with a view to determining the feasibility of removing any remaining citizenship or permanent residency requirement for the licensing or certification of each other's services suppliers. Such consultations will also include consideration of the development of procedures that could contribute to greater transparency of measures described in Article 11.6(1)(c).

Article 11.11: Denial of Benefits

1.   A Party may deny the benefits of this Chapter to a service supplier of the other Party if the service is being supplied by an enterprise owned or controlled by nationals of a non-Party, and the denying Party:

    (a)   does not maintain diplomatic relations with the non-Party; or

(b)   adopts or maintains measures with respect to the non-Party that prohibit transactions with the enterprise or that would be violated or circumvented if the benefits of this Chapter were accorded to the enterprise.

2.   Subject to Article 22.4 (Consultations), a Party may deny the benefits of this Chapter to:

(a)   service suppliers of the other Party where the service is being supplied by an enterprise that is owned or controlled by persons of a non-Party and the enterprise has no substantial business activities in the territory of the other Party, or

(b)   service suppliers of the other Party where the service is being supplied by an enterprise that is owned or controlled by persons of the denying Party and the enterprise has no substantial business activities in the territory of the other Party.

Article 11.12: Definitions

For purposes of this Chapter:

cross-border trade in services or cross-border supply of services means the supply of a service:

(a)   from the territory of one Party into the territory of the other Party;

(b)   in the territory of one Party by a person of that Party to a person of the other Party; or

(c)   by a national of a Party in the territory of the other Party,
but does not include the supply of a service in the territory of a Party by an investor of the other Party as defined in Article 10.27 (Investment-Definitions) or a covered investment;

enterprise means an "enterprise" as defined in Article 2.1 (Definitions of General Application), and a branch of an enterprise;

enterprise of a Party means an enterprise constituted or organized under the law of a Party, and a branch located in the territory of a Party and carrying out business activities there;

professional services means services, the provision of which requires specialized post-secondary education, or equivalent training or experience, and for which the right to practice is granted or restricted by a Party, but does not include services provided by trades-persons or vessel and aircraft crew members;

service supplier of a Party means a person of a Party that seeks to supply or supplies a service; and

specialty air services means any non-transportation air services, such as aerial fire-fighting, sightseeing, spraying, surveying, mapping, photography, parachute jumping, glider towing, and helicopter-lift for logging and construction, and other airborne agricultural, industrial, and inspection services.

Annex 11.6

Express Delivery

1.   The Parties affirm that measures affecting express delivery services are subject to the provisions of this Agreement.

2.   For purposes of this Agreement, express delivery services shall be defined as the expedited collection, transport, delivery, tracking, and maintaining control of documents, printed matter, parcels, and/or other goods throughout the supply of the service.

3.   The Parties express their desire to maintain the level of open market access existing on the date this Agreement is signed.

4.   Chile agrees that it will not impose any restrictions on express delivery services which are not in existence on the date this Agreement is signed. Chile confirms that it has no intention to direct revenues from its postal monopoly to benefit express delivery services as defined in paragraph 2.

Annex 11.9

Professional Services

Section A - General Provisions

Development of Professional Standards

1.   The Parties shall encourage the relevant bodies in their respective territories to develop mutually acceptable standards and criteria for licensing and certification of professional service providers and to provide recommendations on mutual recognition to the Commission.

2.   The standards and criteria referred to in paragraph 1 may be developed with regard to the following matters:

   (a)   education - accreditation of schools or academic programs;

   (b)   examinations - qualifying examinations for licensing, including alternative methods of assessment such as oral examinations and interviews;

   (c)   experience - length and nature of experience required for licensing;

   (d)   conduct and ethics - standards of professional conduct and the nature of disciplinary action for non-conformity with those standards;

   (e)   professional development and re-certification - continuing education and ongoing requirements to maintain professional certification;

   (f)   scope of practice - extent of, or limitations on, permissible activities;

(g)   local knowledge - requirements for knowledge of such matters as local laws, regulations, language, geography, or climate; and

(h)   consumer protection - alternatives to residency requirements, including bonding, professional liability insurance, and client restitution funds, to provide for the protection of consumers.

3.   On receipt of a recommendation referred to in paragraph 1, the Commission shall review the recommendation within a reasonable time to determine whether it is consistent with this Agreement. Based on the Commission's review, each Party shall encourage its respective competent authorities, where appropriate, to implement the recommendation within a mutually agreed time.

Temporary Licensing

4.   Where the Parties agree, each Party shall encourage the relevant bodies in its territory to develop procedures for the temporary licensing of professional service providers of the other Party.

Review

5.   The Commission shall periodically, and at least once every three years, review the implementation of this Section. The Commission shall include within the scope of its review any differences in regulatory approaches between the Parties. Among other issues, a Party may raise issues connected with the development of international standards of relevant international organizations related to professional services.[8]

Section B - Foreign Legal Consultants

1.   Each Party shall, in implementing its obligations and commitments regarding foreign legal consultants as set out in its relevant Schedules to Annex I or II and subject to any non-conforming measures therein, ensure that a national of the other Party is permitted to practice or advise on the law of any country in which that national is authorized to practice as a lawyer.

Consultations With Professional Bodies

2.   Each Party shall consult with its relevant professional bodies to obtain their recommendations on:

(a)   the form of association or partnership between lawyers authorized to practice in its territory and foreign legal consultants;

(b)   the development of standards and criteria for the authorization of foreign legal consultants in conformity with Article 11.9; and

(c)   other matters relating to the provision of foreign legal consultancy services.

---

[8] The term "relevant international organizations" refers to international bodies whose membership is open to the relevant bodies of at least both Parties.

3.   Prior to initiation of consultations under paragraph 7, each Party shall encourage its relevant professional bodies to consult with the relevant professional bodies designated by the other Party regarding the development of joint recommendations on the matters referred to in paragraph 2.

Future Liberalization

4.   Each Party shall establish a work program to develop common procedures throughout its territory for the authorization of foreign legal consultants.

5.   Each Party shall promptly review any recommendation referred to in paragraphs 2 and 3 to ensure its consistency with this Agreement. If the recommendation is consistent with this Agreement, each Party shall encourage its competent authorities to implement the recommendation within one year.

6.   Each Party shall report to the Commission within one year of the date of entry into force of this Agreement, and each year thereafter, on its progress in implementing the work program referred to in paragraph 4.

7.   The Parties shall meet within one year of the date of entry into force of this Agreement with a view to:

(a)   assessing the implementation of paragraphs 2 through 5;

(b)   amending or removing, where appropriate, non-conforming measures on foreign legal consultancy services; and

(c)   assessing further work that may be appropriate regarding foreign legal consultancy services.

Section C - Temporary Licensing of Engineers

1.   The Parties shall meet within one year of the date of entry into force of this Agreement to establish a work program to be undertaken by each Party, in conjunction with its relevant professional bodies, to provide for the temporary licensing in its territory of nationals of the other Party who are licensed as engineers in the territory of that other Party.

2.   To this end, each Party shall consult with its relevant professional bodies to obtain their recommendations on:

(a)   the development of procedures for the temporary licensing of such engineers to permit them to practice their engineering specialties in each jurisdiction in its territory;

(b)   the development of model procedures for adoption by the competent authorities throughout its territory to facilitate the temporary licensing of such engineers;

(c)   the engineering specialties to which priority should be given in developing temporary licensing procedures; and

(d)   other matters relating to the temporary licensing of engineers identified by the Party in such consultations.

3.   Each Party shall request its relevant professional bodies to make recommendations on the matters referred to in paragraph 2 within two years of the date of entry into force of this Agreement.

4.   Each Party shall encourage its relevant professional bodies to meet at the earliest opportunity with the relevant professional bodies of the other Party with a view to cooperating in the development of joint recommendations on the matters referred to in paragraph 2 within two years of the date of entry into force of this Agreement. Each Party shall request an annual report from its relevant professional bodies on the progress achieved in developing those recommendations.

5.   The Parties shall promptly review any recommendation referred to in paragraphs 3 or 4 to ensure its consistency with this Agreement. If the recommendation is consistent with this Agreement, each Party shall encourage its competent authorities to implement the recommendation within one year.

6.   The Commission shall review the implementation of this Section within two years of the date of entry into force of this Section. 7. Appendix 11.9-C applies to the Parties specified therein.

Appendix 11.9-C

Civil Engineers

The rights and obligations of Section C of Annex 11.9 apply to Chile with respect to civil engineers ("ingenieros civiles") and to such other engineering specialties that Chile may designate.

Chapter Twelve

Financial Services

Article 12.1: Scope and Coverage

1.   This Chapter applies to measures adopted or maintained by a Party relating to:

(a)   financial institutions of the other Party;

(b)   investors of the other Party, and investments of such investors, in financial institutions in the Party's territory; and

(c)   cross-border trade in financial services.

2.   Articles 10.8 through 10.12 and 11.11 are hereby incorporated into and made a part of this Chapter. Section B of Chapter Ten (Investment) is hereby incorporated into and made a part of this Chapter solely for breaches by a Party of Articles 10.8 through 10.11, as incorporated into this Chapter.[1] No other provision of Chapter Ten (Investment) or Chapter Eleven (Cross Border Trade in Services) shall apply to a measure described in paragraph 1.

3.   This Chapter does not apply to measures adopted or maintained by a Party relating to:

(a)   activities or services forming part of a public retirement plan or statutory system of social security; or

(b)   activities or services conducted for the account or with the guarantee or using the financial resources of the Party, including its public entities, except that this Chapter shall apply if a Party allows any of the activities or services referred to in subparagraphs (a) or (b) to be conducted by its financial institutions in competition with a public entity or a financial institution.

Article 12.2: National Treatment

1.   Each Party shall accord to investors of the other Party treatment no less favorable than that it accords to its own investors, in like circumstances, with respect to the establishment, acquisition, expansion, management, conduct, operation, and sale or other disposition of financial institutions and investments in financial institutions in its territory.

2.   Each Party shall accord to financial institutions of the other Party and to investments of investors of the other Party in financial institutions treatment no less favorable than that it accords to its own financial institutions, and to investments of its own investors in financial institutions, in like circumstances, with respect to the establishment, acquisition, expansion, management, conduct, operation, and sale or other disposition of financial institutions and investments.

3.   For purposes of the national treatment obligations in Article 12.5(1), a Party shall accord to cross-border financial service suppliers of the other Party treatment no less favorable than that it accords to its own financial service suppliers, in like circumstances, with respect to the supply of the relevant service.

Article 12.3: Most-Favored-Nation Treatment

1.   Each Party shall accord to investors of the other Party, financial institutions of the other Party, investments of investors in financial institutions, and cross-border financial service suppliers of the other Party treatment no less favorable than that it accords to the investors, financial institutions, investments of investors in financial institutions and crossborder financial service suppliers of a non-Party, in like circumstances.

2.   A Party may recognize prudential measures of a non-Party in the application of measures covered by this Chapter. Such recognition may be:

---

[1] For greater certainty, the provisions of Chapter Ten (Investment) hereby incorporated include, are subject to, and shall be interpreted in conformity with, Annexes 10-A through 10-H of that Chapter, as applicable.

(a)   accorded unilaterally;

(b)   achieved through harmonization or other means; or

(c)   based upon an agreement or arrangement with the non-Party.

3.   A Party according recognition of prudential measures under paragraph 2 shall provide adequate opportunity to the other Party to demonstrate that circumstances exist in which there are or will be equivalent regulation, oversight, implementation of regulation, and, if appropriate, procedures concerning the sharing of information between the Parties.

4.   Where a Party accords recognition of prudential measures under paragraph 2(c) and the circumstances set out in paragraph 3 exist, the Party shall provide adequate opportunity to the other Party to negotiate accession to the agreement or arrangement, or to negotiate a comparable agreement or arrangement.

Article 12.4: Market Access for Financial Institutions

Neither Party may, with respect to investors of the other Party, either on the basis of a regional subdivision or on the basis of its entire territory adopt or maintain measures that:

(a)   impose limitations on:

(i)   the number of financial institutions whether in the form of numerical quotas, monopolies, exclusive financial service suppliers, or the requirements of an economic needs test,

(ii)   the total value of financial service transactions or assets in the form of numerical quotas or the requirement of an economic needs test,

(iii)   the total number of financial service operations or on the total quantity of financial services output expressed in terms of designated numerical units in the form of quotas or the requirement of an economic needs test, or

(iv)   the total number of natural persons that may be employed in a particular financial service sector or that a financial institution may employ and who are necessary for, and directly related to, the supply of a specific financial service in the form of a numerical quota or the requirement of an economic needs test; or

(b)   restrict or require specific types of legal entity or joint venture through which a financial institution may supply a service.

Article 12.5: Cross-Border Trade

1.   Each Party shall permit, under terms and conditions that accord national treatment, cross-border financial service suppliers of the other Party to supply the financial services specified in Annex 12.5.

2.   Each Party shall permit persons located in its territory, and its nationals wherever located, to purchase financial services from cross-border financial service suppliers of the other Party

located in the territory of the other Party. This obligation does not require a Party to permit such suppliers to do business or solicit in its territory. Each Party may define "doing business" and "solicitation" for purposes of this Article as long as such definitions are not inconsistent with the obligations of paragraph 1.

3.   Without prejudice to other means of prudential regulation of cross-border trade in financial services, a Party may require the registration of cross-border financial service suppliers of the other Party and of financial instruments.

Article 12.6: New Financial Services[2]

1.   Each Party shall permit a financial institution of the other Party, on request or notification to the relevant regulator, where required, to supply any new financial service that the first Party would permit its own financial institutions, in like circumstances, to supply under its domestic law, provided that the introduction of the financial service does not require the Party to adopt a new law or modify an existing law.

2.   A Party may determine the institutional and juridical form through which the new financial service may be supplied and may require authorization for the supply of the service. Where a Party would permit the new financial service and authorization is required, the decision shall be made within a reasonable time and authorization may only be refused for prudential reasons.

Article 12.7: Treatment of Certain Information

Nothing in this Chapter requires a Party to furnish or allow access to:

(a)   information related to the financial affairs and accounts of individual customers of financial institutions or cross-border financial service suppliers; or

(b)   any confidential information, the disclosure of which would impede law enforcement or otherwise be contrary to the public interest or prejudice legitimate commercial interests of particular enterprises.

Article 12.8: Senior Management and Boards of Directors

1.   Neither Party may require financial institutions of the other Party to engage individuals of any particular nationality as senior managerial or other essential personnel.

2.   Neither Party may require that more than a minority of the board of directors of a financial institution of the other Party be composed of nationals of the Party, persons residing in the territory of the Party, or a combination thereof.

Article 12.9: Non-Conforming Measures

1.   Articles 12.2 through 12.5 and 12.8 and Section A of Annex 12.9 do not apply to:

---

[2] The Parties understand that nothing in Article 12.6 prevents a financial institution of a Party from applying to the other Party to consider authorizing the supply of a financial service that is supplied within neither Party's territory. Such application shall be subject to the domestic law of the Party to which the application is made and, for greater certainty, shall not be subject to the obligations of Article 12.6.

    (a)   any existing non-conforming measure that is maintained by a Party at:

              (i)   the central level of government, as set out by that Party in its Schedule to Annex III,

              (ii)   a regional level of government, as set out by that Party in its Schedule to Annex III, or

              (iii)   a local level of government;

    (b)   the continuation or prompt renewal of any non-conforming measure referred to in subparagraph (a); or

    (c)   an amendment to any non-conforming measure referred to in subparagraph (a) to the extent that the amendment does not decrease the conformity of the measure, as it existed immediately before the amendment, with Articles 12.2, 12.3, 12.4, and 12.8 and Section A of Annex 12.9.

2.   Articles 12.2 through 12.5 and 12.8 and Section A of Annex 12.9 do not apply to any measure that a Party adopts or maintains with respect to sectors, subsectors, or activities, as set out in its Schedule to Annex III.

3.   Annex 12.9 sets out certain specific commitments by each Party.

4.   Where a Party has set out in its Schedule to Annexes I and II a measure that does not conform to Articles 10.2, 10.3, 11.2, 11.3, or 11.4 pursuant to paragraphs 1 and 2 of Articles 10.7 and 11.6, that measure shall be deemed to constitute a non-conforming measure, pursuant to paragraphs 1 and 2 of this Article, with respect to Article 12.2, Article 12.3, or Article 12.4, or Section A of Annex 12.9, as the case may be, to the extent that the measure, sector, sub-sector, or activity set out in the Schedule of non-conforming measures is covered by this Chapter.

Article 12.10: Exceptions

1.   Notwithstanding any other provision of this Chapter or of Chapters Ten (Investment), Eleven (Cross-Border Trade in Services), Thirteen (Telecommunications), Fifteen (Electronic Commerce), and Sixteen (Competition Policy, Designated Monopolies, and State Enterprises), including specifically Article 13.16 (Telecommunications - Relationship to Other Chapters), a Party shall not be prevented from adopting or maintaining measures for prudential reasons,[3] including for the protection of investors, depositors, policy holders, or persons to whom a fiduciary duty is owed by a financial institution or crossborder financial service supplier, or to ensure the integrity and stability of the financial system. Where such measures do not conform with the provisions of this Agreement referred to in this paragraph, they shall not be used as a means of avoiding the Party's commitments or obligations under such provisions.[4]

---

[3] It is understood that the term "prudential reasons" includes the maintenance of the safety, soundness, integrity, or financial responsibility of individual financial institutions or cross-border financial service suppliers.

[4] The Parties understand that a Party may take measures for prudential reasons through regulatory or administrative authorities, in addition to those who have regulatory responsibilities with respect to financial institutions, such as ministries or departments of labor.

2.   Nothing in this Chapter or Chapters Ten (Investment), Eleven (Cross-Border Trade in Services), Thirteen (Telecommunications), Fifteen (Electronic Commerce), and Sixteen (Competition Policy, Designated Monopolies, and State Enterprises), including specifically Article 13.16 (Telecommunications – Relationship to Other Chapters), applies to nondiscriminatory measures of general application taken by any public entity in pursuit of monetary and related credit policies or exchange rate policies. This paragraph shall not effect a Party's obligations under Article 10.5 (Performance Requirements) with respect to measures covered by Chapter Ten (Investment) or Article 10.8 (Transfers).

3.   Notwithstanding Article 10.8 (Transfers), as incorporated into this Chapter, a Party may prevent or limit transfers by a financial institution or cross-border financial service supplier to, or for the benefit of, an affiliate of or person related to such institution or supplier, through the equitable, non-discriminatory and good faith application of measures relating to maintenance of the safety, soundness, integrity, or financial responsibility of financial institutions or cross-border financial service suppliers. This paragraph does not prejudice any other provision of this Agreement that permits a Party to restrict transfers.

4.   For greater certainty, nothing in this Chapter shall be construed to prevent the adoption or enforcement by a Party of measures necessary to secure compliance with laws or regulations that are not inconsistent with this Chapter, including those relating to the prevention of deceptive and fraudulent practices or to deal with the effects of a default on financial services contracts, subject to the requirement that such measures are not applied in a manner which would constitute a means of arbitrary or unjustifiable discrimination between countries where like conditions prevail, or a disguised restriction on investment in financial institutions or cross-border trade in financial services as covered by this Chapter.

Article 12.11: Transparency

1.   The Parties recognize that transparent regulations and policies and reasonable, objective, and impartial administration governing the activities of financial institutions and financial service suppliers are important in facilitating both access of financial institutions and financial service suppliers to, and their operations in, each other's markets.

2.   In lieu of Article 20.2 (Publication), each Party shall, to the extent practicable:

(a)   publish in advance any regulations of general application relating to the subject matter of this Chapter that it proposes to adopt; and

(b)   provide interested persons and the other Party a reasonable opportunity to comment on such proposed regulations.

3.   Each Party's regulatory authorities shall make available to interested persons their requirements, including any documentation required, for completing applications relating to the supply of financial services.

4.   On the request of an applicant, the regulatory authority shall inform the applicant of the status of its application. If such authority requires additional information from the applicant, it shall notify the applicant without undue delay.

5.   A regulatory authority shall make an administrative decision on a completed application of an investor in a financial institution, a financial institution, or a cross-border financial service supplier of the other Party relating to the supply of a financial service within 120 days, and shall promptly notify the applicant of the decision. An application shall not be considered complete until all relevant hearings are held and all necessary information is received. Where it is not practicable for a decision to be made within 120 days, the regulatory authority shall notify the applicant without undue delay and shall endeavor to make the decision within a reasonable time thereafter.

6.   Each Party shall maintain or establish appropriate mechanisms that will respond to inquiries from interested persons regarding measures of general application covered by this Chapter.

7.   Each Party shall ensure that the rules of general application adopted or maintained by self-regulatory organizations of the Party are promptly published or otherwise made available in such a manner as to enable interested persons to become acquainted with them.

8.   To the extent practicable, each Party should allow reasonable time between publication of final regulations and their effective date.

9.   At the time it adopts final regulations, a Party should, to the extent practicable, address in writing substantive comments received from interested persons with respect to the proposed regulations.

Article 12.12: Self-Regulatory Organizations

Where a Party requires a financial institution or a cross-border financial service supplier of the other Party to be a member of, participate in, or have access to, a self regulatory organization to provide a financial service in or into the territory of that Party, the Party shall ensure observance of the obligations of Articles 12.2 and 12.3 by such self regulatory organization.

Article 12.13: Payment and Clearing Systems

Under terms and conditions that accord national treatment, each Party shall grant to financial institutions of the other Party established in its territory access to payment and clearing systems operated by public entities, and to official funding and refinancing facilities available in the normal course of ordinary business. This paragraph is not intended to confer access to the Party's lender of last resort facilities.

Article 12.14: Expedited Availability of Insurance Services

The Parties recognize the importance of maintaining and developing regulatory procedures to expedite the offering of insurance services by licensed suppliers.

Article 12.15: Financial Services Committee

1.   The Parties hereby establish the Financial Services Committee. The principal representative of each Party shall be an official of the Party's authority responsible for financial services set out in Annex 12.15.

2.   In accordance with Article 21.1(2)(d) (The Free Trade Commission), the Committee shall:

(a)   supervise the implementation of this Chapter and its further elaboration;

(b)   consider issues regarding financial services that are referred to it by a Party; and

(c)   participate in the dispute settlement procedures in accordance with Articles 12.17 and 12.18.

3.   The Committee shall meet annually, or as otherwise agreed, to assess the functioning of this Agreement as it applies to financial services. The Committee shall inform the Commission of the results of each meeting.

Article 12.16: Consultations

1.   A Party may request in writing consultations with the other Party regarding any matter arising under this Agreement that affects financial services. The other Party shall give sympathetic consideration to the request. The Parties shall report the results of their consultations to the Committee.

2.   Officials from the authorities specified in Annex 12.15 shall participate in the consultations under this Article.

3.   Nothing in this Article shall be construed to require regulatory authorities participating in consultations under paragraph 1 to disclose information or take any action that would interfere with specific regulatory, supervisory, administrative, or enforcement matters.

4.   Nothing in this Article shall be construed to require a Party to derogate from its relevant law regarding sharing of information among financial regulators or the requirements of an agreement or arrangement between financial authorities of the Parties.

Article 12.17: Dispute Settlement

1.   Chapter Twenty-Two (Dispute Settlement) applies as modified by this Article to the settlement of disputes arising under this Chapter.

2.   For purposes of Article 22.4 (Consultations), consultations held under Article 12.16 with respect to a measure or matter shall be deemed to constitute consultations under Article 22.4(1), unless the Parties otherwise agree. Upon initiation of consultations, the Parties shall provide information and give confidential treatment under Article 22.4(4)(b) to the information exchanged. If the matter has not been resolved within 45 days after commencing consultations under Article 12.16 or 90 days after the delivery of the request for consultations under Article 12.16, whichever is earlier, the complaining Party may request in writing the establishment of an arbitral panel. The Parties shall report the results of their consultations to the Commission.

3.   The Parties shall establish by January 1, 2005, and maintain a roster of up to 10 individuals who are willing and able to serve as financial services panelists, up to four of whom shall be non-Party nationals. The roster members shall be appointed by mutual agreement of the

Parties, and may be reappointed. Once established, a roster shall remain in effect for a minimum of three years, and shall remain in effect thereafter until the Parties constitute a new roster.

4.   Financial services roster members shall:

(a)   have expertise or experience in financial services law or practice, which may include the regulation of financial institutions;

(b)   be chosen strictly on the basis of objectivity, reliability, and sound judgment;

(c)   be independent of, and not affiliated with or take instructions from, either Party; and

(d)   comply with a code of conduct to be established by the Commission.

5.   Where a Party claims that a dispute arises under this Chapter, Article 22.9 (Panel Selection) shall apply, except that, unless the Parties otherwise agree, the panel shall be composed entirely of panelists meeting the qualifications in paragraph 4.

6.   In any dispute where a panel finds a measure to be inconsistent with the obligations of this Agreement and the measure affects:

(a)   only the financial services sector, the complaining Party may suspend benefits only in the financial services sector;

(b)   the financial services sector and any other sector, the complaining Party may suspend benefits in the financial services sector that have an effect equivalent to the effect of the measure in the Party's financial services sector; or

(c)   only a sector other than the financial services sector, the complaining Party may not suspend benefits in the financial services sector.

Article 12.18: Investment Disputes in Financial Services

1.   Where an investor of one Party submits a claim under Article 10.15 (Submission of a Claim to Arbitration) to arbitration under Section B of Chapter Ten (Investment) against the other Party and the respondent invokes Article 12.10, on request of the respondent, the tribunal shall refer the matter in writing to the Committee for a decision. The tribunal may not proceed pending receipt of a decision or report under this Article.

2.   In a referral pursuant to paragraph 1, the Committee shall decide the issue of whether and to what extent Article 12.10 is a valid defense to the claim of the investor. The Committee shall transmit a copy of its decision to the tribunal and to the Commission. The decision shall be binding on the tribunal.

3.   Where the Committee has not decided the issue within 60 days of the receipt of the referral under paragraph 1, the respondent or the Party of the claimant may request the establishment of an arbitral panel under Article 22.6 (Request for an Arbitral Panel). The panel shall be constituted in accordance with Article 12.17. Further to Article 22.13 (Final Report), the

panel shall transmit its final report to the Committee and to the tribunal. The report shall be binding on the tribunal.

4.   Where no request for the establishment of a panel pursuant to paragraph 3 has been made within 10 days of the expiration of the 60-day period referred to in paragraph 3, the tribunal may proceed to decide the matter.

Article 12.19: Definitions

For purposes of this Chapter:

cross-border financial service supplier of a Party means a person of a Party that is engaged in the business of supplying a financial service within the territory of the Party and that seeks to supply or supplies a financial service through the cross-border supply of such services;

cross-border trade in financial services or cross-border supply of financial services means the supply of a financial service:

(a)   from the territory of one Party into the territory of the other Party,

(b)   in the territory of a Party by a person of that Party to a person of the other Party, or

(c)   by a national of a Party in the territory of the other Party, but does not include the supply of a service in the territory of a Party by an investment in that territory;

financial institution means any financial intermediary or other enterprise that is authorized to do business and regulated or supervised as a financial institution under the law of the Party in whose territory it is located;

financial institution of the other Party means a financial institution, including a branch, located in the territory of a Party that is controlled by persons of the other Party;

financial service means any service of a financial nature. Financial services include all insurance and insurance-related services, and all banking and other financial services (excluding insurance), as well as services incidental or auxiliary to a service of a financial nature. Financial services include the following activities:

Insurance and insurance-related services

(a)   Direct insurance (including co-insurance):

(i) life

(ii) non-life

(b)   Reinsurance and retrocession;

(c)   Insurance intermediation, such as brokerage and agency;

(d)   Service auxiliary to insurance, such as consultancy, actuarial, risk assessment, and claim settlement services.

Banking and other financial services (excluding insurance)

(e)   Acceptance of deposits and other repayable funds from the public;

(f)   Lending of all types, including consumer credit, mortgage credit, factoring and financing of commercial transactions;

(g)   Financial leasing;

(h)   All payment and money transmission services, including credit, charge and debit cards, travelers checks, and bankers drafts;

(i)   Guarantees and commitments;

(j)   Trading for own account or for account of customers, whether on an exchange, in an over-the-counter market, or otherwise, the following:

    (i)   money market instruments (including checks, bills, certificates of deposits);

    (ii)   foreign exchange;

    (iii)   derivative products including, futures and options;

    (iv)   exchange rate and interest rate instruments, including products such as swaps, forward rate agreements;

    (v)   transferable securities;

    (vi)   other negotiable instruments and financial assets, including bullion;

(k)   Participation in issues of all kinds of securities, including underwriting and placement as agent (whether publicly or privately) and provision of services related to such issues;

(l)   Money broking;

(m)   Asset management, such as cash or portfolio management, all forms of collective investment management, pension fund management, custodial, depository, and trust services;

(n)   Settlement and clearing services for financial assets, including securities, derivative products, and other negotiable instruments;

(o)   Provision and transfer of financial information, and financial data processing and related software by suppliers of other financial services;

(p)   Advisory, intermediation, and other auxiliary financial services on all the activities listed in subparagraphs (e) through (o), including credit reference and analysis, investment and portfolio research and advice, advice on acquisitions and on corporate restructuring and strategy;

financial service supplier of a Party means a person of a Party that is engaged in the business of supplying a financial service within the territory of that Party;

investment means "investment" as defined in Article 10.27 (Definitions), except that, with respect to "loans" and "debt instruments" referred to in that Article:

(a)   a loan to or debt instrument issued by a financial institution is an investment only where it is treated as regulatory capital by the Party in whose territory the financial institution is located; and

(b)   a loan granted by or debt instrument owned by a financial institution, other than a loan to or debt instrument of a financial institution referred to in subparagraph (a), is not an investment; for greater certainty, a loan granted by or debt instrument owned by a cross-border financial service supplier, other than a loan to or debt instrument issued by a financial institution, is an investment if such loan or debt instrument meets the criteria for investments set out in Article 10.27 (Definitions);

investor of a Party means a Party or state enterprise thereof, or a person of a Party, that attempts to make, is making, or has made an investment in the territory of the other Party; provided, however, that a natural person who is a dual national shall be deemed to be exclusively a national of the State of his/her dominant and effective nationality;

new financial service means a financial service not supplied in the Party's territory that is supplied within the territory of the other Party, and includes any new form of delivery of a financial service or the sale of a financial product that is not sold in the Party's territory;

person of a Party means "person of a Party" as defined in Article 2.1 (General Definitions) and, for greater certainty, does not include a branch of an enterprise of a non-Party;

public entity means a central bank or monetary authority of a Party, or any financial institution owned or controlled by a Party;

self-regulatory organization means any non-governmental body, including any securities or futures exchange or market, clearing agency, other organization or association, that exercises its own or delegated regulatory or supervisory authority over financial service suppliers or financial institutions; and

tribunal means an arbitration tribunal established under Article 10.18 (Selection of Arbitrators).

Annex 12.5

Cross-Border Trade

Insurance and insurance-related services

1.   For the United States, Article 12.5(1) applies to the cross-border supply of or trade in financial services as defined in subparagraph (a) of the definition of cross-border supply of financial services in Article 12.19 with respect to:

(a)   insurance of risks relating to:

      (i)   maritime shipping and commercial aviation and space launching and freight (including satellites), with such insurance to cover any or all of the following: the goods being transported, the vehicle transporting the goods, and any liability arising therefrom; and

      (ii)   goods in international transit;

   (b)   reinsurance and retrocession, services auxiliary to insurance as described in subparagraph (d) of the definition of financial service, and insurance intermediation such as brokerage and agency as described in subparagraph

   (c)   of the definition of financial service.

2.   For the United States, Article 12.5(1) applies to the cross-border supply of or trade in financial services as defined in subparagraph (c) of the definition of cross-border supply of financial services in Article 12.19 with respect to insurance services.

3.   For Chile, Article 12.5(1) applies to the cross-border supply of or trade in financial services as defined in subparagraph (a) of the definition of cross-border supply of financial services in Article 12.19 with respect to:

   (a)   insurance of risk relating to:

      (i)   international maritime transport, international commercial aviation with such insurance to cover any or all of the following: the goods being transported, the vehicle transporting the goods, and any liability deriving therefrom; and

      (ii)   goods in international transit.

   (b)   brokerage of insurance of risks relating to subparagraph (a)(i) and (a)(ii).

   (c)   reinsurance and retrocession; reinsurance brokerage; and consultancy, actuarial, and risk assessment.

4.   Chile's commitments regarding sale and brokerage of insurance for international maritime transport, international commercial aviation, and goods in international transit shall apply one year after the entry into force of this Agreement or when Chile has made and implemented the necessary amendments to its pertinent legislation, whichever occurs first.

Banking and other financial services (excluding insurance)

5.   For the United States, Article 12.5(1) applies with respect to the provision and transfer of financial information and financial data processing as described in subparagraph (o) of the definition of financial service and advisory and other auxiliary financial services, excluding intermediation, relating to banking and other financial services as described in subparagraph (p) of the definition of financial service.

6.   For Chile, Article 12.5(1) applies with respect to:

(a)   provision and transfer of financial information as described in subparagraph (o) of the definition of financial service.

(b)   financial data processing as described in subparagraph (o) of the definition of financial service, subject to prior authorization from the relevant regulator, as required.[5]

(c)   advisory and other auxiliary financial services, excluding intermediation and credit reference and analysis, relating to banking and other financial services as described in subparagraph (p) of the definition of financial service.

Notwithstanding subparagraph (c), in the event that after the date of entry into force of this Agreement Chile allows credit reference and analysis to be supplied by cross-border financial service suppliers, it shall accord national treatment (as specified in Article 12.2(3)) to cross-border financial service suppliers of the United States. Nothing in this commitment shall be construed to prevent Chile from subsequently restricting or prohibiting the supply of credit reference and analysis services by cross-border financial service suppliers.

7.   It is understood that a Party's commitments on cross-border investment advisory services shall not, in and of themselves, be construed to require the Party to permit the public offering of securities (as defined under its relevant law) in the territory of the Party by cross-border suppliers of the other Party who supply or seek to supply such investment advisory services. A Party may subject the cross-border suppliers of investment advisory services to regulatory and registration requirements.

Annex 12.9

Specific Commitments

Section A: Right of Establishment with Respect to Certain Financial Services

1.   In lieu of Article 12.4 with respect to banking and other financial services (excluding insurance):

(a)   Each Party shall permit an investor of the other Party

(i)   that does not own or control a financial institution in the Party's territory to establish in that territory a financial institution permitted to supply financial services that such an institution may supply under the domestic law of the Party at the time of establishment, without the imposition of numerical restrictions, and

(ii)   that owns or controls a financial institution in the Party's territory to establish in that territory such additional financial institutions as may be necessary to permit the supply of the full range of financial services

---

[5] It is understood that where the financial information or financial data processing referred to in subparagraphs (a) and (b) involve personal data, the treatment of such personal data shall be in accordance with Chilean law regulating the protection of such data.

allowed under the domestic law of the Party at the time of establishment of the additional financial institutions.

The right of establishment shall include the acquisition of existing entities.

(b)   Neither Party may restrict or require specific types of juridical form with respect to the initial financial institution that the investor seeks to establish pursuant to subparagraph (a)(i).

(c)   Except with respect to the imposition of numerical or juridical form restrictions on establishment of the initial financial institution described in subparagraph (a)(i), a Party may, consistent with Article 12.2, impose terms and conditions on establishment of additional financial institutions described in subparagraph (a)(ii) and determine the institutional and juridical form through which particular permitted financial services or activities are supplied.

(d)   A Party may, consistent with Article 12.2, prohibit a particular financial service or activity.[6]

2.   For purposes of this Annex:

(a)   an "investor of the other Party" means an investor of the other Party engaged in the business of providing banking and other financial services (excluding insurance) in the territory of that Party.

(b)   "numerical restrictions" means limitations imposed, either on the basis of a regional subdivision or on the basis of the entire territory of the Party, on the number of financial institutions whether in the form of numerical quotas, monopolies, exclusive service suppliers, or the requirements of an economic needs test.

3.   Notwithstanding the inclusion of the non-conforming measures of Chile in Annex III, Section II, referring to social services, Chile, with respect to the establishment by an investor of the United States of an Administradora de Fondos de Pensiones under Decreto Ley 3.500, shall:

(a)   apply subparagraph 1(a) of Section A of this Annex, and

(b)   not apply an economic needs test.

No other modification of the effect of the non-conforming measures referring to social services is intended or shall be construed under this paragraph.

4.   The specific commitments of the United States under paragraph 1 are subject to the headnotes and non-conforming measures set forth in Sections A and B of Annex III with respect to banking and other financial services (excluding insurance).

---

[6] The Parties understand that a Party may not prohibit all financial services or a complete financial services subsector such as banking.

5.   The specific commitments of Chile under paragraphs 1 and 3 are subject to the headnotes and non-conforming measures set forth in Annex III of Chile with respect to banking and other financial services (excluding insurance).

Section B: Voluntary Savings Plans; Non-Discriminatory Treatment of U.S. Investors

1.   Notwithstanding the inclusion of the non-conforming measures of Chile in Annex III, Section II, referring to social services, with respect to voluntary savings pension plans established under Ley 19.768, Chile shall extend the obligations of Article 12.2(1) and (2) and of Article 12.3 to financial institutions of the United States, investors of the United States, and investments of such investors in financial institutions established in Chile. The specific commitment contained in this paragraph shall enter into force by March 1, 2005.

2.   Notwithstanding the inclusion of the nonconforming measures of Chile in Annex III, Section II, referring to social services, Chile, as required by its domestic law, shall not establish arbitrary differences with respect to U.S. investors in Administradoras de Fondos de Pensiones under Decreto Ley 3.500.

Section C: Portfolio Management

1.   Each Party shall allow a financial institution (other than a trust company or insurance company), organized outside its territory, to provide investment advice and portfolio management services, excluding (1) custodial services, (2) trustee services, and (3) execution services that are not related to managing a collective investment scheme, to a collective investment scheme located in the Party's territory. This commitment is subject to Article 12.1 and to the provisions of Article 12.5(3) regarding the right to require registration, without prejudice to other means of prudential regulation.

2.   Notwithstanding paragraph 1, a Party may require the collective investment scheme located in the Party's territory to retain ultimate responsibility for the management of the collective investment scheme or the funds that it manages.

3.   For purposes of paragraphs 1 and 2, collective investment scheme means:

(a)   in the United States, an investment company registered with the Securities and Exchange Commission under the Investment Company Act of 1940; and

(b)   in Chile, the following fund management companies subject to supervision by the Superintendencia de Valores y Seguros:

(i)   Compañías Administradoras de Fondos Mutuos (Decreto Ley 1.328 de 1976);

(ii)   Compañías Administradoras de Fondos de Inversión (Ley 18.815 de 1989);

(iii)   Compañías Administradoras de Fondos de Inversión de Capital Extranjero (Ley 18.657 de 1987);

(iv)   Compañías Administradoras de Fondos para la Vivienda (Ley 18.281 de 1993); and

(v)   Compañías Administradoras Generales de Fondos (Ley 18.045 de 1981).

Section D: Expedited Availability of Insurance Services

Each Party should endeavor to maintain existing opportunities or may wish to consider policies or procedures such as: not requiring product approval for insurance other than sold to individuals or compulsory insurance; allowing introduction of products unless those products are disapproved within a reasonable period of time; and not imposing limitations on the number or frequency of product introductions. This Section does not apply to the specific category of Chilean government-supported insurance programs, such as climate insurance.

Section E: Insurance Branching

1.   Notwithstanding the inclusion of the nonconforming measures of Chile in Annex III, Section II, referring to insurance market access, excluding any portion of those nonconforming measures referring to financial conglomerates and social services, no later than four years after the date of entry into force of this Agreement, Chile shall allow U.S. insurance suppliers to establish in its territory through branches. Chile may choose how to regulate branches, including their characteristics, structure, relationship to their parent company, capital requirements, technical reserves, and obligations regarding risk patrimony and their investments.[7]

2.   Recognizing the principles of federalism under the U.S. Constitution, the history of state regulation of insurance in the United States, and the McCarran-Ferguson Act, the United States will work with the National Association of Insurance Commissioners (NAIC) in its review of those states that do not allow initial entry of a non-US insurance company as a branch to supply life, accident, health (excluding worker's compensation) insurance, non-life insurance, or reinsurance and retrocession to determine whether such entry could be provided in the future. Those states are Arkansas, Arizona, Connecticut, Georgia, Hawaii (branching allowed for reinsurance), Kansas, Maryland, Minnesota, Nebraska, New Jersey, North Carolina, Pennsylvania, Tennessee, Vermont, and Wyoming.

Annex 12.11

The Parties recognize that Chile's implementation of the obligations of paragraphs 2 and 9 of Article 12.11 may require legislative and regulatory changes. Chile shall implement the

---

[7] The Parties understand that for this purpose, Chile may establish the following requirements among others:

(a)   that the capital and reserves that foreign insurance companies assign to their branches must be effectively transferred and converted into domestic currency in conformity with Chilean law;
(b)   that the increases of capital and reserves that do not come from capitalization of other reserves will have the same treatment as initial capital and reserves;
(c)   that in the transactions between a branch and its parent or other related companies each shall be considered as independent entities;
(d) that the branch owners or shareholders meet the solvency and integrity requirements established in Chile's insurance legislation;
(e)   that branches of foreign insurance companies that operate in Chile may transfer liquid profits only if they do not have an investment deficit in their technical reserves and risk patrimony, nor a deficit of risk patrimony.

obligations of these paragraphs no later than two years after the date of entry into force of this Agreement.

Annex 12.15

Authorities Responsible for Financial Services

The authority of each Party responsible for financial services shall be:

(a)   for Chile, the Ministerio de Hacienda; and

(b)   for the United States, the Department of the Treasury for banking and other financial services and the Office of the United States Trade Representative, in coordination with the Department of Commerce and other agencies, for insurance services.

Chapter Seventeen

Intellectual Property Rights

The Parties,

Desiring to reduce distortions and impediments to trade between the Parties;

Desiring to enhance the intellectual property systems of the two Parties to account for the latest technological developments and to ensure that measures and procedures to enforce intellectual property rights do not themselves become barriers to legitimate trade;

Desiring to promote greater efficiency and transparency in the administration of intellectual property systems of the Parties;

Desiring to build on the foundations established in existing international agreements in the field of intellectual property, including the World Trade Organization (WTO) Agreement on Trade-Related Aspects of Intellectual Property Rights (TRIPS Agreement) and affirming the rights and obligations set forth in the TRIPS Agreement;

Recognizing the principles set out in the Declaration on the TRIPS Agreement on Public Health, adopted on November 14, 2001, by the WTO at the Fourth WTO Ministerial Conference, held in Doha, Qatar;

Emphasizing that the protection and enforcement of intellectual property rights is a fundamental principle of this Chapter that helps promote technological innovation as well as the transfer and dissemination of technology to the mutual advantage of technology producers and users, and that encourages the development of social and economic well-being;

Convinced of the importance of efforts to encourage private and public investment for research, development, and innovation;

Recognizing that the business community of each Party should be encouraged to participate in programs and initiatives for research, development, innovation, and the transfer of technology implemented by the other Party;

Recognizing the need to achieve a balance between the rights of right holders and the legitimate interests of users and the community with regard to protected works;

Agree as follows:

Article 17.1: General Provisions

1.   Each Party shall give effect to the provisions of this Chapter and may, but shall not be obliged to, implement in its domestic law more extensive protection than is required by this Chapter, provided that such protection does not contravene the provisions of this Chapter.

2.   Before January 1, 2007, each Party shall ratify or accede to the Patent Cooperation Treaty (1984).

3.   Before January 1, 2009, each Party shall ratify or accede to:

   (a)   the International Convention for the Protection of New Varieties of Plants (1991);

   (b)   the Trademark Law Treaty (1994); and

   (c)   the Convention Relating to the Distribution of Programme-Carrying Signals Transmitted by Satellite (1974).

4.   Each Party shall undertake reasonable efforts to ratify or accede to the following agreements in a manner consistent with its domestic law:

   (a)   the Patent Law Treaty (2000);

   (b)   the Hague Agreement Concerning the International Registration of Industrial Designs (1999); and

   (c)   the Protocol Relating to the Madrid Agreement Concerning the International Registration of Marks (1989).

5.   Nothing in this Chapter concerning intellectual property rights shall derogate from the obligations and rights of one Party with respect to the other by virtue of the TRIPS Agreement or multilateral intellectual property agreements concluded or administered under the auspices of the World Intellectual Property Organization (WIPO).

6.   In respect of all categories of intellectual property covered in this Chapter, each Party shall accord to persons of the other Party treatment no less favorable than it accords to its own persons with regard to the protection[1] and enjoyment of such intellectual property rights and any

---

[1] For purposes of paragraphs 6 and 7, "protection" shall include matters affecting the availability, acquisition, scope, maintenance, and enforcement of intellectual property rights as well as matters affecting the use of intellectual property rights specifically covered by this Chapter. For purposes of paragraphs 6 and 7, "protection"

benefits derived from such rights. With respect to secondary uses of phonograms by means of analog communications and free over-the-air radio broadcasting, however, a Party may limit the rights of the performers and producers of the other Party to the rights its persons are accorded within the jurisdiction of the other Party.

7.   Each Party may derogate from paragraph 6 in relation to its judicial and administrative procedures, including the designation of an address for service or the appointment of an agent within the jurisdiction of that Party, only where such derogations are necessary to secure compliance with laws and regulations that are not inconsistent with the provisions of this Chapter and where such practices are not applied in a manner that would constitute a disguised restriction on trade.

8.   Paragraphs 6 and 7 do not apply to procedures provided in multilateral agreements concluded under the auspices of WIPO relating to the acquisition or maintenance of intellectual property rights.

9.   This Chapter does not give rise to obligations in respect of acts that occurred before the date of entry into force of this Agreement.

10.   Except as otherwise provided for in this Chapter, this Chapter gives rise to obligations in respect of all subject matter existing at the date of entry into force of this Agreement, and which is protected by a Party on that date, or which meets or comes subsequently to meet the criteria for protection under the terms of this Chapter. In respect of paragraphs 10 and 11, copyright and related rights obligations with respect to existing works and phonograms shall be determined solely under Article 17.7(7).

11.   Neither Party shall be obligated to restore protection to subject matter which on the date of entry into force of this Chapter has fallen into the public domain in that Party.

12.   Each Party shall ensure that all laws, regulations, and procedures concerning the protection or enforcement of intellectual property rights, and all final judicial decisions and administrative rulings of general applicability pertaining to the enforcement of such rights, shall be in writing and shall be published,[2] or where such publication is not practicable, made publicly available, in a national language in such a manner as to enable the other Party and right holders to become acquainted with them, with the object of making the protection and enforcement of intellectual property rights transparent. Nothing in this paragraph shall require a Party to disclose confidential information the disclosure of which would impede law enforcement or otherwise be contrary to the public interest or would prejudice the legitimate commercial interests of particular enterprises, public or private.

13.   Nothing in this Chapter prevents a Party from adopting measures necessary to prevent anticompetitive practices that may result from the abuse of the intellectual property rights set forth in this Chapter.

---

shall also include the prohibition on circumvention of effective technological measures pursuant to Article 17.7(5) and the provisions concerning rights management information pursuant to Article 17.7(6).

[2] The requirement for publication is satisfied by making the written document available to the public via the Internet.

14.   For the purposes of strengthening the development and protection of intellectual property, and implementing the obligations of this Chapter, the Parties will cooperate, on mutually agreed terms and subject to the availability of appropriated funds, by means of:

(a)   educational and dissemination projects on the use of intellectual property as a research and innovation tool, as well as on the enforcement of intellectual property;

(b)   appropriate coordination, training, specialization courses, and exchange of information between the intellectual property offices and other institutions of the Parties; and

(c)   enhancing the knowledge, development, and implementation of the electronic systems used for the management of intellectual property.

Article 17.2: Trademarks

1.   Each Party shall provide that trademarks shall include collective, certification, and sound marks, and may include geographical indications[3] and scent marks. Neither Party is obligated to treat certification marks as a separate category in its domestic law, provided that the signs as such are protected.

2.   Each Party shall afford an opportunity for interested parties to oppose the application for a trademark.

3.   Pursuant to Article 20 of the TRIPS Agreement, each Party shall ensure that any measures mandating the use of the term customary in common language as the common name for a good ("common name") including, *inter alia*, requirements concerning the relative size, placement, or style of use of the trademark in relation to the common name, do not impair the use or effectiveness of trademarks used in relation to such good.

4.   Each Party shall provide that the owner of a registered trademark shall have the exclusive right to prevent third parties not having the owner's consent from using in the course of trade identical or similar signs, including subsequent geographical indications, for goods or services that are related to those goods or services in respect of which the trademark is registered, where such use would result in a likelihood of confusion.[4]

5.   Each Party may provide limited exceptions to the rights conferred by a trademark, such as fair use of descriptive terms, provided that such exceptions take account of the legitimate interests of the owner of the trademark and of third parties.

6.   Article 6bis of the Paris Convention for the Protection of Industrial Property (1967) (Paris Convention) shall apply, *mutatis mutandis*, to goods or services which are not similar to those identified by a well-known trademark, whether registered or not, provided that use of that

---

[3] A geographical indication is capable of constituting a trademark to the extent that the geographical indication consists of any sign, or any combination of signs, capable of identifying a good or service as originating in the territory of a Party, or a region or locality in that territory, where a given quality, reputation, or other characteristic of the good or service is essentially attributable to its geographical origin.

[4] It is understood that likelihood of confusion is to be determined under the domestic trademark law of each Party.

trademark in relation to those goods or services would indicate a connection between those goods or services and the owner of the trademark and provided that the interests of the owner of the trademark are likely to be damaged by such use.

7.   Each Party shall, according to its domestic law, provide for appropriate measures to prohibit or cancel the registration of a trademark identical or similar to a well-known trademark, if the use of that trademark by the registration applicant is likely to cause confusion, or to cause mistake, or to deceive or risk associating the trademark with the owner of the well-known trademark, or constitutes unfair exploitation of the reputation of the trademark. Such measures to prohibit or cancel registration shall not apply when the registration applicant is the owner of the well-known trademark.

8.   In determining whether a trademark is well-known, a Party shall not require that the reputation of the trademark extend beyond the sector of the public that normally deals with the relevant goods or services.

9.   Each Party recognizes the importance of the Joint Recommendation Concerning Provisions on the Protection of Well-Known Marks (1999), adopted by the Assembly of the Paris Union for the Protection of Industrial Property and the General Assembly of WIPO and shall be guided by the principles contained in this Recommendation.

10.   Each Party shall provide a system for the registration of trademarks, which shall include:

   (a)   providing to the applicant a communication in writing, which may be electronic, of the reasons for any refusal to register a trademark;

   (b)   providing to the applicant an opportunity to respond to communications from the trademark authorities, contest an initial refusal, and appeal judicially any final refusal to register; and

   (c)   a requirement that decisions in opposition or cancellation proceedings be reasoned and in writing.

11.   Each Party shall work to provide, to the maximum degree practical, a system for the electronic application, processing, registration, and maintenance of trademarks.

12.   In relation to trademarks, Parties are encouraged to classify goods and services according to the classification of the Nice Agreement Concerning the International Classification of Goods and Services for the Purposes of the Registration of Marks (1979). In addition, each Party shall provide that:

   (a)   each registration or publication which concerns a trademark application or registration and which indicates the relevant goods or services shall indicate the goods or services by their names; and

   (b)   goods or services may not be considered as being similar to each other simply on the ground that, in any registration or publication, they appear in the same class of any classification system, including the Nice Classification. Conversely, goods or services may not be considered as being dissimilar from each other simply on the ground that, in any registration or publication, they appear in different classes of any classification system, including the Nice Classification.

Article 17.3: Domain Names on the Internet

1.   Each Party shall require that the management of its country-code top level domain (ccTLD) provide an appropriate procedure for the settlement of disputes, based on the principles established in the Uniform Domain-Name Dispute-Resolution Policy (UDRP), in order to address the problem of trademark cyber-piracy.

2.   Each Party shall, in addition, require that the management of its respective ccTLD provide online public access to a reliable and accurate database of contact information for domain-name registrants, in accordance with each Party's law regarding protection of personal data.

Article 17.4: Geographical Indications [5]

1.   Geographical indications, for the purposes of this Article, are indications which identify a good as originating in the territory of a Party, or a region or locality in that territory, where a given quality, reputation, or other characteristic of the good is essentially attributable to its geographical origin. Any sign or combination of signs (such as words, including geographical and personal names, letters, numerals, figurative elements, and colors), in any form whatsoever, shall be eligible for protection or recognition as a geographical indication.

2.   Chile shall:

(a)   provide the legal means to identify and protect geographical indications of United States persons that meet the criteria in paragraph 1; and

(b)   provide to United States geographical indications of wines and spirits the same recognition as Chile accords to wines and spirits under the Chilean geographical indications registration system.

3.   The United States shall:

(a)   provide the legal means to identify and protect the geographical indications of Chile that meet the criteria in paragraph 1; and

(b)   provide to Chilean geographical indications of wines and spirits the same recognition as the United States accords to wines and spirits under the Certificate of Label Approval (COLA) system as administered by the Alcohol and Tobacco Tax and Trade Bureau, Department of Treasury (TTB), or any successor agencies. Names that Chile desires to be included in the regulation set forth in 27 CFR Part 12 (Foreign Nongeneric), or any successor to that regulation, will be governed by paragraph 4 of this Article.

4.   Each Party shall provide the means for persons of the other Party to apply for protection or petition for recognition of geographical indications. Each Party shall accept applications or

---

[5] For the purposes of this Article, persons of a Party shall also mean government agencies.

petitions, as the case may be, without the requirement for intercession by a Party on behalf of its persons.

5.   Each Party shall process applications or petitions, as the case may be, for geographical indications with a minimum of formalities.

6.   Each Party shall make the regulations governing filing of such applications or petitions, as the case may be, available to the public in both printed and electronic form.

7.   Each Party shall ensure that applications or petitions, as the case may be, for geographical indications are published for opposition, and shall provide procedures to effect opposition of geographical indications that are the subject of applications or petitions. Each Party shall also provide procedures to cancel any registration resulting from an application or a petition.

8.   Each Party shall ensure that measures governing the filing of applications or petitions, as the case may be, for geographical indications set out clearly the procedures for these actions. Such procedures shall include contact information sufficient for applicants or petitioners to obtain specific procedural guidance regarding the processing of applications or petitions.

9.   The Parties acknowledge the principle of exclusivity incorporated in the Paris Convention and TRIPS Agreement, with respect to rights in trademarks.

10.   After the date of entry into force of this Agreement, each Party shall ensure that grounds for refusing protection or registration of a geographical indication include the following:

   (a)   the geographical indication is confusingly similar to a pre-existing pending good faith application for a trademark or a pre-existing trademark registered in that Party; or

   (b)   the geographical indication is confusingly similar to a pre-existing trademark, the rights to which have been acquired through use in good faith in that Party.

11.   Within six months of the entry into force of this Agreement, each Party shall communicate to the public the means by which it intends to implement paragraphs 2 through 10.

Article 17.5: Copyright[6]

1.   Each Party shall provide that authors[7] of literary and artistic works have the right[8] to authorize or prohibit all reproductions of their works, in any manner or form, permanent or temporary (including temporary storage in electronic form).

2.   Without prejudice to the provisions of Articles 11(1)(ii), 11bis(1)(i) and (ii), 11ter(1)(ii), 14(1)(ii), and 14bis(1) of the Berne Convention for the Protection of Literary and Artistic Works (1971) (Berne Convention), each Party shall provide to authors of literary and artistic works the right to authorize or prohibit the communication to the public of their works, by wire or wireless

---

[6] Except as provided in Article 17.12(2), each Party shall give effect to this Article upon the date of entry into force of this Agreement.

[7] References to "authors" in this chapter refer also to any successors in interest.

[8] With respect to copyrights and related rights in this Chapter, a right to authorize or prohibit or a right to authorize shall mean an exclusive right.

means, including the making available to the public of their works in such a way that members of the public may access these works from a place and at a time individually chosen by them.[9]

3.   Each Party shall provide to authors of literary and artistic works the right to authorize the making available to the public of the original and copies[10] of their works through sale or other transfer of ownership.

4.   Each Party shall provide that where the term of protection of a work (including a photographic work) is calculated:

(a)   on the basis of the life of a natural person, the term shall be not less than the life of the author and 70 years after the author's death; and

(b)   on a basis other than the life of a natural person, the term shall be

(i)   not less than 70 years from the end of the calendar year of the first authorized publication of the work, or

(ii)   failing such authorized publication within 50 years from the creation of the work, not less than 70 years from the end of the calendar year of the creation of the work.

Article 17.6: Related Rights[11]

1.   Each Party shall provide that performers and producers of phonograms[12] have the right to authorize or prohibit all reproductions of their performances or phonograms, in any manner or form, permanent or temporary (including temporary storage in electronic form).

2.   Each Party shall provide to performers and producers of phonograms the right to authorize the making available to the public of the original and copies[13] of their performances or phonograms through sale or other transfer of ownership.

3.   Each Party shall accord the rights provided under this Chapter to the performers and producers of phonograms who are persons of the other Party and to performances or phonograms first published or first fixed in a Party. A performance or phonogram shall be considered first published in any Party in which it is published within 30 days of its original publication.[14]

---

[9] It is understood that the mere provision of physical facilities for enabling or making a communication does not in itself amount to communication within the meaning of this Chapter or the Berne Convention. It is further understood that nothing in this Article precludes a Party from applying Article 11bis(2) of the Berne Convention.

[10] The expressions "copies" and "original and copies", being subject to the right of distribution under this paragraph, refer exclusively to fixed copies that can be put into circulation as tangible objects, i.e., for this purpose, "copies" means physical copies.

[11] Except as provided in Article 17.12(2), each Party shall give effect to this Article upon the date of entry into force of this Agreement.

[12] References to "performers and producers of phonograms" in this Chapter refer also to any successors in interest.

[13] The expressions "copies" and "original and copies", being subject to the right of distribution under this paragraph, refer exclusively to fixed copies that can be put into circulation as tangible objects, i.e., for this purpose, "copies" means physical copies.

[14] For the application of Article 17.6(3), fixation means the finalization of the master tape or its equivalent.

4.   Each Party shall provide to performers the right to authorize or prohibit:

(a)   the broadcasting and communication to the public of their unfixed performances except where the performance is already a broadcast performance, and

(b)   the fixation of their unfixed performances.

5.   (a)   Each Party shall provide to performers and producers of phonograms the right to authorize or prohibit the broadcasting or any communication to the public of their fixed performances or phonograms, by wire or wireless means, including the making available to the public of those performances and phonograms in such a way that members of the public may access them from a place and at a time individually chosen by them.

(b)   Notwithstanding paragraph 5(a) and Article 17.7(3), the right to authorize or prohibit the broadcasting or communication to the public of performances or phonograms through analog communication and free over-the-air broadcasting, and the exceptions or limitations to this right for such activities, shall be a matter of domestic law. Each Party may adopt exceptions and limitations, including compulsory licenses, to the right to authorize or prohibit the broadcasting or communication to the public of performances or phonograms in respect of other non interactive transmissions in accordance with Article 17.7(3). Such compulsory licenses shall not prejudice the right of the performer or producer of a phonogram to obtain equitable remuneration.

6.   Neither Party shall subject the enjoyment and exercise of the rights of performers and producers of phonograms provided for in this Chapter to any formality.

7.   Each Party shall provide that where the term of protection of a performance or phonogram is to be calculated on a basis other than the life of a natural person, the term shall be:

(a)   not less than 70 years from the end of the calendar year of the first authorized publication of the performance or phonogram, or

(b)   failing such authorized publication within 50 years from the fixation of the performance or phonogram, not less than 70 years from the end of the calendar year of the fixation of the performance or phonogram.

8.   For the purposes of Articles 17.6 and 17.7, the following definitions apply with respect to performers and producers of phonograms:

(a)   performers means actors, singers, musicians, dancers, and other persons who act, sing, deliver, declaim, play in, interpret, or otherwise perform literary or artistic works or expressions of folklore;

(b)   phonogram means the fixation of the sounds of a performance or of other sounds, or of a representation of sounds, other than in the form of a fixation incorporated in a cinematographic or other audiovisual work;[15]

(c)   fixation means the embodiment of sounds, or of the representations thereof, from which they can be perceived, reproduced, or communicated through a device;

(d)   producer of a phonogram means the person, or the legal entity, who or which takes the initiative and has the responsibility for the first fixation of the sounds of a performance or other sounds, or the representations of sounds;

(e)   publication of a fixed performance or a phonogram means the offering of copies of the fixed performance or the phonogram to the public, with the consent of the right holder, and provided that copies are offered to the public in reasonable quantity;

(f)   broadcasting means the transmission by wireless means for public reception of sounds or of images and sounds or of the representations thereof; such transmission by satellite is also broadcasting; transmission of encrypted signals is broadcasting where the means for decrypting are provided to the public by the broadcasting organization or with its consent; and

(g)   communication to the public of a performance or a phonogram means the transmission to the public by any medium, otherwise than by broadcasting, of sounds of a performance or the sounds or the representations of sounds fixed in a phonogram. For the purposes of Article 17.6(5) "communication to the public" includes making the sounds or representations of sounds fixed in a phonogram audible to the public.

Article 17.7: Obligations Common to Copyright and Related Rights[16]

1.   Each Party shall establish that in cases where authorization is needed from both the author of a work embodied in a phonogram and a performer or producer owning rights in the phonogram, the need for the authorization of the author does not cease to exist because the authorization of the performer and producer is also required. Likewise, each Party shall establish that in cases where authorization is needed from both the author of a work embodied in a phonogram and a performer or producer owning rights in the phonogram, the need for the authorization of the performer or producer does not cease to exist because the authorization of the author is also required.

2.   (a)   Each Party shall provide that for copyright and related rights:

        (i)   any person owning any economic right, i.e., not a moral right, may freely and separately transfer such right by contract; and

---

[15] It is understood that the definition of phonogram provided in this Chapter does not suggest that rights in the phonogram are in any way affected through their incorporation into a cinematographic or other audiovisual work.

[16] Except as provided in Article 17.12(2), each Party shall give effect to this Article upon the date of entry into force of this Agreement.

(ii)   any person who has acquired or owns any such economic right by virtue of a contract, including contracts of employment underlying the creation of works and phonograms, shall be permitted to exercise that right in its own name and enjoy fully the benefits derived from that right.

(b)   Each Party may establish:

(i)   which contracts of employment underlying the creation of works or phonograms shall, in the absence of a written agreement, result in a transfer of economic rights by operation of law; and

(ii)   reasonable limits to the provisions in paragraph 2(a) to protect the interests of the original right holders, taking into account the legitimate interests of the transferees.

3.   Each Party shall confine limitations or exceptions to rights to certain special cases which do not conflict with a normal exploitation of the work, performance, or phonogram, and do not unreasonably prejudice the legitimate interests of the right holder.[17]

4.   In order to confirm that all federal or central government agencies use computer software only as authorized, each Party shall issue appropriate laws, orders, regulations, or administrative or executive decrees to actively regulate the acquisition and management of software for such government use. Such measures may take the form of procedures such as preparing and maintaining inventories of software present on agencies' computers and inventories of software licenses.

5.   In order to provide adequate legal protection and effective legal remedies against the circumvention of effective technological measures that are used by authors, performers, and producers of phonograms in connection with the exercise of their rights and that restrict unauthorized acts in respect of their works, performances, and phonograms, protected by copyright and related rights:

(a)   each Party shall provide that any person who knowingly[18]18 circumvents without authorization of the right holder or law consistent with this Agreement any effective technological measure that controls access to a protected work, performance, or phonogram shall be civilly liable and, in appropriate circumstances, shall be criminally liable, or said conduct shall be considered an

---

[17] Article 17.7(3) permits a Party to carry forward and appropriately extend into the digital environment limitations and exceptions in its domestic laws which have been considered acceptable under the Berne Convention. Similarly, these provisions permit a Party to devise new exceptions and limitations that are appropriate in the digital network environment. For works, other than computer software, and other subject matter, such exceptions and limitations may include temporary acts of reproduction which are transient or incidental and an integral and essential part of a technological process and whose sole purpose is to enable (a) a lawful transmission in a network between third parties by an intermediary; or (b) a lawful use of a work or other subject-matter to be made; and which have no independent economic significance.

Article 17.7(3) neither reduces nor extends the scope of applicability of the limitations and exceptions permitted by the Berne Convention, the WIPO Copyright Treaty (1996), and the WIPO Performances and Phonograms Treaty (1996).

[18] For purposes of paragraph 5, knowledge may be demonstrated through reasonable evidence taking into account the facts and circumstances surrounding the alleged illegal act.

aggravating circumstance of another offense.[19] No Party is required to impose civil or criminal liability for a person who circumvents any effective technological measure that protects any of the exclusive rights of copyright or related rights in a protected work, but does not control access to such work.

(b)   each Party shall also provide administrative or civil measures, and, where the conduct is willful and for prohibited commercial purposes, criminal measures with regard to the manufacture, import, distribution, sale, or rental of devices, products, or components or the provision of services which:

      (i)   are promoted, advertised, or marketed for the purpose of circumvention of any effective technological measure, or

      (ii)   do not have a commercially significant purpose or use other than to circumvent any effective technological measure, or

      (iii)   are primarily designed, produced, adapted, or performed for the purpose of enabling or facilitating the circumvention of any effective technological measures.

Each Party shall ensure that due account is given, *inter alia*, to the scientific or educational purpose of the conduct of the defendant in applying criminal measures under any provisions implementing this subparagraph. A Party may exempt from criminal liability, and if carried out in good faith without knowledge that the conduct is prohibited, from civil liability, acts prohibited under this subparagraph that are carried out in connection with a nonprofit library, archive or educational institution.

(c)   Each Party shall ensure that nothing in subparagraphs (a) and (b) affects rights, remedies, limitations, or defenses with respect to copyright or related rights infringement.

(d)   Each Party shall confine limitations and exceptions to measures implementing subparagraphs (a) and (b) to certain special cases that do not impair the adequacy of legal protection or the effectiveness of legal remedies against the circumvention of effective technological measures. In particular, each Party may establish exemptions and limitations to address the following situations and activities in accordance with subparagraph (e):

      (i)   when an actual or likely adverse effect on non infringing uses with respect to a particular class of works or exceptions or limitation to copyright or related rights with respect to a class of users is demonstrated or recognized through a legislative or administrative proceeding established by law, provided that any limitation or exception adopted in reliance upon this subparagraph (d)(i) shall have effect for a period of not more than three years from the date of conclusion of such proceeding;

---

[19] Paragraph 5 does not obligate a Party to require that the design of, or the design and selection of parts and components for, a consumer electronics, telecommunications, or computing product provide for a response to any particular technological measure, so long as such product does not otherwise violate any measure implementing paragraph 5(b).

(ii)   noninfringing reverse engineering activities with regard to a lawfully obtained copy of a computer program, carried out in good faith with respect to particular elements of that computer program that have not been readily available to that person,[20] for the sole purpose of achieving interoperability of an independently created computer program with other programs;[21]

(iii)   noninfringing good faith activities, carried out by a researcher who has lawfully obtained a copy, performance, or display of a work, and who has made a reasonable attempt to obtain authorization for such activities, to the extent necessary for the sole purpose of identifying and analyzing flaws and vulnerabilities of encryption technologies;[22]

(iv)   the inclusion of a component or part for the sole purpose of preventing the access of minors to inappropriate online content in a technology, product, service, or device that does not itself violate any measures implementing subparagraphs (a) and (b);

(v)   noninfringing good faith activities that are authorized by the owner of a computer, computer system, or computer network for the sole purpose of testing, investigating, or correcting the security of that computer, computer system, or computer network;

(vi)   noninfringing activities for the sole purpose of identifying and disabling a capability to carry out undisclosed collection or dissemination of personally identifying information reflecting the online activities of a natural person in a way that has no other effect on the ability of any person to gain access to any work;

(vii)   lawfully authorized activities carried out by government employees, agents, or contractors for the purpose of law enforcement, intelligence, or similar government activities; and

(viii)   access by a nonprofit library, archive, or educational institution to a work not otherwise available to it, for the sole purpose of making acquisition decisions.

(e)   Each Party may apply the exceptions and limitations for the situations and activities set forth in subparagraph (d) as follows:

(i)   any measure implementing subparagraph (a) may be subject to the exceptions and limitations with respect to each situation and activity set forth in subparagraph (d).

---

[20] For greater certainty, elements of a computer program are not readily available to a person seeking to engage in noninfringing reverse engineering when they cannot be obtained from the literature on the subject, from the copyright holder, or from sources in the public domain.

[21] Such activity occurring in the course of research and development is not excluded from this exception.

[22] Such activity occurring in the course of research and development is not excluded from this exception.

(ii)   any measure implementing subparagraph (b), as it applies to effective technological measures that control access to a work, may be subject to exceptions and limitations with respect to the activities set forth in subparagraphs (d)(ii), (iii), (iv), (v), and (vii).

(iii)   any measure implementing subparagraph (b), as it applies to effective technological measures that protect any copyright or any rights related to copyright, may be subject to exceptions and limitations with respect to the activities set forth in subparagraph (d)(ii) and (vii).

(f)   Effective technological measure means any technology, device, or component that, in the normal course of its operation, controls access to a work, performance, phonogram, or any other protected material, or that protects any copyright or any rights related to copyright, and cannot, in the usual case, be circumvented accidentally.

6.   In order to provide adequate and effective legal remedies to protect rights management information:

(a)   each Party shall provide that any person who without authority, and knowing, or, with respect to civil remedies, having reasonable grounds to know, that it will induce, enable, facilitate, or conceal an infringement of any copyright or related right,

     (i)   knowingly removes or alters any rights management information;

     (ii)   distributes or imports for distribution rights management information knowing that the rights management information has been altered without authority; or

     (iii)   distributes, imports for distribution, broadcasts, communicates, or makes available to the public copies of works or phonograms, knowing that rights management information has been removed or altered without authority, shall be liable, upon the suit of any injured person, and subject to the remedies in Article 17.11(5). Each Party shall provide for application of criminal procedures and remedies at least in cases where acts prohibited in the subparagraph are done willfully and for purposes of commercial advantage. A Party may exempt from criminal liability prohibited acts done in connection with a nonprofit library, archive, educational institution, or broadcasting entity established without a profit-making purpose.

(b)   Rights management information means:

     (i)   information which identifies a work, performance, or phonogram; the author of the work, the performer of the performance, or the producer of the phonogram; or the owner of any right in the work, performance, or phonogram;

(ii)   information about the terms and conditions of the use of the work, performance, or phonogram; and

(iii)   any numbers or codes that represent such information, when any of these items is attached to a copy of the work, performance, or phonogram or appears in conjunction with the communication or making available of a work, performance, or phonogram to the public. Nothing in paragraph 6(a) requires the owner of any right in the work, performance, or phonogram to attach rights management information to copies of the owner's work, performance, or phonogram or to cause rights management information to appear in connection with a communication of the work, performance, or phonogram to the public.

7.   Each Party shall apply Article 18 of the Berne Convention, *mutatis mutandis*, to all the protections of copyright and related rights and effective technological measures and rights management information in Articles 17.5, 17.6, and 17.7.

Article 17.8: Protection of Encrypted Program-Carrying Satellite Signals

1.   Each Party shall make it:

(a)   a civil or criminal offense to manufacture, assemble, modify, import, export, sell, lease, or otherwise distribute a tangible or intangible device or system, knowing[23] that the device or system's principal function is solely to assist in decoding an encrypted program-carrying satellite signal without the authorization of the lawful distributor of such signal; and

(b)   a civil or criminal offense willfully to receive or further distribute an encrypted program-carrying satellite signal knowing that it has been decoded without the authorization of the lawful distributor of the signal.

2.   Each Party shall provide that any person injured by any activity described in subparagraphs 1(a) or 1(b), including any person that holds an interest in the encrypted programming signal or the content of that signal, shall be permitted to initiate a civil action under any measure implementing such subparagraphs.

Article 17.9: Patents

1.   Each Party shall make patents available for any invention, whether a product or a process, in all fields of technology, provided that the invention is new, involves an inventive step, and is capable of industrial application. For purposes of this Article, a Party may treat the terms "inventive step" and "capable of industrial application" as being synonymous with the terms "non-obvious" and "useful", respectively.

2.   Each Party will undertake reasonable efforts, through a transparent and participatory process, to develop and propose legislation within 4 years from the entry into force of this

---

[23] For purposes of paragraph 1, knowledge may be demonstrated through reasonable evidence, taking into account the facts and circumstances surrounding the alleged illegal act.

Agreement that makes available patent protection for plants that are new, involve an inventive step, and are capable of industrial application.

3.   Each Party may provide limited exceptions to the exclusive rights conferred by a patent, provided that such exceptions do not unreasonably conflict with a normal exploitation of the patent and do not unreasonably prejudice the legitimate interests of the patent owner, taking account of the legitimate interests of third parties.

4.   If a Party permits the use by a third party of the subject matter of a subsisting patent to support an application for marketing approval or sanitary permit of a pharmaceutical product, the Party shall provide that any product produced under such authority shall not be made, used, or sold in the territory of the Party other than for purposes related to meeting requirements for marketing approval or the sanitary permit, and if export is permitted, the product shall only be exported outside the territory of the Party for purposes of meeting requirements for issuing marketing approval or sanitary permits in the exporting Party.

5.   A Party may revoke or cancel a patent only when grounds exist that would have justified a refusal to grant the patent.[24]

6.   Each Party shall provide for the adjustment of the term of a patent, at the request of the patent owner, to compensate for unreasonable delays that occur in granting the patent. For the purposes of this paragraph, an unreasonable delay shall be understood to include a delay in the issuance of the patent of more than five years from the date of filing of the application in the Party, or three years after a request for examination of the application has been made, whichever is later, provided that periods of time attributable to actions of the patent applicant need not be included in the determination of such delays.

7.   Neither Party shall use a public disclosure to bar patentability based upon a lack of novelty or inventive step if the public disclosure (a) was made or authorized by, or derived from, the patent applicant and (b) occurs within 12 months prior to the date of filing of the application in the Party.

Article 17.10: Measures Related to Certain Regulated Products

1.   If a Party requires the submission of undisclosed information concerning the safety and efficacy of a pharmaceutical or agricultural chemical product which utilizes a new chemical entity, which product has not been previously approved, to grant a marketing approval or sanitary permit for such product, the Party shall not permit third parties not having the consent of the person providing the information to market a product based on this new chemical entity, on the basis of the approval granted to the party submitting such information. A Party shall maintain this prohibition for a period of at least five years from the date of approval for a pharmaceutical product and ten years from the date of approval for an agricultural chemical product.[25] Each Party shall protect such information against disclosure except where necessary to protect the public.

---

[24] Fraud in obtaining a patent may constitute grounds for revocation or cancellation.

[25] Where a Party, on the date of its implementation of the TRIPS Agreement, had in place a system for protecting pharmaceutical or agricultural chemical products not involving new chemical entities from unfair commercial use which conferred a period of protection shorter than that specified in paragraph 1, that Party may retain such system notwithstanding the obligations of paragraph 1.

2.   With respect to pharmaceutical products that are subject to a patent, each Party shall:

    (a)   make available an extension of the patent term to compensate the patent owner for unreasonable curtailment of the patent term as a result of the marketing approval process;

    (b)   make available to the patent owner the identity of any third party requesting marketing approval effective during the term of the patent; and

    (c)   not grant marketing approval to any third party prior to the expiration of the patent term, unless by consent or acquiescence of the patent owner.

Article 17.11: Enforcement of Intellectual Property Rights

General Obligations

1.   Each Party shall ensure that procedures and remedies set forth in this Article for enforcement of intellectual property rights are established in accordance with its domestic law.[26] Such administrative and judicial procedures and remedies, both civil and criminal, shall be made available to the holders of such rights in accordance with the principles of due process that each Party recognizes as well as with the foundations of its own legal system.

2.   This Article does not create any obligation:

    (a)   to put in place a judicial system for the enforcement of intellectual property rights distinct from that already existing for the enforcement of law in general, or

    (b)   with respect to the distribution of resources for the enforcement of intellectual property rights and the enforcement of law in general.

The distribution of resources for the enforcement of intellectual property rights shall not excuse a Party from compliance with the provisions of this Article.

3.   Final decisions on the merits of a case of general application shall be in writing and shall state the reasons or the legal basis upon which decisions are based.

4.   Each Party shall publicize or make available to the public information that each Party might collect regarding its efforts to provide effective enforcement of intellectual property rights, including statistical information.

5.   Each Party shall make available the civil remedies set forth in this Article for the acts described in the Articles 17.7(5) and 17.7(6).

6.   In civil, administrative, and criminal proceedings involving copyright or related rights, each Party shall provide that:

---

[26] Nothing in this Chapter prevents a Party from establishing or maintaining appropriate judicial or administrative procedural formalities for this purpose that do not impair each Party's rights and obligations under this Agreement.

(a)   the natural person or legal entity whose name is indicated as the author, producer, performer, or publisher of the work, performance, or phonogram in the usual manner,[27] shall, in the absence of proof to the contrary, be presumed to be the designated right holder in such work, performance, or phonogram.

(b)   it shall be presumed, in the absence of proof to the contrary, that the copyright or related right subsists in such subject matter. A Party may require, as a condition for according such presumption of subsistence, that the work appear on its face to be original and that it bear a publication date not more than 70 years prior to the date of the alleged infringement.

Civil and Administrative Procedures[28] and Remedies

7.   Each Party shall make available to right holders[29] civil judicial procedures concerning the enforcement of any intellectual property right.

8.   Each Party shall provide that:

(a)   In civil judicial proceedings, the judicial authorities shall have the authority to order the infringer to pay the right holder:

(i)   damages adequate to compensate for the injury the right holder has suffered because of an infringement of that person's intellectual property right by an infringer engaged in infringing activity, and

(ii)   at least in the case of infringements of trademark, copyright, or related rights, the profits of the infringer that are attributable to the infringement and are not already taken into account in determining injury.

(b)   In determining injury to the right holder, the judicial authorities shall, *inter alia*, consider the legitimate retail value of the infringed goods.

9.   In civil judicial proceedings, each Party shall, at least with respect to works protected by copyright or related rights and trademark counterfeiting, establish pre-established damages, prescribed by each Party's domestic law, that the judicial authorities deem reasonable in light of the goals of the intellectual property system and the objectives set forth in this Chapter.

10.   Each Party shall provide that, except in exceptional circumstances, its judicial authorities have the authority to order, at the conclusion of civil judicial proceedings concerning infringement of copyright or related rights and trademark counterfeiting, that the prevailing right holder shall be paid the court costs or fees and reasonable attorney's fees by the infringing party.

11.   In civil judicial proceedings concerning copyright and related rights infringement and trademark counterfeiting, each Party shall provide that its judicial authorities shall have the

---

[27] Each Party may establish the means by which it shall determine what constitutes the "usual manner" for a particular physical support.

[28] Each Party may establish the means by which it shall determine what constitutes the "usual manner" for a particular physical support.

[29] For the purposes of this Article, the term "right holder" shall include duly authorized licensees as well as federations and associations having legal standing and authorization to assert such rights.

authority to order the seizure of suspected infringing goods, and of material and implements by means of which such goods are produced where necessary to prevent further infringement.

12.   In civil judicial proceedings, each Party shall provide that:

(a)   its judicial authorities shall have the authority to order, at their discretion, the destruction, except in exceptional cases, of the goods determined to be infringing goods;

(b)   the charitable donation of goods that infringe copyright and related rights shall not be ordered by the judicial authorities without the authorization of the right holder other than in special cases that do not conflict with the normal exploitation of the work, performance, or phonogram, and do not unreasonably prejudice the legitimate interests of the right holder;

(c)   the judicial authorities shall have the authority to order, at their discretion, that material and implements actually used in the manufacture of the infringing goods be destroyed. In considering such requests, the judicial authorities shall take into account, *inter alia*, the need for proportionality between the gravity of the infringement and remedies ordered, as well as the interests of third parties holding an ownership, possessory, contractual, or secured interest; and

(d)   in regard to counterfeited trademarked goods, the simple removal of the trademark unlawfully affixed shall not permit release of the goods into the channels of commerce. However, such goods may be donated to charity when the removal of the trademark eliminates the infringing characteristic of the good and the good is no longer identifiable with the removed trademark.

13.   In civil judicial proceedings, each Party shall provide that the judicial authorities shall have the authority to order the infringer to provide any information the infringer may have regarding persons involved in the infringement, and regarding the distribution channels of infringing goods. Judicial authorities shall also have the authority to impose fines or imprisonment on infringers who do not comply with such orders, in accordance with each Party's domestic law.

14.   To the extent that any civil remedy can be ordered as a result of administrative procedures on the merits of a case, such procedures shall conform to principles equivalent in substance to those set forth in paragraphs 1 through 13.

Provisional Measures

15.   Each Party shall provide that requests for relief inaudita altera parte shall be acted upon expeditiously in accordance with the judicial procedural rules of that Party.

16.   Each Party shall provide that:

(a)   its judicial authorities have the authority to require the applicant for any provisional measure to provide any reasonably available evidence in order to satisfy themselves to a sufficient degree of certainty that the applicant is the holder of the right in question[30] and that infringement of such right is imminent, and to order the applicant to provide a reasonable security or equivalent assurance in an amount that is sufficient to protect the defendant and prevent abuse, set at a level so as not to unreasonably deter recourse to such procedures.

(b)   in the event that judicial or other authorities appoint experts, technical or otherwise, that must be paid by the parties, such costs shall be set at a reasonable level taking into account the work performed, or if applicable, based   on standardized fees, and shall not unreasonably deter recourse to provisional relief.

Special Requirements Related to Border Measures

17.   Each Party shall provide that any right holder initiating procedures for suspension by the customs authorities of the release of suspected counterfeit trademark or pirated copyright goods[31] into free circulation is required to provide adequate evidence to satisfy the competent authorities that, under the laws of the Party of importation, there is prima facie an infringement of the right holder's intellectual property right and to supply sufficient information to make the suspected goods reasonably recognizable to the customs authorities.

The sufficient information required shall not unreasonably deter recourse to these procedures.

18.   Each Party shall provide the competent authorities with the authority to require an applicant to provide a reasonable security or equivalent assurance sufficient to protect the defendant and the competent authorities and to prevent abuse. Such security or equivalent assurance shall not unreasonably deter recourse to these procedures.

19.   Where the competent authorities have made a determination that goods are counterfeit or pirated, a Party shall grant the competent authorities the authority to inform the right holder, at the right holder's request, of the names and addresses of the consignor, the importer, and the consignee, and of the quantity of the goods in question.

20.   Each Party shall provide that the competent authorities are permitted to initiate border measures ex officio, without the need for a formal complaint from a person or right holder. Such measures shall be used when there is reason to believe or suspect that goods being imported, destined for export, or moving in transit are counterfeit or pirated. In case of goods in transit, each Party, in conformity with other international agreements subscribed to by it, may provide

---

[30] In accordance with the provisions in paragraph 6(a).

[31] For the purposes of paragraphs 17 through 19:

(a) counterfeit trademark goods means any goods, including packaging, bearing without authorization a trademark which is identical to the trademark validly registered in respect of such goods, or which cannot be distinguished in its essential aspects from such a trademark, and which thereby infringes the rights of the owner of the trademark in question under the law of the country of importation;

(b) pirated copyright goods means any goods which are copies made without the consent of the right holder or person duly authorized by the right holder in the country of production and which are made directly or indirectly from an article where the making of that copy would have constituted an infringement of a copyright or a related right under the law of the country of importation.

that ex officio authority shall be exercised prior to sealing the container, or other means of conveyance, with the customs seal, as applicable.[32]

21.   Each Party shall provide that:

(a)   goods that have been found to be pirated or counterfeit by the competent authorities shall be destroyed, except in exceptional cases.

(b)   in regard to counterfeit trademark goods, the simple removal of the trademark unlawfully affixed shall not be sufficient to permit the release of goods into the channels of commerce.

(c)   in no event shall the competent authorities engage in, or permit, the re-exportation of counterfeit or pirated goods, nor shall they permit such goods to be subject to other customs procedures.

Criminal Procedures and Remedies

22.   Each Party shall provide for application of criminal procedures and penalties at least in cases of willful trademark counterfeiting or piracy, on a commercial scale, of works, performances, or phonograms protected by copyright or related rights. Specifically, each Party shall ensure that:

(a)   (i)   willfull infringement[33] of copyright and related rights for a commercial advantage or financial gain, is subject to criminal procedures and penalties;[34]

(ii)   copyright or related rights piracy on a commercial scale includes the willful infringing reproduction or distribution, including by electronic means, of copies with a significant aggregate monetary value, calculated based on the legitimate retail value of the infringed goods;

(b)   available remedies include sentences of imprisonment and/or monetary fines that are sufficient to provide a deterrent to future infringements and present a level of punishment consistent with the gravity of the offense, which shall be applied by the judicial authorities in light of, *inter alia*, these criteria;

(c)   judicial authorities have the authority to order the seizure of suspected counterfeit or pirated goods, assets legally traceable to the infringing activity, documents and related materials, and implements that constitute evidence of the offense. Each Party shall further provide that its judicial authorities have the authority to seize items in accordance with its domestic law. Items that are subject to seizure

---

[32] The Parties recognize their obligations with respect to technological cooperation and other matters set forth in Chapter Five (Customs Administration), concerning, *inter alia*, improved customs enforcement, including with respect to intellectual property rights.

[33] For purposes of paragraph 22, evidence of reproduction or distribution of a copyrighted work, by itself, shall not be sufficient to establish willful infringement.

[34] For purposes of paragraph 22, commercial advantage or financial gain shall be understood to exclude de minimis infringements. Nothing in this Agreement prevents prosecutors from exercising any discretion that they may have to decline to pursue cases.

pursuant to a search order need not be individually identified so long as they fall within general categories specified in the order;

(d)   judicial authorities have the authority to order, among other measures, the forfeiture of any assets legally traceable to the infringing activity, and the forfeiture and destruction of all counterfeit and pirated goods and, at least with respect to copyright and related rights piracy, any related materials and implements actually used in the manufacture of the pirated goods. Parties shall not make compensation available to the infringer for any such forfeiture or destruction; and

(e)   Appropriate authorities, as determined by each Party, have the authority, in cases of copyright and related rights piracy and trademark counterfeiting, to exercise legal action ex officio without the need for a formal complaint by a person or right holder.

Limitations on Liability for Internet Service Providers

23.   (a)   For the purpose of providing enforcement procedures that permit effective action against any act of infringement of copyright[35] covered under this Chapter, including expeditious remedies to prevent infringements and criminal and civil remedies, each Party shall provide, consistent with the framework set forth in this Article:

(i)   legal incentives for service providers to cooperate with copyright owners in deterring the unauthorized storage and transmission of copyrighted materials; and

(ii)   limitations in its law regarding the scope of remedies available against service providers for copyright infringements that they do not control, initiate, or direct, and that take place through systems or networks controlled or operated by them or on their behalf, as set forth below.

(b)   These limitations shall preclude monetary relief and provide reasonable limitations on court-ordered relief to compel or restrain certain actions for the following functions and shall be confined to those functions:

(i)   transmitting, routing, or providing connections for material without modification of its content;[36]

(ii)   caching carried out through an automatic process;

(iii)   storage at the direction of a user of material residing on a system or network controlled or operated by or for the provider, including e-mails and its attachments stored in the provider's server, and web pages residing on the provider's server; and

---

[35] For purposes of paragraph 23, "copyright" shall also include related rights.

[36] Modification of the content of material shall not include technological manipulation of material for the purpose of facilitating network transmission, such as division into packets.

(iv)   referring or linking users to an online location by using information location tools, including hyperlinks and directories.

These limitations shall apply only where the provider does not initiate the transmission, or select the material or its recipients (except to the extent that a function described in subparagraph (iv) in itself entails some form of selection). This paragraph does not preclude the availability of other defenses to copyright infringement that are of general applicability, and qualification for the limitations as to each function shall be considered separately from qualification for the limitations as to other functions.

(c)   With respect to function (b)(ii), the limitations shall be conditioned on the service provider:

     (i)   complying with conditions on user access and rules regarding the updating of the cached material imposed by the supplier of the material;

     (ii)   not interfering with technology consistent with widely accepted industry standards lawfully used at the originating site to obtain information about the use of the material, and not modifying its content in transmission to subsequent users; and

     (iii)   expeditiously removing or disabling access, upon receipt of an effective notification of claimed infringement in accordance with subparagraph (f), to cached material that has been removed or access to which has been disabled at the originating site.

With respect to functions (b)(iii) and (iv), the limitations shall be conditioned on the service provider:

     (i)   not receiving a financial benefit directly attributable to the infringing activity, in circumstances where it has the right and ability to control such activity;

     (ii)   expeditiously removing or disabling access to the material residing on its system or network upon obtaining actual knowledge of the infringement or becoming aware of facts or circumstances from which the infringement was apparent, including through effective notifications of claimed infringement in accordance with subparagraph (f); and

     (iii)   publicly designating a representative to receive such notifications.

(d)   Eligibility for application of the limitations in this paragraph shall be conditioned on the service provider:

     (i)   adopting and reasonably implementing[37] a policy that provides for termination in appropriate circumstances of the accounts of repeat infringers; and

---

[37] A Party may determine in its domestic law that "reasonably implementing" entails, *inter alia*, making such policy continuously available to its users of its system or network.

> (ii)   accommodating and not interfering with standard technical measures that lawfully protect and identify copyrighted material, that are developed through an open, voluntary process by a broad consensus of interested parties, approved by relevant authorities, as applicable, that are available on reasonable and nondiscriminatory terms, and that do not impose substantial costs on service providers or substantial burdens on their systems or networks.

Eligibility for application of the limitations in this paragraph may not be conditioned on the service provider monitoring its service, or affirmatively seeking facts indicating infringing activity, except to the extent consistent with such technical measures.

(e)   If the service provider qualifies for the limitation with respect to function (b)(i), court-ordered relief to compel or restrain certain actions shall be limited to measures to terminate specified accounts, or to take reasonable steps to block access to a specific, non-domestic online location. If the service provider qualifies for the limitations with respect to any other function in subparagraph (b), court-ordered relief to compel or restrain certain actions shall be limited to removing or disabling access to the infringing material, terminating specified accounts, and other remedies that a court may find necessary provided that such other remedies are the least burdensome to the service provider and users or subscribers among comparably effective forms of relief. Any such relief shall be issued with due regard for the relative burden to the service provider, to users or subscribers and harm to the copyright owner, the technical feasibility and effectiveness of the remedy and whether less burdensome, comparably effective enforcement methods are available. Except for orders ensuring the preservation of evidence, or other orders having no material adverse effect on the operation of the service provider's communications network, such relief shall be available only where the service provider has received notice and an opportunity to appear before the judicial authority.

(f)   For purposes of the notice and take down process for functions (b)(ii), (iii), and (iv), each Party shall establish appropriate procedures through an open and transparent process which is set forth in domestic law, for effective notifications of claimed infringement, and effective counter-notifications by those whose material is removed or disabled through mistake or misidentification. At a minimum, each Party shall require that an effective notification of claimed infringement be a written communication, physically or electronically[38] signed by a person who represents, under penalty of perjury or other criminal penalty, that he is an authorized representative of a right holder in the material that is claimed to have been infringed, and containing information that is reasonably sufficient to enable the service provider to identify and locate material that the complaining party claims in good faith to be infringing and to contact that complaining party. At a minimum, each Party shall require that an effective counter-notification contain the same information, *mutatis mutandis*, as a notification of claimed infringement, and in addition, contain a statement that the subscriber making the counter-notification consents to the jurisdiction of the courts of the Party. Each

---

[38] In accordance with domestic law.

Party shall also provide for monetary remedies against any person who makes a knowing material misrepresentation in a notification or counter-notification which causes injury to any interested party as a result of a service provider relying on the misrepresentation.

(g)   If the service provider removes or disables access to material in good faith based on claimed or apparent infringement, it shall be exempted from liability for any resulting claims, provided that, in the case of material residing on its system or network, it takes reasonable steps promptly to notify the supplier of the material that it has done so and, if the supplier makes an effective counter-notification and is subject to jurisdiction in an infringement suit, to restore the material online unless the original notifying party seeks judicial relief within a reasonable time.

(h)   Each Party shall establish an administrative or judicial procedure enabling copyright owners who have given effective notification of claimed infringement to obtain expeditiously from a service provider information in its possession identifying the alleged infringer.

(i)   Service provider means, for purposes of function (b)(i), a provider of transmission, routing, or connections for digital online communications without modification of their content between or among points specified by the user of material of the user's choosing, or for purposes of functions (b)(ii) through (iv) a provider or operator of facilities for online services (including in cases where network access is provided by another provider) or network access.

Article 17.12: Final Provisions

1.   Except as otherwise provided in this Chapter, each Party shall give effect to the provisions of this Chapter upon the date of entry into force of this Agreement.

2.   In those cases in which the full implementation of the obligations contained in this Chapter requires a Party to amend its domestic legislation or additional financial resources, those amendments and financial resources shall be in force or available as soon as practicable, and in no event later than:

(a)   two years from the date of entry into force of this Agreement, with respect to the obligations in Article 17.2 on trademarks, Article 17.4(1) through 17.4(9) on geographical indications, Article 17.9(1), 17.9(3) through 17.9(7) on patents, and Articles 17.5(1) and 17.6(1) on temporary copies;

(b)   four years from the date of entry into force of this Agreement, with respect to the obligations in Article 17.11 on enforcement (including border measures), and Article 17.6(5) with respect to the right of communication to the public, and non-interactive digital transmissions, for performers and producers of phonograms; and

(c)   five years from the date of entry into force of this Agreement, with respect to the obligations in Article 17.7(5) on effective technological measures.

*

FREE TRADE AGREEMENT BETWEEN THE EFTA STATES AND THE REPUBLIC OF CHILE* [excerpts]

The free trade agreement between the EFTA States and the Republic of Chile was signed on 26 June 2003. It is expected to enter into force on 1 February 2004.

CHAPTER III

TRADE IN SERVICES AND ESTABLISHMENT

SECTION I – TRADE IN SERVICES

ARTICLE 22
Coverage

1.   This Section applies to measures affecting trade in services taken by central, regional or local governments and authorities as well as by non-governmental bodies in the exercise of powers delegated by central, regional or local governments or authorities.

2.   This Section applies to measures affecting trade in all services sectors with the exception of air services, including domestic and international air transportation services, whether scheduled or non-scheduled, and related services in support of air services, other than:

    (a)   aircraft repair and maintenance services;

    (b)   the selling and marketing of air transport services;

    (c)   computer reservation system (CRS) services.[1]

3.   Nothing in this Section shall be construed to impose any obligation with respect to government procurement, which is subject to the Chapter V.

ARTICLE 23
Definitions

For the purposes of this Section:

---

* *Source*: European Free Trade Association and the Government of the Republic of Chile (2003). "Free Trade Agreement Between the EFTA States and the Republic of Chile", available on the Internet (http://www.sice.oas.org/trade/Chi-EFTA_e/ChiEFTAind_e.asp) and (http://secretariat.efta.int/Web/ExternalRelations/PartnerCountries/Chile/CL/CL_FTA.pdf). [Note added by the editor.]

[1] The terms "aircraft repair and maintenance services", "selling and marketing of air transport services" and "computer reservation system (CRS) services" are as defined in paragraph 6 of the Annex on Air Transport Services to the GATS.

(a)   "trade in services" is defined as the supply of a service:

    (i)   from the territory of a Party into the territory of another Party (mode 1);

    (ii)   in the territory of a Party to the service consumer of another Party (mode 2);

    (iii)   by a service supplier of a Party, through commercial presence in the territory of another Party (mode 3);

    (iv)   by a service supplier of a Party, through presence of natural persons in the territory of another Party (mode 4).

(b)   "measure" means any measure by a Party, whether in the form of a law, regulation, rule, procedure, decision, administrative action or any other form;

(c)   "supply of a service" includes the production, distribution, marketing, sale and delivery of a service;

(d)   "measures by a Party affecting trade in services" include measures in respect of:

    (i)   the purchase, payment or use of a service;

    (ii)   the access to and use of, in connection with the supply of a service, services which are required by that Party to be offered to the public generally;

    (iii)   the presence, including commercial presence, of persons of another Party for the supply of a service in the territory of that Party;

(e)   "commercial presence" means any type of business or professional establishment, including through:

    (i)   the constitution, acquisition or maintenance of a juridical person; or

    (ii)   the creation or maintenance of a branch or a representative office; within the territory of a Party for the purpose of supplying a service;

(f)   "service supplier" means any person that seeks to supply or supplies a service;[2]

(g)   "natural person of a Party" is, in accordance with its legislation, a national or a permanent resident of that Party if he or she is accorded substantially the same treatment as nationals in respect of measures affecting trade in services;

(h)   "juridical person" means any legal entity duly constituted or otherwise organised under applicable law, whether for profit or otherwise, and whether privately-owned or governmentally-

---

[2] Where the service is not supplied directly by a juridical person but through other forms of commercial presence such as a branch or a representative office, the service supplier (i.e. the juridical person) shall, nonetheless, through such presence be accorded the treatment provided for service suppliers under this Agreement. Such treatment shall be extended to the presence through which the service is supplied and need not be extended to any other parts of the supplier located outside the territory where the service is supplied.

owned, including any corporation, trust, partnership, joint venture, sole proprietorship or association;

(i)   "services" includes any service in any sector except services supplied in the exercise of governmental authority;

(j)   "juridical person of a Party" means a juridical person which is either:

  (i)   constituted or otherwise organised under the law of Chile or an EFTA State, and that is engaged in substantive business operations in Chile or in the EFTA State concerned, or

  (ii)   in the case of the supply of a service through commercial presence, owned or controlled by:

    (A)   natural persons of that Party; or

    (B)   juridical persons identified under paragraph (j)(i); and (k) "a service supplied in the exercise of governmental authority" means any service which is supplied neither on a commercial basis nor in competition with one or more service suppliers.

ARTICLE 24
Most-favoured nation treatment

1.   The rights and obligations of the Parties with respect to most-favoured nation treatment shall be governed by the GATS.

2.   If a Party enters into an agreement with a non-Party which has been notified under Article V of the GATS, it shall, upon request from another Party, afford adequate opportunity to the other Parties to negotiate, on a mutually advantageous basis, the benefits granted therein.

ARTICLE 25
Market access

1.   With respect to market access through the modes of supply identified in Article 23, each Party shall accord services and service suppliers of another Party treatment no less favourable than that provided for under the terms, limitations and conditions agreed and specified in its Schedule referred to in Article 27.

2.   In sectors where market-access commitments are undertaken, the measures which a Party shall not maintain or adopt either on the basis of a regional subdivision or on the basis of its entire territory, unless otherwise specified in its Schedule, are defined as:

  (a)   limitations on the number of service suppliers whether in the form of numerical quotas, monopolies, exclusive service suppliers or the requirements of an economic needs test;

  (b)   limitations on the total value of service transactions or assets in the form of numerical quotas or the requirement of an economic needs test;

(c)   limitations on the total number of service operations or on the total quantity of service output expressed in the terms of designated numerical units in the form of quotas or the requirement of an economic needs test.[3]

(d)   limitations on the total number of natural persons that may be employed in a particular service sector or that a service supplier may employ and who are necessary for, and directly related to, the supply of a specific service in the form of numerical quotas or a requirement of an economic needs test;

(e)   measures which restrict or require specific types of legal entities or joint ventures through which a service supplier of another Party may supply a service; and

(f)   limitations on the participation of foreign capital in terms of maximum percentage limit on foreign shareholding or the total value of individual or aggregate foreign investment.

ARTICLE 26
National treatment

1.   In the sectors inscribed in its Schedule referred to in Article 27 and subject to the conditions and qualifications set out therein, each Party shall grant to services and services suppliers of another Party, in respect of all measures affecting the supply of services, treatment no less favourable than that it accords to its own like services and services suppliers.[4]

2.   A Party may meet the requirement of paragraph 1 by according to services and service suppliers of another Party, either formally identical treatment or formally different treatment to that it accords to its own like services and service suppliers.

3.   Formally identical or formally different treatment shall be considered to be less favourable if it modifies the conditions of competition in favour of services or service suppliers of the Party compared to like services or service suppliers of another Party.

ARTICLE 27
Trade liberalisation

1.   The Schedule of specific commitments that each Party undertakes under Articles 25 and 26 as well as paragraph 3 of this Article is set out at Annex VIII. With respect to sectors where such commitments are undertaken, each Schedule specifies:

(a)   terms, limitations and conditions on market access;

(b)   conditions and qualifications on national treatment;

(c)   undertakings relating to additional commitments referred to in paragraph 3; and

---

[3] Subparagraph (c) does not cover measures of a Party which limit inputs for the supply of services.

[4] Specific commitments assumed under this Article shall not be construed to require the Parties to compensate for any inherent competitive disadvantage which result from the foreign character of the relevant services and service suppliers.

(d)   where appropriate, the time-frame for implementation of such commitments and the date of entry into force of such commitments.

2.   Measures inconsistent with both Articles 25 and 26 are inscribed in the column relating to Article 25. In this case, the inscription is considered to provide a condition or qualification to Article 26 as well.

3.   Where a Party undertakes a specific commitment on measures affecting trade in services not subject to scheduling under Articles 25 and 26, including those regarding qualifications, standards or licensing matters, such commitments are inscribed in its Schedule as additional commitments.

4.   The Parties undertake to review their Schedules of specific commitments at least every three years, or more frequently, with a view to provide for a reduction or elimination of substantially all remaining discrimination between the Parties with regard to trade in services covered in this Section on a mutually advantageous basis and ensuring an overall balance of rights and obligations.

ARTICLE 28
Domestic regulation

1.   In sectors where specific commitments are undertaken, each Party shall ensure that all measures of general application affecting trade in services are administered in a reasonable, objective and impartial manner.

2.   Each Party shall maintain or institute as soon as practicable judicial, arbitral or administrative tribunals or procedures which provide, at the request of an affected service supplier of another Party, for the prompt review of, and where justified, appropriate remedies for, administrative decisions affecting trade in services. Where such procedures are not independent of the agency entrusted with the administrative decision concerned, the Party shall ensure that the procedures in fact provide for an objective and impartial review.

3.   Where authorisation is required for the supply of a service, the competent authorities of a Party shall promptly, after the submission of an application is considered complete under domestic laws and regulations, inform the applicant of the decision concerning the application. At the request of the applicant, the competent authorities of the Party shall provide, without undue delay, information concerning the status of the application.

4.   The Parties shall jointly review the results of the negotiations on disciplines for measures relating to qualification requirements and procedures, technical standards and licensing requirements pursuant to Article VI.4 of the GATS aiming to ensure that such measure do not constitute unnecessary barriers to trade in services, with a view to their incorporation into this Agreement. The Parties note that such disciplines aim to ensure that such requirements are, *inter alia*:

(a)   based on objective and transparent criteria, such as competence and the ability to supply the service;

(b)   not more burdensome than necessary to ensure the quality of the service;

(c)   in the case of licensing procedures, not in themselves a restriction on the supply of the service.

5.   In sectors in which a Party has undertaken specific commitments, until the incorporation of disciplines developed pursuant to paragraph 4, a Party shall not apply licensing and qualification requirements and technical standards in a manner which:

(a)   does not comply with the criteria outlined in paragraphs 4 (a), (b) or (c); and

(b)   could not reasonably have been expected of that Party at the time of the conclusion of the negotiation of the present agreement.

6.   Whenever a domestic regulation is prepared, adopted and applied in accordance with international standards applied by both Parties, it shall be rebuttably presumed to comply with the provisions of this Article.

7.   Each Party shall provide for adequate procedures to verify the competence of professionals of another Party.

ARTICLE 29
Recognition

1.   The Parties shall encourage the relevant bodies in their respective territories to provide recommendations on mutual recognition, for the purpose of the fulfilment, in whole or in part, by service suppliers of the criteria applied by each Party for the authorisation, licensing, accreditation, operation and certification of service suppliers and, in particular, professional services.

2.   The Joint Committee, within a reasonable period of time and considering the level of correspondence of the respective regulations, shall decide whether a recommendation referred to in paragraph 1 is consistent with this Section. If that is the case, such a recommendation shall be implemented through an agreement on mutual requirements, qualifications, licences and other regulations to be negotiated by the competent authorities.

3.   Any such agreement shall be in conformity with the relevant provisions of the WTO Agreement and, in particular, Article VII of the GATS.

4.   Where the Parties agree, each Party shall encourage its relevant bodies to develop procedures for the temporary licensing of professional services suppliers of another Party.

5.   The Joint Committee shall periodically, and at least once every three years, review the implementation of this Article.

6.   Where a Party recognises, by agreement or arrangement, the education or experience obtained, requirements met or licenses or certifications granted in the territory of a non-Party, that Party shall accord another Party, upon request, adequate opportunity to negotiate its accession to such an agreement or arrangement or to negotiate comparable ones with it. Where a Party accords recognition autonomously, it shall afford adequate opportunity for another Party to demonstrate that the education or experience obtained, requirements met or licenses or certifications granted in the territory of that other Party should also be recognised.

ARTICLE 30
Movement of natural persons

1.   This Section applies to measures affecting natural persons who are service suppliers of a Party, and natural persons of a Party who are employed by a service supplier of a Party, in respect of the supply of a service. Natural persons covered by a Party's specific commitments shall be allowed to supply the service in accordance with the terms of those commitments.

2.   This Section shall not apply to measures affecting natural persons seeking access to the employment market of a Party, nor shall it apply to measures regarding nationality, residence or employment on a permanent basis.

3.   This Section shall not prevent a Party from applying measures to regulate the entry of natural persons of another Party into, or their temporary stay in, its territory, including those measures necessary to protect the integrity of, and to ensure the orderly movement of natural persons across its borders, provided that such measures are not applied in a manner so as to nullify or impair the benefits accruing to a Party under the terms of a specific commitment.[5]

ARTICLE 31
Telecommunications services

Specific provisions on telecommunications services are set out in Annex IX.

SECTION II – ESTABLISHMENT

ARTICLE 32
Coverage

This Section shall apply to establishment in all sectors, with the exception of establishment in services sectors.

ARTICLE 33
Definitions

For the purposes of this Section,

(a)   "juridical person" means any legal entity duly constituted or otherwise organised under applicable law, whether for profit or otherwise, and whether privately-owned or governmentally-owned, including any corporation, trust, partnership, joint venture, sole proprietorship or association;

(b)   "juridical person of a Party" means a juridical person constituted or otherwise organised under the law of an EFTA State or of Chile and that is engaged in substantive business operations in Chile or in the EFTA State concerned;

---

[5] The sole fact of requiring a visa shall not be regarded as nullifying or impairing benefits under a specific commitment.

(c)   "natural person" means a national of an EFTA State or of Chile according to their respective legislation;

(d)   "establishment" means:

      (i)   the constitution, acquisition or maintenance of a juridical person, or

      (ii)   the creation or maintenance of a branch or a representative office, within the territory of a Party for the purpose of performing an economic activity.

As regards natural persons, this shall not extend to seeking or taking employment in the labour market or confer a right of access to the labour market of a Party.

ARTICLE 34
National treatment

With respect to establishment, and subject to the reservations set out in Annex X, each Party shall grant to juridical and natural persons of the other Party treatment no less favourable than that it accords to its own juridical and natural persons performing a like economic activity.

ARTICLE 35
Reservations

1.   National treatment as provided for under Article 34 shall not apply to:

      (a)   any reservation that is listed by a Party in Annex X;

      (b)   an amendment to a reservation covered by paragraph (a) to the extent that the amendment does not decrease the conformity of the reservation with Article 34;

      (c)   any new reservation adopted by a Party, and incorporated into Annex X which does not affect the overall level of commitments of that Party under this Agreement; to the extent that such reservations are inconsistent with Article 34.

2.   As part of the reviews provided for in Article 37 the Parties undertake to review at least every three years the status of the reservations set out in Annex X with a view to reducing or removing such reservations.

3.   A Party may, at any time, either upon the request of another Party or unilaterally, remove in whole or in part reservations set out in Annex X by written notification to the other Parties.

4.   A Party may, at any time, incorporate a new reservation into Annex X in accordance with paragraph 1(c) of this Article by written notification to the other Parties. On receiving such written notification, the other Parties may request consultations regarding the reservation. On receiving the request for consultations, the Party incorporating the new reservation shall enter into consultations with the other Parties.

ARTICLE 36
Right to regulate

Subject to the provisions of Article 34, each Party may regulate the establishment of juridical and natural persons.

ARTICLE 37
Final provisions

With the objective of progressive liberalisation of investment conditions, the Parties affirm their commitment to review the investment legal framework, the investment environment and the flow of investment between them consistent with their commitments in international investment agreements, no later than three years after the entry into force of this Agreement.

SECTION III – PAYMENTS AND CAPITAL MOVEMENTS

ARTICLE 38
Objective and scope

1.   The Parties shall aim at the liberalisation of current payments and capital movements between them, in conformity with the commitments undertaken in the framework of the international financial institutions and with due consideration to each Party's currency stability.

2.   This Section applies to all current payments and capital movements between the Parties. Specific provisions on current payments and capital movements are set out in Annex XI.

ARTICLE 39
Current Account

The Parties shall allow, in freely convertible currency and in accordance with the Articles of Agreement of the International Monetary Fund, any payments and transfers of the Current Account between the Parties.

ARTICLE 40
Capital Account

The Parties shall allow the free movements of capital relating to direct investments made in accordance with the laws of the host country and investments made in accordance with the provisions of Sections Trade in Services and Establishment of this Chapter, and the liquidation or repatriation of these capitals and of any profit stemming therefrom.

ARTICLE 41
Exceptions and safeguard measures

1.   Where, in exceptional circumstances, payments and capital movements between the Parties cause or threaten to cause serious difficulties for the operation of monetary policy or exchange rate policy in any Party, the Party concerned may take safeguard measures with regard to capital movements that are strictly necessary for a period not exceeding one year. The application of safeguard measures may be extended through their formal reintroduction.

2.   The Party adopting the safeguard measures shall inform the other Party forthwith and present, as soon as possible, a time schedule for their removal.

ARTICLE 42
Final provisions

The Parties shall consult each other with a view to facilitating the movement of capital between them in order to promote the objectives of this Agreement.

SECTION IV – COMMON PROVISIONS

ARTICLE 43
Relation to other international agreements

With respect to matters related to this Chapter, the Parties confirm the rights and obligations existing under any bilateral or multilateral agreements to which they are a party.

ARTICLE 44
General exceptions

Article XIV and Article XXVIII paragraph (o) of the GATS are hereby incorporated into and made part of this Chapter.

ARTICLE 45
Financial services

1.   The Parties understand that no commitments have been made in financial services. For greater clarity, financial services are defined as in paragraph 5 of the Annex on Financial Services of the GATS.

2.   Notwithstanding paragraph 1, two years after the entry into force of this Agreement, the Parties will consider the inclusion of financial services in this Chapter on a mutually advantageous basis and securing an overall balance of rights and obligations.

CHAPTER IV

PROTECTION OF INTELLECTUAL PROPERTY

ARTICLE 46
Intellectual property rights

1.   The Parties shall grant and ensure adequate, effective and non-discriminatory protection of intellectual property rights, and provide for measures for the enforcement of such rights against infringement thereof, counterfeiting and piracy, in accordance with the provisions of this Article, Annex XII to this Agreement and the international agreements referred to therein.

2.   The Parties shall accord to each other's nationals treatment no less favourable than that they accord to their own nationals. Exemptions from this obligation must be in accordance with

the substantive provisions of Articles 3 and 5 of the WTO Agreement on Trade-Related Aspects of Intellectual Property Rights (hereinafter referred to as "the TRIPS Agreement").[6]

3.   The Parties shall grant to each other's nationals treatment no less favourable than that accorded to nationals of any other State. Exemptions from this obligation must be in accordance with the substantive provisions of the TRIPS Agreement, in particular Articles 4 and 5 thereof 6

4.   The Parties agree, upon request of any Party to the Joint Committee and subject to its consensus, to review the provisions on the protection of intellectual property rights contained in the present Article and in Annex XII, with a view to further improving the levels of protection and to avoid or remedy trade distortions caused by actual levels of protection of intellectual property rights.

CHAPTER V

GOVERNMENT PROCUREMENT

ARTICLE 47
Objective

In accordance with the provisions of this Chapter, the Parties shall ensure the effective and reciprocal opening of their government procurement markets.

ARTICLE 48
Scope and coverage

1.   This Chapter applies to any law, regulation, procedure or practice regarding any procurement, by the entities of the Parties, of goods[7] and services including works, subject to the conditions specified by each Party in Annexes XIII and XIV.

2.   This Chapter shall not be applicable to:

(a)   contracts awarded pursuant to:

(i)   an international agreement and intended for the joint implementation or exploitation of a project by the contracting Parties;

(ii)   an international agreement relating to the stationing of troops; and

(iii)   the particular procedure of an international organisation;

(b)   non-contractual agreements or any form of government assistance and procurement made in the framework of assistance or co-operation programmes;

(c)   contracts for:

---

[6] It is understood that the reference of paragraphs 2 and 3 to Articles 3 to 5 of the TRIPS Agreement is made for the purpose of outlining their applicability to the provisions on Intellectual Property of this Agreement.
[7] For the purpose of this Chapter, "goods" shall mean goods classified in chapters 1 to 97 of the HS.

> (i)   the acquisition or rental of land, existing buildings, or other immovable property or concerning rights thereon;
>
> (ii)   the acquisition, development, production or co-production of programme material by broadcasters and contracts for broadcasting time;
>
> (iii)   arbitration and conciliation services;
>
> (iv)   employment contracts; and
>
> (v)   research and development services other than those where the benefits accrue exclusively to the entity for its use in the conduct of its own affairs, on condition that the service is wholly remunerated by the entity;

(d)   financial services.

3.   Public works concessions, as defined in Article 49, shall also be subject to this Chapter, as specified in Annexes XIII and XIV.

4.   No Party may prepare, design or otherwise structure any procurement contract in order to avoid the obligations under this Chapter.

ARTICLE 49
Definitions

For the purpose of this Chapter, the following definitions shall apply:

(a)   "entity" means an entity covered in Annex XIII;

(b)   "government procurement" means the process by which a government obtains the use of or acquires goods or services, or any combination thereof, for governmental purposes and not with a view to commercial sale or resale, or use in the production or supply of goods or services for commercial sale or resale;

(c)   "liberalisation" means a process as a result of which an entity enjoys no exclusive or special rights and is exclusively engaged in the provision of goods or services on markets that are subject to effective competition;

(d)   "offsets" means those conditions imposed or considered by an entity prior to, or in the course of its procurement process, that encourage local development or improve its Party's balance of payments accounts by means of requirements of local content, licensing of technology, investment, counter-trade or similar requirements;

(e)   "privatisation" means a process by means of which a public entity is no longer subject to government control, whether by public tender of the shares of that entity or otherwise, as contemplated in the respective Party's legislation in force;

(f)   "public works concessions" means a contract of the same type as the public works procurement contracts, except for the fact that the remuneration for the works to be carried out consists either solely in the right to exploit the construction or in this right together with a payment;

(g)   "supplier" means a natural or legal person that provides or could provide goods or services to an entity;

(h)   "technical specifications" means a specification, which lays down the characteristics of the products or services to be procured, such as quality, performance, safety and dimensions, symbols, terminology, packaging, marking and labelling, or the processes and methods for their production and requirements relating to conformity assessment procedures prescribed by procuring entities; and

(i)   "tenderer" means a supplier who has submitted a tender.

ARTICLE 50
National treatment and non-discrimination

1.   With respect to any laws, regulations, procedures and practices regarding government procurement covered by this Chapter, each Party shall grant the goods, services and suppliers of another Party a treatment no less favourable than that accorded by it to domestic goods, services and suppliers.

2.   With respect to any laws, regulations, procedures and practices regarding government procurement covered by this Chapter, each Party shall ensure:

(a)   that its entities do not treat a locally-established supplier less favourably than another locally-established supplier on the basis of the degree of foreign affiliation to or ownership by, a person of another Party; and

(b)   that its entities do not discriminate against a locally-established supplier on the basis that the goods or services offered by that supplier for a particular procurement are goods or services of another Party.

3.   This Article shall not apply to measures concerning customs duties or other charges of any kind imposed on, or in connection with importation, the method of levying such duties and charges, other import regulations, including restrictions and formalities, nor to measures affecting trade in services other than measures specifically governing procurement covered by this Chapter.

ARTICLE 51
Prohibition of offsets

Each Party shall ensure that its entities do not, in the qualification and selection of suppliers, goods or services, in the evaluation of bids or in the award of contracts, consider, seek or impose offsets.

ARTICLE 52
Valuation rules

1.   Entities shall not split up a procurement, nor use any other method of contract valuation with the intention of evading the application of this Chapter when determining whether a contract is covered by the disciplines thereof, subject to the conditions set out in Annexes XIII and XIV.

2.   In calculating the value of a contract, an entity shall take into account all forms of remuneration, such as premiums, fees, commissions and interests, as well as the maximum permitted total amount, including option clauses, provided for by the contract.

3.   When, due to the nature of the contract, it is not possible to calculate in advance its precise value, entities shall estimate this value on the basis of objective criteria.

ARTICLE 53
Transparency

1.   Each Party shall promptly publish any law, regulation, judicial decision and administrative ruling of general application and procedure, including standard contract clauses, regarding procurement covered by this Chapter in the appropriate publications referred to in Appendix 2 of Annex XIV, including officially designated electronic media.

2.   Each Party shall promptly publish in the same manner all modifications to such measures.

ARTICLE 54
Tendering procedures

1.   Entities shall award their public contracts by open or selective tendering procedures according to their national procedures, in compliance with this Chapter and in a non-discriminatory manner.

2.   For the purposes of this Chapter:

    (a)   open tendering procedures are those procedures whereby any interested supplier may submit a tender.

    (b)   selective tendering procedures are those procedures whereby, consistent with Article 55 and other relevant provisions of this Chapter, only suppliers satisfying qualification requirements established by the entities are invited to submit a tender.

3.   However, in the specific cases and only under the conditions laid down in Article 56, entities may use a procedure other than the open or selective tendering procedures referred to in paragraph 1, in which case the entities may choose not to publish a notice of intended procurement, and may consult the suppliers of their choice and negotiate the terms of contract with one or more of these.

4.   Entities shall treat tenders in confidence. In particular, they shall not provide information intended to assist particular participants to bring their tenders up to the level of other participants.

ARTICLE 55
Selective tendering

1.   In selective tendering, entities may limit the number of qualified suppliers they will invite to tender, consistent with the efficient operation of the procurement process, provided that they select the maximum number of domestic suppliers and suppliers of another Party, and that they make the selection in a fair and non-discriminatory manner and on the basis of the criteria indicated in the notice of intended procurement or in tender documents.

2.   Entities maintaining permanent lists of qualified suppliers may select suppliers to be invited to tender from among those listed, under the conditions foreseen in Article 57(7). Any selection shall allow for equitable opportunities for suppliers on the lists.

ARTICLE 56
Other procedures

1.   Provided that the tendering procedure is not used to avoid maximum possible competition or to protect domestic suppliers, entities shall be allowed to award contracts by means other than an open or selective tendering procedure in the following circumstances and subject to the following conditions, where applicable:

(a)   when no suitable tenders or request to participate have been submitted in response to a prior procurement, on condition that the requirements of the initial procurement are not substantially modified;

(b)   when, for technical or artistic reasons, or for reasons connected with protection of exclusive rights, the contract may be performed only by a particular supplier and no reasonable alternative or substitute exists;

(c)   for reasons of extreme urgency brought about by events unforeseeable by the entity, the products or services could not be obtained in time by means of open or selective tendering procedures;

(d)   for additional deliveries of goods or services by the original supplier where a change of supplier would compel the entity to procure equipment or services not meeting requirements of interchangeability with already existing equipment, software or services;

(e)   when an entity procures prototypes or a first product or service which are developed at its request in the course of, and for, a particular contract for research, experiment, study or original development;

(f)   when additional services which were not included in the initial contract but which were within the objectives of the original tender documentation have, through unforeseeable circumstances, become necessary to complete the services described therein. However, the total value of contracts awarded for the additional construction services may not exceed 50 percent of the amount of the main contract;

(g)   for new services consisting of the repetition of similar services and for which the entity has indicated in the notice concerning the initial service, that tendering procedures other than open or selective might be used in awarding contracts for such new services;

(h)   in the case of contracts awarded to the winner of a design contest, provided that the contest has been organised in a manner which is consistent with the principles of this Chapter; in case of several successful candidates, all successful candidates shall be invited to participate in the negotiations; and

(i)   for quoted goods purchased on a commodity market and for purchases of goods made under exceptionally advantageous conditions which only arise in the very short term in the case of unusual disposals and not for routine purchases from regular suppliers.

2.   The Parties shall ensure that, whenever it is necessary for entities to resort to a procedure other than the open or selective tendering procedures based on the circumstances set forth in paragraph 1, the entities shall maintain a record or prepare a written report providing specific justification for the contract awarded under that paragraph.

ARTICLE 57
Qualification of suppliers

1.   Any conditions for participation in procurement shall be limited to those that are essential to ensure that the potential supplier has the capability to fulfil the requirements of the procurement and the ability to execute the contract in question.

2.   In the process of qualifying suppliers, entities shall not discriminate between domestic suppliers and suppliers of another Party.

3.   A Party shall not impose the condition that, in order for a supplier to participate in a procurement, the supplier has previously been awarded one or more contracts by an entity of that Party or that the supplier has prior work experience in the territory of that Party.

4.   Entities shall recognise as qualified suppliers all suppliers who meet the conditions for participation in a particular intended procurement. Entities shall base their qualification decisions solely on the conditions for participation that have been specified in advance in notices or tender documentation.

5.   Nothing in this Chapter shall preclude the exclusion of any supplier on grounds such as bankruptcy or false declarations or conviction for a serious crime such as participation in criminal organisations.

6.   Entities shall promptly communicate to suppliers that have applied for qualification their decision on whether or not they qualify.

Permanent lists of qualified suppliers

7. Entities may establish permanent lists of qualified suppliers provided that the following rules are respected:

   (a) entities establishing permanent lists shall ensure that suppliers may apply for qualification at any time;

   (b) any supplier having requested to become a qualified supplier shall be notified by the entities concerned of the decision in this regard;

   (c) suppliers requesting to participate in a given intended procurement who are not on the permanent list of qualified suppliers shall be given the possibility to participate in the procurement by presenting the equivalent certifications and other means of proof requested from suppliers who are on the list;

   (d) when an entity operating in the utilities sector uses a notice on the existence of a permanent list as a notice of intended procurement, as provided in Annex XIV, Appendix 5, paragraph 6, suppliers requesting to participate who are not on the permanent list of qualified suppliers shall also be considered for the procurement, provided there is sufficient time to complete the qualification procedure; in this event, the procuring entity shall promptly start procedures for qualification and the process of, and the time required for, qualifying suppliers shall not be used in order to keep suppliers of other Parties off the suppliers' list.

ARTICLE 58
Publication of notices

General provisions

1. Each Party shall ensure that its entities provide for effective dissemination of the tendering opportunities generated by the relevant government procurement processes, providing suppliers of another Party with all the information required to take part in such procurement.

2. For each contract covered by this Chapter, except as set out in Articles 54(3) and 56, entities shall publish in advance a notice inviting interested suppliers to submit tenders, or where appropriate, requests for participation for that contract.

3. The information in each notice of intended procurement shall include at least the following:

   (a) name, address, telefax number, electronic address of the entity and, if different, the address where all documents relating to the procurement may be obtained;

   (b) the tendering procedure chosen and the form of the contract;

   (c) a description of the intended procurement, as well as essential contract requirements to be fulfilled;

   (d) any conditions that suppliers must fulfil to participate in the procurement;

(e) time-limits for submission of tenders and, where appropriate, other time limits;

(f) main criteria to be used for award of the contract; and

(g) if possible, terms of payment and any other terms.

Common provisions

4. Each notice referred to in this Article and Appendix 5 of Annex XIV, shall be accessible during the entire time period established for tendering for the relevant procurement.

5. Entities shall publish the notices in a timely manner through means which offer the widest possible and non-discriminatory access to the interested suppliers of the Parties. These means shall be accessible free of charge through a single point of access specified in Appendix 2 to Annex XIV.

ARTICLE 59
Tender documentation

1. Tender documentation provided to suppliers shall contain all information necessary to permit them to submit responsive tenders.

2. Where contracting entities do not offer free direct access to the entire tender documents and any supporting documents by electronic means, entities shall make promptly available the tender documentation at the request of any supplier of the Parties.

3. Entities shall promptly reply to any reasonable request for relevant information relating to the intended procurement, on condition that such information does not give that supplier an advantage over its competitors.

ARTICLE 60
Technical specifications

1. Technical specifications shall be set out in the notices, tender documents or additional documents.

2. Each Party shall ensure that its entities do not prepare, adopt or apply any technical specifications with a view to, or with the effect of, creating unnecessary obstacles to trade between the Parties.

3. Technical specifications prescribed by entities shall be:

(a) in terms of performance and functional requirements rather than design or descriptive characteristics; and

(b) based on international standards, where these exist or, in their absence, on national technical regulations[8] , recognised national standards[9] , or building codes.

---

[8] For the purpose of this Chapter, a technical regulation is a document which lays down characteristics of a product or a service or their related processes and production methods, including the applicable administrative

4.   The provisions of paragraph 3 do not apply when the entity can objectively demonstrate that the use of technical specifications referred to in that paragraph would be ineffective or inappropriate for the fulfilment of the legitimate objectives pursued.

5.   In all cases, entities shall consider bids which do not comply with the technical specifications but meet the essential requirements thereof and are fit for the purpose intended. The reference to technical specifications in the tender documents must include words such as "or equivalent".

6.   There shall be no requirement or reference to a particular trademark or trade name, patent, design or type, specific origin, producer or supplier, unless there is no sufficiently precise or intelligible way of describing the procurement requirements and provided that words, such as "or equivalent", are included in the tender documentation.

7.   The tenderer shall have the burden of proof to demonstrate that his bid meets the essential requirements.

ARTICLE 61
Time limits

1.   All time limits established by the entities for the receipt of tenders and requests to participate shall be adequate to allow suppliers of another Party, as well as domestic suppliers, to prepare and to submit tenders, and where appropriate, requests for participation or applications for qualifying. In determining any such time limit, entities shall, consistent with their own reasonable needs, take into account such factors as the complexity of the intended procurement and the normal time for transmitting tenders from foreign as well as domestic points.

2.   Each Party shall ensure that its entities shall take due account of publication delays when setting the final date for receipt of tenders or of requests for participation or for qualifying for the suppliers' list.

3.   The minimum time limits for the receipt of tenders are specified in Appendix 3 to Annex XIV.

ARTICLE 62
Negotiations

1.   A Party may provide for its entities to conduct negotiations:

   (a)   in the context of procurements in which they have indicated such intent in the notice of intended procurement; or

---

provisions, with which compliance is mandatory. It may also include or deal exclusively with terminology, symbols, packaging, marking or labeling requirements as they apply to a product, service, process or production method.

[9] For the purpose of this Chapter, a standard is a document approved by a recognised body, that provides, for common and repeated use, rules, guidelines or characteristics for products or services or related processes and production methods, with which compliance is not mandatory. It may also include or deal exclusively with terminology, symbols, packaging, marking or labeling requirements as they apply to a product, service, process or production method.

(b) when it appears from evaluation that no one tender is obviously the most advantageous in terms of the specific evaluation criteria set forth in the notices or tender documentation.

2. Negotiations shall primarily be used to identify the strengths and weaknesses in tenders.

3. Entities shall not, in the course of negotiations, discriminate between tenderers. In particular, they shall ensure that:

(a) any elimination of participants is carried out in accordance with the criteria set forth in the notices and tender documentation;

(b) all modifications to the criteria and to the technical requirements are transmitted in writing to all remaining participants in the negotiations;

(c) on the basis of the revised requirements and/or when negotiations are concluded, all remaining participants are afforded an opportunity to submit new or amended tenders in accordance with a common deadline.

ARTICLE 63
Submission, receipt and opening of tenders

1. Tenders and requests to participate in procedures shall be submitted in writing.

2. Entities shall receive and open bids from tenderers under procedures and conditions guaranteeing the respect of the principles of transparency and non-discrimination.

ARTICLE 64
Awarding of contracts

1. To be considered for award, a tender must, at the time of opening, conform to the essential requirements of the notices or tender documentation and be submitted by a supplier which complies with the conditions for participation.

2. Entities shall make the award to the tenderer whose tender is either the lowest tender or the tender which, in terms of the specific objective evaluation criteria previously set forth in the notices or tender documentation, is determined to be the most advantageous.

ARTICLE 65
Information on contract award

1. Each Party shall ensure that its entities provide for effective dissemination of the results of government procurement processes.

2. Entities shall promptly inform tenderers of decisions regarding the award of the contract and of the characteristics and relative advantages of the selected tender. Upon request, entities shall inform any eliminated tenderer of the reasons for the rejection of its tender.

3. Entities may decide to withhold certain information on the contract award where release of such information would prevent law enforcement or otherwise be contrary to the public

interest, would prejudice the legitimate commercial interests of suppliers, or might prejudice fair competition between them.

ARTICLE 66
Bid challenges

1.   Entities shall accord impartial and timely consideration to any complaints from suppliers regarding an alleged breach of this Chapter in the context of a procurement procedure.

2.   Each Party shall provide non-discriminatory, timely, transparent and effective procedures enabling suppliers to challenge alleged breaches of this Chapter arising in the context of procurements in which they have, or have had, an interest.

3.   Challenges shall be heard by an impartial and independent reviewing authority. A reviewing authority which is not a court shall either be subject to judicial review or shall have procedural guarantees similar to those of a court.

4.   Challenge procedures shall provide for:

   (a)   rapid interim measures to correct breaches of this Chapter and to preserve commercial opportunities. Such action may result in suspension of the procurement process. However, procedures may provide that overriding adverse consequences for the interests concerned, including the public interest, may be taken into account in deciding whether such measures should be applied; and

   (b)   if appropriate, correction of the breach of this Chapter or, in the absence of such correction, compensation for the loss or damages suffered, which may be limited to costs for tender preparation and protest.

ARTICLE 67
Information technology and co-operation

1.   The Parties shall, to the extent possible, endeavour to use electronic means of communication to permit efficient dissemination of information on government procurement, particularly as regards tender opportunities offered by entities, while respecting the principles of transparency and non-discrimination.

2.   The Parties shall endeavour to provide each other with technical co-operation, particularly aimed at small and medium size enterprises, with a view to achieve a better understanding of their respective government procurement systems and statistics, as well as a better access to their respective markets.

ARTICLE 68
Modifications to coverage

1.   A Party may modify its coverage under this Chapter, provided that it:

   (a)   notifies the other Parties of the modification; and

(b)   provides the other Parties, within 30 days following the date of such notification, appropriate compensatory adjustments to its coverage in order to maintain a level of coverage comparable to that existing prior to the modification.

2.   Notwithstanding paragraph 1(b), no compensatory adjustments shall be provided to the other Parties where the modification by a Party of its coverage under this Chapter concerns:

(a)   rectifications of a purely formal nature and minor amendments to Annexes XIII and XIV;

(b)   one or more covered entities on which government control or influence has been effectively eliminated as a result of privatisation or liberalisation.

3.   Where the Parties agree on the modification, the Joint Committee shall give effect to the agreement by amending the relevant Annex.

ARTICLE 69
Further negotiations

In the case that a Party offers, in the future, a third party additional advantages with regard to its respective government procurement market access coverage agreed under this Chapter, it shall agree, upon request of another Party, to enter into negotiations with a view to extending coverage under this Chapter on a reciprocal basis.

ARTICLE 70
Exceptions

Provided that such measures are not applied in a manner that would constitute a means of arbitrary or unjustifiable discrimination between the Parties or a disguised restriction on trade between them, nothing in this Chapter shall be construed to prevent any Party from adopting or maintaining measures necessary to protect:

(a)   public morals, order or safety;

(b)   human life, health or security;

(c)   animal or plant life or health;

(d)   intellectual property; or

(d)   relating to goods or services of handicapped persons, of philanthropic institutions or of prison labour.

ARTICLE 71
Review and implementation

1.   The Joint Committee shall review the implementation of this Chapter every two years, unless otherwise agreed by the Parties; it shall consider any issue arising from it, and take appropriate action in the exercise of its functions.

2.   At the request of a Party, the Parties shall convene a bilateral Working Group to address issues related to the implementation of this Chapter. Such issues may include:

(a)   bilateral cooperation relating to the development and use of electronic communications in government procurement systems;

(b)   the exchange of statistics and other information needed for monitoring procurement conducted by the Parties and the results of the application of this Chapter; and

(c)   exploration of potential interest in further negotiations aimed at further broadening of the scope of market access commitments under this Chapter.

*

Part Two

Prototype Instruments

TRATADO ENTRE EL GOBIERNO DE LA REPUBLICA DE GUATEMALA Y EL GOBIERNO DE LA REPUBLICA DE_____ PARA EL FOMENTO Y PROTECCION DE LAS INVERSIONES*

Tratado Entre el Gobierno de la Republica de Guatemala y el Gobierno de la Republica de_____ para el Fomento y Proteccion de las Inversiones

El Gobierno de la República de Guatemala y el Gobierno de la República de _____ en adelante denominadas las Partes Contratantes;

Animados por el deseo de crear condiciones favorables para que los inversionistas de una Parte Contratante realicen mayores inversiones en el territorio de la otra Parte Contratante;

Reconociendo que el fomento y la protección recíproca mediante acuerdos internacionales de esas inversiones de capital pueden servir para estimular la iniciativa económica individual y aumentar la prosperidad de ambas Partes Contratantes;

Han acordado lo siguiente:

ARÚCULO 1. DEFINICIONES

Para los fines del presente Convenio:

(a)   El término "inversión" significa toda clase de activos tales como bienes, derechos e intereses de toda naturaleza, y en particular, aunque no exclusivamente, comprende.

>   (i)   bienes muebles e inmuebles y derechos reales, tales como hipotecas y prendas;
>
>   (ii)   acciones, títulos y obligaciones de sociedades y otras formas de participación en los bienes de sociedades y personas jurídicas constituidas en una de las Partes Contratantes conforme a la legislación de cada Parte;
>
>   (iii)   derechos de crédito o cualquier prestación   que tenga un valor financiero;
>
>   (iv)   derechos de propiedad intelectual, derechos de llave, procesos y conocimientos técnicos;
>
>   (v)   concesiones de tipo comercial otorgadas por disposición legal o bajo contrato, incluidas las concesiones para la exploración, cultivo, extracción o explotación de recursos naturales.
>
>   Ninguna modificación a la forma original en que se haya realizado fa Inversión afectará su carácter como tal, siempre que dicha modificación no sea contraria a la legislación de la Parte Contratante donde se efectúe la inversión.

---

* *Source*: The Government of the Republic of Guatemala, Ministry of Foreign Affairs (2003).

(b)   El término "rentas" significa las cantidades que rinde una inversión y en particular, aunque no exclusivamente, comprende beneficios, intereses, ganancias de capital, dividendos, cánones y honorarios.

Las rentas, tanto de la inversión original, como de la reinversión gozan de la misma protección.

(c)   El término "inversionista "designa, para cada una de las Partes Contratantes:

(i)   Las personas individuales que, de acuerdo con fa legislación de esa Parte Contratante, son consideradas nacionales de la misma;

(ii)   Las personas jurídicas constituidas en una de las Partes Contratantes, conforme a la legislación de ésta y que tiene allí su sede social, o controladas directa o indirectamente por nacionales de una de las Partes Contratantes o por personas jurídicas que tengan su sede social en una de las Partes Contratantes y constituidas conforme a su legislación.

(d)   El término "territorio" significa:

En relación con la República de Guatemala: el espacio terrestre, marítimo y aéreo, y las zonas marinas y submarinas incluyendo las aguas internas sobre las que el Estado ejerce soberanía de conformidad con la Constitución Política de la República de Guatemala y el Derecho Internacional.

En relación con [   ].

ARTÍCULO 2. FOMENTO Y PROTECCIÓN DE INVERSIONES

(1)   Cada Parte Contratante fomentará y creará condiciones favorables para que los inversionistas de la otra Parte Contratante inviertan capital en su territorio, de conformidad con su legislación.

(2)   A las inversiones de inversionistas de cada Parte Contratante se les concederá en toda ocasión un trato justo y equitativo y gozarán de plena protección y seguridad en el territorio de la otra Parte Contratante. Ninguna de las Partes Contratantes de ningún modo perjudicará, por medidas inmoderadas o discriminatorias, la gestión, mantenimiento, uso, goce o enajenación en su territorio de las inversiones de inversionistas de la otra Parte Contratante. Cada Parte Contratante cumplirá cualquier compromiso que haya contraído en lo referente a las inversiones del inversionista de la otra Parte Contratante.

ARTÍCULO 3. TRATO NACIONAL Y TRATO DE NACIÓN MÁS FAVORECIDA

(1)   Ninguna de las Partes Contratantes someterá en su territorio las inversiones y rentas del inversionista de la otra Parte Contratante a un trato menos favorable del que concede a las inversiones o rentas de sus propios inversionistas o a las inversiones y rentas de los inversionistas de cualquier tercer Estado.

(2)   Ninguna de las Partes Contratantes someterá en su territorio a los inversionistas de la otra Parte Contratante, en cuanto se refiere a la gestión, mantenimiento, uso, goce o enajenación de

sus inversiones, a un trato menos favorable del que concede a sus propios inversionistas, o a los inversionistas de cualquier tercer Estado.

(3)   Queda entendido que el trato previsto en los apartados (1) y (2) precedentes se aplicará a las disposiciones de los Artículos 1 al 12 de este Convenio.

ARTÍCULO 4. INDEMNIZACION EN CASO DE PERDIDAS

Los inversionistas de una de las Partes Contratantes cuyas inversiones en el territorio de la otra Parte Contratante sufran pérdidas a consecuencia de guerra u otro conflicto armado, revolución, estado de emergencia nacional, rebelión, insurrección o motín en el territorio de la otra Parte Contratante, no recibirá de ésta un trato menos favorable del que concede a sus propios inversionistas o a los inversionistas de cualquier tercer Estado en lo referente a - restitución, indemnización, compensación u otro arreglo. Los pagos correspondientes serán libremente transferibles.

ARTÍCULO 5. EXPROPIACIÓN

(1)   Las inversiones de los inversionistas de una Parte Contratante no podrán, en el territorio de la otra Parte Contratante, ser nacionalizadas, expropiadas a sometidas a medidas que en sus efectos equivalgan a nacionalización o expropiación (a las que en lo sucesivo se denomina "expropiación") salvo por razones de utilidad pública relacionadas con las necesidades internas de dicha Parte Contratante a título no discriminatorio y a cambio de compensación puntual, adecuada y efectiva. Dicha compensación equivaldrá al valor real de la inversión expropiada inmediatamente antes de que se expropiara o de que la expropiación inminente se hiciera de conocimiento público, cualquiera que sea anterior y comprenderá los intereses conforme al tipo normal comercial hasta la fecha en que se efectúe el pago. Dicho pago se efectuará sin demora, será efectivamente realizable y libremente transferible. El inversionista tendrá derecho, en virtud de las leyes de la Parte Contratante que efectúe dicha expropiación, a una puntual revisión, por parte de una autoridad judicial u otra autoridad independiente de dicha Parte Contratante, de su causa y de la evaluación de sus inversiones conforme a los principios establecidos en este párrafo.

(2)   En el caso de que una Parte Contratante expropie los bienes de una sociedad incorporada o constituida conforme a las leyes vigentes en cualquier parte de su territorio y en la que los inversionistas de la otra Parte Contratante tengan acciones, se asegurará de que las disposiciones del párrafo (1) de este Artículo se cumplan en todo lo necesario para garantizar la puntual, adecuada y efectiva compensación en lo referente a las inversiones de los inversionistas de la otra Parte Contratante que sean propietarios de dichas acciones.

ARTÍCULO 6. LIBRE TRANSFERENCIA

Cada Parte Contratante, en lo referente a inversiones, garantizará a los inversionistas de la otra Parte Contratante la libre transferencia de sus inversiones y rentas. Las transferencias se efectuarán sin demora en la moneda convertible en la cual se efectuó la inversión de capital originalmente o en cualquier otra moneda convertible convenida por el inversionista y la Parte Contratante interesada. A menos que el inversionista disponga de otro modo, las transferencias se efectuarán al tipo de cambio aplicable en la fecha de la transferencia, de acuerdo con la legislación cambiaría que esté en vigor.

ARTÍCULO 7. EXCEPCIONES

Las disposiciones del Artículo 3 del presente Convenio, no se han de interpretar de modo que obliguen a una Parte Contratante a conceder a los inversionistas de la otra parte Contratante los beneficios de cualquier trato, preferencia o privilegio proveniente de:

(a) cualquier unión aduanera, zona de libre comercio, mercado común, unión económica o cualquier otra forma de organización económica regional existente o futura o cualquier convenio internacional semejante, en el que una u otra de las Partes Contratantes sea o llegue a ser parte; o,

(b) cualquier convenio, acuerdo internacional o legislación interna que esté relacionado en todo o principalmente con tributación.

ARTÍCULO 8. SOLUCION DE DIFERENCIAS ENTRE UN INVERSIONISTA Y UN ESTADO RECEPTOR

Las diferencias entre un inversionista de una Parte Contratante y la otra Parte Contratante concernientes a una obligación de la última conforme a este Convenio y en relación con una inversión de la primera que no hayan sido arregladas amigablemente, serán sometidas, después de un período de tres meses a partir de la notificación escrita del reclamo, a:

(a) los tribunales nacionales competentes o al arbitraje nacional de la Parte Contratante; o,

(b) al Centro Internacional de Arreglo deDiferencias Relativas a Inversiones (CIADI) establecido por las disposiciones del Convenio sobre Arreglo de Diferencias Relativas a Inversiones entre Estados y Nacionales de Otros Estados, abierto a la firma en Washington el 18 de marzo de 1965, y el Mecanismo Complementario para la Administración de Procedimientos de Conciliación, Arbitraje y Encuesta); o,

(c) al Tribunal de Arbitraje de la Cámara de Comercio Internacional; o,

(d) a un árbitro internacional o tribunal de arbitraje ad - hoc a ser designado por un acuerdo especial o establecido conforme al Reglamento de Arbitraje de la Comisión de las Naciones sobre el Derecho Mercantil Internacional.

Si, después de un período de tres meses a partir de la notificación escrita del reclamo, las partes no se pusieren de acuerdo sobre uno de los procedimientos alternativos antes mencionados, la diferencia se someterá, a solicitud por escrito del inversionista en cuestión, a arbitraje conforme al Reglamento de Arbitraje de la Comisión de las Naciones Unidas sobre el Derecho Mercantil Internacional (NUDMI) vigente en ese momento. Las Partes podrán acordar por escrito la modificación de los procedimientos de arbitraje.

ARTÍCULO 9. SOLUCION DE DIFERENCIAS ENTRE LAS PARTES CONTRATANTES

(1) Las diferencias que surgieren entre las Partes Contratantes sobre la interpretación o aplicación del presente Convenio deberán, en lo posible, ser dirimidas por la vía diplomática.

(2) Si una diferencia entre las Partes Contratantes no pudiere ser dirimida de esa manera, "dentro del plazo de seis meses", será sometida a un Tribunal de arbitraje a petición de una u otra de las Partes Contratantes.

(3)   El Tribunal Arbitral estará compuesto de tres miembros y será constituido de la siguiente forma: dentro del plazo de dos meses contados a partir de la fecha de notificación de la solicitud de arbitraje, cada Parte Contratante designará un árbitro. Esos dos árbitros, dentro del plazo de un mes contado a partir de la designación del último de ellos, elegirán de común acuerdo a un tercer miembro quien presidirá el tribunal y deberá ser nacional de un tercer Estado, con el cual ambas Partes Contratantes mantengan relaciones diplomáticas.

(4)   Si dentro de los plazos previstos en el párrafo (3) de este Artículo no se hubieren efectuado los nombramientos necesarios, una u otra de las Partes Contratantes podrá, en ausencia de otro arreglo, invitar al Presidente de la Corte Internacional de Justicia a proceder a los nombramientos necesarios. En caso de que el Presidente sea nacional de una de las dos Partes Contratantes o se halle por otra causa impedido para desempeñar dicha función, Vicepresidente será invitado a efectuar los nombramientos necesarios. Si el Vicepresidente fuere nacional de una de las dos Partes Contratantes o si se hallaré también impedido para desempeñar dicha función, el miembro de la Corte Internacional de Justicia que siga inmediatamente en el orden jerárquico y no sea nacional de una de las dos Partes Contratantes será invitado a ejecutar los nombramientos necesarios.

(5)   El Tribunal Arbitral decidirá sobre la base de las disposiciones de este Convenio y de los principios del derecho internacional. El tribunal decidirá por mayoría de votos y determinará sus propias reglas procesales. Cada una de las Partes Contratantes sufragará los gastos del árbitro respectivo, así como los relativos a su representación en el proceso arbitral.

Los gastos de Presidente y las demás costas dei proceso serán solventados en partes iguales por las Partes Contratantes, salvo que éstas acuerden otra modalidad.

Las decisiones del Tribunal serán definitivas y obligatorias para ambas Partes Contratantes.

ARTÍCULO 10. SUBROGACIÓN

1.   Cuando una Parte Contratante o un organismo autorizado por ésta hubiere otorgado un contrato de seguro o alguna otra garantía financiera contra riesgos no comerciales, con respecto a alguna inversión de uno de sus inversionistas en el territorio de la otra Parte Contratante, ésta última ·deberá reconocer los derechos de la primera Parte Contratante, de subrogarse en los derechos de inversionista, cuando hubiere efectuado un pago en virtud de dicho contrato o garantía.

2.   Cuando una Parte Contratante haya pagado a su inversionista y en tal virtud haya asumido sus derechos, dicho inversionista no podrá reclamar tales derechos a la otra Parte Contratante, salvo autorización expresa de la primera Parte Contratante.

ARTÍCULO 11. AAABITO DE APLICACIÓN

El presente Acuerdo se aplicará a las inversiones establecidas a partir de su entrada en vigor, por inversionistas de una Parte Contratante, conforme a las disposiciones legales de la otra Parte Contratante, en el territorio de esta última.

No obstante, el presente Convenio no se aplicará a divergencias o controversias que hubieran surgido con anterioridad o estén directamente relacionadas con acontecimientos producidos antes de su entrada en vigor.

ARTÍCULO 12. APLICACIÓN DE OTRAS REGLAS

Si las disposiciones de la legislación de cualquier Parte Contratante u obligaciones en virtud del derecho internacional ya existentes o que se establezcan en el futuro entre las Partes Contratantes, además del presente Convenio, contienen reglas ya sean generales o específicas, que conceden a las inversiones realizadas por inversionistas de la otra Parte Contratante un trato más favorable del que se dispone en virtud del presente Convenio, dichas reglas se aplicarán en la medida en que sean más favorables.

ARTÍCULO 13. ENTRADA EN VIGOR

Cada Parte Contratante notificará por escrito a la otra, el cumplimiento de los trámites constitucionales exigidos en su territorio para la entrada en vigor del presente Convenio. El presente Convenio entrará en vigor en la fecha de la última de las dos notificaciones.

ARTÍCULO 14. DURACION Y DENUNCIA

El presente Convenio permanecerá en vigor por un período de diez años. Posteriormente continuará en vigor hasta la expiración de un período de doce meses contado a partir de la fecha en que una de las dos Partes Contratantes haya notificado la denuncia por escrito a la otra. No obstante, en lo referente a inversiones efectuadas en cualquier momento antes de la terminación del Convenio, sus disposiciones continuarán vigentes en lo referente a dichas inversiones por un período de veinte años contado a partir de la fecha de la terminación del mismo y sin perjuicio de la aplicación posterior de las reglas de derecho internacional general.

En fe de lo cual los infrascritos, debidamente autorizados a tal efecto por sus respectivos Gobiernos, firman el presente Convenio.

Hecho en la ciudad de _____ a los ____ días del mes de _____ del 200... en duplicado, en idiomas inglés y español, siendo ambos textos igualmente auténticos.

Por el Gobierno de
la República de Guatemala

Por el Gobierno de
la República de _____

*

AGREEMENT BETWEEN THE GOVERNMENT OF THE ITALIAN REPUBLIC AND THE GOVERNMENT OF THE _____ ON THE PROMOTION AND PROTECTION OF INVESTMENTS[*]

The Government of the Italian Republic and the Government of the _____, hereafter referred to as "Contracting Parties",

DESIRING to establish favourable conditions to enhance economic co-operation between the two Countries, and especially in relation to capital investments by investors of one Contracting Party in the territory of the other Contracting Party, and

ACKNOWLEDGING that offering mutual encouragement and protection to such investments on the basis of international Agreements will contribute to stimulate business ventures which will foster the prosperity of both Contracting Parties;

HAVE agreed as follows:

Article I
Definitions

For the purposes of this Agreement:

1.   The term "investment" shall mean any kind of asset invested, before or after the entry into force of this Agreement, by a natural or legal person of a Contracting Party in the territory of the other Contracting Party, in conformity with the laws and regulations of that Party, irrespective of the legal form chosen, as well as of the legal framework.

Without limiting the generality of the foregoing, the term "investment" shall include in particular, but not exclusively:

a)   movable and immovable property and any ownership rights in rem, including real guarantee rights on a property of a third party, to the extent that it can be invested;

b)   shares, debentures, equity holdings and any other instruments of credit, as well as Government and public securities in general;

c)   credits for sums of money connected with an investment as well as reinvested incomes and capital gains or any service right having an economic value as integral part of an investment;

d)   copyright, commercial trade marks, patents, industrial designs and other intellectual and industrial property rights, know-how, trade secrets, trade names and goodwill;

e)   any economic right accruing by law or by contract and any licence and franchise granted in accordance with the provisions in force on economic activities, including the right to prospect for, extract and exploit natural resources;

---

[*] *Source*: The Government of the Republic of Italy, Ministry of Foreign Affairs (2003).

f)   any increase in value of the original investment.

Any alteration of the legal form chosen for the investments shall not affect their classification as investments.

2.   The term "investor" shall mean any natural or legal person of a Contracting Party investing in the territory of the other Contracting Party as well as any foreign subsidiaries, affiliates and branches controlled in any way by the above natural and legal persons.

3.   The term "natural person", with reference to either Contracting Party, shall mean any natural person having the nationality of that State in accordance with its laws.

4.   The term "legal person", with reference to either Contracting Party, shall mean any entity having its head office in the territory of one of the Contracting Parties and recognised by it, such as public institutions, corporations, partnerships, foundations and associations, regardless of whether their liability is limited or otherwise.

5.   The term "income" shall mean the money accrued or accruing to an investment, including in particular profits or interests, dividends, royalties, payments for assistance or technical services and other services, as well as any considerations in kind.

6.   The term "territory" shall mean in addition to the zones comprised within land borders also the "maritime zones". The latter shall include also marine and submarine zones over which the Contracting Parties exercise sovereignty and sovereign or jurisdictional rights under international law.

7.   The term "investment agreement" shall mean an agreement that a Contracting Party may stipulate with an investor of the other Contracting Party in order to regulate the specific relationship concerning the investment.

8.   The term "non-discriminatory treatment" shall mean treatment that is at least as favourable as the best between national treatment and the most-favoured-nation treatment.

9.   The term "right of access" shall mean the right to be admitted to invest in the territory of the order Contracting Party. Investors of either Contracting Party shall have the right of access to investment activities in the territory of the other Contracting Party, with the exceptions to which the latter is entitled by multilateral agreements.

10.   The term "activities connected with an investment" shall include, inter alia, the organisation, control, operation, maintenance and disposal of companies, branches, agencies, offices or other organisations for the conduct of business; the access to the financial markets; the borrowing of funds, the purchase, sale and issue of shares and other securities and the purchase of foreign exchange for imports necessary for the conduct of business affairs; the marketing of goods and services; the procurement, sale and transport of raw and processed materials, energy, fuels and production means and the dissemination of commercial information.

Article II
Promotion and Protection of investments

1.   Both Contracting Parties shall encourage investors of the other Contracting Party to invest in their territory.

2.   Investors of either Contracting Parties shall have the right of access to investments activities in the territory of the other Contracting Party, which shall be not less favourable than that under Article III, paragraph 1.

3.   Both Contracting Parties shall at all times ensure just and fair treatment to investments of investors of the other Contracting Party. Both Contracting Parties shall ensure that the management, maintenance, use, transformation, enjoyment or assignment of the investments effected in their territory by investors of the other Contracting Party, as well as by companies and enterprises in which these investments have been effected, shall in no way be the object of unjustified or discriminatory measures.

4.   Each Contracting Party shall create and maintain in its territory a legal framework capable of guaranteeing to investors the continuity of legal treatment, including compliance in good faith to all undertakings entered into with regard to each individual investor.

5.   Neither Contracting Parties shall set any conditions for the establishment, expansion or continuation of investments which might imply taking over or imposing any obligations on export production and specifying that goods must be procured locally or similar conditions.

6.   In accordance with its laws and regulations, each Contracting Party shall grant to nationals of the other Contracting Party, who are in its territory in connection with an investment as part this Agreement, adequate working conditions for carrying out their professional activities. Each Contracting Party and shall regulate as favourably as possible the problems connected with the entry, stay, work and movement in its territory of the above nationals of the other Contracting Party and members of their families.

Companies constituted under the laws and regulations of one Contracting Party and which are owned or controlled by investors of the other Contracting Party shall be permitted to engage top managerial personnel of their choice, regardless of nationality, in accordance with the laws of the host Contracting Party.

Article III
National Treatment and the Most Favoured Nation clause

1.   Both Contracting Parties, within their own territory, shall offer investments effected by, and income accruing to, investors of the other Contracting Party no less favourable treatment than that accorded to investments effected by, and income accruing to, its own nationals or investors of Third States. The same treatment will be granted to the activities connected with an investment.

2.   Should, from the legislation of either Contracting Parties or from the international obligations in force or that may come into force in the future for one of the Contracting Parties, come out a legal framework according which investors of the other Contracting Party would be granted a more favourable treatment than the one provided in this Agreement the treatment granted to the investors of such other Party will apply to investors of the relevant Contracting Party also for the outstanding relationships.

3.   The provisions under points 1 and 2 of this Article do not refer to the advantages and privileges which one Contracting Party may grant to investors of Third States by virtue of their membership to a Customs or Economic Union, a Common Market, to a Free Trade Area, to a

regional or sub-regional Agreement, to an international multilateral economic Agreement or under Agreements to avoid double taxation or to facilitate cross border trade.

Article IV
Compensation for Damages or Losses

Should investors of either Contracting Parties incur losses or damages on their investments in the territory of the other Contracting Party due to war, other forms of armed conflict, a state of emergency, civil strife or other similar events, the Contracting Party in which the investment has been effected shall offer adequate compensation in respect of such losses or damages, irrespective of whether they have been caused by governmental forces or other subjects. Compensation payments shall be made in freely convertible currency, freely transferable without undue delay.

The investors concerned shall receive in any case the same treatment as the nationals of the other Contracting Party and, at all events, no less favourable treatment than investors of Third States.

Article V
Nationalisation or Expropriation

1.   Investments covered by this Agreement shall not be subjected to any measure which might limit the right of ownership, possession, control or enjoyment of the investments, permanently or temporarily, unless specifically provided for by current, national or local law and regulations and orders issued by Courts or Tribunals having jurisdictions.

2.   Investments and the activities connected with an investment of investors of one of the Contracting Parties shall not be, de jure or de facto, directly or indirectly, nationalised, expropriated, requisitioned or subjected to any measures having an equivalent effect, including measures affecting companies and their assets controlled by the investor in the territory of the other contracting Party, except for public purpose or national interest and in exchange for immediate, full and effective compensation, and on condition that these measures are taken on a non-discriminatory basis and in conformity with all legal provisions and procedures.

3.   The just compensation shall be equivalent to the fair market value of the expropriated investment immediately prior to the moment in which the decision to nationalise or expropriate was announced or made public.

Whenever there are difficulties in ascertaining the fair market value, it shall be determined according to the internationally acknowledged evaluation standards.

Compensation shall be calculated in a convertible currency at the prevailing exchange rate applicable on the date on which the decision to nationalise or expropriate was announced or made public and shall include interests calculated on the basis of EURIBOR standards from the date of nationalisation or expropriation to the date of payment and shall be freely collectable and transferable.

Once the compensation has been determined, it shall be paid without undue delay and in any case within 1 month.

4.   In case the object of the expropriation is a joint-venture constituted in the territory of either Contracting Party, the compensation to be paid to the investor of a Contracting Party shall be calculated taking into account the value of the share of such investor in the joint-venture, in accordance with its basic documents and adopting the same evaluations criteria referred to in the paragraph 3 of this Article.

5.   A national or company of either Contracting Party asserting that all or part of its investments has been expropriated shall enjoy the right of a prompt review by the appropriate judicial or administrative authorities of the other Contracting Party, in order to determine whether any such expropriation occurred and, if so, whether expropriation and any compensation thereof conform to the principles of international law, and in order to decide all other relevant matters.

6.   If, after the expropriation, the expropriated investment does not serve the anticipated purpose, wholly or partially, the former owner or his/its assignee/s shall be entitled to repurchase it. The price of such expropriated investment shall be calculated with reference to the date in which the repurchasing takes place, adopting the same valuation criteria taken into account when calculating the compensation referred to in paragraph 3 of this Article.

Article VI
Repatriation of Capital, Profits and Income

1.   Each Contracting Party shall ensure that all payments relating to investment in its territory of an investor of the other Contracting Party may be freely transferred into and out of its territory without undue delay after the fiscal obligations have been met. Such transfers shall include, in particular, but not exclusively:

   a)   capital and additional capital, including reinvested income, used to maintain and increase investment;

   b)   the net income, dividends, royalties, payments for assistance and technical services, interests and other profits;

   c)   income deriving from the total or partial sale or the total or partial liquidation of an investment;

   d)   funds to repay loans connected to an investment and the payment of relevant interests;

   e)   remuneration and allowances paid to nationals of the other Contracting Party for work and services performed in relation to an investment effected in the territory of the other Contracting Party, in the amount and manner provided for by national legislation and regulations in force;

   f)   compensation payments under Article IV.

2.   The fiscal obligations under paragraph 1 above are deemed to be complied with when the investor has fulfilled the procedures provided for by the legislation of the Contracting Party on which territory the investment has been taken place.

3.   Without restricting the scope of Article III of this Agreement, both Contracting Parties undertake to apply to the transfers mentioned in paragraph 1 of this Article the same favourable treatment that is accorded to investments effected by investors of third States, in case it is more favourable.

4.   In the event that, due to very serious balance of payments problems, one of Contracting Party were to temporarily restrict tansfer of funds, these restriction shall be applied to the investments related to this Agreement, only if the Contracting Party implements International Found Monetary relevant provisions adopted in the specific case. These restrictions would be adopted on an equitable, non-discriminatory and in good faith basis.

Article VII
Subrogation

In the event that one Contracting Party or an Institution thereof has provided a guarantee in respect of non-commercial risks for the investment effected by one of its investors in the territory of the other Contracting Party, and has effected payment to said investor on the basis of that guarantee, the other Contracting Party shall recognise the assignment of the rights of the investor to the former Contracting Party. In relation to the transfer of payment to the Contracting Party or its Institution by virtue of this assignment, the provisions of Articles IV, V and VI of this Agreement shall apply.

Article VIII
Transfer procedures

The transfers referred to in Articles IV, V, VI and VII shall be effected without undue delay and, in any case, within one month. All transfers shall be made in a freely convertible currency at the prevailing exchange rate applicable on the date on which the investor applied for the related transfer, with the exception of the provision under paragraph 3 of Article V concerning the exchange rate applicable in case of nationalisation or expropriation.

Article IX
Settlement of Dispute between the Contracting Parties

1.   Any dispute, which may arise between the Contracting Parties, relating to the interpretation and application of this Agreement shall, as far as possible, be settled through consultation and negotiation.

2.   In the event that the dispute cannot be settled within six months from the date on which one of the Contracting Parties notify the other Contracting Party in writing, the dispute shall, at the request of one of the Contracting Parties, be laid before and ad hoc Arbitration Tribunal as provided for in this Article.

3.   The Arbitration Tribunal shall be constituted in the following manner: within two months from the moment on which the request for arbitration is received, each of the two Contracting Parties shall appoint a member of the Tribunal. The President shall be appointed within three months from the date on which the other two members are appointed.

4.   If, within the period specified in paragraph 3 of this Article, the appointment has not been made, each of the two Contracting Parties can, in default of other arrangement, asks the President

of the International Court of Justice to make the appointment. In the event that the President of the Court is a national of one of the Contracting Parties or if, for any reason, it is impossible for him to make the appointment, the application shall be made to the Vice-President of the Court. If the Vice-President of the Court is a national of one of the Contracting Parties or, for any reason is unable to make the appointment, the most senior member of the International Court of Justice, who is not a national of one of the Contracting Parties, shall be invited to make the appointment.

5.   The Arbitration Tribunal shall rule with a majority vote, and its decision shall be binding. Both Contracting Parties shall pay the cost of their own arbitration and of their representative at the hearings. The President's cost and any other cost shall be divided equally between the Contracting Parties. The Arbitration Tribunal shall lay down its own procedure.

Article X
Settlement of Dispute between Investors and Contracting Parties

1.   Any dispute which may arise between one of the Contracting Parties and the investor of the other Contracting Party on investment, including dispute relating to the amount of compensation, shall be settled through consultation and negotiation, as far as possible.

2.   In case the investor and one entity of either Contracting Parties stipulated an investment agreement, the procedure foreseen in such investment agreement shall apply.

3.   In the event that such dispute cannot be settled as provided for in paragraph 1 of this Article within six months from the date of the written application for settlement, the investor in question may submit at his choice the dispute for settlement to:

    a)   the Contracting Party' Court having territorial jurisdiction;

    b)   an ad hoc Arbitration Tribunal, in compliance with the arbitration regulation of the UN Commission on International Trade Law (UNCITRAL); the host Contracting Party undertake hereby to accept reference to said arbitration;

    c)   the International Centre for Settlement of Investment Dispute, for the implementation of the arbitration procedure under the Washington Convention of 18 March, 1965, on the Settlement of Investment Dispute between State and Nationals of other State, if or as soon as both Contracting Parties have acceded to it.

4.   Under paragraph 3, lett. b), of this Article, arbitration shall be conducted pursuant to the following provisions:

    the Arbitration Tribunal shall be composed of three arbitrators; if they are not nationals of either Contracting Party, they shall be nationals of States having diplomatic relations with both Contracting Parties, appointed by the President of the Arbitration Institute of the Stockholm/Paris Chamber, in his capacity as Appointing Authority. The arbitration will take place in Stockholm/Paris, unless the two Parties in the arbitration have agreed otherwise. When delivering its decision, the Arbitration Tribunal shall apply the provisions contained in this Agreement, as well as the principles of international law recognized by the two Contracting Parties. Recognition and implementation of the arbitration decision in the territory of the Contracting Parties shall be governed by their respective national legislation, in compliance with the relevant international Conventions they are Parties to.

5.   Both Contracting Parties shall refrain from negotiating through diplomatic channels any matter relating to an arbitration procedure or judicial procedure underway until these procedures have been concluded, and if one of the Contracting Parties has failed to comply with the ruling of the Arbitration Tribunal or the Court of law within the period envisaged by the ruling, or else within the period which can be determined on the basis of the international or domestic law provision which can be applied to the case.

Article XI
Relation between Governments

The provision of this Agreement shall be applied irrespective of whether or not the Contracting Parties have diplomatic or consular relations.

Article XII
Application of other Provisions

1.   If a matter is governed both by this Agreement and another International Agreement to which both Contracting Parties are signatories, and by general international law provision, the most favourable provision shall be applied to the Contracting Parties and to their investors.

2.   Whenever the treatment accorded by one Contracting Party to the investors of the other Contracting Party, according to its laws and regulations or other provisions or specific contract or investment authorisation or agreements, is more favourable than that provided under this Agreement, the most favourable treatment shall apply.

3.   After the date when the investment has been made, any substantial modification in the legislation of the Contracting party regulating directly or indirectly the investment shall not be applied retroactively and the investments made under this Agreement shall therefore be protected.

4.   The provisions of this Agreement shall not, however, limit the application of the national provisions aimed at preventing fiscal evasion and elusion. To this purpose the competent authorities of each Contracting Party commit themselves to provide any useful information upon the other Contracting Party' request.

Article XIII
Entry into Force

This Agreement shall come into force on the date of the receipt of the last of the two notifications by which the two Contracting Parties shall have communicated officially to each other that their respective ratification procedures have been completed.

Article XIV
Duration and Expiry

1.   This Agreement shall remain effective for a period of 10 years and shall remain in force for a further period of 5 years thereafter, unless either Contracting Parties decide to denounce it not later than one year before its expiry date.

2.   In case of investment effected prior to the expiry date, as provided for under paragraph 1 of this Article, the provision of Articles I to XII shall remain effective for a further period of five years after the aforementioned date.

In witness thereof the undersigned Representatives, duly authorised by their respective Governments, have signed the present Agreement.

DONE at ...., on........................in two originals each in the Italian, ... and English languages, both texts been equally authentic. In case of any divergence on interpretation, the English text shall prevail.

*

AGREEMENT ON ENCOURAGEMENT AND RECIPROCAL PROTECTION OF INVESTMENTS BETWEEN THE REPUBLIC OF KENYA AND
_____
*

The Republic of Kenya and the _____ .

Hereinafter referred to as the Contracting Parties

Desiring to strengthen their traditional ties of friendship and to extend and intensify the economic relations between them particularly with respect to investments by the nationals of one Contracting Party in the territory of the other Contracting Party

Recognizing that agreement upon the treatment to be accorded to such investments will stimulate the flow of capital and technology and economic development of the Contracting Parties and that fair and equitable treatment of investment is desirable,

Have agreed as follows;

Article 1
Definitions

For the purpose of this Agreement:

(a)   the term "investments" shall be construed to mean any kind of property invested before or after the entry into force of this Agreement by a natural or legal persons being national of one Contracting Party in the territory of the other, in conformity with the laws and regulations of the latter.

Without limiting the generality of the foregoing, the term "investment" comprises;

(i)   movable and immovable property as well as any other rights in rem in respect of every kind of assets;

(ii)   rights derived from shares, bonds and other kinds of interests in companies and joint ventures;

(iii)   claims to money, to other assets or to any performance having an economic value;

(iv)   rights in the field of intellectual property, technical processes, goodwill and know-how;

(v)   rights granted under public law or under contract, including rights to prospect, explore, extract and win natural resources

(vi)   the minimum volume of investment set at _____ million US dollars or the equivalent.

---

* *Source*: The Government of the Republic of Kenya, Ministry of Foreign Affairs (2003).

(b) "investor" means the following subjects which have made an investment in the territory of the other Contracting Party in accordance with the present Agreement:

(i) natural persons who, according to the law of that Contracting Party, are considered to be its nationals;

(ii) a legal entity, including companies, corporations, business associations and other legally recognized entities, which are constituted or otherwise duly organized under the law of that Contracting Party and have their seat together with effective economic activities in the territory of that same Contracting Party.

c) "returns" means all amounts yielded by an investment and in particular, though not exclusively, include profits, interest, capital gains, dividends, royalties, fees or other incomes.

d) "territory" means in respect of each of the Contracting Party the land territory and territorial waters of each of the Contracting Party, over which it has jurisdiction and sovereign rights pursuant to international law.

Article 2
Promotion and encouragement of investments

1. Either Contracting Party shall, within the framework of its laws and regulations, promote economic cooperation through the protection in its territory of investments of investors of the other Contracting Party, subject to its right to exercise powers conferred by its laws or regulations, each Contracting Party shall admit such investments.

2. Each contracting party shall endeavour to encourage the use of local resources both human and material for the promotion of investment in the country of both contracting parties

Article 3
Most favoured nation treatment

a) Each Contracting Party shall ensure fair and equitable treatment of investment of investors of the other Contracting Party and shall not impair, by unreasonable or discriminatory measures, the operation, management, maintenance, use, enjoyment or disposal thereof.

b) More particularly, each Contracting Party shall accord to such admitted investments and returns on investments treatment that in any case shall not be less favourable than that accorded to admitted investments or returns of investments of investors of any third State.

c) If a Contracting Party has accorded special advantages to investors of any third State by virtue of agreements establishing customs unions, economic unions, monetary unions or similar institutions, or on the basis of interim agreements leading to such unions or institutions, that Contracting Party shall not be obliged to accord such advantages to investors of the other Contracting Party.

Article 4
National treatment

a)   Each Contracting Party shall accord in its territory to the investments or returns of investors of the other Contracting Party treatment that is not less favourable than that it accords to the investments or returns of its own investors.

b)   Each of the Contracting Parties shall extend to the investors of the other Contracting Party, treatment that is not less favourable than that it accords to its own investors in regard to management, control, use enjoyment and disposal in relation to investments which have been received in its territory.

Article 5
Expropriation and Compensation

a)   Neither Contracting Party shall take any measures depriving, directly or indirectly, an investor of the other Contracting Party of an investment unless the following conditions are complied with:

(i)   The measures are taken in the public or national interest and in accordance with the law;

(ii)   The measures are not discriminatory;

(iii)   Provisions for the payment of prompt, adequate and effective compensation accompany the measures.

b)   The compensation shall be based on the market value of the investments affected immediately before the measure became public knowledge. Where that value cannot be readily ascertained, the compensation may be determined in accordance with generally recognised equitable principles of valuation taking into account the capital invested, depreciation, capital already repatriated, replacement value and other relevant factors. This compensation shall carry an interest at the appropriate market rate of interest from the date of expropriation or loss until the date of payment.

c)   The investor affected shall have a right to access, under the law of the Contracting Party making the expropriation, to the judicial authority of that Part, in order to review the amount of compensation and the legality of any such expropriation or comparable measure.

Article 6
Transfer of Payments

(a)   Each Contracting Party shall allow without delay the investors of the other Contracting Party the unrestricted transfer of payments in connection with the investment in a freely convertible currency, subject to the right of the former Contracting Party to impose equitably and in good faith such measures as may be necessary to safeguard the integrity and independence of its currency, its external financial position and balance of payments consistent with its rights and obligations as a member of the International Monetary Fund. Such transfers include in particular:

i.   interests, dividends, profits and other returns;

    ii.   repayments of loans related to investment;

    iii.   the proceeds of partial or total sale of the investment;

    iv.   compensation for dispossession or loss described in Article 5 of this Agreement

    v.   the earnings of foreign employees working in relation to an investment once the legal requirements have been fulfilled.

(b)   A transfer shall be deemed to have been made without delay if carried out within such period as is normally required for the completion of transfer formalities. The said period shall start on the day on which the relevant request has been submitted in due form and may in no case exceed six months. Transfers shall be made at the prevailing rate of exchange on the date of transfer.

(c)   Equity capital can only be transferred one year after it has entered the territory of the Contracting Party unless its legislation provides for a more favourable treatment.

Article 7
Performance requirements

Within the context of its national economic policies and goals, each Party shall endeavour to avoid imposing on the investments of investors of the other Party conditions, which require the export of goods produced, or purchase of goods or services locally. This provision shall not preclude the right of either Contracting Party to impose restrictions on the importation of goods and services into their respective territories.

Article 8
Entry and sojourn of foreign nationals

The Contracting Parties shall within the framework of their national legislation give sympathetic consideration to applications for the entry and sojourn of persons of either Contracting Party who wish to enter the territory of the other Contracting Party in connection with the making and carrying through of an investment; the same shall apply to nationals of either Contracting Party who in connection with an investment wish to enter the territory of the other Contracting Party and sojourn there to take up employment. Application for work permits shall also be given sympathetic consideration.

Article 9
Transparency

Each Contracting Party shall make public all laws, regulations, administrative practices and procedures that pertain to or affect investments

Article 10
Investor-to-State dispute resolution

(a)   In the event of a dispute between a Contracting Party and a national of the other Contracting Party relating to an investment, the parties to the dispute shall initially seek to resolve the dispute by consultations and negotiations.

(b)   If the dispute in question cannot be resolved through consultations and negotiations, either party to the dispute may:

    i.   In accordance with the law of the Contracting Party which has admitted the investment, initiate proceedings before that Contracting Party's competent judicial or administrative bodies;

    ii.   If both Contracting Parties are at the time party to the 1965 Convention on the Settlement of Investment of Investment Disputes between States and Nationals of other States ("the Convention"), refer the dispute to the International Centre for the Settlement of Investment Disputes ("the Centre") for conciliation or arbitration pursuant to Article 28 or 36 of the Convention;

    iii.   If both Contracting Parties are not at the time party to the Convention, refer the dispute to an Arbitral Tribunal constituted in accordance with........or by agreement, to any other arbitral authority.

(c)   Where a dispute is referred to the Centre pursuant to sub-paragraph (b)(ii) of this Article:

    i.   Where the action is taken by a national of one Contracting Party, the other Contracting

    ii.   Party shall consent in writing to the submission of the dispute to the Centre within thirty days of receiving such a request from the national.

    iii.   If the parties to the dispute cannot agree whether conciliation or arbitration is the more appropriate procedure, the national affected shall have the right to choose;

    iv.   A company which is constituted or incorporated under the law in force in the territory of one Contracting Party and in which before the dispute arises the majority of the shares are owned by nationals of the other Contracting Party shall, in accordance with Article 25(2)(b) of the Convention, be treated for the purpose of the Convention as a company of the other Contracting Party.

(d)   Once an action referred to in paragraph (b) of this Article has been taken, neither Contracting Party shall pursue the dispute through diplomatic channels unless:

    i.   The relevant judicial or administrative body, the Secretary General of the Centre, the arbitral authority or tribunal or the conciliation commission, as the case may be, has decided that it has no jurisdiction in relation to the dispute in question; or

    ii.   The other Contracting Party has failed to abide by or comply with any judgement, award, order or other determination made by the body in question.

(e)   In any proceeding involving a dispute relating to an investment, a Contracting Party shall not assert, as a defence, counter-claim right of set-off or otherwise, that the national concerned has received or will receive pursuant to an insurance or guarantee contract, indemnification or other compensation for all or part of any alleged loss

Article 11
Dispute between the Contracting Parties

(a)   Disputes between the Contracting Parties concerning the interpretation or application of this Agreement should, as far as possible, be settled through negotiation.

(b)   If a dispute between the Contracting Parties cannot thus be settled within six months from the time the dispute arose, it shall upon the request of either Contracting Party be submitted to an arbitral tribunal

(c)   Such an arbitral tribunal shall be constituted for each individual case in the following way: Within two months of the receipt of the request for arbitration, each Contracting Party shall appoint one member of the tribunal. Those two members shall then select a national of a third State who on approval by the two Contracting Parties shall be appointed Chairman of the tribunal. The Chairman shall be appointed within two months from the date of appointment of the other two members.

(d)   If within the periods specified in paragraph (3) of this Article the necessary appointments have not been made, either Contracting Party may, in the absence of any other agreement, invite the President of the International Court of Justice to make any necessary appointments. If the President is a national of either Contracting Party or if he is otherwise prevented from discharging the said function, the Vice President shall be invited to make the necessary appointments. If the Vice President is a national of either Contracting Party or if he too is prevented from discharging the said function, the Member of the International Court of Justice next in seniority who is not a national of either Contracting Party shall be invited to make the necessary appointments.

(e)   The arbitral tribunal shall reach its decision by a majority of votes. Such decisions shall be binding on both Contracting Parties. Each Contracting Party shall bear the cost of its own member of the tribunal and of its representation in the arbitral proceedings; the cost of the Chairman and the remaining costs shall be borne in equal parts by the Contracting Parties. The tribunal may, however, in its decision direct that a higher proportion of cost shall be borne by one of the two Contracting Parties, and this award shall be binding on both Contracting Parties. The tribunal shall determine its own procedures

Article 12
Applicable Laws

Except as otherwise provided in this Agreement, all investments shall be governed by the laws in force in the territory of the Contracting Party in which such investments are made including such laws enacted for the protection of its essential security interests or in circumstances of extreme emergency provided however that such laws are reasonably applied on a non-discriminatory basis.

Article 13
Application of other Rules

If the provision of law of either Contracting Party or obligations under international law existing at the present or established hereafter between the Contracting Parties in addition to the present Agreement contain rules, whether general or specific, entitling investments by investors of the other Contracting Party to a treatment more favourable than is provided for by the present Agreement, such rules shall to the extent that they are more favourable prevail over the present Agreement.

Article 14
Entry into force

This Agreement shall be subject to ratification and shall enter into force on the date of exchange of Instruments of Ratification.

Article 15
Duration and termination

(a)   This agreement shall remain in force for a period of ten years and thereafter it shall be deemed to have been automatically extended unless either Contracting Party gives to the other Contracting Party a written notice of its intention to terminate the Agreement. The Agreement shall stand terminated one year from receipt of such written notice

(b)   Notwithstanding termination of this Agreement pursuant to paragraph (1) of this Article, the Agreement shall continue to be effective for a further period of fifteen years from the date of its termination in respect of investment made or acquired before the date of termination of this Agreement.

In witness whereof the undersigned, duly authorised thereto by their respective Governments, have signed this Agreement.

Done at _____on this ___ day of _____, 2003 in two originals each in the ....and English languages, both texts being authoritative.

In case of any divergence, the English text shall prevail.

*

AGREEMENT BETWEEN THE GOVERNMENT OF THE REPUBLIC OF UGANDA AND THE GOVERNMENT OF THE REPUBLIC OF _____ ON THE RECIPROCAL PROMOTION AND PROTECTION OF INVESTMENTS*

The Government of the Republic of Uganda and the Government of the Republic of _____ hereinafter referred to as the Contracting Parties,

DESIRING to strengthen their economic cooperation by creating favourable conditions for investments by nationals of one Contracting Party in the territory of the other Contracting Party,

RECOGNISING that the encouragement and reciprocal protection under international agreement of such investments will be conducive to the stimulation of individual business initiative and will increase prosperity in the territories of both Contracting Parties:
have agreed as follows:

CONVINCED that the promotion and protection of these investments would succeed in stimulating transfers of capital and technology between the two countries in the interest of their economic development,

Have agreed as follows.

ARTICLE 1
Definitions

For the purpose of this Agreement:

1.   The term "investment" means every kind of assets, such as goods, rights and interests of whatever nature, and in particular though not exclusively:

   a)   tangible, intangible, movable and immovable property as well as any other right in rem such as mortgages, liens, usufructs, pledges and similar rights ;

   b)   shares, premium on share and other kinds of interest including minority or indirect forms, in companies constituted in the territory of one Contracting Party ;

   c)   title to money or debentures, or title to any legitimate performance having an economic value ;

   d)   intellectual, commercial and industrial property rights such as copyrights, patents, licenses, trademarks, industrial models and mock-ups, technical processes, know-how, trade-names and goodwill, and any other similar rights ;

   e)   business concessions conferred by law or under contract, including concessions to search for, cultivate, extract or exploit natural resources, including those which are located in the maritime area of the Contracting Parties.

---

* *Source*: The Government of the Republic of Uganda, Ministry of Foreign Affairs (2003).

It is understood that those investments are investments which have already been made or may be made subsequent to the entering into force of this Agreement, in accordance with the legislation of the Contracting Party on the territory or in the maritime area of which the investment is made.

Any alteration of the form in which assets are invested shall not affect their qualification as investments provided that such alteration is not in conflict with the legislation of the Contracting Party on the territory or in the maritime area of which the investment is made.

2.   The term "nationals" means physical persons possessing the nationality of either Contracting Party.

3.   The term "company" means any legal person constituted on the territory of one Contracting Party in accordance with the legislation of that Party and having its head office on the territory of that Party, or controlled directly or indirectly by the nationals of one Contracting Party or by legal persons having their head office in the territory of one contracting Party and constituted in accordance with the legislation of that Party.

4.   The term "returns" means all amounts produced by an investment, such as profits, royalties and interest, during a given period.

Investment returns and, in case of re-investment, re-investment returns shall enjoy the same protection as the investment.

5.   The term "territory" shall mean

      a)   in the case of Uganda, The Republic of Uganda.

      b)   in the case of the Republic of ....,.

6.   This Agreement shall apply to the territory of each Contracting Party, as well as the maritime area of each Contracting Party, hereafter defined as the economic zone and the continental shelf outwards the territorial sea of each Contracting Party over which they have in accordance with International Law sovereign rights and a jurisdiction with a view to prospecting, exploiting and preserving natural resources.

7.   Nothing in this agreement shall be construed to prevent any contracting party from taking any measure to regulate investment of foreign companies and the conditions of activities of these companies in the framework of policies designed to preserve and promote cultural and linguistic diversity.

ARTICLE 2
Promotion and admission of investments

Each Contracting Party shall promote, encourage and admit on its territory and in its maritime area, in accordance with its legislation and with the provisions of this Agreement, investments made by nationals or companies of the other Contracting Party.

ARTICLE 3
Fair and equitable treatment

Either Contracting Party shall extend fair and equitable treatment in accordance with the principles of International Law to investments made by nationals and companies of the other Contracting Party on its territory or in its maritime area, and shall ensure that the exercise of the right thus recognized shall not be hindered by law or in practice. In particular though not exclusively, shall be considered as de jure or de facto impediments to fair and equitable treatment any restriction to free movement, purchase and sale of goods and services, as well as any other measures that have a similar effect.

Within the framework of their internal legislation, the Contracting Parties shall favorably examine requests for entry and authorization to reside, work and travel made by the nationals of one Contracting Party in relation to an investment made on the territory or in the maritime area of the other Contracting Party.

ARTICLE 4
National treatment and Most Favored Nation treatment

1   Each Contracting Party shall apply on its territory and in its maritime area to the nationals and companies of the other Party, with respect to their investments and activities related to the investments, a treatment not less favorable than that granted to its nationals or companies, or the treatment granted to the nationals or companies of the most favored nation, if the latter is more favorable. In this respect, nationals authorized to work on the territory and in the maritime area of one Contracting Party shall enjoy the material facilities relevant to the exercise of their professional activities in accordance with the national labour laws.

This treatment shall not include the privileges granted by one Contracting Party to nationals or companies of a third party State by virtue of its participation or association in a free trade zone, customs union, common market or any other form of regional economic organization.

2   The provisions of this Agreement shall not apply to matters of taxation in the territory of either Contracting Party. Such matters shall be governed by the Double Taxation Treaty Convention between the two Contracting Parties and the domestic laws of each Contracting Party.

ARTICLE 5
Dispossession and indemnification

1.   The investments made by nationals or companies of one Contracting Party shall enjoy full and complete protection and safety on the territory and in the maritime area of the other Contracting Party.

2.   Neither Contracting Party shall take any measures of expropriation or nationalization or any other measures having the effect of dispossession, direct or indirect, of nationals or companies of the other Contracting Party of their investments on its territory and in its maritime area, except in the public interest and provided that these measures are neither discriminatory nor contrary to a specific commitment.

Any measures of dispossession which might be taken shall give rise to prompt and adequate compensation, the amount of which shall be equal to the real value of the investments concerned and shall be set in accordance with the normal economic situation prevailing prior to any threat of dispossession.

The said compensation, the amounts and conditions of payment, shall be set not later than the date of dispossession. This compensation shall be effectively realizable, shall be paid without delay and shall be freely transferable. Until the date of payment, it shall bear interest calculated at the appropriate market rate of interest.

3.   Nationals or companies of one Contracting Party whose investments have sustained losses due to war or any other armed conflict, revolution, national state of emergency or revolt occurring on the territory or in the maritime areas of the other Contracting Party, shall enjoy treatment from the latter Contracting Party that is not less favorable than that granted to its own nationals or companies or to those of the most favored nation.

ARTICLE 6
Free transfer

Each Contracting Party, on the territory or in the maritime area of which the investments have been made by nationals or companies of the other Contracting Party, shall guarantee to these nationals and companies the free transfer of:

a)   interest, dividends, profits and other current income ;

b)   royalties deriving from incorporeal rights as defined in Article 1, Paragraph 1, letters (d) and (e) ;

c)   repayments of loans which have been regularly contracted ;

d)   value of partial or total liquidation or disposition of the investment, including capital gains on the capital invested ;

e)   compensation for dispossession or loss described in Article 5, Paragraphs 2 and 3.

The nationals of either Contracting Party, who have been authorized to work on the territory or in the maritime area of the other Contracting Party, as the result of an approved investment, shall also be permitted to transfer to their country of origin an appropriate proportion of their earnings.

The transfers referred to in the foregoing paragraphs shall be promptly effected at the official exchange rate prevailing on the date of transfer.

In case of a serious balance of payments difficulties and external financial difficulties or the threat thereof, each contracting party may temporarily restrict transfers, provided that this restriction:

   i)   shall be promptly notified to the other party ;

   ii)   shall be consistent with the articles of agreement with the International Monetary Fund;

iii)   shall be within an agreed period ; iv) would be imposed in an equitable, non discriminatory and in good faith basis

ARTICLE 7
Settlement of disputes between an investor and a Contracting Party

1.   Any investment dispute between an investor of one Contracting Party and the other Contracting Party shall be notified in writing by the first party to take action. The notification shall be accompanied by a sufficiently detailed memorandum.

As far as possible, the Parties shall endeavour to settle the dispute through negotiations, if necessary by seeking expert advice from a third party, or by conciliation between the Contracting Parties through diplomatic channels.

2.   In the absence of an amicable settlement by direct agreement between the parties to the dispute or by conciliation through diplomatic channels within six months from the notification, the dispute shall be submitted, at the option of the investor, either to the competent jurisdiction of the State where the investment was made, or to international arbitration.

To this end, each Contracting Party agrees in advance and irrevocably to the settlement of any dispute by this type of arbitration. Such consent implies that both Parties waive the right to demand that all domestic administrative or judiciary remedies be exhausted.

3.   In case of international arbitration, the dispute shall be submitted for settlement by arbitration to one of the hereinafter mentioned organizations, at the option of the investor:

-    an ad hoc arbitral tribunal set up according to the arbitration rules laid down by the United Nations Commission on International Trade Law (U.N.C.I.T.R.A.L.) ;

-    the International Centre for the Settlement of Investment Disputes (I.C.S.I.D.), set up by the Convention on the Settlement of Investment Disputes between States and Nationals of other States, opened for signature at Washington on March 18, 1965, when each State party to this Agreement has become a party to the said Convention.

As long as this requirement is not met, each Contracting Party agrees that the dispute shall be submitted to arbitration pursuant to the Rules of the Additional Facility of the I.C.S.I.D.

-    the Arbitral Court of the International Chamber of Commerce in Paris;

-    an Arbitration Institution of their choice.

If the arbitration procedure has been introduced upon the initiative of a Contracting Party, this Party shall request the investor involved in writing to designate the arbitration organization to which the dispute shall be referred.

4.   At any stage of the arbitration proceedings or of the execution of an arbitral award, none of the Contracting Parties involved in a dispute shall be entitled to raise as an objection the fact that the investor who is the opposing party in the dispute has received compensation totally or partly covering his losses pursuant to an insurance policy or to the guarantee provided for in Article 9 of this Agreement.

5.   The arbitral tribunal shall decide on the basis of the national law, including the rules relating to conflicts of law, of the Contracting Party involved in the dispute in whose territory the investment has been made, as well as on the basis of the provisions of this Agreement, of the terms of the specific agreement which may have been entered into regarding the investment, and of the principles of international law.

6.   The arbitral awards shall be final and binding on the parties to the dispute. Each Contracting Party undertakes to execute the awards in accordance with its national legislation.

ARTICLE 8
Application of other provisions

Where a matter is governed both by this agreement and by an other International Agreement to which both Contracting Parties are signatories, the most favourable provisions shall be applied to the Contracting Parties and to their investors.

ARTICLE 9
Guarantee and subrogation

1.   In the event that the regulations of one Contracting Party contain a guarantee for investments made abroad, this guarantee may be accorded, after examining case by case, to investments made by nationals or companies of this Party on the territory or in the maritime area of the other Party.

2.   Investments made by nationals or companies of one Contracting Party on the territory or in the maritime area of the other Contracting Party may obtain the guarantee referred to in the foregoing paragraph only if they have been previously agreed to by the other Party.

3.   If one Contracting Party, as a result of a guarantee given for an investment made on the territory or in the maritime area of the other Contracting Party, makes payments to its own nationals or companies, the first mentioned Party has in this case full rights of subrogation with regard to the rights and actions of the said national or company.

4.   The said payments shall not affect the rights of the beneficiary of the guarantee to recourse to the ICSID or to continue proceedings submitted to it until completion of the proceedings.

ARTICLE 10
Special Agreements

1.   Investments made pursuant to a specific agreement concluded between one Contracting Party and investors of the other Party shall be covered by the provisions of this Agreement and by those of the specific agreement.

2.   Each Contracting Party undertakes to ensure at all times that the commitments it has entered into vis-à-vis investors of the other Contracting Party shall be observed

ARTICLE 11
Settlement of disputes between Contracting Parties

1.   Any dispute relating to the interpretation or application of this Agreement shall be settled as far as possible through diplomatic channels.

2.   In the absence of a settlement through diplomatic channels, the dispute shall be submitted to a joint commission consisting of representatives of the two Parties; this commission shall convene without undue delay at the request of the first party to take action.

3.   If the joint commission cannot settle the dispute, the latter shall be submitted, at the request of either Contracting Party, to an arbitration court set up as follows for each individual case:

Each Contracting Party shall appoint one arbitrator within a period of two months from the date on which either Contracting Party has informed the other Party of its intention to submit the dispute to arbitration. Within a period of two months following their appointment, these two arbitrators shall appoint by mutual agreement a national of a third State as chairman of the arbitration court.

If these time limits have not been complied with, either Contracting Party shall request the President of the International Court of Justice to make the necessary appointment(s).

If the President of the International Court of Justice is a national of either Contracting Party or of a State with which one of the Contracting Parties has no diplomatic relations or if, for any other reason, he cannot exercise this function, the Vice-President of the International Court of Justice shall be requested to make the appointment(s).

4.   The court thus constituted shall determine its own rules of procedure. Its decisions shall be taken by a majority of the votes; they shall be final and binding on the Contracting Parties.

5.   Each Contracting Party shall bear the costs resulting from the appointment of its arbitrator. The expenses in connection with the appointment of the third arbitrator and the administrative costs of the court shall be borne equally by the Contracting Parties.

ARTICLE 12
Previous Investments

(1)   This Agreement shall also apply to investments made before its entry into force by investors of one Contracting Party in the territory of the other Contracting Party in accordance with the latter's laws and regulations. It shall, however, not be applicable to claims arising out of disputes which occurred prior to its entry into force.

ARTICLE 13
Laws

For the avoidance of any doubt, it is declared that all investments shall, subject to this Agreement, be governed by the laws in force in the territory of the Contracting Party in which such investments are made.

ARTICLE 14
Amendments

The terms of this agreement may be amended by mutual agreement of both contracting parties and such amendments shall be effected by exchange of notes between them through diplomatic channels.

ARTICLE 15
Entry Into Force And Duration

1.   This Agreement shall enter into force one month after the date of exchange of the instruments of ratification by the Contracting Parties. The Agreement shall remain in force for a period of 20 years.

Unless notice of termination is given by either Contracting Party at least six months before the expiry of its period of validity, this Agreement shall be tacitly extended each time for a further period of ten years, it being understood that each Contracting Party reserves the right to terminate the Agreement by notification given at least six months before the date of expiry of the current period of validity.

2.   Investments made prior to the date of termination of this Agreement shall be covered by this Agreement for a period of ten years from the date of termination.

IN WITNESS WHEREOF, the undersigned representatives, duly authorized thereto by their respective Governments, have signed this Agreement.

DONE at ...., on ......, in three original copies, each in the English and .... languages, all texts being equally authentic. The text in the English language shall prevail in case of difference of interpretation.

SELECTED UNCTAD PUBLICATIONS ON TRANSNATIONAL CORPORATIONS AND FOREIGN DIRECT INVESTMENT
(For more information, please visit www.unctad.org/en/pub on the web.)

World Investment Report 2003:FDI Policies for Development: National and International Perspectives. 327 p. Sales No. E.03.II.D.8 $49.
http://www.unctad.org/wir/contents/wir02_dl.htm.

World Investment Report 2003: FDI Policies for Development: National and International Perspectives. An Overview. 48 p. UNCTAD/WIR/2003 (Overview). Free of charge.
http://www.unctad.org/wir/contents/wir02_dl.htm.

World Investment Report 2002: Transnational Corporations and Competitiveness. 384 p. Sales No. E.02.II.D.4 $49. http://www.unctad.org/wir/contents/wir02_dl.htm.

World Investment Report 2002: Transnational Corporations and Competitiveness. An Overview. 44 p. UNCTAD/WIR/2002 (Overview). Free of charge.
http://www.unctad.org/wir/contents/wir02_dl.htm.

World Investment Report 2001: Promoting Linkages. 356 p. Sales No. E.01.II.D.12 $49.
http://www.unctad.org/wir/contents/wir01content.en.htm.

World Investment Report 2001: Promoting Linkages. An Overview. 67 p. UNCTAD/WIR/2001 (Overview). Free of charge. http://www.unctad.org/wir/contents/wir01content.en.htm.

Ten Years of World Investment Reports: The Challenges Ahead. Proceedings of an UNCTAD special event on future challenges in the area of FDI. UNCTAD/ITE/Misc. 45. Free of charge.
http://www.unctad.org/wir/contents/wir_xth.html.

World Investment Report 2000: Cross-border Mergers and Acquisitions and Development. 368 p. Sales No. E.99.II.D.20. $49. http://www.unctad.org/wir/contents/wir00content.en.htm.

World Investment Report 2000: Cross-border Mergers and Acquisitions and Development. An Overview. 75 p. UNCTAD/WIR/2000 (Overview). Free of charge.
http://www.unctad.org/wir/contents/wir00content.en.htm.

World Investment Report 1999: Foreign Direct Investment and the Challenge of Development. 543 p. Sales No. E.99.II.D.3. $49. http://www.unctad.org/wir/contents/wir99content.en.htm.

World Investment Report 1999: Foreign Direct Investment and the Challenge of Development. An Overview. 75 p. UNCTAD/WIR/1999 (Overview). Free of charge.
http://www.unctad.org/wir/contents/wir99content.en.htm.

World Investment Report 1998: Trends and Determinants. 432 p. Sales No. E.98.II.D.5. $45.
http://www.unctad.org/wir/contents/wir98content.en.htm.

World Investment Report 1998: Trends and Determinants. An Overview. 67 p.
UNCTAD/WIR/1998 (Overview). Free of charge.
http://www.unctad.org/wir/contents/wir98content.en.htm.

World Investment Report 1997: Transnational Corporations, Market Structure and Competition Policy. 384 p. Sales No. E.97.II.D.10. $45.
http://www.unctad.org/wir/contents/wir97content.en.htm

World Investment Report 1997: Transnational Corporations, Market Structure and Competition Policy. *An Overview*. 70 p. UNCTAD/ITE/IIT/5 (Overview). Free of charge.
http://www.unctad.org/wir/contents/wir97content.en.htm

World Investment Report 1996: Investment, Trade and International Policy Arrangements.
332 p. Sales No. E.96.II.A.14. $45. http://www.unctad.org/wir/contents/wir96content.en.htm

World Investment Report 1996: Investment, Trade and International Policy Arrangements. *An Overview*. 51 p. UNCTAD/DTCI/32 (Overview). Free of charge.
http://www.unctad.org/wir/contents/wir96content.en.htm

World Investment Report 1995: Transnational Corporations and Competitiveness. 491 p. Sales No. E.95.II.A.9. $45. http://www.unctad.org/wir/contents/wir95content.en.htm

World Investment Report 1995: Transnational Corporations and Competitiveness. *An Overview*.
51 p. UNCTAD/DTCI/26 (Overview). Free of charge.
http://www.unctad.org/wir/contents/wir95content.en.htm

World Investment Report 1994: Transnational Corporations, Employment and the Workplace.
482 p. Sales No. E.94.II.A.14. $45. http://www.unctad.org/wir/contents/wir94content.en.htm

World Investment Report 1994: Transnational Corporations, Employment and the Workplace. *An Executive Summary*. 34 p. UNCTAD/DTCI/10 (Overview). Free of charge.
http://www.unctad.org/wir/contents/wir94content.en.htm

World Investment Report 1993: Transnational Corporations and Integrated International Production. 290 p. Sales No. E.93.II.A.14.
$45.http://www.unctad.org/wir/contents/wir93content.en.htm

World Investment Report 1993: Transnational Corporations and Integrated International Production. *An Executive Summary*. 31 p. ST/CTC/159 (Executive Summary). Free of charge.
http://www.unctad.org/wir/contents/wir93content.en.htm

World Investment Report 1992: Transnational Corporations as Engines of Growth. 356 p.
Sales No. E.92.II.A.19. $45. http://www.unctad.org/wir/contents/wir92content.en.htm

World Investment Report 1992: Transnational Corporations as Engines of Growth. *An Executive Summary*. 30 p. ST/CTC/143 (Executive Summary). Free of charge.
http://www.unctad.org/wir/contents/wir92content.en.htm

World Investment Report 1991: The Triad in Foreign Direct Investment. 108 p. Sales No.E.91.II.A.12. $25. http://www.unctad.org/wir/contents/wir91content.en.htm

World Investment Directories

World Investment Directory: Vol. VIII: Central and Eastern Europe, 2003. 86 p. (Overview)+CD-Rom (country profiles). Sales No. E.03.II.D.12. $25. http://www.unctad.org/en/docs//iteiit20032_en.pdf(Overview); http://www.unctad.org/en/subsites/dite/fdistats_files/WID2.htm (country profiles).

World Investment Directory, Vol. VII (Parts I and II): Asia and the Pacific, 1999. 332+638 p. Sales No. E.00.II.D.21. $80.

World Investment Directory, Vol. VI: West Asia, 1996. 138 p. Sales No. E.97.II.A.2. $35.

World Investment Directory, Vol. V: Africa, 1996. 461 p. Sales No. E.97.II.A.1. $75.

World Investment Directory, Vol. IV: Latin America and the Caribbean, 1994. 478 p. Sales No. E.94.II.A.10. $65.

World Investment Directory, Vol. III: Developed Countries, 1992. 532 p. Sales No. E.93.II.A.9. $75.

World Investment Directory, Vol. II: Central and Eastern Europe, 1992. 432 p. Sales No. E.93.II.A.1. $65. (Joint publication with the United Nations Economic Commission for Europe.)

World Investment Directory, Vol. I: Asia and the Pacific, 1992. 356 p. Sales No. E.92.II.A.11. $65.

Investment Policy Reviews
http://www.unctad.org/ipr/

***Investment Policy Review of Nepal*.** 95 p. Sales No. E.03.II.D.17. http://www.unctad.org/ipr/nepal.pdf

***Investment Policy Review of Lesotho*.** 93 p. UNCTAD/ITE/IPC/Misc. 25. http://www.unctad.org/en/docs//iteipcmisc25corr1_en.pdf.

***Investment Policy Review of Ghana*.** 93 p. Sales No. E.02.II.D.20. http://www.unctad.org/ipr/ghana.pdf.

***Investment Policy Review of Botswana*.** 107 p. Sales No. E.03.II.D.1. http://www.unctad.org/ipr/botswana.pdf.

***Investment Policy Review of the United Republic of Tanzania*.** 98 p. Sales No. 02.E.II.D.6 $20. http://www.unctad.org/ipr/Tanzania.pdf.

***Investment Policy Review of Ecuador*.** 117 p. Sales No. E.01.II D.31. $25. http://www.unctad.org/ipr/Ecuador.pdf.

***Investment and Innovation Policy Review of Ethiopia*.** 115 p. UNCTAD/ITE/IPC/Misc. 4. Free of charge. http://www.unctad.org/ipr/Ethiopia.pdf.

Investment Policy Review of Mauritius. 84 p. Sales No. E.01.II.D.11. $22.
http://www.unctad.org/ipr/Mauritius.pdf.

Investment Policy Review of Peru. 108 p. Sales No. E.00.II.D.7. $22.
http://www.unctad.org/ipr/Peru.pdf.

Investment Policy Review of Uganda. 75 p. Sales No. E.99.II.D.24. $15.
http://www.unctad.org/ipr/UGANDA.PDF.

Investment Policy Review of Egypt. 113 p. Sales No. E.99.II.D.20. $19.
http://www.unctad.org/ipr/EGYFIN1.PDF.

Investment Policy Review of Uzbekistan. 64 p. UNCTAD/ITE/IIP/Misc.13. Free of charge.
http://www.unctad.org/ipr/Uzbekistan.pdf.

Investment Guides
http://www.unctad.org/en/pub/investguide.en.htm

An Investment Guide to Nepal: Opportunities and Conditions. 88 p.
UNCTAD/ITE/IPC/MISC/2003/1. Free of charge.

An Investment Guide to Mozambique: Opportunities and Conditions. 72 p.
UNCTAD/ITE/IIA/4. Free of charge. http://www.unctad.org/en/docs/poiteiiad4.en.pdf.

An Investment Guide to Uganda: Opportunities and Conditions. 76 p. UNCTAD/ITE/IIT/Misc.
30. Free of charge. http://www.unctad.org/en/docs/poiteiitm30.en.pdf.

An Investment Guide to Bangladesh: Opportunities and Conditions. 66 p.
UNCTAD/ITE/IIT/Misc. 29. Free of charge. http://www.unctad.org/en/docs/poiteiitm29.en.pdf.

An Investment Guide to Mali. 105 p. UNCTAD/ITE/IIT/Misc. 24. Free of charge.
http://www.unctad.org/en/docs/poiteiitm24.en.pdf (joint publication with the International
Chamber of Commerce, in association with PricewaterhouseCoopers).

An Investment Guide to Ethiopia: Opportunities and Conditions. 69 p.
UNCTAD/ITE/IIT/Misc. 19. Free of charge. http://www.unctad.org/en/docs/poiteiitm19.en.pdf
(joint publication with the International Chamber of Commerce, in association with
PricewaterhouseCoopers).

Issues in International Investment Agreements
http://www.unctad.org/en/subsites/dite/iia/IIA_Series/iia_series.htm

Admission and Establishment. 72 p. Sales No. E.99.II.D.10. $12.
http://www.unctad.org/en/subsites/dite/iia/IIA_Series/admission.pdf.

Dispute Settlement (Investor-State). Sales No. E.03.II.D.5. $15.

Dispute Settlement (State-State). Sales No. E.03.II.D.6. $15.

Employment. 69 p. http://www.unctad.org/en/subsites/dite/iia/IIA_Series/employment.pdf.

Environment. 105 p. Sales No. E.01.II.D.3. $15.
http://www.unctad.org/en/subsites/dite/iia/IIA_Series/environment.pdf.

Fair and Equitable Treatment. 64 p. Sales No. E.99.II.D.15. $12.
http://www.unctad.org/en/subsites/dite/iia/IIA_Series/fair.pdf.

Foreign Direct Investment and Development. 88 p. Sales No. E.98.II.D.15. $12.
http://www.unctad.org/en/subsites/dite/iia/IIA_Series/fdi&dev.pdf.

Home Country Measures. 96 p. Sales No.E.01.II.D.19. $12.
http://www.unctad.org/en/subsites/dite/iia/IIA_Series/homecm.pdf.

Host Country Operational Measures. 109 p. Sales No E.01.II.D.18. $15.
http://www.unctad.org/en/subsites/dite/iia/IIA_Series/hostcom.pdf.

Illicit Payments. 108 p. Sales No. E.01.II.D.20. $13.
http://www.unctad.org/en/subsites/dite/iia/IIA_Series/illicitpayments.pdf.

International Investment Agreements: Flexibility for Development. 185 p. Sales No.
E.00.II.D.6. $12. http://www.unctad.org/en/subsites/dite/iia/IIA_Series/flexibilitynew.pdf.

Investment-Related Trade Measures. 64 p. Sales No. E.99.II.D.12. $12.
http://www.unctad.org/en/subsites/dite/iia/IIA_Series/IRTM.pdf.

Lessons from the MAI. 31 p. Sales No. E.99.II.D.26. $12.
http://www.unctad.org/en/subsites/dite/iia/IIA_Series/lessons.pdf.

Most-Favoured-Nation Treatment. 72 p. Sales No. E.99.II.D.11. $12.
http://www.unctad.org/en/subsites/dite/iia/IIA_Series/mfnt.pdf.

National Treatment. 104 p. Sales No. E.99.II.D.16. $12.
http://www.unctad.org/en/subsites/dite/iia/IIA_Series/national.pdf.

Scope and Definition. 96 p. Sales No. E.99.II.D.9. $12.
http://www.unctad.org/en/subsites/dite/iia/IIA_Series/scopedef.pdf.

Social Responsibility. 91 p. Sales No. E.01.II.D.4. $15.
http://www.unctad.org/en/subsites/dite/iia/IIA_Series/socialresp.pdf.

Taking of Property. 83 p. Sales No. E.00.II.D.4. $12.
http://www.unctad.org/en/subsites/dite/iia/IIA_Series/taking.pdf.

Taxation. 111 p. Sales No. E.00.II.D.5. $12.
http://www.unctad.org/en/subsites/dite/iia/IIA_Series/taxation1.pdf.

Transfer of Funds. 68 p. Sales No. E.00.II.D.27. $12.
http://www.unctad.org/en/subsites/dite/iia/IIA_Series/transferoffunds.pdf.

Transfer of Technology. 138p. Sales No. E.01.II.D.33. $18.
http://www.unctad.org/en/subsites/dite/iia/IIA_Series/TRANSFEROFTECH.pdf.

Transfer Pricing. 72 p. Sales No. E.99.II.D.8. $12.

Trends in International Investment Agreements: An Overview. 112 p. Sales No. E.99.II.D.23.
$12. http://www.unctad.org/en/subsites/dite/iia/IIA_Series/trends.pdf.

***Progress Report on Work undertaken within UNCTAD's work programme on international
investment agreements between the 10th Conference of UNCTAD, Bangkok, February 2000
and July 2002***. 90 p. UNCTAD/ITE/IIT/2002. Free of charge.
http://www.unctad.org/en/docs//poiteiit02.en.pdf.

International Investment Instruments

International Investment Instruments: A Compendium. Vol. X. 343 p. Sales No. E.02.II.D.21.
$60. http://www.unctad.org/en/docs//dite3vol10_en.pdf.

International Investment Instruments: A Compendium. Vol. IX. 353 p. Sales No. E.02.II.D.16.
$60. http://www.unctad.org/en/docs/psdited3v9.en.pdf.

International Investment Instruments: A Compendium. Vol. VIII. 335 p. Sales No.
E.02.II.D.15. $60. http://www.unctad.org/en/docs/psdited3v8.en.pdf.

International Investment Instruments: A Compendium. Vol. VII. 339 p. Sales No.
E.02.II.D.14. $60. http://www.unctad.org/en/docs/psdited3v7.en.pdf.

International Investment Instruments: A Compendium. Vol. VI. 568 p. Sales No. E.01.II.D.34.
$60. http://www.unctad.org/en/docs/ps1dited2v6_p1.en.pdf (part one).

International Investment Instruments: A Compendium. Vol. V. 505 p. Sales No. E.00.II.D.14.
$55.

International Investment Instruments: A Compendium. Vol. IV. 319 p. Sales No. E.00.II.D.13.
$55.

International Investment Instruments: A Compendium. Vol. I. 371 p. Sales No. E.96.II.A.9;
Vol. II. 577 p. Sales No. E.96.II.A.10; ***Vol. III***. 389 p. Sales No. E.96.II.A.11; the 3-volume set,
Sales No. E.96.II.A.12. $125.

Bilateral Investment Treaties 1959-1999. 143 p. UNCTAD/ITE/IIA/2, Free of charge. Available
only in electronic version from http://www.unctad.org/en/docs//poiteiiad2.en.pdf.

Bilateral Investment Treaties in the Mid-1990s. 314 p. Sales No. E.98.II.D.8. $46.

ASIT Advisory Studies
http://www.unctad.org/asit/index2.html

No. 17. ***The World of Investment Promotion at a Glance: A Survey of Investment Promotion Practices***. UNCTAD/ITE/IPC/3. Free of charge.
http://www.unctad.org/en/docs//poiteipcd3.en.pdf.

No. 16. ***Tax Incentives and Foreign Direct Investment: A Global Survey***. 180 p. Sales No. E.01.II.D.5. $23. http://www.unctad.org/en/docs//iteipcmisc3_en.pdf.

No. 15. ***Investment Regimes in the Arab World: Issues and Policies***. 232 p. Sales No. E/F.00.II.D.32. Summary at: http://www.unctad.org/asit/index2.html.

No. 14. ***Handbook on Outward Investment Promotion Agencies and Institutions***. 50 p. Sales No. E.99.II.D.22. $15.

No. 13. ***Survey of Best Practices in Investment Promotion***. 71 p. Sales No. E.97.II.D.11. $35. http://www.unctad.org/en/docs//psiteiipd1.en.pdf.

B. Individual Studies

FDI in Least Developed Countries at a Glance: 2002 edition. 150 p. UNCTAD/ITE/IIA/3. Free of charge. http://www.unctad.org/en/subsites/dite/LDCs/fdi_ldcs.htm.

FDI in ACP Economies: Recent Trends and Developments. 36 p. UNCTAD/ITE/IIA/Misc. 2. Free of charge. http://www.unctad.org/en/docs//iteiiamisc2_en.pdf.

Transfer of Technology for Successful Integration into the Global Economy: A Case Study of the Pharmaceutical Industry in India. 58 p. UNCTAD/ITE/IPC/Misc. 22. Free of charge. http://www.unctad.org/en/docs//iteipcmisc22_en.pdf.

Transfer of Technology for Successful Integration into the Global Economy: A Case Study of the South African Automotive Industry. 38 p. UNCTAD/ITE/IPC/Misc. 21. Free of charge. http://www.unctad.org/en/docs//iteipcmisc21_en.pdf.

Transfer of Technology for Successful Integration into the Global Economy: A Case Study of Embraer in Brazil. 64 p. UNCTAD/ITE/IPC/Misc. 20. Free of charge. http://www.unctad.org/en/docs//iteipcmisc20_en.pdf.

Managing the Environment across Borders. 38 p. UNCTAD/ITE/IPC/Misc. 12. Free of charge. http://www.unctad.org/en/docs//iteipcmisc12_en.pdf.

The Tradability of Consulting Services and its implications for developing countries. 189 p. UNCTAD/ITE/IPC/Misc. 8. Free of charge. http://www.unctad.org/en/docs/poiteipcm8.en.pdf.

Compendium of International Arrangements on Transfer of Technology: Selected Instruments. 308 p. Sales No. E.01.II.D.28. $45. http://www.unctad.org/en/docs//psiteipcm5.en.pdf.

Measures of the Transnationalization of Economic Activity. 93 p. Sales No. E.01.II.D.2. $20.

The Competitiveness Challenge: Transnational Corporations and Industrial Restructuring in Developing Countries. 283p. Sales No. E.00.II.D.35. $42.

Integrating International and Financial Performance at the Enterprise Level. 116 p. Sales No. E.00.II.D.28. $18.

FDI Determinants and TNC Strategies: The Case of Brazil. 195 p. Sales No. E.00.II.D.2. $35.

TNC-SME Linkages for Development: Issues-Experiences-Best Practices. *Proceedings of the Special Round Table on TNCs, SMEs and Development, UNCTAD X, 15 February 2000, Bangkok, Thailand*. 113 p. UNCTAD/ITE/TEB/1. Free of charge.

Foreign Direct Investment in Africa: Performance and Potential. 89 p. UNCTAD/ITE/IIT/Misc. 15. Free of charge. http://www.unctad.org/en/docs/poiteiitm15.pdf.

The Social Responsibility of Transnational Corporations. 75 p. UNCTAD/ITE/IIT/Misc. 21. Free-of- charge. [Printed version is out of stock.] http://www.unctad.org/en/docs/poiteiitm21.en.pdf.

Handbook on Foreign Direct Investment by Small and Medium-sized Enterprises: Lessons from Asia. 200 p. Sales No. E.98.II.D.4. $48.

Handbook on Foreign Direct Investment by Small and Medium-sized Enterprises: Lessons from Asia. *Executive Summary and Report of the Kunming Conference*. 74 p. Free of charge.

The Financial Crisis in Asia and Foreign Direct Investment: An Assessment. 101 p. Sales No. GV.E.98.0.29. $20. http://www.unctad.org/en/docs//poiteiitd8.en.pdf.

International Investment towards the Year 2002. 166 p. Sales No. GV.E.98.0.15. $29. (Joint publication with Invest in France Mission and Arthur Andersen, in collaboration with DATAR.)

Sharing Asia's Dynamism: Asian Direct Investment in the European Union. 192 p. Sales No. E.97.II.D.1. $26.

Investing in Asia's Dynamism: European Union Direct Investment in Asia. 124 p. ISBN 92-827-7675-1. €14. (Joint publication with the European Commission.)

Electronic materials
Available in electronic version only from the Division's web page at:
http://www.unctad.org/en/subsites/dite/index.html

Prospects for Global and Regional FDI flows: UNCTAD's Worldwide Survey of Investment Promotion Agencies. 15 p. Free of charge. Available at:
http://www.unctad.org/en/subsites/dite/docs/rnote031405.pdf.

Outward FDI from Central and Eastern European Countries. 17 p. Free of charge. Available at: http://www.unctad.org/en/subsites/dite/pdfs/CEE_outward_en.pdf.

China: WTO Accession and Growing FDI Flows. 24 p. Free of charge. Available at:
http://www.unctad.org/en/subsites/dite/pdfs/PRChina.pdf.

C. Journals

Transnational Corporations Journal (formerly ***The CTC Reporter***). Published three times a year. Annual subscription price: $45; individual issues $20.
http://www.unctad.org/en/subsites/dite/1_itncs/1_tncs.htm.
United Nations publications may be obtained from bookstores and distributors throughout the world. Please consult your bookstore or write to:

For Africa and Europe to

Sales Section
United Nations Office at Geneva
Palais des Nations
CH-1211 Geneva 10
Switzerland
Tel: (41-22) 917-1234
Fax: (41-22) 917-0123
E-mail: unpubli@unog.ch

For Asia and the Pacific, the Caribbean, Latin America and North America to:

Sales Section
Room DC2-0853
United Nations Secretariat
New York, NY 10017
United States
Tel: (1-212) 963-8302 or (800) 253-9646
Fax: (1-212) 963-3489
E-mail: publications@un.org

All prices are quoted in United States dollars.

For further information on the work of the Division on Investment, Technology and Enterprise Development, UNCTAD, please address inquiries to:

United Nations Conference on Trade and Development
Division on Investment, Technology and Enterprise Development
Palais des Nations, Room E-10054
CH-1211 Geneva 10, Switzerland
Telephone: (41-22) 907-5534
Fax: (41-22) 907-0498
E-mail: virginie.noblat-pianta@unctad.org
http://www.unctad.org

QUESTIONNAIRE

International Investment Instruments: A Compendium

Volume XII

In order to improve the quality and relevance of the work of the UNCTAD Division on Investment, Technology and Enterprise Development, it would be useful to receive the views of readers on this publication. It would therefore be greatly appreciated if you could complete the following questionnaire and return it to:

Readership Survey
UNCTAD Division on Investment, Technology and Enterprise Development
United Nations Office in Geneva
Palais des Nations
Room E-9123
CH-1211 Geneva 10
Switzerland
Fax: 41-22-907-0194

1. Name and address of respondent (optional):

_____

_____

2. Which of the following best describes your area of work?

Government ☐   Public enterprise ☐

Private enterprise ☐   Academic or research institution ☐

International organization ☐   Media ☐

Not-for-profit organization ☐   Other (specify) _____

3. In which country do you work? _____

4. What is your assessment of the contents of this publication?

Excellent ☐   Adequate ☐

Good ☐   Poor ☐

5. How useful is this publication to your work?

Very useful ☐   Of some use ☐   Irrelevant ☐

6. Please indicate the three things you liked best about this publication:

_____
_____
_____

7. Please indicate the three things you liked least about this publication:

_____
_____
_____

8. Are you a regular recipient of *Transnational Corporations* (formerly *The CTC Reporter*), UNCTAD-DITE's tri-annual refereed journal?

Yes ☐   No ☐

If not, please check here if you would like to receive
a sample copy sent to the name and address you have   ☐
given above

*